The Heritage of American Catholicism

A TWENTY-EIGHT-VOLUME SERIES DOCUMENTING THE HISTORY OF AMERICA'S LARGEST RELIGIOUS DENOMINATION

EDITED BY

Timothy Walch

ASSOCIATE EDITOR
U.S. Catholic Historian

A Garland Series

Orestes A. Brownson and Nineteenth-Century Catholic Education

JAMES M. MCDONNELL

Garland Publishing, Inc.
New York & London
1988

LIBRARY OF CONGRESS CATALOGING-IN-PUBLICATION DATA

McDonnell, James M. (James Michael)
    Orestes A. Brownson and nineteenth-century Catholic education / James M. McDonnell.
    p. cm. -- (The Heritage of American Catholicism)
    Originally presented as the author's thesis (doctoral)--University of Notre Dame, South Bend, 1988.
    Bibliography: p.
    ISBN 0-8240-4094-5 (alk. paper)
    1. Catholic Church--Education--United States--History--19th century. 2. Brownson, Orestes Augustus, 1803-1876. 3. Catholic schools--United States--History--19th century. I. Title. II. Series.
LC501.M38 1988
377'.82'73--dc19   88-11000
                                                                                          CIP

DESIGN BY MARY BETH BRENNAN

PRINTED ON ACID-FREE, 250-YEAR-LIFE PAPER.
MANUFACTURED IN THE UNITED STATES OF AMERICA

TABLE OF CONTENTS

i

PREFACE

Orestes Augustus Brownson (1803-1876) was a controversial figure who never hesitated to state his positions vigorously. But to his contemporaries, Brownson's words were not always clear, and sometimes seemed inconsistent. His position on Catholic schools was a case in point. Catholic bishops such as John Hughes and John B. Purcell construed Brownson's criticism of Catholic schools to mean their condemnation and abandonment. In the ensuing arguments, Brownson was often considered a proponent of the common school, and thus, anti-Catholic in regard to the school question. Similarly, the essay "Catholic Schools and Education" (1862) is usually considered as Brownson's position on the school question. However, Brownson often stated that no single essay from his pen could be understood as "final" or "definitive." When he wrote a series of essays on any issue, he expected his readers to view each article in terms of the others. Catholic audiences have failed to accord Brownson this request. Scholars have misinterpreted much of what Brownson wrote; and they have ignored many of his writings, especially those of the late 1860's and 1870's.

Although Brownson was indeed interested in schooling, his definition of education went far beyond tne confines of the school-room. Besides the formal educational agencies such as schools, colleges, and universities, Brownson envisioned informal and popular agencies such as the family, Church, press, literature,

iii

adult societies, lyceums, and lectures as viable educational agencies. One thing is certain: Brownson never considered the school, Catholic or common, as the single most important agency in the educative process. Also, Brownson viewed education as an ongoing process, for youth and adult alike. The fact that he was largely a self-educated man significantly influenced his views on education and his role as an educator. In addition, Brownson was highly influenced by a belief that he had a scholarly duty to perform in life--the mental, moral, religious, and social amelioration of the human race; his mission ultimately arose from his persistent concerns for religion, for his own salvation and that of his nation. It is hoped that this dissertation sheds new light both on Brownson and on the education of nineteenth-century American Catholics, both youths and adults.

In the preparation of this dissertation, I owe a special thanks to all those who have encouraged, aided, and guided my educational endeavors--to my teachers at Our Mother of Good Counsel School (Blasdell, N.Y.); at Bishop Timon High School (Buffalo, N.Y.); at Siena College, especially the late Reverend Noel A. Fitzpatrick, OFM, whose untimely and premature death has compelled me to thank him posthumously; and at the University of Notre Dame; to my wife's parents, Jerry and Alice Joyce, whose encouragement and other assistance are deeply appreciated; and to my parents, Jim and Rose McDonnell, whose dreams and visions for my academic success have continually kept me going on my own scholar's mission. To classmates Norlene Kunkel, Timothy Morrissey, and Robert O'Gorman whose comments, encouragements, and stamina have helped me realize the common plight of all dissertation writers. To the staff of the University of Notre Dame

Memorial Library, especially Frank Clark of the microfilm department, Reverend Thomas Blantz, C.S.C., and Mercedes Muenz of the Notre Dame archives, and to all the information and check-out personnel for their consideration. To those who helped in the original proposal, especially Dr. George N. Shuster and Dr. Philip Gleason; to readers, Dr. Harold Burgess, Dr. Morton Kelsey, and Dr. William Tageson; to Dr. Lawrence Bradley, Assistant Archivist, for digging out the Brownson Papers, for sitting on the proposal board, and for many helpful suggestions in the preparation of the final draft. And to Dr. Vincent Lannie I owe a special thanks for his guidance throughout my doctoral studies, for his friendship, and for his editorial assistance, both organizational and stylistic, without which this dissertation might not have been. He and the others are responsible for whatever merits this work possesses; we may all share the praise, but I alone am responsible for the shortcomings. I owe a special thanks to Mrs. Pat Fujawa for typing this final draft. My wife Colleen seldom complained about typing one draft after another and never asked why my first drafts needed to be redone. Thanks. And finally, I want to dedicate this publication to Colleen, Jimmy, Bobby, Erin and Megan.

LIST OF TABLES

CHAPTER I

ORESTES A. BROWNSON (1803-1876): SCHOLAR

i

THE SCHOLAR'S MISSION

Among the many speaking engagements he received during the
spring of 1843, Orestes Brownson accepted invitations to lecture at
Dartmouth College and the University of Vermont.[1] He chose "The
Scholar's Mission" as his topic for both addresses. Students,
alumni and friends admired the address so much that they requested
copies for publication.[2]

Although he overtly designed his remarks as a "charge" for
recent graduates and present students of these two institutions,

---

[1]This first chapter, and the succeeding one, are not meant
in any way to be a comprehensive biography of Brownson. They focus
on his psychological, intellectual, and religious dimensions,
including his own development and the intellectual, religious, and
political climate of his day.

[2]Orestes A. Brownson, An Oration on the Scholar's Mission
(Burlington, Vt.: V. Harrington, 1843). Hereafter cited as The
Scholar's Mission. Brownson delivered his lectures on July 26
at Dartmouth, and on August 1 at Vermont. The letters requesting
publication of the oration are printed on p. 3. The invitation
to speak at Vermont resulted in a somewhat comical situation. It
seems that Brownson had accepted the original invitation, but the
Phi Sigma Nu and University Institute had proffered the invitation
without legitimate authority. Brownson was therefore asked to
write a second acceptance letter, since his first acceptance letter
was also illegal. See H. S. Haskell and Moses Lane to Orestes A.
Brownson, May 1, 1843 and Moses Lane to Orestes A. Brownson, May
9, 1843, Orestes Augustus Brownson Papers, University of Notre Dame
Archives. Hereafter cited as O.A.B., OABP, UNDA.

1

in reality Brownson presented the students with a revealing autobiography. His self-portrait became even more pronounced as he
smoothly interwove first and third person points-of-view in the
address. By the end of the oration, it became obvious that the
ideal scholar worthy of emulation was none other than Brownson
himself.

The scholar was a learner, one who continually sought to
discover more and more infinite truth. He rose above the level of
student, and became a master.

> I understand by the scholar no mere pedant, dilettante,
> literary epicure, or dandy; but a serious, hearty,
> robust, full-grown man; who feels that life is a
> serious affair, and that he has a serious part to
> act in its eventful drama; and must therefore do his
> best to act well his part, so as to leave behind him,
> in the good he has done, a grateful remembrance of his
> having been. He may be a theologian, a politician, a
> naturalist, a poet, a moralist, or a metaphysician;
> but whichever or whatever he is, he is it with all his
> heart and soul, with high, noble,--in one word, _reli-
> gious_ aims and aspirations . . . for which he counts
> it honorable to live, and sweet to die.[3]

Brownson certainly considered himself a master with a serious part
to play in life's drama. He wanted to be remembered for the good
he had done. Religion dominated his aims and aspirations; he
lived and died in the cause of religion. This then, was Brownson's
primary psychological motivation--to fulfill the scholar's mission.

Accordingly, Brownson believed it the scholar's principal
responsibility to master those sciences which answered the

---

[3]_The Scholar's Mission_, pp. 6-8 (Italics Brownson's).

questions "what is our duty?" and "what are our means of fulfilling

it?" To know man's destiny, and to labor to accomplish it became

Brownson's life-long work. He found the answer to both questions

in religion. "Religion has a two-fold office,--to answer the

question, what is my destiny? and to be to me the 'wisdom of God,

and the power of God'; to struggle, without fatigue and success-

fully, for its realization."[4] Religion was "indispensible to the

Scholar,"[5] for without it, he was unable to understand his end and

to love and pursue it unfalteringly through life.

Man's chief end was "to glorify God and enjoy him forever

. . . . The end for which God made us, and placed us here, is

PROGRESS, growth, to be eternally approaching the Infinite God,

communion with whom is the consummation of the soul's good."[6]

Understanding clearly the end of man, the scholar played a peculiar

role in helping to bring about this progress. He instructed and

inspired mankind for the accomplishment of its destiny. "The

Scholar is always one who stands out from and above the mass, to

instruct them as to what is their duty, and to inspire them with

zeal and energy to perform it."[7]

---

[4]Ibid., p. 10.

[5]Ibidem.

[6]Ibid., pp. 11-12. Brownson here recites his catechism that he knew so well. Also, Brownson in 1843 was on the verge of converting to Catholicism. Highly influential in his conversion was the idea of "communion with God" to which he refers. See a series of articles that Brownson wrote at this time in the Christian World entitled the "Mission of Jesus."

[7]Ibid., p. 12.

Brownson anticipated the objections raised against his expression "stands out from and above the mass." The Jacksonian era and the era of reform emphasized equality, and some even contended "that every man is fitted by nature to succeed equally in every thing." Brownson believed that all men were equal, "that all men are equally men, equally accountable to God," but this did not mean the "dead level equality of the mass." Brownson maintained that such a concept could not carry forward the race. Although the theory was popular, it would "not abide the wear and tear of active life; it is a mere dream, a silly dream, unsustained by a single fact tangible to waking sense." The race can only be carried forward "by suffering individuals to stand from and above the multitude, the prophets of a more advanced stage, and the ministers of God to help reach it."[8] Just as an army needed generals to lead the privates, so too humanity needed scholars to lead the masses.

Everywhere life reflected this hierarchy and infinite diversity. Each man had his own special mission, one which no one else had, or could be fitted to perform. However, each was to labor "for the advancement of all." All men were assigned a different work--some artists, some scientists, some industrialists. "All cannot be prophets and priests; all cannot be kings and rulers, all cannot be poets and philosophers; and all, I dare add, cannot be scholars."[9] For as St. Paul remarked, "Now there are

[8]Ibid., pp. 12-13.
[9]Ibid., p. 14.

diversities of gifts but the same Spirit."[10] Brownson believed

that the diversity of gifts and callings was essential to the very

conception of society. It was a

> fact which there is no getting over . . . . I care
> not how much you war against it; you will never fit
> every man to succeed equally in every thing. I care
> not how universal you may make education /‾schooling‾7,
> nor how nearly equal the advantages you may extend
> to all the children of the land; only a small, a very
> small number of those you educate will become Scholars.[11]

Although gifts and callings were diverse, all were alike necessary,

honorable, and noble. All possessed the same spirit; all were

directed to the same end.

Nonetheless, the diversity and the inequality growing out of

it were essential for the progress of humanity. "The mass are not

carried forward without individuals, who rise above the general

average."[12] Level all things, Brownson maintained, and society

lost its activity, charm, and variety, and became as putrid as a

stagnant pool. Where would the world be without Socrates, Plato,

St. Thomas, Bacon, Descartes, Alexander, Caesar, Charlemagne,

Napoleon, Washington, or without inspired prophets and messengers

like Noah, Abraham, Moses, David, Paul, John, or Augustine. "It

is only by the life, love, labors, and sacrifices of these, and

such as these, that the race is quickened, instructed, inspired,

and enabled to make its way through the ages to the accomplish-

ment of its destiny."[13]

---

[10]Corinthians XIII, 4; also used by Brownson in his oration,
p. 14.
[11]The Scholar's Mission, pp. 15-16.
[12]Ibid., p. 17.
[13]Ibid., p. 18.

Moreover, Brownson argued, it was undeniable that there are
certain labors indispensable to the progress of mankind--in moral,
religious, intellectual, and social aspects--which can only be
performed "by men who stand out, and are distinguished by their
capacity, virtues and attainments, from the multitude."[14] These
few were the scholars; the results of their work, though, bene-
fitted all. The few received the glory and honor of labor, while
many enjoyed the fruit.

The scholar, instructor and inspirer of his race, advanced
the progress of mankind only if he bore in mind that his office
was of providential origin, and not for special benefit of the
incumbent. Too many who passed for scholars had overlooked this
very fact and considered their superior capacities and attainments
as marks of special Divine favor upon themselves, conferred for
their own personal good. It was this error, selfishness, that had
caused many to distrust the "Scholar."

> No man is really offended, that there is inequality
> in men's capacities, attainments, and virtues. But
> the prejudice grows out of the fact, that our edu-
> cated men are exceedingly prone to forget, that their
> superior capacities and attainments are to be held by
> them, not for their own private benefit, but as sacred
> trusts, to be used for the moral, religious, social,
> and intellectual advancement of mankind.[15]

Brownson believed the mortal sin of every aristocracy--literary,
scientific, military, or political--was not the inequality
implied, produced, or perpetuated, but the fact that aristocracy

---

[14]Ibidem.
[15]Ibid., p. 20.

regarded itself as a privileged class, master of all classes,
rather than as a servant. After all, "to whom much is given, of
him much is required." Those who were given more carried a
heavier burden. "Greatness is conferred not to be ministered
unto, but to minister. He is the greatest who best serves his
race; and he proves himself not great, but little, who seeks to
serve not his race, but himself."[16]

True distinction lay not in how far above the multitude one
advanced himself, but how much one contributed to the real progress
of his race. The scholar who sought only his own ease was worthy
of unmitigated contempt.

> Of all men, the Scholar is he who needs most thoroughly
> to understand and practice the abnegation of self; who
> more than any other is to be laborious and self-
> sacrificing, feeling himself charged to work out a
> higher good for his brethren; and that where-ever
> he is, or whatever he does, the Infinite Eye rests
> upon him, and his honor as a man, as well as a Scholar,
> is staked on the wisdom and fidelity with which he
> labors to execute his mission.[17]

After discussing the general character of the scholar's mission,
found at all times and in all places, Brownson proceeded to consider the scholar's /¯his¯/ role in nineteenth century America.

Whatever the circumstances, "it never is, it never can be,
the Mission of the Scholar to do over again for the progress of
his race, what has already been done; but that which has not as
yet been done, and which must be done, before another step forward

---

[16]Ibid., p. 21.
[17]Ibid., p. 22.

can be taken."[18]   The scholar must stand above the mass as a

prophet and a priest.   He cannot join in with the multitude, not

blindly and passively submit to their pressure.   The scholar,

though above the people, possessed neither scorn nor contempt for

the people, but a deep and enduring love that enabled him to live,

and labor, and if necessary, suffer and die for their redemption.

He must remember:

> he is their instructor, their guide, their chief, not
> their echo, their slave, their tool. He believes, and
> proceeds on the belief, that there is a standard of
> truth and justice, of wisdom and virtue, above popular
> convictions, ay, or popular instincts; and that to
> this standard both he and the people are bound to
> conform. To this standard he aims to bring his own
> convictions, and by it to rectify his own judgments;
> and having so done, instead of going with the multitude
> when they depart from it, swimming with the popular
> current when it sets in against it, he throws himself
> before the multitude, and with a bold face and a firm
> voice commands them to pause, for their onward course
> is their death. He resists the popular current, he
> braves popular opinion, wherever he believes it wrong
> or mischievous, be the consequences to himself what
> they may. This he must do, for Providence, in giving
> him the capacity and means to be a Scholar, that is,
> a leader and chief of his race, has made him responsi-
> ble, to the full measure of his ability, for the wisdom
> and virtue of the multitude.
>   Here is the law that must govern the Scholar. He
> must labor to lead public opinion where right, and
> correct it where wrong.[19]

Brownson envisioned himself, then, as playing a significant role

in the formation, direction, and elevation of public opinion. He

believed that a God-given mandate required him to elucidate man's

---

[18]Ibid., p. 23.

[19]Ibid., pp. 24-25.

chief duty in life, and to expedite man's means of achieving his truly religious end. For this reason, Orestes Brownson devoted his life to instructing and inspiring his fellow man. He labored for the moral, religious, intellectual, and social amelioration of the human race.

In attempting to elevate the human race, Brownson confronted what he called a "leveling" tendency in American society, and a downward tendency at that, one that was everywhere in evidence--in literature, religion, morals, philosophy, education, church, and state. The scholar's special mission in nineteenth century America, Brownson argued, was to labor and to battle against this equalizing trend before it completely dragged thought down to the lowest level of common intelligence.[20] The voice of God was being replaced by the will of the people.

> We have broken down the old nobilities, and hier-
> archies; we have abolished all that was formerly held
> to be noble and venerable, and made the scholar, the
> moralist, the politician, and last but not least, the
> minister of religion, responsible to THE PEOPLE; that

---

[20] See The Scholar's Mission, pp. 25-30 for a discussion of Brownson's objections to the many institutional leveling tendencies. Also in late 1842, Brownson began writing for John L. O'Sullivan's United States Magazine and Democratic Review. The popular democratic organ's editor soon began to disapprove of Brownson's articles. O'Sullivan advised him to tone down his articles, for the readers were not interested in Brownson's profound metaphysics. O'Sullivan's philosophy was "the greatest entertainment of the greatest number," to vary the Benthamic formula. (See John L. O'Sullivan to O.A.B., February 12, 1843, OABP, UNDA.) Needless to say, the short interlude of 1843 convinced Brownson that he must revive his Boston Quarterly Review (1838-1842) if he intended to write forcefully once again. January, 1844 saw the emergence of Brownson's Quarterly Review, leaving no doubt regarding Brownson's seriousness in his desire to be heard on his own terms and at his own level.

is, to public opinion. Whether we write, preach,
moralize, or _politize_, we do it with the fear of the
people before our eyes, and with the desire to obtain
their approbation. In a word, it has come to this:
our study is to _follow_, to _echo_ the public opinion,
not to form it.[21]

Brownson could not allow this pattern to continue. To do so would

mean abandoning the religious cause of progress--a progress that

could be achieved only if scholars performed their God-given tasks.

The scholar must sacrifice himself "_for_ the masses, not _to_

them," Brownson told his audience.

Who knows not, that if you would save the people, you
must often oppose them? No advance has ever yet been
made, but it has been opposed by them, especially by
those they follow as their trusted leaders. Every
true prophet and priest is at first martyred by them
. . . . It cannot be otherwise. They are of the
future and must look to the future for their reward.
Their views, hopes, wishes, are dark mysteries to
their contemporaries, and how can they be the favor-
ites of their age. They are the prophets of a better
age, of which they must be the builders, as well as
the heralds.[22]

---

[21]_Ibid._, p. 31 (italics Brownson's). One Universalist
minister, Edward Turner, complained to Brownson that his congregation merely wished to hear that "all men will be happy at death,
irrespective of their moral characters while living." See Edward
Turner to O.A.B., July 3, 1834, OABP, UNDA. A more intimate friend
and correspondent of Brownson, Isaac B. Peirce, often complained
about the lack of true religious spirit and actions on the part
of his congregations. In addition, Peirce felt himself a victim
of the times. Congregations preferred young, modern, progressive
ministers, recent graduates of Theological or Divinity Schools,
whom Peirce called "inexperienced boys." The hard-working, self-
denying minister of old could not expect to remain a minister
past age 50. See letters of Isaac B. Peirce to O.A.B., June 20,
1831, June 27, 1831, October 12, 1833, December 19, 1833, August
14, 1841, and March 4, 1842, OABP, UNDA.

[22]_Ibid._, pp. 32-33.

11

Time and time again, Brownson would either remind himself or be reminded by trusted friends that recognition, esteem, and reward would come in the future, probably after death. Only by keeping this in mind was Brownson able to withstand constant popular criticism throughout his life.

Brownson warned his scholarly audience of the temptations facing the scholar to court popular applause. He must withstand such allurements, and must correct and form the public conscience by appealing to God's law; this required a high degree of moral heroism. Scholars must always look "to a higher and nobler plaudit, than that of the multitude, and for a more terrible execration than its."[23] The scholar must take a high and noble view of this mission, his duty, his responsibility; he must ascertain his special work in the progress of mankind; and finally, must go forth and do it--with or without public approbation.

> Ask not what your age wants, but what it needs; not
> what it will reward, but what, without which, it
> cannot be saved; and that go and do; do it well; do
> it thoroughly; and find your reward in the conscious-
> ness of having done your duty, and above all in the
> reflection, that you have been accounted worthy to
> suffer somewhat for mankind.[24]

Brownson concluded this oration by proposing that the progress of society could be advanced only by the creation of an army of genuine scholars--"educated men, gifted with a brave,

[23]Ibid., pp. 35-36.

[24]Ibid., p. 38; the reader might recall the famous lines of John F. Kennedy's Inaugural Address, January 30, 1961. His indebtedness to Brownson is clearly discernible.

heroic, self-denying spirit," devoted and obedient to the spirit
and letter of God's Law. He urged the young men to go forth and
instruct and inspire their countrymen. He suggested to them that
they had taken consecrated vows to be prophets and priests of their
race. Finally, he reminded them that their God-given gifts of
birth and education were not for their own pleasure, nor for
getting their living out of the people. Too many college and
university graduates had already caused the scholarly profession
to fall into disrepute. The scholar must dedicate his life to
better serving the people. He must devote himself, heart and soul,
to the progress of the race, to the moral, religious, intellectual
and social elevation of all men. In so doing, the scholar would
magnify his profession, fulfill his mission, do honor to his
country, and receive the approbation of God.[25]

Brownson's advice to the young men of Dartmouth and Vermont
was much more than abstract theorizing. He had drawn a map for the
scholar to follow. He had explained and forewarned about the unpleasant possibility of meeting popular disapproval. He placed the
will of God above the caprice of man, and he anticipated his reward
from God and posterity. The oration may not have been enough to
instill and inspire the scholarly life into the young New Englanders.
To Brownson, however, it served as his guide on life's journey--
The Scholar's Mission.

In essence, the scholar was an educator--one who led and
drew out the God-given gifts in his fellow human beings. This was

---

[25]Ibid., pp. 39-40.

Brownson's self-proclaimed mission in life. Nearly forty years old when he delivered An Oration on the Scholar's Mission, Brownson would live another thirty-three years to continue practicing what he had theorized and preached. He would attempt to lead his fellow Catholic and non-Catholic countrymen to higher moral, religious, intellectual and social levels. Thus, Brownson, the scholar, was an educator. Yet, how did he become a scholar? What factors influenced his life and learning? How would his learning influence his views on education? Hence, it is essential to examine the ways in which Brownson learned.

ii

THE EDUCATION OF ORESTES BROWNSON

Shortly before his thirty-sixth birthday in 1839 Brownson wrote:

> I am almost wholly an uneducated man. I was a poor boy, thrown upon the (wicked?) world alone, at a tender age, and have been compelled to make my way without assistance. I have no learning but such as I picked up myself, having never received even the ordinary advantages of our common schools. My whole life, till within a few months, has been a continual struggle with poverty. For the most part of my life, I have lived away from books and the great centres of ideas. I have had intercourse with learned man, and access to books only during the last four or five years.[26]

When he delivered "The Scholar's Mission" four years later, Brownson advised his audiences that he had "no recollections

_____

[26]O.A.B. to Victor Cousin, September 6, 1839, OABP, UNDA.

or associations connected with college halls or academic bowers."
Hence, he modestly announced his topic, "though but ill-qualified
to do the subject justice."[27] No common school; no college or
university; a continual struggle with poverty; a country boy
unacquainted with learned men and having had only limited access
to books--this sounds like the successful nineteenth century
American farmer rags-to-riches story. Surprisingly, this person
became one of the leading intellectual figures of nineteenth
century America. This uneducated and ill-qualified man was, nonetheless, in the words of Theodore Maynard, "the greatest and most
luminous mind that has so far appeared among Catholics in this
country."[28] Indeed, Orestes Brownson was a scholar--a self-taught
and a self-made scholar.

Born to a poor Stockbridge, Vermont family in 1803, Orestes
Brownson was orphaned away by his mother in 1809 after his father's
death. He lived with an elderly couple, aged 60 and 50, in nearby
Royalton[29] who served as his first teachers. In addition to
religious and moral training,[30] this couple taught Orestes the

---

[27] The Scholar's Mission, p. 5.

[28] Theodore Maynard, Orestes Brownson Yankee, Radical,
Catholic (New York: The Macmillan Company, 1943) Introduction, xiv.

[29] Brownson was later re-united with his mother in 1817 and
remained with her, in all probability, for a few years. Brownson
never mentions the name of the elderly couple with whom he resided.
However, in the Henry Brownson Collection is a letter from a George
Severance to Henry F. Brownson, dated December 15, 1879. Severance
wrote that he constantly passes the old house of Luther Hunting,
where Henry's father lived as a teenager. He also told Henry that
Orestes' brother, Orin, had been sent to live at Mrs. Benemi
Wight's house.

[30] His religious and moral training are discussed in Chapter
II.

rudiments of reading and writing. He studied The Franklin Primer

and read a weekly newspaper during the War of 1812. But his foster

parents' small library was hardly enough to satisfy Orestes'

voracious appetite for reading. His neighborhood provided few

playmates, but it did enable Orestes to borrow books. Having no

access to a public library, he canvassed the neighborhood and

obtained the English classics of Queen Anne's reign, some fifty

volumes of English poets, Locke's Essay on the Human Understanding,

Pope's Homer, works on American history, the planting of the

colonies, wars with the Indians, Robinson Crusoe, Philip Quarles,

and A Thousand and One Arabian Nights.

> I have never known or imagined on earth greater
> enjoyment than I had as a boy lying on the hearth
> in a miserable shanty reading by the light of burning
> pine-knots some book I had just borrowed. I felt
> neither hunger nor thirst, and no want of sleep, my
> book was meat and drink, home and raiment, friend and
> guardian, father and mother . . . . Good reading be-
> came my greatest delight, and my greatest want was
> books . . . . I had a book in my hand whenever I had
> a leisure moment.[31]

Unable to attend school during his early years, Brownson regarded

the family as the primary educational agency, for it provided his

character training, moral and religious, as well as academic

training. This early training provided Brownson with a quality

he possessed throughout his entire life--the love of reading.

Besides this early moral and academic learning, several

significant events helped shape the young Orestes. First of all,

---

[31]Contained in Henry F. Brownson, Brownson's Early Life
1803-1844 (Detroit: H. F. Brownson, 1898), pp. 6-7.

sometime between 1817 and 1822, during the period that Orestes was
re-united with his mother again in Ballston Spa, Saratoga County,
New York, he attended an academy where he learned some Latin and
Greek and, in all probability, some arithmetic, English, geography
and history. This stay provided him with new vistas for learning.
Having had the rudiments, Brownson later delved more deeply into
the study of Latin and Greek, as well as Spanish, French, and
German. During the same period, Orestes obtained employment in a
printing office which furnished him with instruction in spelling,
grammar, paragraphing and style. In addition, he obtained invaluable experience in the editing and publishing of newspapers and
magazines. Although neither Brownson nor his biographers have
drawn much attention to this period of employment, nonetheless the
importance stands clear. From his mid-twenties until his death,
Brownson worked continually as a writer and editor of newspapers
and periodical literature. Moreover, from about age 19 to 22,
Brownson kept a diary in which he recorded his feelings and
experiences. Again, neither he nor his biographers emphasize this,
but, the experience existed and the results stand out: he recorded
his thoughts, he practiced his writing, and eventually, he became
a proficient writer.[32]

---

[32]One should recall to mind the tremendous significance that
Benjamin Franklin attributed to very similar experiences in his
Autobiography. Franklin also worked in a printing office and
practiced his writing. Perhaps the importance of Orestes' early
intellectual development and experiences can be amplified by a
comparison to his twin sister, Daphne Augusta. After their
father's death, the twins were separated. Orestes learned to read,
found reading material, briefly attended an academy, worked as a
printer's aid, and kept a "Notebook of Reflections." Daphne,
deprived of these formal and informal means of education, remained

As a consequence of his early love of learning, primarily by informal means and without the aid of much formal schooling, it was not surprising that Orestes Brownson eventually became a teacher. In 1823, he accepted a position in Stillwater, New York,[33] and in 1824, moved to Detroit where he taught briefly until illness forced him to resign. He returned to Elbridge, New York and taught during 1825.[34] These three years coincided with the dates that Brownson kept his "Notebook of Reflections." Perhaps the most surprising thing about this period was that he never wrote about his own teaching and seldom discussed education. The two glimpses obtained, though, were significant nonetheless.

During the summer of 1823, Brownson recorded in his diary: "Tis Education forms the common mind / Just as the twig is bent the tree's inclined."[35] He marvelled at the thought that the human mind, when properly cultivated, produced "towering geniuses which astound the world." However, he was "surprised that parents take no more pains to draw out these hidden virtues of the mind."[36] In another entry, perhaps copied, Brownson related the story of

---

to her death a pitifully ignorant and uneducated, though good-hearted, woman. Her letters to her brother are replete with spelling, grammatical, and punctuation errors. Her concerns were personal, and quite often petty. Her brother became an accomplished writer and thinker, with worldly, universal concerns.

[33]He turned down an offer to teach in Halfmoon, New York. See Elisha G. Calkins to O.A.B., March 27, 1823, OABP, UNDA.

[34]It was here that he met his wife, Sarah Healy, one of his pupils.

[35]"Notebook of Reflections," p. 84, OABP, UNDA (probably in July or August, 1823).

[36]Ibid.

a boy who hated his teacher, considered school a dungeon, and complained to his parents about physical beatings at school. The enraged parents "anathamatize/_d_7" /_sic_7 the teacher and kept their boy at home.[37]

Although he was optimistic that man's mind could vastly improve with proper training, the Brownson of 20 believed that a teacher alone could not produce significant results without parental cooperation. In addition, physical punishment of students produced fear and hatred of a teacher rather than a love of learning. Nowhere in this diary did Brownson express hope or confidence in the common schools of this time. Moreover, he devoted fewer than two pages of this 150 page diary to education at a time when he spent nearly three years as a teacher! Just as Brownson himself had not spent much time as a student in a school room, he would not teach long in a school room. Even while in the midst of teaching, his main concerns were primarily religious. His "Notebook of Reflections" abounds in religious matters. It is quite understandable that within the next year, 1826, Brownson launched a new career as a minister.

From the late 1820's until his death in 1876, Brownson continued to learn. The primary resource of this learning was books, journals, periodicals, and newspapers.[38] An insight into Brownson's character, especially his love of reading and learning,

---

[37]Ibid., p. 11 (January 14, 1823).

[38]Chapter II covers in detail Brownson's philosophical and religious reading during the 1830's and 1840's.

is captured by several letters. He decided to leave Walpole,
Massachusetts in early 1834 to search for a new location to serve
as minister. Brownson wrote his wife that he was much pleased
with his visit to Canton because of its proximity to the Boston
and Cambridge libraries. He refused William Ellery Channing's
offer to reside at Fall River, likewise, because it was too far
away from the intellectual center of Boston.[39] Shortly afterwards,
one of Brownson's former parishioners in Walpole wrote and asked,
"Do you read and study as much as ever?"[40] And finally, Brownson's
correspondence with George Ripley, Isaac Peirce, Victor Cousin and
Henry David Thoreau during this period reveals a love of learning,
a constant discussion of ideas, and an ongoing inquiry about and
search for different books.[41] So important were books that
Brownson established a parish library during his ministerial
position in Canton (1834-1836). And when he moved to Boston to
establish his Society for Christian Union and Progress, he again
set up a library.

Brownson learned more from reading than from any other
source. By the 1830's, he could manage Latin, Greek, French,
Spanish, German, and Italian. And it was essential to his life's
work. From 1838 until his death, Brownson served as a reviewer;
and practically every essay he wrote took another piece of writing
as its starting point. To do his work, he continually read,

[39]O.A.B. to Sarah Healy Brownson, February 19, 1834, Odiorne
Collection, UNDA.
[40]Wm. M. Prichard to O.A.B., June 12, 1834, OABP, UNDA.
[41]These letters during the 1830's are contained in the OABP,
UNDA.

evaluated, criticized, and wrote. Augustine Hewit and Isaac Hecker
of the Catholic World constantly procurred for Brownson every major
book or essay they or he considered important. The elder Brownson
insisted that Denis and James Sadlier, proprietors of the New York
Tablet, provide him with Blackwood's Magazine, The London Quarterly
Review, The Westminster Review, London Tablet and Weekly Register,
The Dublin Review and The Nation, in order for him to do his job
properly.[42]

Brownson himself acknowledged that he was a borrower of ideas
and that he learned from what others wrote. "I lay no claim to
inventive genius, and I can work only with materials furnished me;
I therefore feel grateful to every man who helps me to a principle."[43] He was a devout reader, always hoping to learn something
new, and eventually to synthesize it with his previous knowledge.
Brownson explained his approach to reading and learning to his
son, Henry.

> Indeed I never master any one till I have made myself
> his disciple, and allowed him to master me . . . . We
> understand by sympathy, and never master an author
> till we have seen his doctrine under an aspect which
> it is not false, or till we see what has led him to
> believe it true. Never begin an author, a real author
> I mean, in a critical spirit. Allow him to enlist
> your sympathies as far as he can, and to carry you
> away, provisorily /_?_/ with him; see with his eyes,
> and think with his thought, till you have taken all
> there is of him up into yourself. Then you may turn
> him over and criticise him as if he were yourself,
> and thus master him and criticise him in his place.
> Read always with an open, not, a closed mind and

---

[42] D. & J. Sadlier to O.A.B., December 16, 1868, OABP, UNDA.
[43] O.A.B. to John C. Hurd, December 28, 1865, OABP, UNDA.

heart. This has been my method of study through
life. The draw back in my case has been that the
circumstances of my life compelled me to write and
publish while the process was going on, before I had
time to complete it. Thus the charge of fickleness
and frequent changes of opinion. The world has never
known and never will know the steadiness with which
I had adhered to my principles, any more than it will
know the loving heart and generous sympathy with which
I have always studied. The loving heart is the true
auxiliary of the comprehensive mind. -The truth Plato
had in mind when he made love and intelligence the two
wings of the soul on which it soars to the Empyrean.[44]

Not having had a thorough and systematic academic background,

Brownson almost had to approach books in this fashion. But before

he could digest and analyze these new ideas thoroughly, his edi-

torial position called on him to publish his views. The natural

dialectical process that he followed seemed to others merely a

trial-and-error procedure. This method caused Brownson heavy

criticism and even mockery for his "shifts of opinion." Neverthe-

less, as Ralph Waldo Emerson put it, "A foolish consistency is

the hobgoblin of little minds."[45] Brownson was consistent though,

in that he continually searched for the truth. His method, even

with its side-stepping and back-peddling, nonetheless constantly

brought him to a deeper level of understanding. If Brownson was

impaired by such a self-learning system, it would appear to be in

the field of philosophy where a sound professor of metaphysics

probably could have aided him in his search for truth and spared

---

[44]O.A.B. to Henry F. Brownson, April 24, 1867, HFB Collection, UNDA.

[45]See an apparently unpublished draft entitled "Consistency"
in which Brownson argues that because we are finite we are capable
of error. Since we must continually seek the truth, "the sooner a
man gets rid of an erroneous opinion the better," OABP, UNDA.

him much of the criticism he received. On the other hand, the
fact that he was self-educated enabled him to discuss education in
the broadest sense, to place schools within the overall context of
society, and to perceive the relationship between schools, education, and society.

Just as the printed word had contributed significantly to
Brownson's education, he believed reading should be an integral
part of everyone's learning. And because he considered it his
mission to instruct and elevate others, Orestes Brownson, almost
continually from 1829 until 1876, edited various journals and
contributed thousands of pages of articles and books. Beginning
with his editorship of the Gospel Advocate and Impartial Investigator (1829), Brownson launched a distinguished journalistic and
literary career that included editorial positions on the Genesee
Republican and Herald of Reform (1829), Free Enquirer (1829), and
The Philanthopist (1831-32). He contributed to the Christian
Register (1833), Unitarian (1833), and Christian Examiner (1833-
36). He briefly edited the Boston Reformer (1836) and the Boston
Quarterly Review (1838-42). His articles appeared in the United
States Magazine and Democratic Review (1843) and the Christian World
(1843). In addition, two books, Charles Elwood (written in 1834,
published in 1840), and New Views of Christianity, Society, and the
Church (1836) appeared before his conversion to Catholicism.

He was indeed a man with a mission, and he continued throughout his Catholic period to teach by means of the press and literature. His Brownson's Quarterly Review (1844-1864; 1873-1875)
remains the most distinguished nineteenth century American Catholic

journal. He also contributed to <u>Ave</u> <u>Maria</u>, <u>Catholic</u> <u>World</u>, and

the <u>New</u> <u>York</u> <u>Tablet</u> between 1865-1872. His books included <u>The</u>

<u>Spirit-Rapper</u> (1854), <u>The</u> <u>Convert</u> (1857), the <u>American</u> <u>Republic</u>

(1865) and <u>Liberalism</u> <u>and</u> <u>the</u> <u>Church</u> (1869). This vast amount of

literature penned by Brownson attempted to teach, to elevate, to

ameliorate man's mental, moral, and religious condition on earth.

As he had learned by reading, so he hoped others would.

He worked relentlessly, often against much opposition. He

hoped to elevate the populace, to get them to think for them-

selves.[46] Brownson's friend Montalembert attempted the same thing

in France, but he too met opposition and was discouraged. Brownson

wrote:

> I have had all my lifetime to fight against fearful
> odds, but I have never seen anything to do, but to
> keep on fighting. No man must stand up for truth and
> justice, God and heaven, but he had to complain of
> opposition from all quarters. He is sure to be
> opposed, and to be deserted by friends, and left to
> struggle on almost single handed. God gives him this
> trial, to prove him, and to let him see that his
> strength is in the Almighty.[47]

Carried onward by this divine calling, he often seemed alone in

his untiring efforts to fulfill his scholarly mission. And alone

he must have felt when <u>Brownson's</u> <u>Quarterly</u> <u>Review</u> folded in

1864.[48] Despite all his efforts on behalf of American Catholics

---

[46]See letter from O.A.B. to (Lord) John Dalberg Acton,
March 28, 1860, OABP, UNDA.

[47]O.A.B. to Montalembert, November 15, 1851, OABP, UNDA.

[48]Brownson had gradually lost the support of the hierarchy
for his <u>Review</u>. Articles on nativism, schools, and temporal power
of the pope had caused the erosion of support. Also, the Civil

and despite occasional letters of good will, Brownson at times
felt forgotten and discouraged. In 1865, he wrote Montalembert
that "I am now a nobody."[49] Neither the Pope, Bishops, clergy or
laity had supported him enough to sustain the Review. Deep inside,
it seems, Brownson considered himself impotent without his powerful
journal.

He soon realized, though, that his efforts had been appreciated, and could still be valuable. Father Edward Sorin of the
University of Notre Dame and Ave Maria soon enlisted Brownson's
pen, as did Catholic World and New York Tablet. Even though he
constantly wrote for these journals, Brownson often felt constrained. He complained to Fathers Augustine Hewit and Isaac
Hecker that they were restraining his rough vigor and robustness
by their editorial policies. Furthermore, Brownson felt that the
Catholic World needed an editor, and that it had too many feminine
writers "whether they wear skirts or breeches. It wants as a whole
robustness . . . . I feel that in writing for the C.W. I am only
half a man, and that I must suppress the rough vigor of thought and
expression that is natural to me."[50] Not agreeing with some of the
liberal notions of the Catholic World and not finding the
desperately needed Catholic leadership and scholarship there

War, with its disruptions of the mails, and his stand against
slavery, seriously diminished his subscriptions. Perhaps most
importantly, the deaths of two of his sons during the Civil War
(1864) drained much of his energy. See Chapter VII.

[49]O.A.B. to Montalembert, June 25, 1865, photostat of
letter from Archives du Chateau de la Roche-en-Breny, UNDA.

[50]O.A.B. to Fr. A.F. Hewit, February 28, 1870, OABP, UNDA;
see also H.S. Hewit to O.A.B., July 30, 1870, OABP, UNDA.

either, Orestes Brownson revived his Quarterly Review. With the

appearance of its first new issue in January, 1873, Brownson wrote

his son that "it is a luxury to feel that I am once more my own

master."[51] He continued writing and editing his Review until

October, 1875. Old age, poor health, and weak eyes all contributed

to Brownson's decision to close the Review.

Yet, for the last half of his life, Brownson employed his

pen for the moral, religious, intellectual, and social advancement

of American Catholics. With his retirement, and eventual death,

Catholics had lost their "Samson."[52] But, as one close friend

remarked, Brownson and his work would continue to live, to

influence, and to uplift the Catholic population. Although criti-

cized during his lifetime, the man whose words often went unheeded

would one day be regarded as a champion of the Catholic cause.

> Posthumous fame will be yours without doubt, and when
> the rising generation shall have reached your stand-
> point of view, words now ignored, or ridiculed, or
> scorned, shall burn like living fires into the brains
> of men and kindle in their hearts the love you will
> then be reaping. There is no mission so great, so
> honorable . . . as bearing the Cross after our divine
> Master.[53]

The person who had learned so much from reading contributed

thousands of pages for the elevation and instruction of his fellow

Catholics and countrymen.

---

[51] O.A.B. to H.F.B., January 7, 1873, HFB Collection, UNDA.

[52] Fr. David J. Doherty to O.A.B., October 12, 1874, OABP,
UNDA.

[53] Sr. M. Eulalia Pearce to O.A.B., May 26, 1865, OABP, UNDA.

Besides the printed word, the spoken word served as a vehicle of education. During his pre-Catholic period, Brownson attended many public lectures, and heard such noted speakers as Fanny Wright, William Ellery Channing and Theodore Parker. He recognized the public lecture as a viable means of instruction. During his ministry in Canton, Brownson established, in addition to a library, a lyceum that attracted outstanding speakers and leading minds of the day to that community. Shortly after his arrival in Boston, his reputation as a speaker spread and from 1837 on, he himself played a significant role as a lecturer not only in the New England area but throughout the entire country as well. This activity became another way of fulfilling the scholar's mission. He had something to say and it was his duty to say it. In the same manner that he learned, so too he effectively instructed others--by teaching, preaching, writing, and lecturing. Just as he himself learned so much after his thirtieth birthday, Brownson directed most of his sermons, writings, and lectures toward adults.

Besides the library and lyceum that Brownson initiated, he took part in several other cooperative ventures. For a time he met with the Transcendental Club of Margaret Fuller, Bronson Alcott, Frederic Henry Hedge, George Ripley, and others. In addition Brownson played a part in the discussions at Brook Farm. Its founder, George Ripley, acknowledged that Brownson had served as the inspiration for such an experiment.[54] Almost five years

---

[54]George Ripley to O.A.B., December 12, 1842, OABP, UNDA.

earlier, Brownson had received a similar letter from Henry David
Thoreau, recalling the six-week joint learning experience the two
had shared at Brownson's home.[55] Brownson served as Thoreau's
informal teacher, much the same as he influenced Isaac Hecker and
others at Brook Farm.

Brownson's own Society for Christian Union and Progress was
basically an attempt at mutual improvement. With Brownson as the
leading figure, the society's overriding goal was the mental, moral,
and social amelioration of the poorer and more numerous classes of
the Boston vicinity. Brownson was active not only in his own
society but cooperated with several other voluntary organizations.
In 1836, the Boston and Vicinity Female Improvement Society called
on him for assistance in the formation of a seminary to train
teachers for common schools. The United Brothers Society of Brown
University asked him to attend one of their meetings in 1841. The
Philomathean Society of Pennsylvania College, Gettysburg, formed
"to cultivate a taste for learning and to create and cherish mutual
regard and friendship among its members," elected Brownson an
honorary member because of his promotion of literature and ethics.
The Mechanic Apprentices Library Association of Boston thanked
Brownson for donating a subscription of his Review to its library.
The secretary, Charles W. Slack, noted how the Review would be
conducive to "their mental and moral improvement and establish
their self-respect as a class." Nor was it inappropriate for the
University Institute of Vermont to elect Brownson an honorary

---

[55]Henry D. Thoreau to O.A.B., December 30, 1837, OABP, UNDA.

member for his fine oration, "The Scholar's Mission."[56]

Brownson, then, joined adult improvement societies and enhanced his own learning. He aided in the formation of several organizations and contributed writings and lectures to hundreds of other associations, lyceums, institutes, and societies.[57] Why? Because he saw these adult mutual benefit societies as viable educational agencies. Education was an ongoing process, and it was only proper that Brownson who had learned from such organizations would contribute significantly to the religious, moral, mental and social improvement of his fellow citizens. At times, Brownson considered the education of adults more important than the education of children. Just as his foster parents taught him, he expected all other parents to teach their children. Logically, Brownson devoted most of his efforts toward the education of adults.

Brownson, in attempting to fulfill the scholarly mission of educator, was highly influenced by the very education that he had received. For Orestes Brownson, this education precluded much formal schooling--just a brief period at an academy. Most of his learning was by informal means and employed a self-help Franklin model: learning from foster parents, the Church and a printing job;

_____

[56]See the following: Letter to the President and Directors of the Franklin Bank, April 6, 1836, OABP, UNDA (Female Improvement Society); Charles Hart and C. George Fenner to O.A.B., January 9, 1841, OABP, UNDA (Brown); Benj. F. Hany to O.A.B., January 16, 1841, OABP UNDA (Gettysburg); Charles E. Tefft to O.A.B., July 21, 1843, OABP, UNDA (Milledgville); Charles W. Slack to O.A.B., June 10, 1844, OABP UNDA (Mechanic Apprentices); Moses Lane to O.A.B., September 13, 1843, OABP, UNDA (Vermont).

[57]Although Brownson's connection with only a few of these adult societies has been evidenced so far, more extensive treatment will be given in Chapter IX.

writing a diary; constantly reading books, newspapers, and periodicals; listening to lectures; and joining mutual improvement societies. Brownson served as an educator in much the same way that he himself had learned. He briefly was a teacher. Always convinced of the importance of religion, he became a minister and wrote articles on religion. He learned from others' writings and taught through his own journals, essays, and books. He became a popular speaker, giving hundreds of lectures. Finally, he cooperated with numerous mutual improvement societies through his lectures and writings. In short, he became a scholar with a duty.

Looking back upon Brownson's education, one might wonder whether or not we place too much emphasis on formal education today. Certainly, there is no shortage of rhetoric on the value of a high school diploma (often stated in terms of earning power) or of a bachelor's degree (or even a master's degree or doctorate). Hiring practices reinforce this belief. The popular mind indeed equates education with schooling. But who could claim even today that all learning takes place in a classroom? The role of the family, peer group, television, radio, movies, books, newspapers, magazines lectures and concerts--all form part of the educational process.

If Brownson had emphasized the role of the "scholar" in his oration, he also stressed the pervading importance and necessity of religion. Without religion, neither the scholar nor mankind could properly fulfill the destiny which God envisioned. Thus, it is crucial to examine Brownson's own religious development and attempt to explain the overwhelming influence that religion played in his life.

CHAPTER II

RELIGION AND THE SCHOLAR

i

BROWNSON'S RELIGIOUS FORMATION

The earliest wish I recollect to have formed with
regard to my future life, was to be a minister of
religion, and to devote myself to the work of bringing
people to the knowledge and the love of God. For this
I longed to go to school, to get learning, to grow up,
and to be a man. I early looked upon myself as one
called and set apart to the service of religion.[1]

Much of Brownson's early upbringing was quite typical of

Congregational New England. His foster parents taught him to be

honest, upright, and strictly moral; to be frugal and industrious;

to speak the truth and never lie; to never steal, even the value

of a pin; to keep the Sabbath; to never let the sun set on his

wrath. He learned the Shorter Catechism, Apostles' Creed, Lord's

Prayer, and the "Now I lay me down to sleep" evening rhyme. He had

read the Bible by age 8, and mastered it by age 14. In addition,

he had read Watts' Psalms and Divine Songs, Edwards' History of

Redemption, and Davies' Sermons. Needless to say, his early

training was heavily moral and religious.

Even during the War of 1812, Brownson's thoughts "took a

religious turn." He delighted in religious conversations--whether

---

[1]Orestes A. Brownson, The Convert, or Leaves from My Experience (New York: Edward Dunnigan and Brother, 1857), p. 6.

31

as a participant or listener. He vividly remembered, at age 9,
taking part in a theological discussion of free will and election,
and remained affected by the mystery of Christ's Redemption to
save man.[2]

Yet, religious certitudes of his childhood eventually gave
way to doubts during his adolescence. "My youth was not as blame-
less as my childhood, and it was far less happy. Religion, however,
never lost its place in my thoughts. But unhappily, while I had
strong religious affections, and the elements of Christian belief,
I belonged to no Church and had no definite creed."[3] The vagueness
of his religious instruction caused confusion to the groping
adolescent. "Getting" or "experiencing" religion, "changing heart,"
and "being born again" were passwords to which Orestes could attach
but little meaning.

He remembered the various religious bodies near his home,
especially the Methodists' loud and noisy sermons on hell fire.
His love of God turned into terror, as Orestes feared his soul's
capture by the devil. At age twelve, he sought religious counsel
from an old lady who lived nearby. It is apparent that even at
this early age, Brownson was searching for true religion. By
fourteen, he was filled with confusion, doubt, and bewilderment.
All religion seemed but a delusion.[4]

However, during September and October of 1822, Brownson's
need for religious security was temporarily satisfied when he

[2]Ibid., pp. 1-3.
[3]Ibid., p. 7.
[4]Ibid., pp. 8-13.

submitted himself for baptism into the Presbyterian Church. As
Orestes recalled later, he had decided to relinquish his free
exercise of reason for an authoritative teacher, but instead,
found that he had obtained no such teacher. He had joined the
church because he had despaired of himself and of his reason--"the
act of an intellectual desperado."[5]

From late 1822 until 1825, Brownson kept a "Notebook of
Reflections" or diary. In it one traces his religious transforma-
tion from Calvinism to Universalism. His religious wanderings,
self-doubt, notions about man's depravity, and the evils contained
in novels, surrounded his occasional serene exclamations: "How
beautiful is religion!"[6] In a section of the diary entitled
"Meditations on the fall of Empires," Brownson attributed the
decline of great nations to God taking out his wrath in vengeance
for man's rebelling against God, polluting His temples, defiling
His altars, reviling His priests, and murdering His saints.[7] Not
only did Brownson worry about his own personal religious condition,
but also he noted the catastrophic results when an entire people
or nation became religiously lax or indifferent.[8]

---

[5]Ibid., pp. 18-25.

[6]Orestes A. Brownson, "Notebook of Reflections," OABP, UNDA,
p. 17.

[7]Ibid., pp. 46-47.

[8]Brownson remarked emphatically that whenever man pursued the
love of ease, ignorance, and especially the path of vice, inevitable
evil was certain to follow. The worst vice, according to Brownson,
was excessive drinking. He pointed to the hard-working, industrious man as beloved by society. The drunkard, however, neglected
to keep up his home and fields, to feed and clothe his family
properly, or to educate his children.

In sum, Brownson was aghast at man's idolatry, vice and ignorance. This early preoccupation with man's religious, moral, and intellectual state became fastened in Brownson's mind. Young and confused, groping for truth, he was unable to find solutions to the problems he encountered. Soon, however, he would plot his course to work for the amelioration of the conditions of the human race--its religious, moral, and intellectual improvement.

About 1824 or 1825, a noticeable change occurred in the religious beliefs of Orestes Brownson. Still writing in his diary, he saw God in a new light. No longer was God taking out revenge on man. Instead, Brownson wrote that "Amor est Deus" and "Veritas /¯est_7 filius Dei." God was infinite in power, wisdom, and un-bounded goodness, and Jesus Christ was His son. The doctrines He taught were eternal truth, and He exhibited the true character of God. All men would be reconciled to their creator; all discord would cease; sorrow and sighing would flee away--when this true character of Christ was exhibited and preached to every creature on earth. The changes in doctrine were obvious. He rejected the doctrines of total depravity, unconditional election and reproba-tion. He refused to believe that God foreordained the wicked to sin. And so, at age 21, his religious views turned an about face-- from the supernaturalism of Orthodox Christianity to the rational-ism of liberal Christianity. He had become a Universalist.[9]

Brownson accepted Universalism because he no longer had any good reason to believe in Prestyterianism. It had not provided

---

[9] The Convert, pp. 31-37; see also "Notebook of Reflections," p. 98.

him with the authoritative, infallible religious security that he
sought. Presbyterianism never claimed infallibility. While it
conceded the possibility of error, it never showed proof of its
institution by Christ and his Apostles, and never claimed its
founders had acted under divine commission.[10] To the man searching
after certitude, all that prevailed was uncertainty.

In 1825, he received a letter of fellowship as a preacher
from the General Convention of Universalists which had met that
year in Hartland, Vt. On June 15, 1826, he was ordained a minister
by the Universalist Association of Jaffrey, New Hampshire.[11] From
this time, until about 1830, Brownson continued to work as a
minister, spending time in Fort Ann, Whitehall, Litchfield, Ithaca,
Geneva, and Auburn, New York.[12] But Universalism did not provide
the ultimate security Brownson so eagerly sought. If his reason
was no longer able to accept the principles of Presbyterianism, it
soon questioned and eventually denied the tenets of Universalism.
If salvation was a right for all men (no longer a favor granted by
God), vice had no punishment and virtue no reward. As unreasonable
as eternal punishment seemed, universal salvation could not be
defended on logical grounds either.

"It is a contradiction in terms to say that you believe what
you hold to be unreasonable," Brownson wrote. He spent his last
two years as a Universalist preaching and professing "more" than

[10]Ibid., p. 38.
[11]Edward Turner to O.A.B., June 15, 1826, OABP, UNDA.
[12]The Convert, p. 64.

he believed. Finally, he admitted the dichotomy in his thought and
action and left the Universalists. He later remarked that these
last two years were probably the most "anti-Christian" of his life.[13]
Shortly after leaving Universalism, Brownson began to regain his
balance of mind.

What is important is not only that Brownson was searching for
religious certitude in his decisions to join and to leave the
Universalists. Equally important is the basic change of belief.
If man was not doomed to eternal punishment, if God was good, if
all men could be elevated through instruction in the eternal
truths of Christ, then man needed to obligate himself to bring
about the religious, moral, and intellectual amelioration of the
human race. Brownson was unable to do this work as a Presbyterian.
As a Universalist, he became a minister, a primary agent in the
work of improving man's lot. And this was the important change
that took place in Brownson during the mid 1820's.

In addition to his preaching, he began a long and distinguished career as an editor and journalist in the cause of ameliorating man's condition on earth. Prior to 1830, he had edited
the Universalist journal, Gospel Advocate and Impartial Investigator. He exerted much time to social issues, as evidenced by his
position as a corresponding editor of the Free Enquirer, a
periodical published by Robert Owen and Fanny Wright, and his
editorship of the Genesee Republican and Herald of Reform. From

_____

[13]Ibid., pp. 70, 81-82.

his mid-20's until he died, Brownson considered the pen and press, priest and pulpit as powerful agents in the cause of improving man's condition.

He continued working for man's betterment throughout the 1830's and 1840's. In 1857, when he reviewed his early years, Brownson, now the staunch Catholic, remarked about this period of his life (1838-1842): "My end was man's earthly happiness, and my creed was progress."[14] He attributed this "change" from concern for the ultimate religious truth to concern for the material order to the doubts he acquired as a Universalist. Brownson claimed he no longer saw the utility of laboring for another world. He therefore became a "world reformer," and focused on earthly life.

> I had a firm belief in progress, full confidence in philosophy, and a strong desire to contribute to the welfare of my fellow-men, to reform the world, and create an earthly paradise for the human race; but I had very little thought or sense of my duty to God, and no serious care for anything beyond the service of my neighbor in relation to this life. I recognized God, but only in man, and I held that he exists for us only in human nature.[15]

But the facts of his life seem to indicate that Brownson was more concerned with religion than he would have us believe. His uncertainty and groping for religious truth were surely apparent, but he was religious in his concerns nonetheless. No matter how weak his theological knowledge, religious concerns, along with earthly matters, continued to dominate his life.

---

[14]_Ibid._, p. 102.
[15]_Ibid._, p. 103.

Brownson became involved in several "earthly" causes, such
as that of the workingman, and labored with Frances Wright, Robert
Dale Owen, and R. L. Jennings. He cooperated with The Daily
Sentinel, and edited the Genesee Republican and Herald of Reform
until the autumn of 1830. However, Brownson soon realized that a
void existed in all of his reform efforts.

> The moment I avowedly threw off all religion and began
> to work without it, I found myself impotent. I did
> not need religion to pull down or destroy society, but
> the moment I wished to build up, to effect something
> positive, I found I could not proceed a single step
> without it. I was compelled to make brick without
> straw.[16]

Without religion, progress and reform were but dreams. The
actions of man ought to be directed toward his own best interest.
But Brownson regretfully perceived that man acted "from habit, from
routine, from appetite and passion, and will sacrifice /_his_7
highest and best good to /_his_7 momentary lusts. It is an old
complaint," Brownson remarked, "that men do not act as well as
they know. They see the right, approve it, and yet pursue the
wrong."[17] Man needed a power to overcome such temptations,
passions, and lusts, and Brownson found it in religion. Only
through religious ideas and principles--belief in God and immortality, moral duty and accountability--could man be induced to make
the sacrifices required to work out the reform of society and to
secure for man his earthly felicity. And so, shortly after

[16]Ibid., p. 141.
[17]Ibid., p. 142.

quitting his journal in late 1830, Brownson resumed his old pro-
fession--that of a preacher.

Not even Brownson knew exactly what religion he preached in
1831. William Ellery Channing's sermon on the "Dignity of Human
Nature" soon led Brownson to affiliate with Unitarianism. The
liberal, rational, and independent nature of the religion attracted
the young Brownson, still not 30 years old. Again he wrote that
"my great aim was not to serve God, but to serve man; the love of
my race, not the love of my Maker, moved me."[18] But again, the
facts of his life throughout the Unitarian period (1831-1842) seem
to refute his own contention that he was not concerned with God and
religious salvation.

Numerous examples of his deep concern and interest in
religious matters are noteworthy. First of all, Brownson did in
fact become a minister. He traveled for months preaching in
various areas of New York, Vermont, New Hampshire, and Massachusetts. He resided as Gospel Minister in Walpole, New Hampshire
from 1833 until 1834, when he left to assume a similar post in
Canton, Massachusetts, a post which he held until 1836. At the
suggestion of George Ripley and Ezra Stiles Gannett, Brownson
moved to Boston in 1836 and established a ministry among the
working classes which lasted until the 1840's. This became

---

[18]Ibid., p. 148. See also Dr. William Ellery Channing to
O.A.B., January 11, 1834, OABP, UNDA, in which Channing expressed
gratification that Brownson considers Christianity as a principle
of reform.

Brownson's own Society for Christian Union and Progress.[19] He was
not merely concerned with earthly happiness; religious and inner
growth were much a part of his ministerial endeavors. In an incomplete letter, tentatively dated 1834, Brownson wrote: "Make
man right within, and you will have no difficulty in making him
right without, at least such is the philosophy of yours respect-
fully, O.A. Brownson."[20]

Secondly, besides his ministerial work, Brownson engaged
himself as a serious religious writer during this "sublunary"
period of his life. During 1831-1832, he edited and published a
journal of religion and benevolence, The Philanthropist. In 1832,
he wrote "Letters to an Unbeliever," a 184 page manuscript that
apparently was never published.[21] This, however, apparently

---

[19]See the following letters in the OABP, UNDA: J. Crosley
and Addison Brown to O.A.B., May 23, 1833, relative to the position
at Walpole; Thomas Bellows and John Bellows to O.A.B., March 10,
1834, Leonard Everett and Thomas French to O.A.B., March 3, 1834,
and William Gruber, Thomas Dunbar, Jonathan Messinger, Thomas
French, and Leonard Everett to O.A.B., March 18, 1834, relative to
position in Canton; George Ripley to O.A.B., March 26, 1834, E. S.
Gannett to O.A.B., April 9, 1835, and Joseph Allen to O.A.B., April
25, 1835, relative to formation of a society in Boston. Brownson,
Gannett, and Allen apparently were working together on a committee
that was considering the Boston experiment. Some of their recommendations, besides preaching Unitarianism, were to develop and
circulate a new translation and commentary of the Bible, to publish
books illustrative of Scripture, devotional works, and treatises on
Christian character. Finally, they hoped to encourage new recruits
to the ministry and to obtain new ministers from Theology schools.
Several letters from Brownson to his wife, contained in the Odiorne
Collection, UNDA, indicate the intensity and seriousness of his job-
hunting ventures. See O.A.B. to Sarah Healy Brownson, August 24,
1832, October 15, 1832, and February 19, 1834. In these letters,
Brownson assesses his preaching abilities, views on religion, on
his fellow ministers, and on various congregations that he met.
[20]Incomplete letter of O.A.B. to ?, 1834(?), OABP, UNDA.
[21]See OABP, UNDA.

provided the basis for a book finished in 1834, Charles Elwood, or
the Infidel Converted. The book was partly autobiographical, and
centered on the passage of its hero "from infidelity to an un-
wavering belief in God and the supernatural origin of Christianity."[22] Between 1833-1836, Brownson contributed articles to
several religious journals such as George Ripley's Christian
Register, Bernard Whitman's Unitarian, and James Walker's Christian
Examiner.

Brownson continued his writings when he moved to Boston. In
conjunction with the formation of his new society, he wrote New
Views of Christianity, Society and the Church, a work in which he
attempted to reconcile, in eclectic fashion, the excesses of
Catholic spiritualism and Protestant materialism. His overriding
theme was progress. "There is progress; there will be progress.
Humanity must go forward. Encouraging is the future."[23] Brownson
cited the re-examination and progress in institutions such as
religion, government, philanthropy, and also efforts aimed at
improving the individual. The central issue, the springboard of
progress was education. "All eyes and hearts are turned to education. The cultivation of the child's moral and spiritual nature
becomes the worship of God. The priest rises to the educator, and
the school-room is the temple in which he is to minister."[24] The

---

[22]Orestes A. Brownson, Charles Elwood, or the Infidel Converted (London: Chapman Brothers, 1840), p. 185. Brownson had
withheld the book from publication for the six year period.

[23]Orestes A. Brownson, New Views of Christianity, Society,
and the Church (Boston: James Munroe & Company, 1836), p. 116.

[24]Ibidem.

theme of progress via education, in reality, was intimately linked
to the moral and spiritual elevation of the populace. The religious
element permeated Brownson's scheme of progress.

In addition to his ministerial work and religious writings,
Brownson also served as editor of the _Boston Reformer_ during 1836.
Although the _Reformer_ was overtly concerned with worldly reforms,
complaints about "too much religion" crept into its columns during
Brownson's editorship. He responded by refusing to condemn the
clergy as others were doing. Brownson argued that the clergy were
essential in the work of reforming society, and that as long as he
was editor, the articles in the _Reformer_ would continue to breathe
a moral and religious tone![25]

It would appear that Brownson, writing his autobiography in
1857, certainly underestimated the deep religious feelings that he
actually possessed during the 1830's and early 1840's. He was not
merely concerned with man's earthly existence and happiness. In
fact, in a sermon delivered in 1835, Brownson warned the youth of
Canton not to seek wealth, rank, or money. Rather, riches of the
soul, moral wealth, goodness, righteousness, honesty, and virtue
were the only real distinctions and worth they should seek.
Man's chief end was to achieve moral virtue and goodness.

> He who exemplifies, in its perfection, a single moral
> virtue, he who discovers and places in the world, a
> single new truth in morals, in religion or in the
> philosophy of mind, outdoes the proudest of earth's
> heroes, exerts a power greater than any king or

[25]Brownson kept a "Notebook of Clippings" during the brief
time he was editor of the _Boston Reformer_ in 1836. See OABP,
UNDA.

emperor ever did or ever can exert . . . . /¯B¯/e able
to say in your dying hour, that the world has been the
better for your having lived.[26]

These were certainly words not spoken by a man of mere "sublunary"
interests.

It was during the 1830's that Brownson became influenced by
two ideas in Benjamin Constant's Religion, Considered in its Origin,
its Forms and its Development. First of all, Constant argued that
man's religious beliefs were progressive, in that they proceeded
from the lowest forms of fetishism to the highest forms of
Christian monotheism. Brownson easily appended his own theory of
human progress to this--and arrived at a formula maintaining that
human progress was essentially intertwined with religious progress.
Secondly, Constant alleged that man naturally sought to embody his
religious ideas and sentiments in institutional forms, and that
these institutions, in turn, served as instruments of progress.
Brownson turned to institutionalized religion to effect reform in
society; he now looked for the Church of the Future.

Believing that Catholicism had outlived its day by over-
stressing the spiritual, and that Protestantism had served as an
agency of destruction by overemphasizing the material, Brownson
attempted to find, and even build, the necessary religious organization. For a while he considered William Ellery Channing as the
new Messiah. Brownson even considered himself as a precursor of

[26]O. A. Brownson, Sermon Delivered to the Young People of
the First Congregational Society in Canton, on Sunday, May 24th,
1835 (Dedham, 1835), pp. 16, 18.

the new Messiah. Not only did Brownson proclaim the necessity of

a new Church, he even began one--The Society for Christian Union

and Progress--that lasted from July, 1836 until the latter part of

1843.[27]

Another major influence on Brownson during this period was

Claude Henri, Count de Saint-Simon. Henri's work Nouveau

Christianisme (1825) pointed to the need for religion in the proper

organization of the human race. Henri himself had led a life of

dissipation and vice, but was brought to a realization of the need

for religion. Henri and his followers, the Saint-Simonians,

asserted that the future progress of the human race was linked to

religion, and that religion, in the future as well as in the past,

needed an organization and an hierarchical structure. Brownson

reassured himself of the necessity of religion in life, and

gradually removed from his mind the popular prejudice against the

Papacy that so engulfed his countrymen.[28]

But Brownson was no immediate convert to Catholicism. In

1840, he published his "Essay on the Laboring Classes" in which he

spoke of eliminating priests altogether. Arthur M. Schlesinger,

Jr., considered this essay as Brownson's best, and even called

Brownson a "pre-Marxian Marx." Brownson himself later called these

---

[27]The Convert, pp. 152-178; see also New Views of Christianity, Society, and the Church. Brownson also acknowledges the
influence of Victor Cousin's eclecticism on his thinking at this
time. Brownson and Cousin corresponded briefly during the 1836-
1838 period, after Brownson wrote an article on Cousin's philosophy
in the Christian Examiner of September, 1836.

[28]The Convert, pp. 199-216.

Page 45

views his "horrible doctrines," for he was speaking of Protestantism as he knew it, and of Catholicism as it had been misrepresented to him by Protestants. In defense of Brownson, Leonard Gilhooley maintains that Schlesinger's appelation is unfortunate and incorrect. Gilhooley argues that Brownson was not nearly as radical as Schlesinger thinks. After examining Brownson's many other writings prior to and after the "Essay on the Labor Classes," he concludes that Brownson was basically more conservative than has been thought, and certainly no "pre-Marxian Marx." Gilhooley believes that the essay must be read in the context of the panic of 1837 and seen as an attempt to alleviate pressing social and economic problems that were still very much in evidence in 1840.[29] Brownson maintained that whereas he tried to establish a new Church in 1836, he attempted in 1840 to found a new State based on Christian democratic principles.

Following the election of 1840 when Van Buren was defeated by the hard cider followers of William Henry Harrison, Brownson began studying political philosophy. He became more conservative and advocated the need for a firm, strong, and efficient government.

> The condition of liberty is order . . . . Liberty is
> not in the absence of authority, but in being held to
> obey only just and legitimate authority . . . .

[29]See Orestes A. Brownson, "The Laboring Classes," BoQR, III (1840), pp. 358-395, and 420-512; Arthur M. Schlesinger, Jr., Orestes A. Brownson - A Pilgrim's Progress (New York: Octagon Books, Inc., 1939), pp. 88-111; Leonard Gilhooley, Contradiction and Dilemma: Orestes Brownson and the American Idea (New York: Fordham University Press, 1972), pp. 44-63. For Brownson's reflections on the essay, see The Convert, pp. 240-267.

Government was no longer the mere agent of society as my Democratic masters had taught me, but an authority having the right and the power to govern society, and direct and aid it, as a wise Providence, in fulfilling its destiny.[30]

Just as Brownson became a political conservative, he advanced rapidly toward religious conservatism as well. Under the chapter heading "Man No Church Builder," Brownson argued the case for religious authority.

There is no true liberty without order, and no order without a constituted authority. Then, since no progress without liberty, my new church, necessary to the maintenance of order, instead of coming after progress and being its result, must precede it, and be the condition of effecting it.[31]

Just as governmental authority was essential for political order, liberty, and progress, so too, religious authority was necessary as a starting point for all order, liberty, and progress. For Brownson, religion, and an authoritative religious institution at that, became the sine qua non of true order and liberty within society, and hence, of all true progress.

And yet, Brownson still had not found the authoritative religion necessary for the preservation and sustenance of true progress. What Brownson considered beyond dispute was the fact that man was an imperfect being who could not lift himself up. Man could only be lifted by direct communion with a higher and elevating object. "Human life," he argued, "is the resultant of

[30] The Convert, p. 267.
[31] Ibid., p. 268.

two forces, of the intercommunion of subject and object." Only
God was a complete being who was capable of living in, from, and
by himself. Man, the incomplete being, could be elevated only by
communion with that which was not himself. "Man is not and cannot
be in himself progressive, and his progress depends on the objective element of his life, or, in other words, on his living in
communion with God, and not only in a natural communion, . . .
but also in a supernatural communion."[32]

All life was the joint product of subject and object. Man,
the subject, did not live by himself, but through communion with
an object not himself. The object, however, was not merely a
passive entity but an active entity which acted on the subject no
less than the subject acted on the object. "They mutually act
and react on each other, and in their mutual action and reaction
the fact of life is generated. The object by its action flows
into the subject, and becomes a real element of the life of the
subject." If the object was supernatural (God), the life of the
subject would be elevated, and true progress secured. The Divine
could flow into the human, and "by a Providential elevation of
individuals by the Creator to an extraordinary or supernatural
communion with himself, they would live a divine life, and we by
communion with them would also be elevated, and live a higher and
more advanced life."[33] And thus, through these providential men,

---

[32]Ibid., p. 291. Brownson here is influenced by Pierre Leroux
and his doctrine of communion. Brownson, however, extended Leroux's
argument beyond the natural to include supernatural communion as
well. [33]Ibid., pp. 294-295.

God secured the elevation and progress of the human race. Brownson
argued that throughout history "the race has always believed that
men are elevated and set forward by supernatural assistance,
obtained through the agency of specially inspired individuals; or
what I call Providential Men . . . . This is the essential, the
vital principle of all the religions which are or ever have been."[34]
In this way, the supernatural element flowed into the natural and
elevated human action. Only thus was true progress achieved and
assured.

Brownson's doctrine of life and communion explain the effi-
cacy of Christ. Since He was the Divine object, Christ was able
to elevate the human race. Life was supernaturally elevated and
progress was assured. Communion with God--through Christ and his
duly-appointed Apostles and their successors--was actualized
through Holy Communion, whereby Divine life was infused into man
and supernaturalized his life.[35]

In late 1842 and early 1843, Brownson commenced a series of
articles on "The Mission of Jesus" that appeared in The Christian
World. The eighth article, which was to answer the question,
"which is the true Church or Body of Christ?", was rejected by
the editor. A Catholic editor offered to publish it, but even
Brownson hesitated and evaded the logical answer. His logic had
brought him to the brink of Roman Catholicism, but he refused to
follow his own principles and "betrayed inexcusable weakness in

[34]Ibid., p. 315.
[35]See an article that Brownson wrote in 1842, "The Media-
torial Life of Jesus," BoQR, V (July, 1842), 383-384.

not submitting to her /‾the Catholic Church‾7 sooner than /‾he‾7

did."[36] Indeed Brownson repeatedly denied that he was heading

Romeward, and tried to satisfy his religious beliefs in the Oxford

or Tractarian movement of the Episcopal Church.[37] But his close

friends, Isaac B. Peirce and Anne C. Lynch, and other observers

too, clearly saw the road to Rome that Brownson was walking.[38]

Brownson was certainly familiar with all of the popular argu-

ments against the Catholic Church. These surely accounted for much

of his long delay in submitting. Finally, in late May, 1844, he

obtained an interview with Bishop Benedict J. Fenwick of Boston,

---

[36] The Convert, p. 355.

[37] See BrQR I (January, 1844), 15-28; and O.A.B. to Isaac
Hecker, September 2, 1843, photostat of letter in the Paulist
Archives, contained in OABP, UNDA.

[38] Anne C. Lynch to O.A.B., April 10, 1843, OABP, UNDA; Isaac
B. Peirce to O.A.B., July 28, 1843, OABP, UNDA; Anonymous letter
signed Benj. Franklin to O.A.B., February 21, 1843, OABP, UNDA;
and an undated newspaper clipping contained in the New York Public
Library commented upon Brownson's sermons becoming more and more
conservative. It flatly predicted that before long, Brownson
would be a Catholic. As early as July 2, 1836, the Boston Pilot
advised Brownson that his efforts in the Society for Christian
Union and Progress were futile, unless he turned to the Catholic
Church. The Pilot seemed confident that should Brownson system-
atically study the character and doctrines of the Catholic Church,
he would become a very good Catholic. Brownson's response was:
"We assure the Pilot, that we are at this late day under no
necessity of examining catholicism. We have examined it, and that
too, perhaps, with as much patience and candour as the editor of
the Pilot. We know its pretensions, its truths and its errors; we
have always treated it with respect, and given it credit for the
good it has done. We share in none of the common protestant
hostility to it, but we must tell those who would convert us to
Catholicism, it is TOO LATE. The Mission of the catholic church is
ended. It is now only a cumberer of the ground. Its symbols no
longer have any life," from Brownson's "Notebook of Clippings--
Boston Reformer, 1836," OABP, UNDA. That Brownson was open-minded
toward Catholicism, and quite opposed to Protestant bigotry can be
seen in his review of the Life of Cardinal Cheverus, Archbishop of
Bordeaux, formerly Bishop of Boston, Massachusetts in "Literary
Notices," BoQR, II (1839), 387-389, and his review of My progress

who immediately placed Brownson under the instruction of the
Reverend John B. Fitzpatrick, future Bishop of Boston. On October
20, 1844, Brownson officially entered the Catholic Church. His
long search for an authoritative religion had ended. Despite the
many predictions that he would soon renounce his Catholicism,
Brownson remained a steadfast Catholic until death, nearly thirty-
two years later. Undoubtedly, Brownson felt assured that he had
found the one religion with authority--divinely instituted by
Christ, and through the doctrines of life and communion, continually endowed with internal authority.

Brownson's conversion to Catholicism led many of his contemporaries to label him fickle and to picture him as a weather-
vane, swaying whichever way the wind blew. On the surface, the
charges are understandable, for anyone who had passed through
Presbyterianism, Universalism, Unitarianism, and Transcendental-
ism, and ended in Catholicism, certainly appeared to be changeable,
if not unsound as a thinker. But many of these charges arose only
when he submitted to "anti-Christ," "the whore of Rome." Although
his logical, dialectical mind had constantly matured, his Protestant contemporaries viewed his changes as mental aberrations.
Consequently, Brownson's reputation has suffered immensely. Recent
scholarship, however, indicates that most of these charges were
unwarranted. Per Sveino, in his Orestes A. Brownson's Road to
Catholicism (Oslo: Universitetsforlaget, 1970), by far the most
thorough presentation of Brownson's early thought, making wide use

_____

in Error, and recovery to Truth: or a Tour through Universalism,
Unitarianism, and Skepticism in "Literary Notices," BoQR, V (1842),
127-128.

of all of his writings that appeared before the inception of the
Boston Quarterly Review in 1838, has argued convincingly that
Brownson maintained a basic consistency in his religious and
intellectual development that led to his entering the Catholic
Church.

Authority was essential for Brownson. "Authority for
believing is always necessary, and nothing is more unreasonable
than to believe without authority. Belief without authority is
credulity, is folly, or madness; not an act of reason, but an act
of unreason."[39] Having found the true divinely authorized
religion, Brownson would re-commence his mission, working for the
mental, social, moral, and religious amelioration of the human
race, especially of its Catholic portion. Because he had found
the authoritative religion, order, liberty, and progress could now
be secured for himself, his fellow Catholics, and hopefully, for
his fellow citizens as well. It was appropriate that just prior
to his actual conversion to Catholicism, Brownson delivered his
Oration on the Scholar's Mission. Much of this mission was essentially religious in nature.

Throughout the remainder of his life, Brownson wrote un-
tiringly on religious matters. In all, at least 300-400 articles
on religious topics were penned by Brownson himself in the pages
of his own Brownson's Quarterly Review (1844-1864, 1873-1875),
Ave Maria, the Catholic World, and the New York Tablet (1865-1872).

_____

[39]The Convert, p. 413.

In general, these articles fall into four categories:[40] 1) those defending and explaining Catholic doctrine against misrepresentations by Protestants and bigots; 2) those pointing out the errors of non-Catholic religions; 3) those instructing Catholics in their own religion; and 4) those showing not only the compatibility of Catholicity to American government, but also the indispensability of Catholicity to American growth and progress. These several thousand pages of religious essays reveal the basic and primary concern, and perhaps obsession, of Orestes Brownson for religion. They demonstrate his belief that religion lay at the heart of all true order, liberty, reform, and progress. If one accepted the above proposition, as Brownson did, and if one believed he possessed a God-given mission to perform a service for the mental, social, moral and religious amelioration of the human race, as Brownson did, then it was only logical that one devoted so much of his energy to furthering the cause of the Catholic religion in America; and this, Brownson did.[41]

---

[40]I use these four categories as a matter of convenience. I am certain other categories may just as easily be devised.

[41]It would be beyond the scope of our central purpose to delve further into the first three categories of religious articles at this time. A sampling of these writings will be included in the Bibliographical essay. Also, a discussion of these essays will constitute a part of the chapter dealing with the educational role of the Catholic press.

ii

SCHOLAR'S GOAL: AMERICANIZE CATHOLICISM, CATHOLICIZE AMERICA

From the time that he first recorded his "Notebook of
Reflections" in the early 1820's until his death in 1876, Orestes
Brownson linked a country's greatness to its religious progress.
Religious laxity had caused the fall of Rome; only religious
strength could secure future greatness for America.[42] In a
lecture before a trade union about 1840, Brownson remarked: "the
mighty power that is to carry society forward to its perfection is
Christian morality."[43] A dozen or so years later, Brownson equated
Christian morality with Catholic morality; Protestant morality was
no morality at all. In the "True Catholic Spirit," Brownson
criticized the Yankee, Protestant definition of man: "an animal
that makes money." Real wealth was divine grace. "The love of
the world, the scramble for wealth, for places, for power, are
threatening our Republic with ruin, and there is no redeeming power
in Protestantism to arrest the danger."[44] This earthly philosophy
was destroying man's faith, hope, and charity, and was supplanting

---

[42]See "Notebook of Reflections," pp. 46-47. See William
Ellery Channing to O.A.B., January 11, 1834, OABP, UNDA. In this
letter Channing praised Brownson's view of Christianity as a
principle of reform--"to work in individuals, in the community,
in the whole fabric of society, in social relations and intercourse, in education publick / sic 7 and private."

[43]Orestes A. Brownson, "A Lecture Before the Trades Union,"
undated manuscript, OABP, UNDA. By the tone and handwriting, the
date of the lecture would seem to be around 1840.

[44]Orestes A. Brownson, "True Catholic Spirit," undated manuscript, OABP, UNDA, pp. 24-25. The date of this lecture would
appear to be in the mid-1850's.

them with the worship of mammon and worldly goods. Only Catholi-
cism possessed the power to arrest those materialistic tendencies.
If America were to rise to greatness, a strong religion, notably
Roman Catholicism, was essential.

As he progressed toward Catholicism in 1844, Brownson
published several important articles in his own Brownson's Quarterly
Review. In a January article, "The Church Question," he called
for the return of the Christian world to the "unity and catholicity"
of the Church under "one fold and one shepherd." In an April
essay, "No Church, No Reform," Brownson advocated the proposition
that this return to catholicity and unity constituted the first
and paramount question for America, because, "till this question
is settled, and the Church rehabilitated in its authority and glory,
no scheme of practical Reform, individual or social, political or
industrial, can be successfully attempted." In July, "Church Unity
and Social Amelioration" appeared, and called for catholicity and
unity of the Church as a prerequisite for reform and progress.
When the October issue came out, just twenty days before his
baptism and confirmation, Brownson parted company with "The
Anglican Church Schismatic" in favor of the Roman Catholic Church.
He was obliged "to look beyond Anglicanism, to a Church which at
least claims to be infallible, and which demands our obedience
only on the ground that it is infallible."[45] At long last, he had
found the authoritative religion that he needed and, more

---

[45]All four articles appeared in BrQR, I (1844) on the following pages: "The Church Question," 57-84; "No Church, No Reform,"
175-194; "Church Unity and Social Amelioration," 310-327; "The
Anglican Church Schismatic," 487-514.

importantly, he found the religion America needed. From this time on, Brownson advocated the essential relationship between Catholicity and America.

Toward the end of his first full year as a Catholic, Brownson published an essay that contained the basic arguments that he would advocate until death: "Catholicity Necessary to Sustain Popular Liberty."[46] Ever since the election of 1828, Brownson believed, the United States had become in practice "a pure democracy, with no effective constitution but the will of the majority for the time being."[47] The theory of democracy was excellent, but because people were infallible, both individually and collectively, their passions and interests governed their decisions and often led them astray.

What resulted was but a series of governmental blunders. What was to prevent this from continuing to happen? Brownson stressed the need to elevate the virtue and intelligence of the American citizenry.

> Our free institutions cannot be sustained without an augmentation of popular virtue and intelligence. We do not say, nor do we pretend, that the people are not capable of a sufficient degree of virtue and intelligence to sustain a democracy; all we say is, they cannot do it without virtue and intelligence, nor without a higher degree of virtue and intelligence than they have as yet attained to.[48]

---

[46]Orestes A. Brownson, "Catholicity Necessary to Sustain Popular Liberty," BrQR, II (October, 1845), 514-530.

[47]Ibid., p. 515.

[48]Ibid., p. 517.

And so, the major problem of sustaining American democracy resolved
itself into the question of "augmenting the virtue and intelligence
of the people."[49]

"What are the means of augmenting the virtue and intelligence
of the people?" Brownson asked. Certainly not the press, newspapers, or popular literature in their present form, for all echoed
and exaggerated popular errors, tastes, passions, prejudices, and
ignorance; and none enhanced virtue and intelligence. Only "education" could secure both virtue and intelligence. Yet Brownson
denied that Frances Wright, Horace Mann, Abner Kneelard, or educa-
tionists generally had the right idea of "education." Speaking of
Horace Mann, Brownson warned:

> We regard his whole theory of education as founded in
> error, and we cannot but believe that all attempts to
> reduce it to practice are opposed to the cause of
> genuine education. Mr. Mann knows nothing of the
> philosophy of education, for he knows nothing of the
> philosophy of human nature, and nothing of Christian
> morals and Theology. His theory is derived from
> German quacks, and can only rear up a generation of
> infidels. Our common-school system needs an entire
> reform, and to be organized on other principles, and
> after another model. It does little or no good as it
> now is; or, at least, the evil which it occasions goes
> far to overbalance the good it effects. The growing
> immorality of the times, and particularly of New
> England, and of Boston even, in which filthy and cor-
> rupting publications find a readier sale and more
> greedy readers than in any other part of the Union,
> should admonish us that something is wrong in our
> system of education.[50]

---

[49]Ibidem.

[50]Orestes A. Brownson, "Literary Notices and Miscellanies--
Remarks on the Seventh Annual Report of Hon. Horace Mann,
Secretary of the Board of Education," BrQR, I (October, 1844),
547.

The attempts to incorporate non-denominational, non-sectarian
Christianity into the common school had failed, and would continue
failing to produce virtuous citizens. "Virtue without intelligence will only fit the mass to be duped by the artful and
designing; and intelligence without virtue only makes one the
abler and more successful villain. Education must be of the right
sort, if it is to answer our purpose; for a bad education is worse
than none."[51]

What will sustain government? What will provide proper
education? Brownson knew but one answer--religion.

> There is no foundation for virtue but in religion,
> and it is only religion that can command that degree
> of popular virtue and intelligence requisite to insure
> to popular government the right direction and a wise
> and just administration. A people without religion,
> however successful they may be in throwing off old
> institutions, or in introducing new ones, have no power
> to secure the free, orderly, and wholesome working of
> any institutions. For the people can bring to the
> support of institutions only the degree of virtue and
> intelligence they have; and we need not stop to prove
> that an infidel people can have very little either of
> virtue or intelligence, since, in this professedly
> Christian country, this will and must be conceded us.
> We shall, therefore, assume, without stopping to defend
> our assumption, that religion is the power or influence
> we need to take care of the people, and secure the
> degree of virtue and intelligence necessary to sustain
> popular liberty. We say, then, if democracy commits
> the government to the people to be taken care of,
> religion is to take care that they take proper care
> of the government, rightly direct and wisely administer
> it.[52]

---

[51]"Catholicity Necessary to Sustain Popular Liberty," p.
17. [52]Ibid., p. 518.

Indeed, Brownson's assumption--that religion was the essential
element in securing sufficient virtue and intelligence to sustain
popular liberty--had long been the motto of American Protestants.
But the similarity ended there.

The religion Brownson discussed needed to be "a religion
which is above the people and controls them, or it will not answer
the purpose." He boldly declared "it cannot be Protestantism, in
all or any of its forms; for Protestantism assumes as its point
of departure that Almighty God has indeed given us a religion,
but has given it to us not to take care of us, but to be taken
care of by us."[53] The entire character of the Reformation,
Brownson believed, had placed religion to the care of man, who
served as its guardians and governed it.

Protestantism accomplished the feat of placing religion to
the care of man in three stages. First of all, Protestantism
placed religion under the charge of the civil government. Instead
of religion and religious principles exercising power over princes
in temporal affairs, religion was brought under the subjection of
the temporal authority. Thus, Protestantism freed the government
from the restraints of religion. "We want religion . . . to
control the people, and through its spiritual governance to cause
them to give the temporal government always a wise and just direction. But if government control the religion, it can exercise no
control over the sovereign people, for they control the government."[54]

---

[53]Ibid., p. 519.
[54]Ibid., p. 520.

And so, it was through the government that the people took care of religion. The basic problem remained: Who or what was to take care of the people?

Secondly, Protestantism rejected the authority of the temporal government in matters of religion, and subjected religion to the control of the faithful. "The people determine their faith and worship, select, sustain, or dismiss their own religious teachers. They who are to be taught judge him who is to teach, and say whether he teaches them truth or falsehood, wholesome doctrine or unwholesome. The patient directs the physician what to prescribe."[55] Again, religion was placed under the control of the people, who also controlled the government. The same problem remained.

Third, and last, Protestantism resulted in individualism. The individual "selects his own creed, or makes a creed to suit himself, devises his own worship and discipline, and submits to no restraints but such as are self-imposed. This makes a man's religion the effect of his virtue and intelligence, and denies it all power to augment or to direct them."[56] Again, the dilemma arose. "The individual takes care of his religion, but who or what takes care of the individual? The State? But who takes care of the state? The People? But who takes care of the people?"[57]

Thus, it was obvious that Protestantism was not the religion to sustain democracy, for like democracy itself, it could not command and teach, but followed the people and subjected itself to

[55] Ibidem.
[56] Ibid., p. 521.
[57] Ibidem.

control by their passions, interests, and caprices. Furthermore,
democracy had a direct tendency to favor inequality and injustice.
Because democracy obeyed the people, it followed the stronger
passions and interests of the people. The predominance of material
interests presented the greatest danger facing America, for certain
interests commanded the government, took possession of the government, and wielded it for their own special advantage. These
interests secured legislation taxing all other interest in the
country for their special advancement. "This leads to inequality
and injustice, which are incompatible with the free, orderly, and
wholesome working of the government." What was needed was "some
power to prevent this, to moderate the passion for wealth, and to
inspire the people with a true and firm sense of justice."[58]

Brownson realized the objections that Protestants would
raise against his essay.

> The burden of their accusation will be, that we labor
> to withdraw religion from the control of the people,
> and to free it from the necessity of following their
> will; that we seek to make it the master, and not the
> slave, of the people. And this is good proof of our
> position, that Protestantism cannot govern the people,--
> for they govern it,--and therefore that Protestantism is
> not the religion wanted; for it is precisely a religion
> that can and will govern the people, be their master,
> that we need.[59]

What religion possessed the power to govern the people? "The Roman
Catholic, or none," for it "assumes, as its point of departure,
that it is instituted not to be taken care of by the people, but

---

[58]Ibid., p. 522.
[59]Ibid., pp. 524-525.

to take care of the people; not to be governed by them, but to

govern them." The people needed governing, or nothing but anarchy

and destruction awaited them. "THE PEOPLE MUST HAVE A MASTER."[60]

Religion must be above the people, and able to command them.

Brownson again returned to his syllogistic reasoning:

> Popular liberty can be sustained only by a religion
> free from popular control and above the people.

> Only the Catholic religion speaks from above and is
> able to command the people.

The Roman Catholic religion was necessary to sustain popular

liberty. The Catholic religion was not only adequate but necessary

as well, since it alone governed the people, and served as their

master.

In what way was the Church to govern and master? "The

authority of the church is spiritual, not temporal; and the only

sense in which we have urged or do urge its necessity is as the

means of augmenting the virtue and intelligence of the people."[61]

Brownson considered Catholicism necessary as a religious power,

not as a political power.

> The only restriction on their will we contend for is
> a moral restriction; and the master we contend for
> is not a master that prevents them from doing politi-
> cally what they will, but who, by his moral and
> spiritual influence, prevents them from willing what
> they ought not to will. The only influence on the
> political or governmental action of the people which
> we ask, which we wish, or expect, or believe in, from
> Catholicity, is that which it exerts on the mind, the
> heart, and the conscience;--an influence which it
> exerts by enlightening the mind to see the true end

---

[60]Ibid., p. 525 /¯capitals Brownson's_7.
[61]Ibid., p. 527.

of man, the relative value of all worldly pursuits,
by moderating the passions, by weaning the affections
from the world, inflaming the heart with true charity,
and by making each act in all seriously, honestly,
conscientiously. The people will thus come to see
and to will what is equitable and right, and will give
to the government a wise and just direction . . . .
This is the kind of master we demand for the people.[62]

Less than one year a Catholic, Brownson had called for the spiritual
permeation of Catholic faith, morals, and principles in directing
the actions of people individually, and collectively through the
arm of government. His cry was not merely to show the adequacy
and the compatibility between Catholicity and popular liberty, but
the necessity and indispensability of Catholicity to the sustenance
of American democracy.

He would proclaim this theme over and over again. Perhaps
circumstances might change, but the conclusion remained the same:
Catholicity was necessary to sustain popular liberty. In 1846,
Brownson reworked the theme in "National Greatness"; in 1851, "The
Higher Law"; in 1856, "The Church and the Republic" and "The Mission of America"; in 1863, "New England Brahminism"; in 1870, four
articles on "The Future of Protestantism and Catholicity"; in 1873,
"The Papacy and the Republic"; in 1874, "Constitutional Guarantees";
and in 1875, "Reforms and Reformers."[63] Brownson's wish was
perhaps too idealistic, yet he persisted. He wished "to see all

[62]Ibidem.

[63]This is a sampling and not a conclusive list. The four
articles listed for 1870 were published in The Catholic World,
from January through April. The third and fourth articles are
also listed under alternate titles: "Civil and Political
Liberty" and "Religious Liberty." The other essays listed
appeared in Brownson's Quarterly Review.

classes of our community, of whatever birth or origin, absorbed

by this common spirit of Catholic zeal. We wish particularly to

see this spirit pervade the whole body of the Catholic clergy and

laity."[64]

Brownson realized the difficulties in trying to make the

spirit of Catholic zeal pervade American thought and action. The

Catholic population was highly foreign and lower class, and by

1850, the Catholic Church was an immigrant Church. Brownson

believed that the first step must be to dispel any thoughts that

the Catholic population was un-American or hostile to American

constitutional liberties. During the 1840's and 1850's, Brownson

addressed himself to the political and religious opposition con-

fronting Catholics. In addition to trying to uplift the Catholic

population, Brownson also attempted to make American society more

receptive to Catholic principles. In essence, Brownson emphasized

the dual theme of "Catholicizing America" and "Americanizing

Catholicism," with a special effort directed on the latter.[65]

When Brownson converted to Catholicism, he was fully aware

of the traditional opposition to the Roman Catholic Church in this

---

[64]Orestes A. Brownson, "New England Brahminism," BrQR, XX
(October, 1863), 444.

[65]Brownson often tried to establish a "balance of power."
Whenever he thought society lacked something, he would try to
emphasize the need in order to fill the gap. In this particular
case, although he desired to Catholicize America, he saw the need to
Americanize the immigrant population as a first step. Only when
the American population considered Catholics as acceptable citizens
would there be any serious hope of Catholicizing America. Brownson
never lost sight of the Catholicizing goal; rather, he felt that
he had to be a catalyst for the Americanization process also. As
we shall see, during the late 1860's and 1870's, Brownson would
reverse these priorities.

country. As a Protestant he had been reared in anti-Catholic
sentiment and admitted that had it not been for this lifelong antipathy towards Catholicism, he would have converted sooner.
Immediately after his conversion most of his "old friends" no
longer included him in their circles.[66] This had been the story of
Catholicism in America--from colonial times up to the nineteenth
century. John Tracy Ellis had commented that Catholicism was more
hated in the English colonies than any other Christian faith, so
much that anti-Catholic prejudice "struck such enduring roots in
the new soil that it became one of the major traditions in a
people's religious life."[67]

---

[66]Brownson received numerous letters from other Catholic
converts who experienced a similar social and religious isolation.
Brownson wrote in The Convert how one could pass from one Protestant sect to another without serious loss of reputation or any
gross disturbance in social or domestic relations. "But to pass
from Protestantism to Catholicity is a very different thing. We
break the whole world in which we have hitherto lived; we enter
into what is to us a new and untried region, and we fear the dis-
coveries we may make there, when it is too late to draw back. To
the Protestant mind this old Catholic Church is veiled in mystery,
and leaves ample room to the imagination to people it with all
manners of monsters, chimeras, and hydras dire" (p. 360). For
17th and 18th century background, see the following: for Protestant unity, Winthrop S. Hudson, American Protestantism (Chicago,
1961); for anti-Catholic thought, Sister Mary Augustina Ray,
American Opinion of Roman Catholicism in the Eighteenth Century
(New York, 1936); for the political, legal, and religious aspects,
John Tracy Ellis, Catholics in Colonial America (Baltimore, 1965),
pp. 315-380, and American Catholicism, pp. 18-40; for Catholic
attitudes, C. J. Nuesse, The Social Thought of American Catholics
1634-1829 (Westminster, Maryland, 1945), and Charles H. Metzger,
Catholics and the American Revolution (Chicago, 1962); for the roots
of anti-Catholic prejudice, Ray Allen Billington, The Protestant
Crusade 1800-1860 (New York, 1938), pp. 1-31.

[67]John Tracy Ellis, American Catholicism, 2nd ed. (Chicago,
1969) p. 20. This anti-Catholic spirit was part of a larger movement known as nativism, which John Higham defined as the "intense
opposition to an internal minority on the ground of its foreign
(i.e., Un-American) connections." See John Higham, Strangers in
the Land: Patterns of American Nativism 1860-1925, 2nd ed. (New

In the eighteenth century, Americans, engaged in war against
Catholic France, heightened their cries against Catholicism,
Popery, and the French. When England allowed Canadian Catholics
the free exercise of their religion, Americans vehemently protested against the Quebec Act. When Irish and French immigrants
increased during the 1790's, Protestants became alarmed at the
large number of Catholics, while conservatives feared the increasing
number of foreign radicals entering the country. The large clamor
resulted in the Alien and Sedition Acts.

This pattern would continue; whenever the proper forces were
brought into play, nativism easily rose up. Because nativism was
linked to nationalism, nativists invariably attacked the foreign
or un-American character, the disloyalty, or the failure of
assimilation of the suspected group. The specific antagonism
could vary from one group to another, and even within the same
group depending on "the changing character of minority irritants
to the larger society, and the shifting conditions of the day."[68]

And shift the conditions did. Following the War of 1812
and the constant European warfare that had ended with Napoleon's

---

York, 1967), p. 4. Billington equated nativism with anti-Catholicism, while Higham included anti-radicalism and racialism as well.
Nativism is continuously involved in the larger movement of American
nationalism, and hence, it rises and falls in relation to intense
national feelings of other kinds. Nativism could flare up--as it
did in the latter part of the eighteenth century during the French
and Indian War (1774), and prior to the passage of the Alien and
Sedition Acts (1798)--or it could lie dormant as it did from 1800-
1820. Billington considered the Alien and Sedition Acts to be anti-
Catholic (pp. 23-24), while Higham viewed the legislation as both
anti-Catholic and anti-radical (pp. 7-9). See also John C. Miller,
Crises in Freedom: The Alien and Sedition Acts (Boston, 1951).

[68]Higham, p. 4.

defeat in 1815, the surplus population of European countries sought
its way to the new world. The fears of Americans increased as
the number of Catholics, paupers and criminals rose rapidly after
1820. Americans feared that European powers were dumping their
poor on America. By 1837, over one-half of the paupers in the
United States were immigrants. Major cities like New York,
Philadelphia, Boston, and Baltimore experienced hitherto unknown
problems which appeared to be directly traceable to the alien
flood.[69] The number of Catholics increased rapidly also. Only
77,000 Catholic immigrants entered the United States in the thirty-
year period from 1790-1820. But the figures increased to 54,000
in the 1830's; 240,000 in the 1830's; 700,000 in the 1840's;
985,000 in the 1850's; and 741,000 in the 1860's. The Catholic
population boomed from a meager 35,000 in 1790 to 1,606,000 in
1850.

"Nativists, charged with the Protestant evangelical fervor
of the day, considered the immigrants minions of the Roman despot,
dispatched here to subvert American institutions."[70] The character of American institutions, with the concept of individual
freedom and political liberty deeply imbedded in the national
culture, seemed threatened by the authoritarian organization of
the Catholic Church and its customary association with monarchical
governments. Some Americans viewed European popery and American
liberty as irreconcilable, and some excited patriots even detected

[69]Billington, pp. 32-48.
[70]Higham, p. 6.

a vast European plot to take over America--with the Pope master-minding the entire project.[71]

Both Protestant and native organizations and publications attempted to combat the growing menace. Evangelical Protestants had been unifying and organizing since the early part of the nineteenth century. A vast array of societies--the American Education Society (1816), American Bible Society (1816), American Sunday School Union (1824), American Tract Society (1825), American Home Missionary Society (1826), American Protestant Reformation Society (1836), American Protestant Union (1841) and the American and Foreign Christian Union (1848)--organized to spread Protestantism and to check the growth and spread of Catholicism. The societies employed lectures, tracts, books, Sunday schools, religious periodicals, schools, academies, colleges, charitable causes and social reforms as part of the strategy of a united front. It was indeed the religious Manifest Destiny of America to see the land become totally Protestant.[72]

Publications attacking Catholicism, such as The Protestant and The Anti-Romanist, became popular. The burning of the Ursuline Convent, school, and farmhouse at Charlestown, Massachusetts in 1834, gave impetus to a new genre of expose literature, none more fraudulent than Maria Monk's Awful Disclosures of the Hotel Dieu Nunnery of Montreal (1836).[73]

---

[71]Ibidem. See also Billington, Chs. 3-9.

[72]See Hudson, pp. 62-85.

[73]Other significant works were Samuel F. B. Morse's Foreign Conspiracy and Lyman Beecher's Plea for the West. These are small samplings of the anti-Catholic literature. Billington has provided

Lyman Beecher contended that it was through schools and colleges that Catholics were attempting to convert and destroy America. When Catholics in New York under Bishop John Hughes petitioned for a share of the common school fund to establish schools of their own, objecting to the use of the Protestant Bible in public schools, Protestants became alarmed. A Catholic priest in Carbeau, New York (1842) further enraged Protestants by publicly burning Protestant Bibles. When Catholics in Philadelphia under Bishop Francis P. Kenrick attempted to exempt Catholic children from reading all except their own version of the Bible, and to exclude them from sectarian religious instruction in schools, indignant Protestants rioted, causing bloodshed, destruction of property, and the burning of churches (1844).

The explosiveness of the religious climate of the mid-1840's was further enhanced by the appearance of the Native American Party, which polarized political opposition against Catholics and foreigners. Orestes Brownson, former Protestant, native American, and now Catholic, hoped to abate the mounting anti-Catholic, anti-foreign sentiment.[74]

As early as 1838, Brownson had defended Irish and German immigrants to America. In reviewing Francis J. Grund's The Americans in their Moral, Social, and Political Relations (1837),

---

an excellent bibliography of anti-Catholic newspapers, periodicals, reports of anti-Catholic societies, publications of nativist parties, books, and pamphlets on pp. 445-482.

[74]I discuss Brownson and nativism at length because of the important connection between Brownson's attempt to mitigate anti-Catholic feeling and his views on the school question during the 1840's, 1850's, and early 1860's.

Brownson spoke out "against those who are raising a cry about the

Irish." Admitting the poverty of the Irish, nonetheless he added:

"A country may be corrupted and destroyed by riches; by poverty,

never." The Irish were not as burdensome as was often pretended.

> After the second or third generation they have become
> amalgamated with our native population, and are among
> our most useful and often our most enterprising citizens.
> Instead of sending them back home when they come, or
> declaiming against them when here, we should do well
> to seek to elevate them, to make their adopted country
> the means of raising them to the true dignity of man-
> hood.[75]

Grund had spoken favorably of the German immigrants' unity and

strength. Brownson cautioned:

> We have none but kindly feelings toward the German
> immigrants to this country; but when they have once
> taken up their residence with us and become national-
> ized, we do not choose to look upon them as Germans.
> We would regard them as Americans and fellow citizens.
> But in order to be so regarded, by us, they must so
> regard themselves. Nothing can be more detrimental
> to them, or tend more to create prejudices against
> them, than a disposition on their part to form a
> distinct population by themselves, and especially
> to band together as a German party in politics. Let
> them act in political and social life as Americans,
> not as Germans; let them consider themselves an
> integral part of our common population, not as
> foreigners, if they would have this country become
> a second home, and its citizens their brothers. We
> always welcome foreigners who come to amalgamate with
> us and to account themselves of us; but emigrants
> from any foreign nation will find this an uncomfort-
> able residence, if they undertake to get up parties
> in their own favor, and by combination among them-
> selves to control the politics of the country.[76]

---

[75]Orestes A. Brownson, "Grund's Americans," BoQR, I (April,
.838) p. 172.

[76]Ibid., pp. 185-186.

Prior to his conversion, then, Brownson favored immigration. Problems of poverty, drunkenness, and petty criminality would generally disappear after two or three generations. And as long as immigrants became part of the American population, and chose to be identified as Americans, the amalgamation process would be smoother and less irritating.

As immigration increased, however, the traditional hatred of Popery and the added fear of foreigners threatening the American economic, political, and social structure drew many voters to the Native American position. Fear of pauperism, foreign competition for American jobs, and ignorant immigrant block voting led to investigations of the naturalization process. Brownson, in the very first Catholic number of his review, felt compelled to discuss the problem.[77]

Brownson became a mediator, a middle-man between his fellow Catholics, especially foreign, and his fellow citizens, especially Protestant and native American. He attempted to break down the hostility between the two groups. In "Native Americanism," Brownson recommended a pamphlet, "Catholicism compatible with Republican Government, and in full Accordance with Popular Institutions," to members of the American Protestant Society and especially to those of the Native American party. Because of his genuine patriotism, Brownson argued, he could not sympathize with Native Americanism which possessed many un-American attributes. He had long regarded the United States as a

---

[77]This is January, 1845. Brownson's October issue of 1844 was published about 20 days before he officially entered the Church.

> chosen land, not for one race, or one people, but for
> the wronged and down-trodden of all nations, tongues, and
> kindreds, where they might come as to a holy asylum of
> peace and charity . . . to which man might flee from
> oppression, be free from the trammels of tyranny, regain
> their rights as human beings, and dwell in security.
> Here . . . every man, no matter where born, in what
> language trained, or faith baptized, was to be regarded
> as a man,--as nothing more, as nothing less.[78]

Native Americanism, on the other hand, contradicted the principles

and destiny of the New World. In this sense, he regarded Native

Americanism as a retrogression. It opposed true Americanism by

denying the great principle that merit makes the man. Brownson

called the Native American party "contemptible," and then illus-

trated the good that foreigners had accomplished for America while

fighting in the Revolution and laboring on projects of internal

improvement. He maintained that political opposition to foreigners

was advocated by Whigs--indeed because immigrants understood

democratic politics too well, and not because they were ignorant.

If immigrants were politically intelligent and economically

advantageous, then the real objection to foreigners lay even deeper.

Brownson declared the real basis of opposition was anti-Catholicism,

especially hatred for Irish Catholics. In addition, he believed

that many members of the Native American party, especially those

who had recently rifled and burned Catholic churches, seminaries,

and dwellings in Philadelphia, were foreigners themselves, many of

them Orangemen. This religious opposition was directly contrary

to the Constitution, which "recognizes and guarantees to all men

---

[78]Orestes A. Brownson, "Native Americanism," BrQR, II
(January, 1845), 77.

the free exercise of their religion." Attempts to prohibit the
exercise of the Catholic religion were clearly un-American in the
truest sense of religious liberty.[79] Again, Brownson reasserted
the compatibility and necessity of Catholicism in America. He
expressed hope and confidence that the Church would survive and
even strengthen itself as a result of Native American hostility.

> Here is our hope for our Republic. We look for our
> safety to the spread of Catholicism. We render solid
> and imperishable our free institutions just in propor-
> tion as we extend the kingdom of God among our people,
> and establish in their hearts the reign of justice
> and charity. And here, then, is our answer to those
> who tell us Catholicism is incompatible with free
> institutions. We tell them that they cannot maintain
> free institutions without it.[80]

In addition, Brownson advised immigrant Catholics to avoid
confrontation with native Americans. "To our Catholic brethren,
who may be called on to suffer for their faith, we would counsel
patience and resignation."[81] He deemed it unwise to oppose force
with force; rather, vengeance was God's work. He foresaw the
controversy that was growing out of the Native American party movement and advocated that the entire controversy be left in the hands
of native American citizens. Finally, Brownson compared the
current unrest to that of the late 1790's. He assured Catholic
immigrants that the Alien and Sedition laws would not be revived.
Americans would see the sins of Native Americanism and

[79] Ibid., pp. 84-86.
[80] Ibid., p. 94 (Italics Brownson's).
[81] Ibid., p. 97.

wholeheartedly reject it as opposed to American democracy.[82]

And so, during his very first year as a Catholic, Brownson attempted to make Americans more tolerant of Catholics and Catholics more acceptable to Americans. These dual goals seemed inseparable to Brownson. The findings of one student seem to corroborate Brownson. Robert F. Hueston maintains that the hostility of the early 1840's reached an explosion point when "foreigners, under the mantle of an alien religion, directly challenged a developing American institution, the public school."[83] When Catholics, with an expanding institutional Church and growing alien population, challenged the status quo by political involvement and by attempts to alter local school systems, they helped to increase the hostility of Americans toward them which culminated in the Philadelphia riots of 1844. Following the riots, Hueston maintains that the Catholic newspapers and journals helped direct the retreat of Catholics, especially the Irish, from areas of value and social conflicts.[84] Brownson certainly was foremost among those urging avoidance of conflict at this time. Overall, Brownson's essays of 1845 caused little stir. But when he felt compelled to address

---

[82]Ibid., pp. 97-98. Brownson also criticized Native Americanism later that year. See "Native American Civility," BrQR, II (October, 1845), 530-540. He repeated many of the same arguments, but stressed the necessity of religious liberty. If Catholics were not free to practice religion, a time would come when Prestyterians, Methodists, or Baptists would also be restricted.

[83]Robert F. Hueston, "The Catholic Press and Nativism, 1840-1860" (Unpublished doctoral dissertation, University of Notre Dame, 1972), p. 31.

[84]Ibid., pp. 108-109.

74

these same issues nine years later, Brownson met both Catholic and native American opposition.

With increased Catholic immigration in the late 1840's, nativist cries returned, objecting again to social and economic evils, poverty and criminality, the lowering of wages, and the traditional religious animosity. In addition, immigrants retained separate ethnic and religious communities which, as Hueston maintains, posed unprecedented threats to established American society which itself had recently undergone the crises of war and depression.[85]

A series of events transpired within the immigrant community which tended to offend native Americans. Considered together, these Catholic activities posed a major social threat to existing American institutions. For example, the Catholic press, especially the *Irish American*, continued to re-inforce Catholic and Irish identity by reporting news of the old country and by advertising ethnic social events. Catholics revived their interest in aiding Ireland and formed a militia to combat Great Britain. "Paddy funerals," drunkenness, and brawling offended native sensibilities. The Irish assumed a greater role in American politics, and together with the Irish press, became more aggressive than natives would have preferred. The Catholic press reported, and often exaggerated, the already high immigration figures. Church institutions multiplied to meet the needs of immigrants. The First Plenary Council convened in 1852, just two years after the restoration of the

[85]Ibid., p. 137.

English hierarchy in 1850. Bishop Hughes' speech in 1850 on "The
Decline of Protestantism and its Cause" marked a new Catholic
aggressiveness--no longer apologetic and defensive, but now
vigorously offensive. Finally, beginning in 1849, Catholics
renewed their interest in the school question.[86]

American Catholics intensified efforts to establish more
schools and to obtain financial aid from the various state governments. And as states attempted to enact legislation to establish
more schools, Catholics feared that secularists were taking over
American schools. Or if the schools were not secular, they were
at least Protestant, if not anti-Catholic. The use of certain
textbooks and the King James Version of the Bible offended Catholic
sensibilities. Catholics generally advocated a series of related
positions: first of all, they attempted to remove offensive texts
from the curriculum, or if this proved futile, to exempt Catholic
students from having to read such material; secondly, Catholics
attempted to obtain a portion of state tax funds to establish
schools free from such sectarian biases; or thirdly, Catholics
attempted, nonetheless, to found and support schools on their own,
rather than have their children attend common schools.

---

[86]Ibid., Ch. 5, "Immigrants and Catholics on the Advance,"
pp. 137-184. Brownson reviewed Hughes' lecture in an article "The
Decline of Protestantism," BrQR, VIII (January, 1851), 97-120. He
remarked that Hughes' lecture was the "commencement of a new era"
and that "Catholics are beginning to shake off their timidity, to
assume in controversy their legitimate position, and to speak in
the bold and energetic tones which become them; that, instead of
stopping to refute anew objections which have been refuted a
thousand times, and to repel calumnies which will be repeated as
often as repelled, they are carrying the war into the enemy's
country, and compelling Protestantism to defend itself. This is
a great and important change of tactics" (p. 97).

The Church had expanded to six archdioceses by 1850, and in
its first Plenary Council of Baltimore (1852), the Prelates urged
all Catholics to "make every sacrifice which may be necessary" for
the establishment and support of Catholic schools.[87] Moreover,
they cited Pope Pius IX's encyclical of November, 1851, which
called on "all Bishops of the Catholic world, to provide for the
religious education of youth."[88] Hence what took place from the
late 1840's through the mid-1850's was a concerted Catholic effort
to alter existing school patterns. Catholic efforts intensified
in New York, Pittsburgh, Cincinnati, Baltimore, Mobile, Detroit,
San Francisco, Newark, Portland, Charleston, and even in Philadelphia (still remembering 1844) where Bishop John N. Neumann made
a concerted effort to build schools in 1852. Only in Boston was
no crusade launched "either to expand the Catholic system or to
raid the state treasury," even though it sympathized with other
campaigns, objected to the Protestant bias of public schooling,
and opposed the 1853 state constitution which forbade appropriating
funds for sectarian schools.[89]

This "Catholic crusade against the new public school systems,
in conjunction with renewed emphasis on building parochial institutions, must rank as a prime cause for the revival of nativism in

[87]Quoted in Neil G. McCluskey, ed., Catholic Education in
America, A Documentary History (New York: Teachers College,
Columbia University, 1964), p. 80.

[88]Ibid., p. 81.

[89]Hueston, op. cit., pp. 167-179 for an analysis of the
revived Catholic interest in the school question. Quote on p.
178.

the 1850's."[90] Yet, the only member of the Catholic press to
dissent on this issue was Orestes Brownson. Just as he discussed
the Native American-immigrant conflict of the 1840's, Brownson
returned to it again in 1854 and 1855. The problems of 1845 had
multiplied tremendously by 1854, and the strength of Catholic
opposition had also mounted in a similar fashion. It is in light
of this new Catholic aggressiveness, of which Brownson was certainly
a part, that one must examine Brownson's essays of 1854 and 1855.

"After God, our first and truest love has always been, and
we trust always will be, for our country."[91] Love of country,
combined with love of God (especially through the Roman Catholic
Church), caused Brownson to work diligently for the assimilation
of his co-religionists and for the conversion of his fellow
citizens.

> Here is the difficulty in this country with the
> great body of our Catholics. Catholicity is their old
> national religion. They embrace, cherish, and defend
> it as the religion of their fathers, and identify it
> so closely with their own nationality, that they hardly
> conceive the possibility of the one without the other,
> and are therefore exceedingly apt in Americanizing to
> lose their Catholicity. Hence the question has two
> grave aspects, the one affecting non-Catholic Ameri-
> cans, and the other the Catholic immigrants themselves.
> It is necessary to convince the former that they can,
> so to speak, Catholicize without ceasing to be Ameri-
> cans, and to enable the latter to Americanize without

---

[90]Ibid., p.179. In addition to all the social and political
threats that Catholics posed, Hueston, in Ch. 6, "American Catholics and the Liberals," discusses the basic ideological clash
between Catholics and liberal Americans over the Revolution of
1848, personages like Kossuth, Meagher, and Bedini visiting the
United States, liberalism and various reform movements, and the
constant bickering between the Catholic and secular press. For a
fuller treatment, see Hueston, pp. 185-225.

[91]Orestes A. Brownson, "Native Americanism," BrQR, XI (July,
1854), 335.

> ceasing to be Catholics . . . . To this end, the Catholic
> who embraces the question under both of its aspects is
> required to present Catholicity solely as the religion
> of God, and to repulse all appeals to any particular
> nationality as an auxiliary.[92]

Brownson regarded as a "fixed fact" that "no nationality here can stand a moment before the Anglo-American. It is the all-absorbing power, and cannot be absorbed or essentially modified by any other." He further advised foreigners that the American character would never be Irish, German, French, Spanish, or Chinese. "It is and will be a peculiar modification of the Anglo-Saxon, or, if you prefer, Anglo-Norman, maintaining its own essential character, however enriched by contributions from other sources."[93] Immigrants from foreign countries "should understand in the outset, if they would avoid unpleasant collision, that they must ultimately lose their own nationality and become assimilated in general character to the Anglo-American race."[94] Brownson proceeded to analyze immigrant habits and actions and corresponding native grievances. In so doing, he wounded the pride of many Irishmen and caused serious opposition to his Americanization views. Brownson did not deliberately intend to upset the Irish but hoped to elevate the Catholic population. He believed that American culture (excluding its Protestant dimension) was the greatest that had yet been achieved by man. He desired to elevate Catholics to that

---

[92] Orestes A. Brownson, "The Know-Nothings," BrQR, XI (October, 1854), 472.

[93] "Native Americanism," BrQR, XI (July, 1854), 336.

[94] Ibid., pp. 336-337.

same culture and prevent any open conflict between the two groups.[95]

It was not sheer coincidence that in 1854, the essay that immediately followed "Native Americanism" was entitled "Schools and Education." It must be read in the light of the previous discussion, and in view of the conclusion that opposition to the common or public schools was a primary reason for the re-emergence of nativism in the 1850's. Although Brownson expressed a definite preference for Catholic schools and religious education, he realized the practical aspects of the immigrant situation. Catholics had neither the financial means nor the requisite number of competent teachers to staff Catholic schools for all the children in Boston.[96]

---

[95]It is beyond the scope of this dissertation to thoroughly examine the Irish-Brownson controversy. Nowhere has the conflict been adequately explained. Brownson is believed to have been anti-Irish. However, there is much evidence to suggest the contrary as true. Repeatedly, in essays and in book reviews, Brownson reflected a love for the Irish. What he did oppose was native and foreign radicalism and demagoguery. Brownson advised immigrants not to antagonize natives. He severely criticized the Native American party and the Know-Nothings--because they were un-American, composed in part of foreign anti-Catholic radicals, and were themselves the real danger of American Republicanism. After the storm created by Brownson's essay on "Native Americanism" in July, 1854, he wrote a series of articles directly attacking the Know-Nothing movement. See "Know-Nothingism; or Satan warring against Christ," BrQR, XI (October, 1854), 447-487; "The Know-Nothings," BrQR, XII (January, 1855), 114-135; "A Know-Nothing Legislature," BrQR, XII (July, 1855), 393-411; "The Know-Nothing Platform," BrQR, XII (October, 1855), 473-498. In 1856, Brownson also refuted attacks on Catholics by Rev. Rufus W. Clark in "Romanism in America," BrQR, XII (April, 1855), 145-183 and by Edward Beecher in "The Papal Conspiracy Exposed," BrQR, XII (April, 1855), 246-270. See also, Philip J. Mitchell, "A Study of Orestes A. Brownson's Views on the Know-Nothing Movement (Unpublished Master's thesis, University of Notre Dame, 1945).

[96]Keeping in mind Hueston's conclusion, that the Diocese of Boston did not attempt to build more schools or to obtain state aid since it would logically be unnecessary), helps to clarify Brownson's position. When this essay was written, Brownson himself was a resident of Boston and had submitted his essays to Bishop

Few of the Catholic children could be educated in Catholic schools;
for the mass of these children, "the only alternative is the public
schools or no education except that of the streets, and the education of the streets is several degrees more injurious, in our
opinion, to faith and piety, than that of the common school room."[97]
More importantly, "our children, if educated in public school,
will at a very early age become Americanized."[98] The current and
strongest arguments against Catholics--that they are foreigners,
and therefore un-American, in tastes, habits, and manners--would
no longer hold.

> The Church will then cease to be a foreign Church here;
> it will be nationalized, and Catholicity become an
> integral element in the national life. The Catholic
> population will assume their rightful position, and
> have their moral weight. This will be a gain to the
> Catholic cause of no little importance, for we can
> assure our non-Catholic friends that their belief that
> to Americanize is to Protestantize is wholly unfounded.[99]

Brownson did "not wish to recommend the common schools to
Catholics . . . . All we say is, that we think these schools, in
our own city and State--we say nothing of them elsewhere--are far
better than none, far better than any we are ourselves at present
able, in a sufficient number for all our children, to institute in
their place."[100] For Catholics to elevate themselves, they needed

---

Fitzpatrick for approval before publication. I make no attempt to
hoist responsibility onto the Bishop, but merely to point out the
Boston educational milieu that Brownson lived in. This issue will
be explored more deeply in Chapter III.

[97]Orestes A. Brownson, "Schools and Education," BrQR, XI
(July, 1854), 370.

[98]Ibid., p. 372.
[99]Ibid., pp. 372-373.
[100]Ibid., p. 375.

at least a good secular education. If this secular education could
be acquired in the common school, and if Catholic pastors and
parents managed religious training in Church and at home, then
Catholics could "prove to non-Catholics that the ignorance which
they complain of, and which we cannot deny, in many foreign
Catholics, is due, not to their religion, but to their political
and social condition in their native country."[101]

And so, during the 1840's and 1850's Brownson urged his
fellow Catholics not to antagonize the native population. On the
very sensitive issue of common schools versus Catholic schools, he
cited several gains to be acquired by Catholic attendance at public
schools. And because he loved his God and his country, Orestes
Brownson sought to Americanize immigrant Catholics, and Catholicize
native Americans. In this union Brownson hoped to achieve the
highest civilization possible.

During the 1854-1856 period, Brownson succeeded in antagonizing a large portion of Irish Catholics--in the United States,
Canada, and Ireland, and aroused the ire of Know-Nothings as well.
In his attempts to further the Catholic position, Brownson un-
wittingly provided political ammunition for Know-Nothings to use
against Catholics during elections. In both 1854 and 1855, he
penned articles on the indirect temporal power of the Pope.[102]
Know-Nothings quoted, misquoted, and used in any way possible
Brownson's arguments to "prove" that Catholics owed civil

[101]Ibid., pp. 375-376.

[102]See O. A. Brownson, "Temporal Power of the Popes," BrQR,
I (April, 1854), 187-218, and "The Temporal Power of the Pope,"
rQR, XII (October, 1855), 417-445.

allegiance to the Pope, and hence, were an un-American alien mob

bent on destroying the free institutions of America. Anti-Catholic

office holders and candidates in Washington, Maryland, New York,

Massachusetts, Vermont, North Carolina, South Carolina, Mississippi,

Ohio and Missouri read the pages of Brownson's Quarterly Review to

legislative sessions and to voters.[103] No matter how loudly

Catholics protested and insisted on their loyalty, Know-Nothings

were able to quote one Catholic position to refute another Catholic

position.[104] When Joseph R. Chandler, a distinguished member of

the House of Representatives and recent Catholic convert, spoke in

defense of Catholics in Washington, his opponents used a fellow

convert, Brownson, to refute him.[105] Know-Nothings argued that

Brownson's views represented official Church policy; after all the

Review was the only Catholic quarterly, and it had had affixed on

its cover since 1849 a letter of approbation from twenty-five

members of the hierarchy. In Poolsville, Maryland, Know-Nothings

---

[103]In the OABP, UNDA are several letters revealing the widespread use of Brownson's articles against the Catholic cause. See
Wm. H. Duncan to O.A.B., January 27, 1855; R. H. Clarke to O.A.B.,
February 17, 1855; O.A.B. to Fr. Cummings, February 21, 1855; John
P. McAuliffe to O.A.B., March 27, 1855; Hugh Davis to O.A.B., June
18, 1855 and July 11, 1855; Q. C. Grasty to O.A.B., August 9, 1855;
(Six men) to O.A.B., October 1, 1855; O.A.B. responds to six Demo-
crats, October 8, 1855; F. H. Churchhill to O.A.B., November 4,
1855; E. H. Platt to O.A.B., December 27, 1855; G. H. Hilton to
O.A.B., February 13, 1856 and March 4, 1856; J. P. Chazal to O.A.B.,
August 3, 1856; and A. W. Chenoweth to O.A.B., August 23, 1857.

[104]R. H. Clarke to O.A.B., February 17, 1855, OABP, UNDA.

[105]Chandler's speech, in January, 1855, was in reply to
Nathaniel Banks who had charged Catholics with treason. So effec-
tive and eloquent was Chandler that even his opponents congratu-
lated him afterwards. The American hierarchy highly approved of
Chandler's attempt to abate Know-Nothing attempts to pass anti-
Catholic legislation. Brownson's disagreement concerned Chandler's
"Gallican views"; Brownson was an Ultra-montanist.

charged that the Review was the acknowledged organ of the Catholic
Church in the United States, and that the Bishops recognized
Brownson as the propounder of Catholic faith.[106]

Catholic Bishops found themselves in embarrassing and irritating situations. Their signatures were being employed in
political campaigns intended to secure office for anti-Catholic
candidates who would eventually pass legislation restricting
Catholic rights. Episcopal letters crossed paths, most of which
were headed to and from Cincinnati, with a substantial number also
going to Baltimore. Shortly, Brownson was asked to voluntarily
remove the letter of approbation so that all would know that what
appeared in the pages of the Review was not in any way to be construed as official Church doctrine. He complied with the request
because it seemed "necessary for the peace of the Church."[107]

Brownson, then, in his attempts to Americanize his fellow
Catholics by not agitating the school question and to Catholicize
Americans by asserting a strong and bold role for the Church ended
up antagonizing both groups. Catholics who disliked his views on
Americanization and schooling became enraged when Know-Nothings
quoted Brownson to support anti-Catholic political arguments. To

[106]Six men to O.A.B., October 1, 1855, OABP, UNDA. In
Brownson's "Scrapbook of Newspaper Clippings," OABP, UNDA, an
article entitled "The Christian Union" contained the substance of
remarks made by Rev. S. Robinson at a meeting of the American and
Foreign Christian Union on May 10, 1853. Robinson denounced the
entire Catholic press, but especially Brownson, because the letter
of approbation signified the Review and its tenets "to be taken
as of the highest authority."

[107]See O.A.B. to Fr. Cummings, February 21, 1855, OABP, UNDA.
In this letter, Brownson told Cummings that the article on "Native
Americanism" had not hurt the Review, but he was unable to say how
badly the "Pope" article would.

many non-Catholics, his essays, or at least the misrepresentations of them, confirmed their deep-rooted prejudices that
Catholics were indeed an un-American lot.[108] Brownson's
early attempts, especially his emphasis on Americanizing Catholicism, failed. Within a decade, though, he reversed his priorities--
America needed Catholicism much more than Catholics needed America.

Brownson's deep love of country and his supreme optimism for
its future were dealt severe blows during the 1860's and 1870's.
The Civil War calamity and the ensuing Reconstruction problems
disturbed Brownson. Even more shattering were the deaths of two
of his sons only weeks apart in 1864. Brownson's Quarterly Review,
in dire financial straits, folded in the same year. The Syllabus
of Errors (1864) cautioned all Catholics that the Church must not
accommodate itself to the world on matters involving moral and
religious principles. Brownson, the ever obedient son of the
Church, took its message to heart. Moreover, chronic pain
resulting from a severe case of the gout tended to curb his
earthly enjoyment. The corruption of the Grant administration
also lessened his confidence in American government. In 1872, his
dear wife Sally died, leaving a wide and sad gap in his life.
In all, Brownson gradually grew more disillusioned with American
society and admitted this much to the liberal Father Isaac Hecker:

> The truth is I am beginning to be once more an
> oscurantist, and can hardly be said to belong to
> the Catholic Movement. I am become a convert to

---

[108]Not all Protestants felt this way though. In the midst
of the Know-Nothing clamor, several Protestants defended Brownson's
views and supported the rights of Catholics.

the Encyclical, and am almost beginning to despair of the success of the American $\sqrt{\text{e}}$ xperiment. I never had a spice of real radicalism in my composition . . . . There is no use denying I have my eyes in my hindhead, and regret more than I hope. I think I am turning Paddy. I have lost confidence in my countrymen, and become ashamed of them.[109]

In addition to the personal and political setbacks that he suffered, Brownson was also deeply concerned over the Church in Europe. He bemoaned to his son Henry that the Church was suffering great losses in Europe. Protestants, Jews, infidels, schismatics, and lukewarm Catholics were ruining Europe and the "Church has nearly all her work to do over again. The world has to be reconverted."[110] In sum, the entire European and American political and religious states of affair deeply disturbed Brownson.

Earlier Brownson had stated that the only religion capable of sustaining democracy was Roman Catholicism. In the late 1860's, he questioned the idea that democracy was favorable to, or even compatible with, Catholicity. He told his son that he no longer believed in democracy or in Hecker's notion that democracy was favorable to Catholicity. "No people that makes popular opinion its criterion of right and wrong, is or can be Catholic. Catholicity spreads among people only in proportion as they habitually act from the law of God, which is above kings and peoples, alike above popular opinion."[111] Although willing to accept the notion

---

[109]Orestes A. Brownson to Fr. Isaac Hecker, March 10, 1868, photostat of letter in Paulist Archives, OABP UNDA.

[110]O.A.B. to Henry F. Brownson, August 7, 1870, HFB Collection, UNDA.

[111]O.A.B. to H.F.B., November 12, 1870, HFB Collection, UNDA.

on the theoretical level, Brownson thought that Catholicity and
democracy were incompatible on the practical level. Not one in a
thousand American Catholics were willing to accept the doctrines
embodied in the Syllabus.

> How many Catholics can you find /¯Brownson asked
> Hecker_7, born and brought up in this country that
> do in reality hold the Church to be higher than the
> people, or who do not consider her /¯?_7 authoritative
> only when it coincides with that of the people?
> These considerations make me feel that the whole
> influence of democratic ideas and tendencies is
> directly antagonistic to Catholicity.[112]

No longer did Brownson talk about creating a harmony between
the Church and American society. Protestantism, democracy, and
materialism were enemies to be combatted. No longer did Brownson
urge the Irish to Americanize; instead, he lamented that they had
Americanized too rapidly. "So long as they retain their Irish
characteristics and their invincible attachment to their religion
and their traditional civilization, they supply the very element
the population of this country most needs."[113] Brownson sadly
regretted his own earlier attempts to prematurely Americanize the
Irish.

> The danger to their mission here is, that they will
> Americanize too much and too rapidly, and become too
> prosperous in the American sense of prosperity
> /¯materialism_7. They have done much to Catholicize,
> still more to hibernicize the country, but what they
> have now to do, is, to guard against becoming them-
> selves Americanized; whence the significance of the

---

[112]O.A.B. to Fr. Isaac Hecker, August 25, 1870, photostat of
letter in Paulist Archives, OABP, UNDA.

[113]Orestes A. Brownson, "Father Thebaud's Irish Race,"
BrQR, XXII (October, 1873), 500.

movement for Catholic schools. The moment they
exchange their original Irish characteristics for
those of the country, they lose the principal part
of their power . . . . It is doubtful, if completely Americanized and severed from their traditional relations, they would retain even their
faith beyond the second generation.[114]

And in a somewhat prophetic tone, Brownson predicted that if

Catholics retained American modes of thought, manners, and usages,

and received nothing from the example of "old and persistent"

Catholic people, then Catholicity would be pared down until it was

hardly distinguishable from Protestantism.

The mission of the Church was no longer to seek harmony with

American civilization. The Graeco-Roman type civilization, as

developed in the American Constitution, no longer seemed to be the

highest type of civilization to Brownson. Earlier, he had supposed

that it only needed Catholic faith and worship to be perfected as

a civilized order. Now Brownson esteemed the Irish supernatural

power of endurance which long survived "the ever-renewed efforts

of their powerful enemies to extinguish them."[115] The Irish had

long been preserved by Providence and trained to be a missionary

people, especially to the English speaking world. Brownson wrote

to his son Henry: "The Church is now if Catholics could see it,

a missionary Church in an infidel world, and is now compelled to

begin anew and reconvert the people."[116]

---

[114]Ibid., pp. 504-505.
[115]Ibid., p. 499.
[116]O.A.B. to H.F.B., October 23, 1871, HFB Collection, UNDA.

This infidel world--materialistic, Protestant, and individual-
istic--warred against Catholicity, at least as Brownson now viewed
things. It is precisely because of this attitude--call it a
personal siege mentality--that during the late 1860's and the
1870's, Brownson decided to support and defend Catholic schools
and to work for their reform and improvement. In a letter to
Hecker, Brownson explained his position.

> I have defended Catholic education as my duty bound,
> but I hope little from it, for it will prove impotent
> against the spirit of the country. I have heretofore
> worked to effect a harmony of the American and the
> Catholic idea, but I believe such harmony impracti-
> cable except by sacrificing the Catholic idea to the
> national.[117]

Sacrifice religion to the state? Never! "The Church does not need
the State; the state needs her, and cannot subsist without her."[118]
Because the country so desperately needed the Church, Brownson
became more adamant on Catholic positions. Thus, he now supported
the movement for Catholic schools. Yet the school alone could not
effect much good against the spirit of the country; a total educational effort was essential. Moreover, America seemingly had gone
so far adrift that only divine intervention--the grace of God
through the Catholic Church--could now save her.

How drastic a change was this? Was it yet another mental
aberration? If anything, Brownson merely seems to have grown less
optimistic and more conservative. He had not changed from a

---

[117]O.A.B. to Fr. Isaac Hecker, August 25, 1870, photostat
of letter in Paulist Archives, OABP,UNDA.

[118]O.A.B. to H.F.B., October 23, 1871, HFB Collection, UNDA.

radical to a conservative. And even his so-called liberal period

of the late 1850's and early 1860's had a strain of conservatism

and pessimism in it. Leonard Gilhooley in his recent work

Contradiction and Dilemma: Orestes Brownson and the American Idea

(New York: Fordham University Press, 1972) has re-examined

Brownson's pre-Civil War writings on the "American Idea"--the

American dream, experiment, and mission--and concludes that

Brownson's conservatism dates back prior to 1840. Brownson's

attitudes toward the "American Idea"--the idea of progress, a

confident air of optimism, belief in the perfectibility of man,

and the indispensability of democracy and Christianity in American

society--all reflect a basic conservatism in his thought.

As far back as the 1830's he had repudiated the tendencies

and implications of Protestantism and for at least thirty years

had argued the need for a strong religious authority to direct

society. Even as early as 1840 he had objected to unlimited

democracy and favored constitutional republicanism. His belief

in progress was not unbridled; because of original sin man's

progress depended on the acceptance or rejection of supernatural

grace which only the Catholic Church was capable of imparting.

Brownson's optimism for America's future was linked to religion.

He had held this view years before his conversion; his Catholicism

only embedded the belief more deeply. His essays of the mid-1850's

on the temporal power of the popes had asserted a strong ultra-

montanist position. Perhaps there was more truth than error in

his statement to Hecker that "I never had a spice of real radical-

ism in my composition."

It would appear that Brownson's conservatism was deep-rooted
and that his views of the late 1860's and 1870's were not reactionary. His retreat seems to reflect an increasing pessimism concerning American society and its receptiveness to Catholicity.
Although his faith in America's greatness became dampened, he
still had hope for her conversion. During the last few years of
his life, Brownson addressed essays to his readers on the role of
the family and Church, Catholic press and literature, adult
societies, Catholic schools and colleges. Only this type of
Catholic "education"--the total educational environment--could
possibly be capable of withstanding the infidel world and of in-
fusing a Catholic spirit into the national life of Americans. And
now, more than ever, America needed the grace of God.

The Orestes Brownson of the 1840's and 1850's is the one
who is usually remembered by Catholics today. He was very much
concerned throughout this Catholic period with Catholicizing
America. During these early years he felt compelled to Americanize the Catholic immigrant and to effect a harmony between
Catholicity and Americanism. He exuded confidence that the
American nation and people were receptive to Catholicity and would
one day be converted to it.[119]

But the little remembered Orestes Brownson of the 1860's
and 1870's was also significant. Although in many respects he

---

[119]See an early letter, O.A.B. to Fr. I. Hecker, August 5,
1857, photostat of letter in Paulist Archives, OABP, UNDA; and
Orestes A. Brownson, "Questions of the Soul," BrQR, XII (April,
1855), 209-227, and "Aspirations of Nature," BrQR, XIV (October,
1857), 459-503.

retained the same positions--as in his views of the educational role of the family, Church, press, and literature--he seemed to materially change his views on the school question. He no longer regarded the common school as an Americanizing agent for the good of immigrant Catholics; instead he believed that Catholic schools were essential to the preservation of Catholic faith and principles against the corrupting spirit of American society. Yet, even this modification in his thought upon close scrutiny will not reveal any radicalness or reactionary tendencies. His major arguments after 1862 do not constitute a break with his earlier views, but a re-focusing of them in relation to his increased pessimism over American religious and civil affairs. As a thinker, Brownson was dialectical, always synthesizing one view in juxtaposition to another. His views on schooling are inextricably linked to his perception of the positive or negative influences which prevailed in American society. In the 1840's and 1850's, the good seemed to outweigh the bad; in the 1860's and 1870's, the bad appeared to dominate, and might even smother the good. His position on Catholic schooling must be seen in relation to these societal factors.

The relationship of Brownson's religious development, views, and attitudes to his views on education are clear: 1) he was deeply concerned over his own personal salvation, and that of his country; 2) viewing himself as a scholar with a God-given mission, he devoted much of his time working for the moral, religious, intellectual, and social amelioration of his fellow Catholics and countrymen; 3) salvation and progress would be achieved through education; 4) education involved much more than schooling, and, it aimed at permeating American society with a Roman Catholic religious base; 5) if American democracy was to be sustained and advanced, it would be by Roman Catholicism, or not at all.

Brownson's remedy for America's ills and prescription for its good health boiled down to an educational cure. Driven by this heavenly-ordained and self-proclaimed mission in life, Orestes Brownson obligated himself to work for the moral, religious, intellectual, and social advancement of mankind. He not only functioned as an educator but he also expressed opinions, attitudes, and views on the meaning of "education," on crucial educational issues, and on the roles of formal and informal educational agencies.

CHAPTER III

EDUCATION AND SCHOOLING

i

THE MEANING OF EDUCATION

We have instituted a free government; we have adopted the principle of universal suffrage; we have made, in some sort, every man in this country a legislator, given him a direct legal voice in the affairs of the state and nation . . . . Power has passed out of the hands of the few; it has passed into the hands of the many . . . . But this fact imposes upon every friend of law and order, upon every friend of the human race, and lover of individual or social progress, a solemn and imperious duty. Power in the hands of an ignorant and vicious populace, is a dangerous thing. With this power should go the virtue and intelligence needed to wield it with safety and with beneficial results to Humanity. This virtue and this intelligence do not yet exist in any community on earth. They do not exist with us. We are yet far, very far, from the virtue which wills nought but the public good, and the intelligence which clearly perceives what good is, and seizes at once the proper means for securing it.[1]

When Orestes Brownson spoke on that summer evening in 1837, he partially summed up one of the primary arguments of America's educational tradition: a free government demands a virtuous and intelligent citizenry for the sustenance of law and order, for the progress of individuals and for the social progress of the

----

[1]O. A. Brownson, An Address on Popular Education Delivered in Winnisimmet Village, on Sunday Evening July 23, 1837 (Boston, Press of John Putnam, 1837), p. 5. Hereafter cited as: Winnisimmet Address.

American nation.[2] Brownson, however, departed somewhat from the
exuberant optimism uttered by many of his contemporaries. Even
though he believed in progress, he still thought America and its
people had a long way to go before reaching an adequate level of
virtue and intelligence. Besides the leveling tendencies he noted
in The Scholar's Mission, Brownson worried about the frequent
occurrences of mobs and lynchings that had recently taken place.
Neither riot laws, nor the military, nor sermons, nor patriotic or
moral lectures could provide security for America. "Your only
safety," he told his audience, "is in education, in an education
which trains up the whole people to love law and order, . . . to
love virtue and freedom, and which fits them to maintain freedom
in the state, by first maintaining it in themselves."[3] He called
for the complete education of all people, both male and female,

---

[2]Although this section will be taken primarily from Brownson's
writings before his conversion to Catholicism, it should be noted
that he does not change his views after entering the Church. His
overall educational philosophy remained basically the same. Also,
I have deliberately omitted any reference to "Observations and
Hints on Education" which appeared in the BoQR, III (April, 1840),
137-166. Although certain ideas are similar to Brownson's, and
despite the fact that Alvin Ryan included a portion of this essay
in A Brownson Reader (New York: P. J. Kenedy & Sons, 1955), pp.
106-113, there are serious reasons for believing Brownson did not
write the essay. Nicholas R. Ayo, "A Study of Brownson's Quarterly
Review" (Unpublished Master's Dissertation, University of Notre
Dame, 1962), examined the authorship of every article appearing in
BoQR. He concluded that Brownson's authorship of "Observations and
Hints on Education" should be doubted for three reasons: "1)
Brownson had promised to announce his own work, and from Jan., 1840
onward this article would make the only exception of the year; 2)
there is no indication of his authorship in Brownson's annotated
gift copy to Harvard University, Widener Library; 3) the article is
not found in the collected writings (XX vols.) by Henry F. Brownson" (p. 84). In addition, the stylistic differences and wording of
key phrases are not consistent with Brownson's other writings on
education during this period.

[3]Ibid., p. 6.

black and white, rich and poor, bond and free. "Nothing else can

save us. Liberty is a mere dream when not coupled with universal

education."[4]

What type of education did Brownson have in mind? Was he

talking about the emerging common school that Horace Mann, Henry

Barnard, and others envisioned as the panacea that would guarantee

American greatness? Did he mean the 3-R's? Just what did Brownson

mean by the term "education"?

> Education is something more than is commonly under-
> stood by the term. Education is something more than
> the ability to read and write and cypher, with a
> smattering of Grammar, Geography and History into the
> bargain. Education is the formation of character.
> It is not acquired in schools only, in the few months
> or the few years our children are in the school-room.
> It begins with the first impression made on the senses
> of the infant, and ends only with the last made on
> those of the man before he sinks into the grave; and
> it embraces the results of all the circumstances and
> influences which have, or which have had, the least
> possible bearing in making up or determining the
> individual character. Its process is ever going on.
> The conversation, habits and conduct of parents; the
> spirit, manners and morals of brothers and sisters,
> of playmates, companions, associates and of the whole
> society, all contribute to it and aid in determining
> its character. These influences make up the real
> education received. Our schools do, and can do but
> little. Even their good influences may be more than
> overbalanced by the evil influences at home, in the
> streets, or in society at large.
> Education will go on; there is no earthly power
> that can stop it. Our children will be educated in
> spite of all our efforts. But shall they be educated
> for good, or for evil? This is a question for the
> community to determine.[5]

----

[4]Ibid., p. 7; see also O. A. Brownson, "Education of the
eople," BoQR, II (October, 1839), p. 50. In the latter, Brownson
emarked that "a popular government unsupported by popular educa-
ion is a baseless fabric" (p. 5).

[5]Ibid., pp. 3-4.

Basically, then, Brownson considered education to be an on-going process--from birth to death. It involved a host of agencies; the school was but one of them. Education took place, within or without a school, even despite societal efforts. In addition, Brownson was not content to merely call for "education" and then rest assured that all was well. For he realized that only education of the right sort would secure American greatness.

> They /‾people‾7 are educated for good, only when they are educated for their destiny; trained up, fitted to discharge the mission which Almighty God has given to each one. No education is a good one which does not take the child from his mother's arms, and train it up to be a Man, with a lofty soul, with generous sympathies, high aims, conscious of his destiny, and prepared to leave his trace on his age and country, for good. God has given to each human being born into the world, a high and important mission, a solemn and responsible charge; and that only is a good education which recognizes that mission, charge, and creates the power, and forms the character to fulfil it. This is the education we want.[6]

Man's true end in life, his God-given mission, was to glorify God and enjoy him forever.[7] Accordingly, the right sort of education had to be religious and moral. Time after time during his pre-Catholic period he noted "that our only hope for the full development and perpetuity of our free institutions, is in the moral soundness of the people."[8] Yet, Brownson believed more was necessary. "There is no security to virtue independent of a high mental

---

[6]Ibid., p. 4.

[7]See an unpublished and undated lecture by Brownson, "Means of Effecting a Reform," probably given in the 1830's or early 1840's, contained in the OABP, UNDA.

[8]O. A. Brownson, An Address on the Fifty-Fifth Anniversary of American Independence, Delivered at Ovid, Seneca Co., N.Y., July 4, 1831 (Ithaca, 1831), pp. 7-8 (Italics Brownson's). Hereafter cited as: Ovid Address. See also 1 above; O. A. Brownson, An Address

cultivation."[9] Fulfilling man's individual destiny, and securing
the destiny of America, required both moral integrity and mental
elevation. Without them, serious dangers confronted individual
and social progress. "There are no chains like those which fetter
the mind, no despotism like that of vice."[10] Without mental and
moral advancement, the American nation would collapse and fold up
as did Egypt, Athens and Rome.

The major weakness of these ancient civilizations was that
only the few possessed knowledge, enlightenment and cultivation,
while the many remained ignorant. "The knowledge of the few was
too weak to dispel the surrounding darkness; it gave but a feeble
glare, and was soon overpowered by universal night."[11] This,
America must avoid. How? Brownson's answer was universal education; all must be educated. And if all were educated, what must
they learn, and how? It is precisely on these two major points,
the subject matter of education and the epistemological question,
that Brownson most objected to the educational practices of his
day. "We are very far from regarding everything which passes or
may pass under the name of education, as something to be approved
and never condemned."[12]

Delivered at Dedham, on the Fifty-Eight Anniversary of American
Independence, July 4, 1834 (Published by Request, Dedham, 1834).
Hereafter cited as: Dedham Address.

[9]Ovid Address, p. 14.

[10]Ibid., p. 6.

[11]Ibid., p. 13; see also Winnisimmet Address, pp. 6-7 in
which Brownson stated: "The feeble lights gleaming out from the
windows of a few solitary students, were lost in the thick darkness which brooded over the many. And so, will it ever be. We
must have an educated people" (p. 7, Italics Brownson's).

[12]"Education of the People," op. cit., 393-394.

What was wrong with the content of education, at least as
Brownson saw it? He felt that the American people had done relatively little to preserve the free government they had established.
The American value system taught people first to make a good
bargain, then to get rich, next to look out for themselves alone,
and finally to thank God they were not among the wretched who were
unhappy or poor. As "long as such an education is the best we
have, we cannot accomplish that grand and beneficent work which
the Deity has assigned us."[13] This type of materialistic education that emphasized wealth and social distinction and produced
legislation for the few and not for the many, was not the education America needed for her people. What was required was an
education based on the true end of man as an individual and as a
social being.

The true end of education was "to fit the individual man to
fulfill his destiny, to train him to go forth as a man, in all the
deep significance of that term."[14] The content of education,
therefore, must teach man the full significance of this end.
Education must regard man's whole nature in all its relations.
It must see him endowed with rights and bound by duties

> as a creature and child of God; as a personal, individ-
> ual, and in a large sense an independent being; as a
> member of society and the state, between which and

---

[13]Dedham Address, p. 21.

[14]Orestes A. Brownson, "Social Evils and their Remedies,"
draft of an article, apparently unpublished, written no later than
1842, contained in OABP, UNDA. An essay by Brownson, "Social
Evils, and their Remedy," appeared in his BoQR, IV (July, 1841),
pp. 265-291; however, it bears no resemblance to the above.

> himself exist reciprocal rights and obligations; as
> one of the great human family, united to the race by
> the infinite ties of a common nature, and a common
> destination; and in a still wider relation, as an
> integral one of the universal spiritual creation of
> God. In all these relations, he has rights and
> duties, a mission and a destiny which it is the
> business of education to enable him to understand and
> to fulfil. None of these are distinct and indepen-
> dent of the others; all are intimately connected in
> a divine, harmonious oneness, so that to overlook,
> or neglect any, destroys the unity and completeness
> of his being. The education which does not aim to
> draw out the whole man, is partial, incomplete, and
> in so far worthless.[15]

The type of education that best considered man's whole nature--as

an individual and as a social being--and answered the questions

of individual destiny and the destiny of society, must be, in

essence, both republican and Christian.

Republican education, for Brownson, meant an education that

breathed into people the spirit of the assertion "God has created

all men equal." People would then judge other people according to

their intrinsic worth without regard for factitious distinctions

of society. A republican education taught people to object to

tyranny and injustice, and to stand up in defense of the rights

of man. Republican education must be political, based on achieving

the true ends of American democratic society. Just as education in

Russia, Prussia, and Austria was political, so too must education

in America be political. But, contrary to those European systems

with their glorification of empire or state, American education

adopted as its starting point that society existed not for the

government, but government for society. The mission of government

---

[15]Ibid.

was to aid society in achieving its destiny--equality for all.
European education for political absolutism had no place in
America, where republican and democratic ends were the true mission
of society.[16]

Christian education taught that all men were members of the
brotherhood of man--rich and poor alike. It taught that a wrong
done against one human being hurt all of human society. It taught
manhood, truth, and love of mankind. It taught man his true
destiny--to glorify God and enjoy him forever--and showed him the
intimate connections between his rights and duties as an individual,
social, and spiritual being.[17] "Education, to be complete, to be
what it ought to be, must be religious. An education which is not
religious is a solemn mockery. Those, who would exclude religion
from education, are not yet in the condition to be teachers."[18]

Nowhere to his satisfaction, though, did Brownson see such
a republican and Christian education. Certainly there were many
attempts in American society; unfortunately, Brownson believed,
none were as effective as they might be. The right sort of education did not exist. Brownson's first objection to nineteenth
century education, then, was a protest against its content. In
essence, he objected to the basic values which seemed to dominate
American society.

---

[16]"Education of the People," pp. 401-402.
[17]Dedham Address, pp. 19-21.
[18]"Education of the People," p. 399.

Brownson also objected to the common understanding of the
word "education." The way one defined "education" significantly
influenced the way one attempted to educate. The "what" determined
the "how." The theory of knowing and how knowledge was acquired
depend on the definition of education that one adopted. If the
premise was false, then the results would be less significant, if
not totally worthless. Brownson believed that the wrong definition
of education was nonetheless the dominant one, especially in
American schools.

"To educate is not to teach; it is to draw forth; it is to
unfold the mind. All is in the mind, but is there enveloped. To
bring it out is the business of education."[19]   Schools, Brownson
believed, did not attempt to "draw out," but rather to "pour in."
This type of instruction, based on the philosophy of materialism,
concentrated on presenting the external world as the primary
source of knowledge, and regarded it as the only inlet of knowledge
to the mind. It ignored knowledge already in the mind. Principles
or spiritual facts it considered inferior to visible facts.
Instead, it gathered facts from the external world and presented
them to develop the faculty of memory. Brownson's objection to
materialism has already been established. In addition, he disagreed that developing man's memory was the best or even an
adequate means of acquiring knowledge.

----

[19]"Social Evils and their Remedies," op. cit.

Speaking before a lyceum audience around 1840, Brownson elucidated his views on the means of acquiring knowledge.[20] Knowledge began with an "acquaintance with all the facts, realities, or real /‾e‾/xistences which there are in this outward and in this inward world, in matter or in spirit."[21] Man, a finite and imperfect being, could never attain perfect knowledge, but he was able to approach closer to absolute knowledge than he was at present. Science classified this vast, unattainable amount of knowledge; however, acquaintance with names and classifications did not consitute knowledge. Man must look for causes and connections among other existences; he must look for results. He could only do this by reflection--"thought taking thought for its object, acting upon thought, weighing, /‾e‾/xamining thought. It is then itself thought in one of its modes of activity."[22] How does man acquire knowledge then? By thinking, under the condition of reflection. Observing the material world and reading books did not constitute knowledge; rather, they provided the mind with materials for the action of reflection. Brownson urged his audience to read extensively and to observe reality with ears and eyes open and with minds awake, to reason and reflect.

If knowledge was thus acquired by thinking, reasoning and reflecting, Brownson contended that knowledge must be self-acquired; one man can not reflect for another man.

---

[20] O. A. Brownson, "Means and End of Knowledge," unpublished lecture, probably around 1840, contained in OABP, UNDA.

[21] Ibidem.

[22] Ibidem.

> One man cannot give another man knowledge. He may impart, or rather awaken the desire for knowledge, but knowledge itself he does not, cannot impart. Schools, seminaries, books, professors, teachers, tutors do not, cannot impart knowledge. All they can do is to /¯e¯/xcite the desire and furnish the material for knowledge, but knowledge itself is our own creation, wrought out in the depths of our own intellectual world. The pupil must think, reason, reflect, and he must do it for himself, for no power on earth or in heaven can do it for him. Knowledge then is self acquired.[23]

Since knowledge was self-acquired, a person who had not been to school ought not despair. Teachers and institutions were not indispensable. Certainly they could facilitate knowledge, but each man possessed within himself the power to behold, observe, think, reason and reflect.

Schools, as Brownson saw them, sought to develop man's memory, not his ability to think, reason and reflect. Certainly Brownson considered the latter functions far superior to memory, which he would probably place between observing and thinking.[24] Brownson believed that the redeeming features of schooling were vastly exaggerated. Schools were not only poor educators but also poor facilitators. He granted that in a few cases common schools had possibly provided the first impulse; nonetheless, "it is an impulse they fail of communicating in a vast majority of cases."[25]

---

[23]Ibidem.

[24]See also Ovid Address, pp. 14-15.

[25]"Social Evils and their Remedies," op. cit.

If knowledge, then, was self-acquired, were its uses merely self-aggrandizement? Was knowledge an end in itself? Brownson admitted that knowledge was no doubt an advantage to its possessor, but its usefulness must be extended beyond the individual. Since man was linked with man, the good of each was obtained by making the good of all the end of one's labor. Man, the social being, was required to put his knowledge to work for the advancement of humanity. All acquired knowledge must have this aim. The possessor of knowledge must be able to answer affirmatively the question "Have you made society the better for your having lived in it?"[26] This was, after all, the scholar's mission. Indeed, it was the mission of all people to acquire as much knowledge as possible and to put that knowledge to work for the moral, religious, intellec-tual and social amelioration of the human race.[27] And Brownson saw no other way to improve society. The learned must help others, who in turn helped others. "In education lie the only genuine elements of true social progress."[28]

It is at this point that Brownson's definition of education becomes so crucial. Education was character training--moral and intellectual. Knowledge was acquired not through the memory but

---

[26]"Means and End of Knowledge," op. cit.

[27]When Brownson discusses the "amelioration" of the human race, he often equates it with the "reform" of society or "social progress." Similarly, when he talks about the "preservation" of American democracy, he usually refers to the ideal of American democracy, not as it is but as it should be. Consequently, to preserve an ideal means, in effect, to reform, to improve, to ameliorate man's condition, to strive for social progress.

[28]"Social Evils and their Remedies," op. cit.

through the modes of thought, reason, and reflection. He wanted
the right sort of education, one that stressed republican and
Christian values in contrast to the materialistic views that permeated society. He wanted a useful education, one that would
improve society. Only this type of education would enable America
to achieve greatness as a republican and Christian nation. Many
of his contemporaries agreed with Brownson that education was the
"palladium of our safety";[29] however, most of them equated education with schooling. Brownson, having attended school but briefly
and believing that knowledge was self-acquired, did not share the
same faith in the effectiveness of schooling. "For the problems
of man's destiny and the destiny of society, the common schools,
as things now are, do not, and perhaps never can, furnish even the
alphabet."[30] Yet Brownson was not a pessimist. At the same time
that he mitigated the role of common schools, he still believed and
was able to write that America was following a path toward progress.[31]

American progress, Brownson still maintained, was to be
achieved through "education" in the broad sense of the term.
"Education" would take place; hence the need for "educators." The
character of educators determined the quality and character of
education. Great care then must be taken to rear up well-qualified
educators--for

---

[29]Ovid Address, p. 15.

[30]"Social Evils and their Remedies," op. cit.

[31]See O. A. Brownson, "Progress our Law," BoQR, III (October,
1840), pp. 397-409. This article was a reprint of a sermon
Brownson gave to his Society for Christian Union and Progress in
1838.

> the real educators of the young are the grown-up
> generation. The rising generation will always receive
> as good, as thorough an education as the actual
> generation is prepared to give, and no better. The
> great work, then, which needs to be done in order
> to advance education, is to qualify the actual genera-
> tion for imparting a more complete and finished
> education to its successor, that is to say, educate
> not the young, but the grown-up generation.[32]

This is what Brownson meant by the education of the people.
"Society at large must be regarded as a vast Normal School, in
which the whole active, doing, and driving generation of the day
are pupils, qualifying themselves to educate the young."[33] In
other words, Brownson regarded the improvement of adults as the
chief means of advancing the child, rather than viewing the education of the child as a means for advancing adults. He considered
criticism of such a scheme inevitable.

> We shall probably be told that in this we put the
> cart before the horse; but we respectfully suggest
> whether it be not possible that they, who may be
> disposed to tell us so, have not made the slight
> mistake of deeming the horse a cart, and the cart
> a horse?[34]

For the horse to pull the cart down the right road, the horse must
know the right road himself. So, adults became learners themselves, and in turn, directed the young. This, no doubt, was
what Brownson meant by saying that education was an on-going
process from cradle to grave.

---

[32]"Education of the People," p. 418.
[33]Ibidem.
[34]Ibid., p. 419.

Education of young and adult alike was Brownson's scheme for
achieving progress. Schools, common or collegiate, with proper
redirection, could play an important role in the progress of
society. Informal educational agencies, like the family and
Church, and popular educational agencies, like the press, literature and the Lyceum, could all aid in the proper education of
society, and hence, foster American progress.

Brownson himself witnessed education as it existed, objected
when he perceived it heading in the wrong direction, and offered
constructive criticism for its improvement. He was a reviewer, a
critic and, in striving to reach an unreachable ideal, a true
reformer. Brownson told an audience in 1834 that man must never
say "It has never been, therefore it cannot be."[35]

ii

VIEWS ON SCHOOLING: PRE-CATHOLIC PERIOD

Beginning with his "Notebook of Reflections," and continuing
throughout the rest of his life, Orestes Brownson entertained
ambivalent feelings about the importance of schooling. During
Brownson's years as a teacher (1823-1825), he had expressed joy
at the thought of improving man's mind; however, schools charac-
terized by corporal punishment were not the place where mind could
be expanded. In addition, parental concern and encouragement

---

[35]Dedham Address, p. 13.

seemed lacking. Indeed his early experience with schooling can be described, at best, as unimpressive.

In the late 1820's, Brownson became acquainted with the educational schemes of Robert Owen, his son Robert Dale Owen, Robert L. Jennings, and Fanny Wright.[36] For a time, he became involved in spreading ideas which found their basis in the thought of Robert Owen. Owen had come from New Lanark, Scotland and established at New Harmony, Indiana an experimental community in which he attempted to mold the character of its inhabitants into the highest wisdom and most heroic virtue. The community would consist of between 1000 and 2000 residents, and traditional notions of property, marriage, and religion were abolished. Owen placed education at the heart of his scheme. He believed that man was a passive being, not active in the formation of his character; that man's character was formed for him, not by him; that man was like clay in the hands of a potter, waiting to be molded and shaped into whatever the potter intended.[37]

Owen's son, Jennings, and Wright, who together edited The Free Enquirer in New York, adopted this view of man and depended, according to Brownson, on the system of public schools rather than experimental communities for ultimate success in their plans.

---

[36]Fanny Wright, after her famous Nashoba experiment, had prepared a course of lectures on knowledge. In 1828, she toured the country, giving speeches in Cincinnati, New York, Boston, Philadelphia, Albany, Buffalo, Auburn, and Utica. Brownson heard her speak in Utica, and invited her to speak at Auburn where he was then located.

[37]This is Brownson's appraisal of Owen. See The Convert, pp. 88 ff.

After Brownson heard Fanny Wright speak in Utica, he too became interested in these plans. He became a corresponding editor of their journal, established the Genesee Republican and Herald of Reform in Western New York, and cooperated with The Daily Sentinel. Brownson and the others involved themselves in the cause of the workingman whom they believed would benefit most by this educational scheme.[38]

The proposed plan called for the maintenance, instruction, and education of all children who would be taken from their parents by the state at the age of one or two. The state would then entirely manage these children, providing housing, governors, and teachers until they reached the "age of majority." The aim of the program was to relieve marriage of its burden of raising children; to provide a rational upbringing of children, unhampered by superstition, belief in the invisible, in God, in immortality; and to promote earthly happiness and enjoyment as its only end. Almost as quickly as Brownson gained enthusiasm for such a program, he withdrew his support by the autumn of 1830.[39]

Although it was more than twenty years later that he recorded his reasons for departing from the movement, the reasons are significant nonetheless. He did not believe that man or the child was passive in the hands of an educator, nor that the human mind was a tabula rasa--a slate upon which one poured experience. He

[38]The Working Man's Party was established in 1828 in Philadelphia, and 1829 in New York.

[39]The Convert, pp. 128-136; see also, O. A. Brownson, An Oration on Liberal Studies (Baltimore: Hedian & Obrien, 1853), pp. 18-20.

did not approve of a curriculum based on the physical sciences and geared only to the five senses; and with religion eliminated, how could society be built up or reformed. No religion, no God, no morals, no accountability--this was the education of animals, not people. And perhaps most important of all, Brownson did not want to see the institution of marriage injured or destroyed. He was married and a father and did not relish the idea of breaking up the family or delegating his children to the state. This plan also assumed that parents were incompetent to educate their children. Brownson objected to this, and doubted that there was any guarantee that the state was better qualified to perform such a task. He saw no assurance that these schools were more conducive to the moral and intellectual development of children than the family.[40]

On July 4, 1831, less than one year after his experience with the schemes of Owen and Wright, Brownson pointed out the need for an education that combined both mental and moral discipline, and for schools that would teach children to think, reason, and reflect. The pendulum had come full swing. Moreover, he launched,

---

[40]In 1843, Brownson wrote to Parke Godwin and stated his objections to Fourierism, which considered only the Phalanx essential for progress. Brownson believed the Church, State, Family, and Community (Phalanx) were essential in his social theory of reform. O. A. B. to Parke Godwin, May 9, 1843, N.Y. Public Library, copied and contained in OABP, UNDA. Also, see The Convert, pp. 128-141. Brownson remarked about Fanny Wright: "She did great harm, and the morals of the American people feel even today the injury she did them; but she acted according to her lights, and was at least no hypocrite" (p. 127). Another interesting aside in this matter is that Richard Owen, brother of Robert Dale Owen, also at New Harmony, asked Brownson, in 1842, for information regarding the common schools of the east, and manual labor schools. Owen proposed a national system of education, capped by a National Normal School whose graduates would filter down into every school-room in the country.

as he rarely did, into excessive praise of schools: "Let our
schools become nurseries of intellect, of moral feeling and virtuous
habits, and then let them embosom all the children of the land, and
we have a bulwark no power can break . . . . Each school becomes
a palladium of our safety."[41]

Exactly three years later in 1834, whatever optimism he may
have had about schools seemed to vanish. The type of education he
advocated, the formation of moral, religious, intellectual, social,
and physical character, he found no where. "Our common schools do
not do this. They are better than nothing, but they do not educate
us."[42]

For a time during 1836, Brownson believed he had found the
right sort of school--the manual labor school. William Ellery
Channing, who thought these schools were the only present means of
giving a thorough education to the mass of the people,[43] encouraged
Brownson, then editor of the *Boston Reformer* and also director of
the Society for Christian Union and Progress, to initiate discussion of this topic. In less than four days, Brownson announced:
"We believe in them, and if we have any practical measure, on
which our heart is set, it is manual labour schools."[44] Whether
he really was convinced, or whether he hoped to please Channing

---

[41]*Ovid Address*, pp. 14-15.

[42]*Dedham Address*, p. 19.

[43]William E. Channing to O.A.B., July 19, 1836, OABP, UNDA.

[44]O. A. Brownson, "Manual Labour Schools," *Boston Reformer*,
July 23, 1836, contained in a scrapbook of newspaper clippings
kept while Brownson was editor of the *Reformer*, OABP, UNDA.

whom he so much admired, Brownson enthusiastically, and perhaps too
hastily, endorsed these schools. But at the same time he asked
his readers for more information to "enlighten us respecting the
manual labour schools already established . . . , the manner in
which they are conducted, the general principles on which such
schools should be established, also on the advantages or dis-
advantages of such schools as they do or may exist."[45] While
admitting that he knew very little about these schools, Brownson
nonetheless called them practical; he believed they would be self-
supporting and would provide the best education within the reach
of the poor. He was anxious that a manual labour school be established as a model school for the whole community and as a school
for preparing teachers to conduct these schools.

     After communicating with Governor Edward Everett of Massa-
chusetts in August, 1836[46] about manual labor schools, Brownson
wrote three more articles in the Reformer in favor of them. He
argued that all the children of a community, rich and poor, would
be educated equally. The rich would respect labor and the poor
would appreciate literature, art, science and other refinements.
These schools would then have a tendency to elevate the status of
manual labor and, consequently, to lessen crime and diminish the
evils of society. The character of the laborer would be elevated--
his moral feelings and mind cultivated, and his tastes and manners

----

     [45]Ibidem.
     [46]Brownson wrote Everett on August 12; Everett's response
came on August 16. Cf. E. Everett to O.A.B., August 16, 1836,
OABP, UNDA. Brownson published Everett's response in the Reformer
in late August.

refined. Brownson felt the rich would support and attend such
schools; and children of all classes would meet, study, and work
together, creating "a charming picture." Finally, these schools
would promote the health and virtue of the students by providing
physical exercise for the body.

> Cure the body and you would banish no small share of
> the moral evils of society. Every body acknowledges
> a close connection between the body and the intellect,
> and to be just they must admit a connexion /‾sic‾/
> equally close between the body and the heart. Moral
> and physical nature, in this mode of being are
> intimately connected, and unsoundness in either will
> generate disease in the other.[47]

All the praise he showered on manual labor schools was short-
lived. Less than one year later, in An Address on Popular Education Delivered in Winnisimmet Village, On Sunday Evening, July 23,
1837, Brownson declared: "Education, in the broad sense in which
I have defined it, nowhere exists among us, and nowhere is there
provision made or begun to be made, that it may exist among us."[48]
Brownson called for quick and effective action and reform as the
first business of the people. Although he believed perfection of
schools to be impossible, their improvement was indeed possible
and necessary.

First of all, parents and guardians needed to take a deeper
and more personal interest in school matters, by attending its

---

[47]Boston Reformer, contained in Brownson's scrapbook of
newspaper clippings. Brownson cited what he considered an
alarming death rate among the young, especially the brighter
ones attending college.

[48]Op. cit., p. 8.

meetings and not leaving its affairs to be managed by the few.

They should know how the school was conducted and managed in all

respects, what progress the children were making, and what good or

bad influences prevailed in the school and on the playground. If

not all baneful surroundings could be eliminated, parental

scrutiny would at least lessen the evil.[49]

Secondly, communities had to pay closer attention to the

construction of school-houses. The average school room seemed to

be constructed "on the principle of occupying as little room and

of being as inconvenient as possible." An 18 x 20 box, placed at

corners of streets or a crotch in the roads, with four or five

small windows, furnished with a few hard benches without support

for children's backs, had been considered suitable accommodation

for anywhere from thirty to a hundred pupils, ranging from ages

four to eighteen. In this crowded, narrow space, children were

"compelled to breathe a confined and unwholesome air, to sit, with

but a few minutes recess, to sit still too, for three long hours,

poring over a dull unintelligible lesson." As a result, children

were neither healthy, nor fond of school and study. Brownson

believed these evils of schools could be remedied by

> enlarging our school-houses, making them spacious,
> light and airy; in which there shall be room for the
> lungs and the mind to expand--for the young thought
> to grow. We should furnish, on the score of school-
> houses, every possible accommodation. The school-
> room should be as richly and tastefully fitted up
> as the drawing-room.[50]

[49]Ibid., pp. 8-9.
[50]Ibid., pp. 9-10.

Brownson's third suggestion called for more care in the selection of teachers. In many instances, teachers hired had been persons fitted for almost anything else except teaching. Although complaints grew louder about incompetent teachers, Brownson reminded his audience that first-rate teachers had not been in any great demand nor had any provision been made for securing them. Was a good teacher one who disciplined well, who paid great attention to subject matter, or who worked for low wages? Without any conception of what constituted a first-rate educator, no plan could be devised for selecting teachers.

An educator (Brownson preferred the term to "teacher") must be no common man of ordinary mind; he must be a man of talent, enlarged and comprehensive intellect, warm heart and generous sympathies--a man of observation, thought, reflection, of pure moral feelings, and a correct moral and religious character. "He should be well versed in the philosophy of mind," its laws of development, growth, and perfection; he should comprehend men and things, the philosophy of history and society--"man's destiny in this world, and the means by which it is to be achieved."[51]

Securing good teachers was another matter. Parents themselves needed better education--so they would recognize and sustain a true educator. The profession of school teaching was not yet lucrative enough to attract qualified persons for a life-time career. Finally, one "grand defect" prevailed: not enough normal schools existed for preparing persons to teach.

---

[51]Ibid., pp. 10-11.

> We are not willing to rely on chance for a supply of
> lawyers, physicians and clergymen, but apparently
> willing to rely on nothing else for a supply of edu-
> cators, more vitally essential to the life and health
> and virtue of the people than they all . . . . The
> school-master, if he be the school-master, makes and
> executes our laws, pleads our cases, writes our
> sermons; for he forms the mind from which these
> emanate.[52]

Brownson urged the legislature to authorize the people in several counties of Massachusetts to establish normal schools. In the meantime, high schools, academies, and higher seminaries would have to provide the supply of teachers for common schools.

In his closing remarks, Brownson encouraged the residents of Winnisimmet to support the proposed construction of an academy in their village. Common schools, though they did some good, were nonetheless inadequate to the educational needs of the community. Academies could secure a better education for all children. Other- wise, with only a few academies scattered throughout the state, only the rich would be able to attend them, and hence, the gap of educational inequality would widen.

By 1837, then, Brownson had lost interest in manual labor schools, felt that common schools were inadequate, and believed that more academies were needed. He encouraged better construction of school houses, more local parental interest in the affairs of schools, and urged the State to authorize local communities to establish normal schools to prepare better teachers.

---

[52]Ibid., pp. 11-12.

At the same time that Brownson was pointing out needed improvements in schooling, Massachusetts established a Board of Education to be headed by Horace Mann. From 1837 to 1848, Mann, as Secretary of the Board, issued a series of annual reports.[53] Brownson, however, often was critical of Mann's reports, at least on crucial issues.

In 1839, Brownson used Mann's Second Annual Report as a springboard for his article, "Education of the People." Brownson found "no leading idea, no enlarged views, no comprehensive measures; nothing . . . as a means of aiding us to an education worthy of a free and Christian Commonwealth."[54] He agreed with Mann that teaching methods should be improved, and that Normal Schools should be established. These measures would no doubt improve the mechanism of teaching. But what would be taught in the Normal Schools? Brownson, who had stressed the importance of religious (Christian) and political (Republican) education, found only shallowness in the Report.

> The Board assure us Christianity shall be insisted on
> so far, and only so far, as it is common to all sects.
> This, if it mean anything, means nothing at all. All,
> who attempt to proceed on the principle here laid
> down, will find their Christianity ending in nothing-
> ness.[55]

No common ground existed between all the various religious denominations in the state. Fundamental differences existed between

---

[53]See Lawrence A. Cremin, ed., The Republic and the School.
Horace Mann on the Education of Free Man (Teachers College Press,
Teachers College, Columbia University, 1957), p. 6.
[54]"Education of the People," p. 403.
[55]Ibid., p. 404.

every group, whether Unitarian, Trinitarian, or Calvinist. No
sect could be satisfied, but all would be dissatisfied.

Politically, Brownson viewed the Board's composition as Whig,
except that one Democrat was added "to save appearances." The
teachers in the Normal Schools would also be Whigs. If they could
not outwardly teach Whig doctrines, at least they would imbibe all
teachers and students with a Whig philosophy. "Now the Whig
doctrines on society are directly hostile to the democratic
doctrines. Whiggism is but another name for Hobbism. It is based
on materialism, and is atheistical in its logical tendencies."[56]

What made matters worse, Brownson commented, was the Board's
imitation of the Prussian system. Prussia's educational system
was good for Prussia; it was despotic and absolutist. Just as King
Frederic of Prussia enlisted the school-master to further his cause,
were not the Whigs also attempting to perpetuate their power? By
establishing a Whig Board of Education, by enabling the Board to
establish Normal Schools, and through them, to educate all the
children, "we have done all that can be done to give Whiggism a
self-perpetuating power; all that we can do to make a community of
practical infidels."[57] If such a system were adopted here, "adieu
then to republicanism, to social progress."[58]

Lest Brownson be construed as merely anti-Whig, he was also
opposed to a Democratic government doing the same thing.

[56]Ibid., p. 405.
[57]Ibid., p. 406.
[58]Ibid., p. 408.

Government should not dictate, at least in this country, where our

philosophy holds the people to be wiser than the government.

> Here, the people do not look to the government for
> light, for instruction, but the government looks to
> the people. The people give the law to the government.
> To entrust, then, the government with the power of
> determining the education which our children shall
> receive, is entrusting our servant with the power to
> be our master . . . . We may as well have a religion
> established by law, as a system of education, and
> the government educate and appoint the pastors of
> our churches, as well as the instructers /¯sic¯/ of
> our children.[59]

Brownson contended that such governmental intrusion into education

tended to destroy the progressive nature of man and society.

One of Brownson's major concerns was the attempt by the Board

to control school libraries. Owing to the emphasis he had placed

on reading in his own education, Brownson remarked that a library

"of the right stamp, is of more importance to the district than

the school itself."[60] Besides all the other needed improvements,

the development of well-selected libraries was a necessary measure

in improving common schools. Although libraries were being estab-

lished, Brownson objected to them on several grounds. First of

all, the State Board had officially sanctioned the book list.

Brownson considered such a step an insult to local control, taking

management away from the people. Secondly, he doubted the legality

of the Board's action of sanctioning books. Thirdly, he opposed

---

[59]Ibid., p. 409. Brownson had earlier asserted that "no
government, no government on earth, is qualified to determine the
education to be given the people"; see the Christian Examiner and
General Review, XX (May, 1836), 155.

[60]O. A. Brownson, "The School Library," BoQR, III (April,
1840), 255.

the selection and recommendation of the same books to all districts; variety, not uniformity, Brownson considered essential, for without conflict of opinion, no progress was possible. In this way, students would read thousands of books rather than merely one or two hundred. Fourthly, Brownson believed the Board approached censorship of the press by encouraging the publication of books sanctioned by it, and consequently, by impairing the publication and sales of books in which an author poured out "his whole thought." Hence, not the best books but the least objectionable ones were selected. Finally, the Board professed to adopt, as a rule, the exclusion of any books that were of sectarian character in religion or partisan character in politics. Brownson believed that every book of value on religion and politics was indeed sectarian or partisan; rather than exclude all these books, Brownson wanted all parties represented in the library. "When a book is introduced giving one side of a question in religion or politics, the best book that can be found treating the opposite side shall be procured and admitted." Brownson believed this the only practical path to follow, "if the library is to possess any positive value, and the rights of all concerned are to be respected."[61] Although Brownson was extremely critical of the Board, he did want to see education promoted. In this instance, he urged that inhabitants of towns or school districts be allowed to select books for their libraries, unimpeded and uninfluenced by the extra-official sanctions and recommendations of the Board.

---

[61]*Ibid.*, p. 232.

Another cause of concern to Brownson was the Board's operation of Normal Schools. He feared that the Board would require
schools to hire only graduates of state-sanctioned Normal Schools.
The teachers in Normal Schools posed another problem. With the
state in control, who would be appointed as professors? Brownson
sensed that appointments would go to men of reputation and respectability, who upheld things as they now existed and who dared not to
disturb the world with a new idea or reforming word. Vitality and
progressiveness would be lost, and man would not be educated for
his true destiny. Instead, the Board seemed to promote universal
education "because they esteem it the most effectual means possible
of checking pauperism and crime, and making the rich secure in
their possessions."[62] The idea of educating a human being to be a
man, to fulfill his destiny, to contribute to the progress of
society, to attain the end God desired, was not within the juris-
diction of a Board or any centralized government.

The purpose of government was to reflect the will of the
people, not lead it; hence, it could never be an educator of the
people. Its province was not to control opinions, whether moral,
literary, political, philosophical, religious, or educational.

> No system of education, no system of schools, which
> can be instituted and sustained by government, can
> be adequate to the educational wants of the community.
> Nothing desirable in matters of education, beyond
> what relates to the finances of the schools, comes
> within the province of the legislature. More than
> this the legislature should not attempt; more than
> this the friends of education should not ask. Let the
> legislature provide ample funds for the support of as

---

[62]Ibid., p. 412.

many schools as are needed for the best education
possible of all the children of the community, and
there let it stop. The selection of teachers, the
choice of studies, and of books to be read or studied,
all that pertains to the methods of teaching, and
the matters to be taught or learned, are best left
to the School District. In these matters, the
District should be paramount to the State. The evils
we have alluded to are in some degree inseparable
from all possible systems of education, which are
capable of being put into practice; but they will
be best avoided by placing the individual school under
the control of a community composed merely of the
number of families having children to be educated in
it.[63]

For all these reasons, Brownson regarded the establishment of the

Board of Education as "unwise."[64] Government should provide funds

for schools, but nothing more. The control of educational matters

must be local, within the school district itself.

Yet even a common school controlled at the district level

could not actually achieve Brownson's ideal; ideals can only be

approached but never perfectly realized. Furthermore, no system

of schools can supply the kind of education Brownson desired,

because the part of education they provide, "in their best organiza-

tion, is the smallest part of the education we do and must

receive."[65] The greater part of education is received from the

---

[63]Ibidem. Brownson believed that American society had been
structured on the democratic principle of Federalism: 1) Congress
takes care of all material interests of the States; 2) State
congresses legislate for Counties; 3) Counties legislate for Wards
and Townships; 4) Townships and Wards legislate for Districts; 5)
Districts legislate all remaining interests, including the Grammar
School. The smallest division, the District, is confided the whole
matter of common school education.

[64]Ibid., p. 415.

[65]Ibid., p. 417.

influences of society--adults, clergy, press, literature, lyceum
and lectures.

> Shut up your school-houses, and in all essential
> matter your children would grow up about the same,
> they would they were open. This is a consideration
> it is not wise to overlook. No matter what your
> schools are, the characters of your children will
> be determined by that intangible, invisible,
> indescribable, but very real personage, called
> the Spirit of the Age.[66]

What did Brownson expect from schools? Quite simply, instruction
in the arts of reading and writing and in the physical sciences.
Schools provided instruction but never education. The community
could only be educated by the free action of mind on mind. "Whatever means we have for bringing mind to act on mind, so many means
we have for educating the people."[67]

Brownson's pessimism over the inability of schools to educate, his criticisms of the Massachusetts Board of Education,
Horace Mann, prevalent teaching methods and philosophies of education, continued almost without abatement throughout the remainder
of his pre-Catholic period.[68] His occasional commendations of

---

[66]Ibid., p. 418.

[67]Ibid., p. 434.

[68]See the following Brownson reviews: A. B. Muzzey, The
Sunday School Guide, and Parents' Manual (Boston: James Munroe &
Co. and Benjamin Greene, 1838) in BoQR, I (July, 1838), 387; Miss
Sedgwick, Means and Ends; or Self Training (Boston: Marsh, Capen,
Lyon, and Webb, 1839) in BoQR, II (July, 1839), 389-390; "The
School Library," BoQR, III (April, 1840), 225-237; Theory of
Teaching, with a Few Practical Illustrations by a Teacher (Boston:
C. P. Peabody, 1841) in BoQR (January, 1842), 123-124; Remarks on
the Seventh Annual Report of the Hon. Horace Mann, Secretary of
the Board of Education (Boston: Little & Brown, 1844) in BrQR
(October, 1844), 547. See also "Social Evils and their Remedies,"
op. cit. About the only favorable review of any educational

schools seem insignificant in contrast to his steady, and at times severe, criticisms of them. That he educated himself without schools was undoubtedly a reason for his belief that others could succeed with no schools.

iii

CATHOLIC SCHOOLS, PUBLIC SCHOOLS, AND EDUCATION

The period from 1830-1860 has been called an "Era of Reform."[69] Springing from the pervading belief in the infinite worthiness and perfectibility of man, it fostered the notion that in due time man would remove all obstacles and claim his true divinity. Utopian experiments, political reform, women's rights, economic reform, land reform, the peace crusade, abolitionism, and assistance for debtors, prisoners, orphans, drunkards and the insane engaged the efforts of thousands of Americans.[70] There was no reform movement that promised more than the common school movement. Its sponsors claimed "education" as the great panacea

ventures is Brownson's estimation of A. Bronson Alcott; see O. A. Brownson, "Alcott on Human Culture," BoQR (October, 1838), 417-432. For an interesting note about Brownson's repeated criticisms of Horace Mann, see Arthur E. Bestor, Jr., "Horace Mann, Elizabeth P. Peabody, and Orestes A. Brownson, An Unpublished Letter, with Commentary," Proceedings of the Middle States Association of History and Social Sciences Teachers (New York: Teachers College, Columbia University, 1940-41), 47-53.

[69]Henry Stelle Commager, The Era of Reform, 1830-1860 (Princeton: D. Van Nostrand Company, 1960).

[70]See ibid.; also, Alice Felt Tyler, Freedom's Ferment: Phases of American Social History from the Colonial Period to the Outbreak of the Civil War (The University of Minnesota Press, 1944); Merle Curti, The Growth of American Thought (New York: Harper & Row, 1943), pp. 283-413; and Timothy L. Smith, Revivalism and Social Reform in Mid-Nineteenth Century America (New York: Abingdon Press, 1957).

that would "right the unrightable wrongs" of society. The entire
national existence depended on "education," they argued, and free
government would be safely secured and assured. Economic benefits
of enterprise and industry would bless the nation and democracy
would be advanced and religion sustained.[71]

Robert Cross has pointed out the general consensus of opinion
during the 1830-1860 period: "Education was too important to be
entrusted to informal processes" and "all youth required formal
education."[72] By mid-nineteenth century, the Protestant churches
were expanding their efforts in higher education, developing and
improving Sunday schools, and sending missionaries at home and
abroad. Confidently they relegated to the state the function of

---

[71]Intimately connected with the promotion of the common
school was the non-denominational character of the schools. The
theme of "PATRIOTISM - PROTESTANTISM - SCHOOL - BIBLE" has been
well documented as the dominant cultural-religious emphasis of
mid-nineteenth century American schooling. See the following:
David B. Tyack, "Onward Christian Soldiers: Religion in the
American Common School," in Paul Nash, History and Education (New
York: Random House, 1970), pp. 212-255; Timothy Smith, "Parochial
Education and American Culture," in Nash, op. cit., pp. 192-211;
Charles Bidwell, "The Moral Significance of the Common School: A
Sociological Study of Common Patterns of School Control and Moral
Education in Massachusetts and New York, 1837-1840," History of
Education Quarterly, VI (1966), 50-91; Timothy Smith, "Protestant
Schooling and American Nationality, 1800-1850," Journal of American
History, LIII (March, 1967) 679-685; David Tyack, "The Kingdom of
God and the Common School: Protestant Ministers and the Educa-
tional Awakening in the West," Harvard Educational Review, XXXVI
Fall, 1966), 447-469; Robert W. Lynn, Protestant Strategies in
Education (New York: Association Press, 1964); William Bean
Kennedy, The Shaping of Protestant Education (New York: Associa-
tion Press, 1966); see also Robert W. Lynn and Elliot Wright, The
Big Little School, Sunday Child of American Protestantism (New York:
Harper & Row, 1971) for an analysis of the Sunday School Movement.

[72]"Origins of the Catholic Parochial Schools in America," The
American Benedictine Review, XVI (1965), 194; see also Jonathan
Messerli, "To Broaden Schooling Was to Narrow Education," Notre Dame
Journal of Education, I (Spring, 1970), 5-16 for a discussion of the
school's role in gradually assuming (or being handed) the responsibilities previously carried on by other non-school educative agencies.

formal daily education. The schools were Protestant and employed
the Bible, textbooks, prayers, hymns, teachers, and school officials
that shared the Protestant viewpoint. The churches certainly could
justify their acquiescence in "public education."[73] As another
student remarked, "Christianity merged imperceptibly with Americanism; a generalized Protestantism was part of the common wisdom of
the common school."[74] Little wonder that many Catholic immigrants
and Church leaders found themselves victims of "alienation in
America,"[75] especially in its schools.

In its public pronouncements on schooling, the Catholic
hierarchy gradually became more outspoken. In 1829, the Pastoral
Letter reminded Catholics of the importance of selecting a school
that will "cultivate the seeds which you have sown." In 1837 the
hierarchy commended the efforts of the Sisterhoods and their work
in the schools, and explained attempts to improve the schools. By
1840 the Bishops expressed a fear that the faith of Catholic
children might be undermined by either sectarian or godless
instruction received in public schools. Catholic schools were
available, yet in many cases Protestants rather than Catholics
attended and supported these schools. The Church has

> always deemed it to be one of our most pressing
> obligations to use our best and earliest efforts

[73]Cross, op. cit., p. 195.
[74]David Tyack, "Onward Christian Soldiers," op. cit., p. 212.
[75]Vincent P. Lannie, "Alienation in America: The Immigrant
Catholic and Public Education in Pre-Civil War America," Review of
Politics, XXXII (October, 1970), 503-521; for a slightly different
version of the same article see "The Emergence of Catholic Education
in America," Notre Dame Journal of Education, III (Winter, 1973),
297-309.

in providing establishments where they /‾children_7
may be carefully educated by competent persons in all
that is necessary for their prosperity in this life,
whilst they were taught by admonition and example
to walk in that path which leads to heaven.[76]

The Bishops charged that public schools were poisoned with a

sectarian hue and that Catholic children were forced to read "a

version of the Bible made under sectarian bias." School books

were "replete with offensive and dangerous matter" and insidious

efforts made "to misrepresent our principles, to distort our tenets,

to vilify our practices and to bring contempt upon our Church and

its members." Because of failure at attempts to bring about a

reconciliation on these issues, as in New York and Philadelphia,

"we are always better pleased to have a separate system of educa-

tion for the children of our communion."[77]

The most serious objection made by Catholics was leveled

against the reading of the Sacred Scriptures "without note or

comment" in the public schools. Letting the Bible speak for itself

had been the lifeblood of Protestantism. Any opposition to the

Bible was considered un-Christian, anti-Protestant, un-American,

and anti-common school. Protestants viewed this complaint by

Catholics as a threat to the very existence of America.

In the Pastoral Letter of 1837, the Bishops denied the alleged

n-Americanism of the Catholic Church, and responded that "we owe

---

[76]"Pastoral Letter (1840)," p. 89.
[77]"Pastoral Letter (1840)" and "Pastoral Letter (1843)," pp.
09, 94; see also Sister Marie Leonore Fell, The Foundations of
ativism in American Textbooks (Washington, D.C.: The Catholic
niversity of America Press, 1941). Sister Fell examined over
,000 school readers, histories, and geographies and concluded
hat the texts were anti-Catholic and pro-Protestant. Considering

civil and political allegiance to the several States in which we reside, and also, to our general government." Catholic immigrants were admitted to this country by the American government and they had taken oaths renouncing all allegiance to any foreign prince, power, state, or potentate in civil and political matters. Moreover, Catholics

> owe no religious allegiance to any State in this Union, nor to its general government. No one of them claims any supremacy or dominion over us in our spiritual or ecclesiastical concerns: nor does it claim any such right or power over any of our fellow citizens, of whatsoever religion they may be: and if such a claim was made, neither would our fellow citizens, nor would we submit thereto.[78]

In 1840 the hierarchy answered charges that the Catholic Church was opposed to the Bible. "We are desirous that all under our charge should be as well acquainted with the doctrines found in the Holy Scriptures as with any other portion of the word of God." But the Bishops objected to unauthorized versions of the Bible being used in schools; moreover, they doubted the value of employing the Bible in the way schools were using it.

> We are disposed to doubt seriously whether the introduction of this sacred volume as an ordinary class book into schools, is beneficial to religion. It is thereby exposed to that irreverend familiarity, which is calculated to produce more contempt than veneration.[79]

---

the Protestant nature of society, books with Protestant sympathies are certainly understandable. See Lannie, "Alienation in America," op. cit., p. 513; Lannie points out the difference between anti-Catholic and Protestant in sympathy: the former is reprehensible, the latter understandable.

[78]"Pastoral Letter (1837)," pp. 66-67.
[79]"Pastoral Letter (1840)," p. 94.

The Bible was being placed side by side with fables and mythology and was made the "subject of vulgar jest," sinking to the level of a task-book. Even the introduction of the Catholic Bible needed to be approached cautiously.

> If the authorized version be used in a school, it should
> be under circumstances very different from those which
> are usually found in the public institutions of our
> States, and this shows the necessity of your $\underline{/}$ to
> Catholics $\underline{/}$ better exertions to establish and uphold
> seminaries and schools, fitted according to our own
> principles, and for the education of the children who
> are daily rising up, and numbers of whom are lost for
> want of such institutions.[80]

With such ambivalent language, it is certainly understandable how Protestants could accuse Catholics of trying to force the Bible from the schools. For Catholics had indeed objected to the very purposes for which the common schools used the Bible.

Catholic attempts to alter existing common school patterns in New York, Philadelphia, and Boston were met vociferously and violently.[81] The Bible had assumed a "symbolic meaning" by this

---

[80]Ibidem.

[81]See Vincent P. Lannie, Public Money and Parochial Education: Bishop Hughes, Governor Seward, and the New York School Controversy (Cleveland: The Press of Case Western Reserve University, 1968) and Austin Flynn, "The School Controversy in New York, 1840-842, and Its Effect on the Formulation of Catholic Elementary Policy" (Unpublished doctoral dissertation, University of Notre Dame, 1962) for an analysis of Bishop Hughes' attempts to secure state funds for parochial schools; see Robert F. Hueston, "The Catholic Press and Nativism, 1840-1860," pp. 50-66 for a discussion of the New York school controversy, and pp. 66-109 for a discussion of the Philadelphia Bible riots of 1844; also, see Vincent P. Lannie and Bernard C. Diethorn, "For the Honor and Glory of God: The Philadelphia Bible Riots of 1840 $\underline{/}$ sic $\underline{/}$," History of Education Quarterly, VIII (Spring, 1968), 44-106; for the Boston "whipping case," see Robert H. Lord, John E. Sexton, and Edward T. Harrington, History of the Archdiocese of Boston (New York: Sheed and Ward, 1944), II, 585-601. It must be noted that the beating administered to eleven year-old Thomas Wall in Boston did not occur until 1859.

time.[82] The defensive measures undertaken by Catholics were perceived by Protestants as gross effrontery to the precepts of
enlightened Christianity. Even though Catholics objected to
several practices within the common schools, no definite decision
was made at this time to commit the Catholic Church to the Catholic
school. There were no compulsory school laws to force a decision
between the common school and the Catholic school. A person could,
and often did, decide not to send his children to any school. In
fact few Catholic children were in school of any kind.[83]

According to Timothy Smith, the immigrant was committed to
becoming Americanized in a new country. But the common school was
determined to wrench the child loose from his cultural and religious roots. The immigrant family resisted the efforts of the
common school and elected to support the Catholic school or none at
all. It was the parish schools, where the teachers understood and
sympathized with the immigrant child and family, that were the
prime agents of adjustment to American life.[84]

---

[82]David Tyack, "Onward Christian Soldiers," discusses the
Bible having symbolic meaning for Protestants at this time.

[83]See Robert Cross, "The Origins of the Catholic Parochial
Schools in America."

[84]"Parochial Education and American Culture," pp. 203-205;
John Tracy Ellis makes a similar statement in American Catholicism,
p. 53; see two articles by Thomas T. McAvoy, "The Catholic Minority in the United States, 1789-1821," Historical Records and
Studies, XXXIX-XL (1952), 33-50, and "The Formation of the Catholic
Minority in the United States, 1820-1860," Review of Politics, X
(1948), 13-34. In the latter, McAvoy argues that the Church maintained its Anglo-American character because Catholics generally
looked to the Anglo-Americans for cultural and normative leadership. Also, a brief examination of the Pastoral Letters of the
hierarchy reveals some truly American phraseology in their exhorta-
tions to the laity and clergy. In other words, many of the things
advocated by the Bishops were quite compatible with the American,
and even Protestant, ethic. The following is a list of such items:

Equally important were the attitudes, values, sensibilities, and skills that were imparted to the immigrant group by the Church and its educational agents. Were the goals sought by the bishops, clergy, and teachers compatible with the American form of government and way of life? Smith maintains that even though to an "outsider" of the immigrant group the parish school "seemed bent upon binding the children of immigrants to outmoded traditions," the school was actually Americanizing youngsters.[85]

This twofold question--whether common schools were destroying the faith of Catholics and whether Catholic schools were impeding or advancing the Americanization of immigrants--absorbed the mind of Orestes Brownson for almost thirty years.

During his first year as a Catholic, Brownson stated that Catholic efforts to establish and multiply schools were aimed at making the whole country Catholic; unfortunately, Catholics had little financial means to accomplish much, and their attempts were made "though not with half the zeal and energy that could be wished."[86] A few years later though, Brownson came out in support

Christian education"; "habits of virtue and religion"; "inspire in them the love and fear of God"; "obedience"; "dread of cursing and swearing, of fraud and duplicity, of lewdness and drunkenness"; respectful and dutiful behavior to their fathers and mothers"; teach him to be industrious, to be frugal"; "You labour for the reservation and increase of true religion, for the benefit of our common country, whose welfare depends on the morals of its citizens." Pastoral Letters, 1792-1843).

[85]"Parochial Education and American Culture," pp. 203-205. Smith does not think the term "Americanization" is precise. The Irish have been "Americanized"--yet not "Protestantized." The term "cultural pluralism" is more exact here--adjustment to both American life along with a modification of the cultures of both the immigrant and host society.

[86]O. A. Brownson, "Native American Civility," BrQR, II (October, 1845), 539.

of common schools for all the children in the Commonwealth of
Massachusetts. Realizing the difficulties of religious neutrality,
he favored the present arrangement with nothing more positive or
sectarian than the inclusion of Christian truths common to all
denominations. The "relation of the public schools to religion
must be negative, excluding what is peculiar to each denomination."[87]
Brownson, who had earlier criticized Horace Mann on this same
issue, saw this as the only condition upon which a school system
could be established and maintained. At the same time, he
cautioned that public schools must not meddle with religion--this
was the province of denominational schools, the churches, and
parents. Moreover, freedom of religion demanded that the State
allow each denomination to establish its own schools,[88] to be
supported not by public tax funds, but by the denominations themselves. Not to permit religious schools would amount in practice
to an educational system with no religion at all.

Brownson expected Catholic children to attend either
Catholic schools or public schools. If the latter, the home and
Church would obviously take care of religious instruction. In the
public schools, Catholic children would at least receive the
benefits of a good common school education that the State had
rightfully provided.[89] The low level of morals and culture,

----

[87]O.A. Brownson, "The College of the Holy Cross," BrQR, VI
(July, 1849), 390.

[88]The purpose of this essay was to support the incorporation
of the College of the Holy Cross as an exclusively Catholic institution of higher learning. The State had recently denied the
petition for incorporation.

[89]Brownson stated that one-third of all children in the
public schools of Boston were Catholics; see ibid., p. 391. He

particularly of Irish immigrants, would be improved. More impor-

tantly, lower class Catholics would not be isolated in the common

schools and tied to an inferior civilization.[90] Furthermore, he

felt that Catholics as a class derived more benefits from these

schools than any other group.[91] Nonetheless, Brownson denied that

common schools were sufficient for all; higher education was

required, especially in institutions founded by religious denomina-

tions that would train students in religion and morality. Common

schools, Brownson believed, would provide basic instruction,

elevate poor and ignorant immigrants, and thus serve as a catalyst

in Americanizing Catholics.

In his next major essay on education in 1852, Brownson

refuted a contention that claimed evil in society resulted from

---

had also received a letter, Sarah F. Stearns to O.A.B., December
19, 1847, OABP, UNDA in which Stearns, a convert, explains the
tremendous financial difficulty of trying to run an Irish Catholic
school in Springfield, Massachusetts. In addition, she cited the
lack of a full-time, permanent priest as a hindrance to her efforts.

[90]See O.A.B. to James A. McMaster, March 14, 1849, OABP,
UNDA.

[91]Brownson's first critic on this issue was James A. McMaster
in early 1849. McMaster responded: "The matter of education,
which you introduce in your letter, is one that I doubt if we could
agree upon. My firm opinion is that any possible form of education
in mixed schools must produce and perpetuate the continual apostacy
of the great body of Catholic youth. I would rather keep them in
the worst Irish schools, or out of school altogether. The civilization of this country is greater than that of Ireland, but it is a
heathen civilization; and I do not believe that the Apostles would
ever have told the faithful of their days to send their children
to Pagan Schools--no matter how much more civilized they might have
been than the Christian." See James A. McMaster to O.A.B., March
8, 1849, OABP, UNDA. See also James A. McMaster to O.A.B.,
November, 1849, OABP, UNDA for McMaster's criticism of Brownson's
July issue. For a discussion of McMaster's views on Catholic
schools after the 1860's, see Thomas T. McAvoy, "Public Schools vs.
Catholic Schools and James McMaster," Review of Politics, XXVIII
January, 1966), 19-46.

evil in the schools. Instead, he claimed the opposite was true; evil influences in society brought about paganism in the schools.[92] How did a pagan society develop under Christian education in the first place? Brownson, retracing events back to the Reformation, stated that education was not omnipotent as some had assumed. A child was not "as ductile as wax in the hands of an educator," nor was he passive. Because of individual differences and free will, "the same regimen will not produce the same effects in all."[93] Furthermore, due to his fallen nature, man was not capable of overcoming evil tendencies without the grace of God. Mere human education could not root out the paganism in individuals or in society. Accordingly, one could not remove paganism in society merely by banishing certain books from schools (or by banning Catholic attendance at public schools). "The education which forms our character is given far less in schools and colleges than in the family and in society, and far less by the textbooks studied than by the personal character of school-mates, and of teachers and professors."[94] Brownson did not mean to derogate education (schools), but he did want to guard against attributing to it a virtue it did not possess—being given credit for the good in society; nor did he want to impute it with a vice it did not possess—being blamed for the evil in society. At least one person asked logically of Brownson: "Do you not conflict with

[92]See O. A. Brownson, "Paganism in Education," BrQR, IX (April, 1852), 227-247.
[93]Ibid., p. 239.
[94]Ibid., pp. 240-241.

Archbishop /‾John Hughes‾7, and leave the advocates of godless
education room to say as they do even now 'go to work in your own
field, then, and leave us to educate the children of the Republic,
in an useful and practical manner.'"[95] The implications were
obvious; if schooling did not produce either good or evil in
society, Catholic fears of public schools were unfounded or at
least exaggerated, and Catholic goals in establishing schools of
their own would not eliminate the evil influences of society, and
do very little for securing a Catholic environment.

What Brownson may have implied in 1852 became explicitly
stated in an 1854 essay, "Schools and Education."[96] Paganism in
society would not be eliminated by the schooling given to children;
"for whatever the lessons of the schoolroom, the character of the
man is not determined by them, but by the various and complex
action of society."[97] The common error, he stated, was that the
age had attributed too much to the school. The solution lay in
conforming the political and social order to the spirit of
Catholicism. Only then could schools help effect and train a
Catholic nation.

Also, this 1854 article was the beginning of a controversy
over the question of public schools versus Catholic schools; and
this dispute flared up with the major essays that Brownson devoted

---

[95]Benjamin Canavan to O.A.B., April 18, 1852, OABP, UNDA.
Canavan was a resident of New York and obviously referred to
Hughes, and not to Fitzpatrick of Boston.

[96]O.A. Brownson, "Schools and Education," BrQR, XI (July,
1854), 354-376. This essay immediately followed his "Native
Americanism" article.

[97]Ibid., p. 360.

to the school issue in 1858, 1859, and 1862.[98] If others had
found an easy solution to the question, Brownson was not among them.
As usual, in his thorough and logical fashion, he examined the
problem at the roots. Apparently, the roots lay too deep for some
to understand.

In "Schools and Education," Brownson answered charges that
he was hostile to common schools and had disparaged them. Even
though he felt these schools were not perfect, had grave defects,
and were partially objectionable in principle, Brownson declared
he was not absolutely opposed to them, nor did he wish to destroy
or impede them. Even though the schools fell far short of his
ideal, and certainly below the "exaggerated boasts an unwise
patriotism is accustomed to make of /‾their_7 perfection and
wonderful effects," Brownson thought very highly of public schools
"when the question lay between /‾them_7 and no common schools at
all."[99]

Still, Brownson objected to certain abuses in public education. First of all, he disapproved of the avowed purpose of the
common school--"to operate against Catholicism" and "to detach
/‾Catholic_7 children from the religion of their parents."[100]
Nonetheless, he had no fear that the schools were capable of doing

[98]See O. A. Brownson, "Conversations of Our Club," BrQR, XV
(October, 1858), 425-444; O. A. Brownson, "Public and Parochial
Schools," BrQR, XVI (July, 1859), 324-342; and O. A. Brownson,
"Catholic Schools and Education," BrQR, XIX (January, 1862), 66-85.
[99]"Schools and Education," p. 362. Brownson obviously
attempted to allay Native American arguments that Catholics
completely opposed common schools.
[100]Ibidem.

such damage to the faith of Catholic children, for non-Catholics

had overstated the potency of schooling. Just as schools could

not insure a good society, they would not be able to effect evil

against a sufficiently robust and tenacious faith. Secondly,

Brownson complained about the state's takeover of education; at no

time should the state be allowed to tax citizens for the support of

schools they conscientiously opposed or to place a school tax on

people with no children. He considered education the right and

duty of parents, not the right of the state. Furthermore, he

considered the centralizing tendency, together with its bureaucracy,

a curse.[101] Education rightfully belonged to families, to towns,

and to municipalities. Thirdly, he objected to state schools

because education was a spiritual affair; states were limited only

to temporal functions. In addition, he disliked schools because

they took no account of religious differences between Catholics

and Protestants. Ideally, separate schools should exist; however,

Brownson realized that no concessions were possible on this issue,

for "no considerations of justice or of good policy will induce

/‾Protestants_7 to forego their vain hope of Protestantizing

/‾Catholic_7 children by means of the common schools."[102]

Fourthly, Brownson especially condemned common schools for not

conforming to either the spirit or letter of the law prohibiting

---

[101]Ibid., pp. 364-368. Brownson pointed to New York and
Massachusetts as leaders in this "bad work." New York had established a Board of Regents and a Superintendent of Common Schools,
while Massachusetts had her Board of Education. Also, Brownson
referred to the stand he had taken against centralized administration of common schools even while he was a Protestant.
 [102]Ibid., p. 369.

sectarianism into the classroom. He did not expect Catholicism to be taught, but neither should it be insulted or tampered with. Textbooks contained material that maligned and misrepresented the Catholic religion, while zealous teachers often attempted to Protestantize Catholic children under their care. This last reason--non-compliance with the provisions of state law--had caused the greatest Catholic dissatisfaction with public schools. Remove these objections, Brownson believed, and Catholic reluctance "to send their children to the public schools will not be greater than that of the more reputable Protestant sects."[103]

Despite these grave objections that Catholics raised against common schools, Brownson felt non-Catholics would be disappointed in discovering that the schools were unable to root out Catholicity. Even if Catholic religious instruction was excluded from the school, Catholics would not settle for godless education. "Besides the school, there is the Church, and there is the home."[104] Catholic losses existed certainly, but they were children who neither went to school, attended Mass, nor received any domestic education. Those in public schools who received religious instruction two or three times per week were not seriously injured in their faith or morals. Moreover, they learned to read and at least were able to understand their catechism which was more than could be said of the street roamers.

> Where the Catholic population is provided with
> churches and priests in sufficient number, and

---

[103]Ibidem.
[104]Ibidem.

parents understand and do their duty, there is
little difficulty in keeping our children in the
faith till their school days are over.[105]

Besides public schools being unable to destroy the Catholic

faith, Brownson believed they actually rendered benefits to

Catholics who had neither enough money nor competent teachers to

educate all the children. In some localities, such as Boston, the

only alternatives were common school or the streets. Because

Catholic children were forewarned to disbelieve anything in school

concerning religion, the public school was less injurious to faith

and piety than the crime, violence and "iniquity" of the street.

Catholics would not lose their faith by attending these schools

(except of course in some individual cases); instead, they would

strengthen their faith by becoming familiar with Protestants, by

hearing their objections, and by learning to answer and refute

their claims. This early mingling of Catholic and Protestant

children, if supplemented by parental and pastoral instruction,

would "work more good than injury to our religion."[106]

Another benefit, contrary to the hopes of non-Catholics, was

that no longer would the label of "foreigner" stand up against

Catholics. Children would be Americanized and Catholicity eventu-

ally would become an integral part of the national life. Common

schools would assist the Catholic population to assume their

rightful position and to exert a moral influence upon society.

The stigma of being foreign, with all the prejudices it entailed,

[105]*Ibid.*, p. 370.
[106]*Ibid.*, p. 372.

no longer would limit Catholic effectiveness in directing American thought and action.[107]

After examining all sides of the question, Brownson concluded that common schools were an advantage rather than a disadvantage to Catholics. As long as parents and pastors were vigilant, the common schools would not "do us any permanent injury as Catholics."[108] Brownson, however, was not recommending public schools to Catholics; he merely wanted to inform Protestants that Catholics did not fear these schools. Brownson did not place a high value on common school education. At the same time, he believed Catholics could not afford to neglect the education of their children or allow them to grow up in ignorance. Besides religious instruction, the age demanded a good secular education either in a Catholic or public school.

Brownson believed it was up to the bishops and clergy to designate the kind of school. When and where they deemed Catholic schools practicable and necessary, "they must be instituted and supported as a matter of course, and no one would rejoice more than we to see such schools established for all the children of the land."[109] Brownson expressed a preference for Catholic schools. But in his own city (Boston) and in his own state, he believed the common schools, where no Catholic schools existed, were

---

[107]Ibid., pp. 373-374.
[108]Ibid., p. 374.
[109]Ibidem.

far better than none, far better than any we are ourselves at present able, in a sufficient number for
all our children, to institute in their place; and
that, however objectionable we may feel it to be
obliged to send our children to them along with
Protestant children, the education acquired in them
is far better than none at all, or that of the
streets.[110]

Brownson felt the schools provided at least secular education,

which Catholics could receive with no harm done to their religious

beliefs, as long as parents and pastors took care of moral and

religious instruction. He considered public schools an asset--

where no Catholic school existed. He spoke only about Massachu-

setts where compulsory attendance laws had been passed in 1852.

He emphasized that his remarks about schools were not to be

generalized to cover the entire country--"we say nothing of them

elsewhere."[111]

Nonetheless, a flurry of criticism charged that Brownson

directly interfered with the movement for Catholic schools. Nearly

every Catholic journal and newspaper disagreed with Brownson, and

only three of them--the Metropolitan Magazine, The Catholic Herald,

and The Pittsburgh Catholic--disagreed in a courteous manner; the

rest denounced his views in rather harsh terms.[112] If Brownson's

essay of 1852 did not directly arouse the ire of Archbishop John

---

[110]Ibid., p. 375.
[111]Ibidem.
[112]See Brownson's response in O.A.B. to the Editor of The
Pittsburgh Catholic, August 1, 1854, OABP, UNDA. Brownson also
defended his "Native Americanism" essay in the same letter. Many
newspapers reprinted parts of "Schools and Education," apparently
making it easy to misinterpret what Brownson actually intended.
See J. S. Ballantyne to O.A.B., November 24, 1854, OABP, UNDA in
which the writer recalls how Bishop Peter Paul Lefevere of Detroit
disagreed with Brownson's article for its "commendation" of the

Hughes, "Schools and Education" certainly did. Brownson responded
to Hughes by repeating many arguments he had written in the essay.
Furthermore, he emphasized that he did not speak against the school
policy that Hughes and others were pursuing; nor did it ever enter
his mind, Brownson noted, that public schools were better or even
as good as Catholic schools. Public schools, quite simply, were
better than none at all. He insisted that his remarks applied only
to Boston where Catholic children attended public schools with
Bishop Fitzpatrick's permission. "The Bishop says to send our
children to the public schools is the best thing we can do, but
not the best he could wish."[113] Finally, Brownson believed the
school question was still an "open" question, since he knew of no
papal decree or national Pastoral Letter which had forbidden
Catholics to attend public schools. He declared that if legitimate
episcopal authority could show him that in fact he had gone against
Church policy, he would retract his words freely "in specific terms
and as publicly as possible."[114] The Plenary Council of 1852 had
indeed encouraged the building of Catholic schools and had asked
Catholics to make every sacrifice necessary to sustain them; but
it did not command them.

---

common school system. Ballantyne, favorable to the essay, suggested
to the Bishop that he reread the article--aside from newspaper mis-
representations--and he would find that Brownson did everything but
commend the common schools.

[113]O.A.B. to Archbishop John Hughes, July 3, 1854, Photostat
from the New York Archdiocesan Archives.

[114]Exact wording taken from O.A.B. to the Editor of The
Pittsburgh Catholic, op. cit.; in substance Brownson told Hughes
the same thing.

Even though the Church did not absolutely require Catholic
schools, it more and more stressed their importance. In January,
1858, Brownson published Bishop Martin John Spalding's essay
"Common Schools" which called for free religious common schools for
all denominations patterned after the European system. He began
his article by stating that

> the great question of the day, for us Americans, is
> undoubtedly, that of Common School Education. Its
> practical importance can scarcely be exaggerated. Upon
> the system adopted for the education of our children,
> probably more than upon any thing else, depends the
> future of our Republic.[115]

Later in the same year, Brownson picked up Spalding's argument that
common school education was the great question of the day; however,
the similarity ended abruptly.

In "Conversations of Our Club" for October, 1858, Brownson
advanced the thesis that a good secular education was essential,
whether acquired in a Catholic or public school. He believed that
the common schools were actually a victory for Catholics, for they
had removed the dominance of Calvinism from the schools.[116] He
supported compulsory attendance; and if religion were not included

---

[115]Martin John Spalding, "Common Schools," BrQR, XV (January,
1858), 70-71.
[116]See James Johonnot to O.A.B., January 17, 1857, OABP, UNDA,
in which the writer told Brownson of attempts by the Onondaga
Teachers' Institute (Syracuse, New York) to squelch ultra Presbyterian efforts to make the schools sectarian. Johonnot asked
Brownson to give assistance to their cause of removing sectarianism
from the schools, and to come to Syracuse and urge Catholics to
send their children to these schools. Hopefully, "hundreds of
children who now rarely see the inside of a school room, and who
most need the advantages of education" would be able to gain the
benefits of a common school education.

in the school, Church and home were to provide it. Catholics just did not have enough schools, teachers, or money. In New York, only one-sixth or one-seventh of Catholic children were enrolled in Catholic schools. Were the rest to receive a street education? And in Boston, about one-half of the public school students were Catholics. Since Boston spent $330,000 annually to run its schools, where would Catholics get half that sum each year to keep the schools in operation? And what about the original outlay of money, probably $1,000,000, to erect schools? The choice was clearcut: either send children to public schools where they would at least acquire a sense of order and learn the elements of a good secular education; or allow these Catholic children to roam the streets and become ruffians through associating with all that is vile, worthless, vicious, and criminal.[117]

Previously, Brownson had merely argued for Catholic children to attend public schools where no Catholic ones existed. In 1858, he qualified his remarks: "where we have not and cannot have good schools of our own, I think the best thing we can do is to send our children to the public schools."[118] Citizenship required intelligence and Catholics certainly needed a good secular education just as well as non-Catholics. Furthermore, most people eventually became parents. How were they to instruct their children without having received an education? Both citizenship and parenthood required a sound education. Public safety demanded that the state

---

[117]O. A. Brownson, "Conversations of Our Club," BrQR (October, 1858), 425-431.

[118]Ibid., p. 433 (Italics Brownson's).

provide secular education, devoid of sectarianism in the curriculum,
textbooks, library materials, the Bible, selection of teachers, and
treatment of students. Brownson stated that the type of education
the state provided had to be secular; but he was not opting for a
godless education. "The assumption is unfounded. After the Common
School, there still remain the family, the Church, and the Sunday-
school."[119] Hence, Brownson called for good secular education and
for religious education.

However, Brownson found Catholic schools inferior, "save under
the religious point of view," to the public schools of Boston and
New York. He believed Catholic schools perpetuated a foreign
colony, reinforced a sense of inferiority, and failed to make
students an integral part of American society and able to stand
on equal footing with non-Catholics. Furthermore, incompetent
teachers--half-educated, half-paid, hardly able to speak the
language of the school, coming from Old World traditions and sur-
roundings--would fail not only as social educators but as religious
instructors as well. Brownson suggested that students of such
schools would have "perhaps, even more difficulty in preserving
_their_7 faith . . . than those educated in the public schools of
the country."[120] This consideration, coupled with the terrible
economic plight of many parishes, created a situation that practically precluded the possibility of first-class schools. Brownson
did not see the rationale for requiring schools to be built and
sustained where the pastors and parishioners were unable or were

[119]Ibid., p. 439.
[120]Ibid., p. 442.

greatly inconvenienced. No longer was Brownson willing to support

an institution merely because it was run by Catholics; Catholic

schools had to meet the same standards that public schools did in

secular studies. In concluding, Brownson took his boldest step to

date:

> I think the public schools, sectarian as they frequently
> are, preferable to very poor parochial schools, under
> the charge of wholly incompetent teachers, and dragging
> out a painful, lingering half-dying existence.[121]

Brownson's remarks were certain to cause denunciation once again.

As one friend remarked, "there are few persons can hear with com-

posure unpleasant truths, bluntly told,"[122] especially when the

truth indicated that Catholic schools were in the hands of unfit

educators. Quite understandably, Brownson was called a Protestant

and one in opposition to the hierarchy's movement for schools. The

Review, some said, was no longer Catholic and its editor would soon

face excommunication; and if he had not already, would soon return

to Protestantism or no religion at all.[123]

---

[121]Ibid., pp. 443-444. Privately, Brownson wrote Montalembert: "The design of the movement here in behalf of Catholic
schools is a movement to train up our children in anti-American
sentiments, to perpetuate the low and servile sentiments generated
by despotism and to keep the population simply a foreign colony in
the country." See O.A.B. to Montalembert, December 27, 1858,
Photostat of letter in Archives du Chateau d'Ecotay, OABP, UNDA.

[122]Fr. P. Barker to O.A.B., December 30, 1858, OABP, UNDA.
Barker was pastor of St. Bridget's Church, Rochester, New York.

[123]Brownson mentioned and answered these charges in O. A.
Brownson, "Public and Parochial Schools," BrQR, XVI (July, 1859),
324-342. One person who agreed with Brownson was George Hilton of
Cincinnati. See George H. Hilton to O.A.B., February 16, 1859,
OABP, UNDA.

To clarify his position, the following year Brownson reviewed Bishop John Baptist Purcell's Pastoral Letter on the Decrees of the Second Provincial Council of Cincinnati (1859). In "Public and Parochial Schools," Brownson agreed that the Church was supreme in the education of faith and morals. Furthermore, she had "full and supreme authority to say what secular schools are or are not imminently dangerous to faith and morals, and to those she declares to be thus dangerous no Catholic parent can lawfully send his child."[124] However, the Church had not condemned any such schools yet, and hence, the issue was still an open question.

He reiterated his stand that he was always "decidedly in favor of really Catholic schools"[125] where Catholic children were well taught in religion and in secular education. But he did not want to build up "a wall of separation" between the Catholic community and American society by tying Catholics to an outmoded European and despotic type of education. Although he did not wholeheartedly commend common schools, he would not categorically condemn them either. They at least provided secular education; moreover, Brownson insisted that he did not "advocate secular education without adequate religious education, and it has never entered our head that any Catholic could be so insane as to do it."[126] This, of course, was the work of parents and pastors. Whether religious instruction was done at home, in Sunday-school,

---

[124]Ibid., p. 329.
[125]Ibid., p. 331 (Italics Brownson's).
[126]Ibid., p. 334.

in the District School, or the Parochial School, "we have supposed
could be a matter of no real importance."[127] All that was necessary was that education be religious; otherwise it was no education
at all.

Since religious education did not have to occur in school,
Brownson felt that secular public schools could aid Catholics.
Furthermore, merely to decry the district schools would not
accomplish much, for these schools were "American pets."[128] He
believed undue and exaggerated criticism by Catholics only served
to exacerbate the wrath already excited against Catholics.
Brownson doubted that the district school system could be broken
up or that Catholics could induce the State to divide funds for
separate religious schools. All that could be done was to insist
on the practical enforcement of existing laws that barred sectarianism in public schools and to remove offensive textbooks and
teachers. These last two measures would be even more difficult
to accomplish when

> it is contended that even then we could not, or would
> not use them/ ._7 /¯H_/ow are we to persuade those
> who have no great fondness for us, and who neither
> believe nor respect our religion, to exert themselves
> to do so much since assured in advance that it will
> not conciliate us in the least? If it were clearly
> announced by the Pastors of the Church that they
> would use, as others, these Common Schools in case
> whatever is repugnant to the Catholic conscience be
> excluded from them, we could, in time, far sooner
> than we can build up schools of our own, get it ex-
> cluded, for no new law is needed for that purpose.[129]

---

[127] Ibid., p. 335.

[128] Ibid., p. 337.

[129] Ibid., p. 338.

Brownson urged the Catholic bishops and clergy to take every
measure practicable or expedient for the moral and religious
training of youth, "without making any war on the public school
system of the country, or unnecessarily provoking the hostility of
our non-Catholic countrymen."[130] Brownson did not want a revival
of the recent Know-Nothing movement against Catholics; he hoped
to effect the Americanization of immigrant Catholics, to earn the
respect of non-Catholics for Catholics, and eventually to Catholicize America. Above all, he wanted Catholicity to flourish in
harmony with American institutions.

Brownson's own respect for American institutions suffered
a setback with the advent of the Civil War. The importance of
education and of Catholic education became paramount. In "Catholic
Schools and Education" (1862), Brownson attempted to analyze and
find answers why the Catholic community had not as yet wholeheartedly and unanimously supported the movement for Catholic
schools, female academies, and colleges. He felt it was a matter
which needs and must receive an answer."[131]

---

[130]Ibid., p. 339. Shortly after this essay appeared, one
priest cancelled his subscription to the Review, since he was no
longer able to present it to his parishioners without prejudicing
his Catholic school and without wounding their national feelings.
See Fr. Ed Joos to O.A.B., October 25, 1859, OABP, UNDA.

[131]O. A. Brownson, "Catholic Schools and Education," BrQR,
IX (January, 1862), 67. Brownson began this essay by praising
the Metropolitan Readers published by D. and J. Sadlier and edited
by Mother Mary Gillespie, C.S.C. (St. Mary's, Notre Dame, Indiana)
as the best series of Catholic readers available. He had given a
brief review of them the previous October, and had compared them
to a reading series by the Christian Brothers. See O. A. Brownson,
"Literary Notices and Criticisms," BrQR, XVIII (October, 1861),
536-537. Brownson's publisher, James Sadlier, requested him to
delete or modify a sentence which said "that the worst reading you
ever listened to was in the schools of the Christian Brothers in

Brownson believed the founders of Catholic schools need not be questioned "as to the/ir_7 purity of motive and the/ir_7 honesty of intention."[132] However, this did not mean that these schools possessed infallibility or were beyond the scrutiny of the Catholic public. His first objection to Catholic schools involved its uncatholic character. He believed many schools were not universal but instead heterodox, sectarian and national. "Catholic education must recognize the catholicity of truth under all its aspects, and tend to actualize it in all the relations of life, in religion and civilization."[133] It must be dialectic and combine the human and the Divine; it must

> tend to harmonize all opposites, the creature and the
> Creator, the natural with the supernatural, the indi-
> vidual with the race, social duties with religious
> duties, order with liberty, authority with freedom,
> the immutability of the dogma, that is, of the
> mysteries, with the progress of intelligence, con-
> servatism with reform; for such is the aim of the
> Church herself, and such the mission given her by the
> Word made flesh, whose Spouse she is.[134]

Brownson did not expect this ideal to be achieved, of course, but he did believe that Catholic education must aim to realize this objective. This ideal became his standard for evaluating Catholic schools.

Montreal." Sadlier feared losing the entire American and Canadian Christian Brothers' schools as customers. Brownson acceded to his publisher's financial concerns and showed that even the best of us would be willing to sacrifice truth to money!

[132]"Catholic Schools and Education," p. 68.
[133]Ibid., p. 70.
[134]Ibid., p. 71.

He estimated, with little hazard, that Catholic schools
tended rather "to depart from the standard than to approach it."
They generally failed to recognize human progress; did not educate
pupils to be at home in America; and did not produce "living,
thinking, and energetic men, prepared for the work which actually
awaits them in either Church or state."[135] Graduates' minds were
more repressed than quickened; they were more unfit than prepared
for living; they seemed misplaced and mistimed in life, apparently
prepared for a world which ceased to exist; they left school
ignorant of contemporary ideas, habits of mind, intelligence and
tendencies; and even worse, they turned their backs on the Church
and her work.[136]

Yet, despite this scathing denunciation of deficient
Catholic schooling, Brownson saw hope. Catholic schools possessed
a merit that none others had: they scrupulously taught the dogmas
and mysteries of the Church. "This fact is of the first importance,
and must never be lost sight of or underrated."[137] And in a quite
surprising way, almost a turnabout, Brownson declared:

> The education given in our schools, however defective
> it may be, must always be preferred to that given in
> schools in which the dogma is rejected or mutilated,
> and can never be justly answered, save when compared
> with its own ideal, or with what it should and would
> be, were it truly and thoroughly Catholic.[138]

[135]Ibidem.
[136]Ibid., pp. 71-72.
[137]Ibid., p. 73.
[138]Ibidem.

Oddly, he abruptly reverted to an extended criticism of Catholic schools, reviewing for eight and one-half pages the various objections to their present status. Suddenly, in contrast to the critical tone of his essay, Brownson uttered words that seemed to signify a tremendous reversal of position.

> After long reflection and much hesitation, some would say opposition, we must say that we do not regard these objections as sufficient reasons for abandoning the movement for Catholic schools and education supported by our bishops and clergy. It may be that the movement was premature, and that it would have been better to have used for a longer time the schools of the country, as the early Christians did those of the Empire, before attempting to establish schools of our own, save for the education of the clergy. But it is too late to discuss that question now. The movement has, wisely or unwisely, been set on foot, and gone too far to be arrested, even if it were desirable to arrest it. Our bishops and clergy have decided that the movement shall go on, and the Catholic cause can never be promoted by any anti-hierarchical action. Much good may be done that is not done by or under the direction of the hierarchy; but no good end can ever be obtained in opposition to it. This consideration is of itself sufficient to deter us from opposing the movement, and of inducing us to accept it at least as un fait accompli, and to make the best we can of it.
> That we are to have schools and colleges of our own, under the control of Catholics, we take it as a "fixed fact." Whether the movement for them is premature or not, it is idle, if nothing worse, to war against it. Let us say, then, to those who regard the education actually given by Catholics as we do, and who have not seen their way clear to the support of primary schools under the control of Catholics as a substitute, in the case of Catholic children, for the Common Schools of the country, that we regard it as our duty now to accept the movement, and labor not to arrest it, or to embarrass it, but to reform and render truly Catholic the whole system of Catholic education, from the highest grade to the lowest. Let it be our work not to destroy Catholic education, but to reform and advance it.[139]

---

[139]Ibid., pp. 82-83.

Brownson was not satisfied with the present state of Catholic schools, but believed they were capable of progress. He would work for combining religious with secular education, for he now accepted as truth that public schools were indeed more dangerous to Catholic faith than he had previously argued, and that the damage to religious faith was more important a consideration than the benefit of mere secular education.

Brownson saw this period as one of Catholic fermentation and reform. Catholics were becoming Americanized, as evidenced by calls for reform not only in parochial schools but in conventual schools for girls and colleges for boys. He trusted that when the fratricidal war ended, Catholic schools would begin to assume their true character and position and exert a truly Catholic influence in society. "Let us console ourselves for what Catholic education now is with what it may become, and with what we may by well-directed effort aid it in becoming."[140]

Brownson's endorsement of the movement for Catholic schools and his goal of reforming and advancing Catholic education preceded the appearance of the Syllabus of Errors by two years. Specifically, Pius IX, in propositions XLV, XLVII, and XLVIII of the Syllabus, condemned as modern errors: 1) that the Church could only be concerned with seminary education, thus allowing civil authorities complete right in the government of public schools, the discipline, arrangement of studies, conferring of degrees and approval of teachers; 2) that popular schools should

---

[140]Ibid., p. 84.

be freed from all ecclesiastical control, authority and interference and be fully subjected to the political power of the
rulers; and 3) that Catholics were allowed to educate youth in a
system unconnected with Catholic faith or the Church, and that
knowledge of only natural things was the true end of earthly social
life.[141] If in 1862 Brownson had perhaps questioned the school
movement as premature, little doubt was evident after that time.

Unfortunately, however, the publishing of the Syllabus
occurred at the same time that Brownson's Quarterly Review folded
in 1864. From 1865 until 1872, Brownson's writings for Ave Maria,
Catholic World and New York Tablet appeared without a by-line.
One student has commented on this period:

> This rather lengthy interlude in which Brownson found
> himself without a personal vehicle wherein to express
> his views seems a relatively unimportant and uninspired
> period of Brownson's life. The articles he wrote . . .
> are largely repetitive and summations of much that he
> had already presented in his own medium. It would
> probably be too much to expect that such a confirmed
> individualist as Brownson would have been able, after
> a quarter of century of free and independent personal
> journalism, to have accomplished very much in the way
> of fresh and constructive ideas in this unfamiliar
> capacity.[142]

Speaking of the period from 1873-1875 when Brownson revived the
Review, this same student added:

[141]Paraphrased from "The Syllabus for the People. A Review
of the Propositions Concerned by His Holiness Pope Pius IX, With
Text of the Condemned List," in The Syllabus of Pius IX (New York:
The Catholic Publication Society, 1875), pp. 17-18.

[142]James W. McGrath, "The Catholicism of Orestes A. Brownson"
(Unpublished doctoral dissertation, The University of New Mexico,
1961), pp. 145-146.

Brownson had reached that point in life when one cannot
do more than play old tunes over again. He dusted off
a few old principles but built no new ideas. The last
series remains unremarkable, significant only as proof
of his ultimate consistency. His powers at last were
losing their strength, and Brownson terminated his
epilogue with the last number for 1875.[143]

No doubt these statements are to a degree true in certain fields

of Brownson's thought; but in the area of the school question,

Brownson's ideas seemed to undergo a dramatic change. Nor was he

too much of an individualist to reject duly constituted authority.

He had always claimed to be an obedient son of the Church, willing

to obey God, the Pope, and the Bishops; in the final dozen years

of his life Brownson was not only a staunch follower of the Church,

but also played a significant role in advocating Catholic schools.

Immediately after the Civil War, the American hierarchy

convened the Second Plenary Council (1866) at Baltimore. They

reiterated their firm belief "that religious teaching and reli-

gious training should form part of every system of school educa-

tion."[144] Previously, Brownson had argued that Catholics could

without detriment to their faith attend public schools for purely

secular education, while religious education would be provided by

---

[143]Ibid., pp. 146-147. Actually, McGrath allowed Brownson to
linger ten more days than anyone else did. He lists April 27,
1876 rather than April 17, 1876 as the day Brownson died. In all
fairness to McGrath, much of the dissertation is quite good. In
fact, his section on "Education and Reform" (pp. 185-205), which I
read after charting my course, reassured me that schools and
colleges were only a part of Brownson's educational ideas.
McGrath briefly mentions the home, ministers, lyceums, and press
as educational agencies.

[144]Quoted in McCluskey, op. cit., p. 82.

156

parents, pastors, and Sunday-schools. But he had also said that
when the Church declared certain schools dangerous to faith and
morals, Catholics had to obey their Prelates. His first application of this principle came in 1869, and it struck close to
home.[145]

Brownson's namesake, Orestes Jr., was employed as a public
school teacher and principal earning $1500 in Dubuque, Iowa. In
his school, ten out of the twelve teachers were Catholics as well
as nearly all the children. In 1869, Bishop John Hennessey ordered
all Catholic children to attend the Catholic school. When Orestes
refused to send his children, the Bishop responded by not allowing
them either the Sacraments or catechism as long as they attended
the public school. The situation was even more acute because
Orestes might also lose his job or part of his salary if everyone
else obeyed the Bishop's orders. He became quite bitter at the
Bishop and the Church for depriving his school of pupils by what
he considered questionable means.[146] His father wrote him at least

[145]It was also during this year that Brownson wrote an 183
page book defending the Church against the objections of liberalism,
progress, and modern civilization. He called his book "rigidly
orthodox," making no concessions nor seeking to conform to the
spirit of the age. See O. A. Brownson, Liberalism and the Church
(New York: D. & J. Sadlier, 1869).

[146]Eventually, about 1875, Orestes Jr. gave up teaching in
Iowa and moved to Missouri where he rejoined his family whom he
had settled on a farm there about two years before. He hoped that
now he too could once more practice his faith without having to
make temporal sacrifices. See Sarah Healy Brownson to H. F.
Brownson, August 15, 1869, HFB Collection, UNDA; O.A.B. to H.F.B.,
November 16, 1869, HFB Collection, UNDA; O.A.B. Jr., to O.A.B.,
November 7, 1873, OABP, UNDA; O.A.B. Jr., to O.A.B., February 23,
1874, OABP UNDA; O.A.B. Jr., to O.A.B., March 13, 1874, OABP,
UNDA; O.A.B. Jr., to O.A.B. March 14, 1875, OABP, UNDA. The
younger Brownson eventually became a playwright and also authored
several books on chess.

two long letters prior to October 21, 1869. Although these letters are not among the Brownson Papers, other family correspondence indicates that the father told his son that "it is the settled policy of the Church to forbid all Catholic children attending the public schools, and this is right";[147] and this despite the fact that the son no doubt kept a good school. Mrs. Brownson prayed that her son "may live and die an obedient child of the Church."[148] Brownson supported the Bishop because the school his son taught, by Orestes Jr.'s own admission, inculcated "no particular dogmas on doubtful or disputed points of religion" and taught only what was "purely temporal," leaving to the ministers and parents the duty of imparting religious and sectarian creeds.[149] Brownson had accepted the goal set by the American hierarchy--"religious teaching and religious training should form part of every system of school education."

---

[147]Sarah Healy Brownson to H. F. Brownson, September 26, 1869, HFB Collection, UNDA.

[148]Sarah Healy Brownson to H. F. Brownson, October 21, 1869, HFB Collection, UNDA.

[149]These words are from a speech he delivered at the Dubuque County Teachers Association meeting in August, 1869. See O. A. Brownson, Jr., Our Public Schools and Their Just Claims (Dubuque, Iowa: Barnes & Ryan, 1869), 4 pp. Ironically, the first three pages of this address on the benefits and practical philosophy of public schools can be traced directly to his father's writings. On the last page, Orestes Jr. showed his animosity toward Catholic schools in Dubuque. "Some particular sectarian party hires the cheapest teacher to teach the greatest numbers that can be squeezed into the poorest accommodations of inadequate or dilapidated buildings. Such schools are often sustained by ecclesiastical errors and superstitious fears of an ignorant multitude."

Almost simultaneous to this personal matter, Brownson wrote

"Our Established Church" for the August, 1869 issue of Catholic

World. Archbishop John McCloskey had specifically requested that

Hecker get Brownson because McCloskey "liked your way of treating

the school question."[150] Boss William Marcy Tweed had inserted

into the annual tax levy bill for New York City a school provision

that reserved twenty per cent of the excise funds received during

1868 to support schools that educated children gratuitously other

than in common schools. No major outburst occurred until after the

bill became law;[151] then cries arose that state and city officials

had violated Church-state provisions of law. All accusations

stemmed from the fact that most of this money appeared to be headed

toward Catholic schools.[152] Brownson, however, felt differently

and attempted to turn the tables on the issue. Arguing that all

schools in New York were sectarian, Brownson felt that this

legislative act did not breach any existing patterns. In fact,

---

[150]Isaac Hecker to O.A.B., June 18, 1869, OABP, UNDA. This
letter obviously implies that Brownson had been writing on the
school issue--either in the Tablet or in the Catholic World.
Earlier articles on schools do appear in both publications but
absolute certainty of Brownson's authorship is still in doubt. I
will use only what is certain. See also, Isaac Hecker to O.A.B.,
March 18, 1869, OABP, UNDA in which Hecker told Brownson about the
prospects of an educational bill being passed on a broad and unsectarian basis.

[151]See John Webb Pratt, Religion, Politics, and Diversity:
The Church-State Theme in New York History (Ithaca, New York:
Cornell University Press, 1967), 195-203. Pratt argues that Tweed
used devious means--secrecy and bribery--to get the bill passed.
The New York Times apparently did not know about Section 10 until
two days after its passage.

[152]Another controversy involved appropriations for charitable
institutions such as hospitals, orphan asylums, reformatories, etc.
See Pratt, pp. 204-224.

the provisions of the law provided a mere pittance to Catholics while Protestants received funds in excess of their proportion. The school budget of $3,000,000 provided only $200,000 for Catholic schools, whereas the Catholic population composed one-third of New York City. How could Protestants claim that Catholics were being favored, when in reality they received only "a tithe of what is honestly or justly their share--whether estimated according to their numbers or according to the amount of public taxes . . . levied on them."[153]

Of course charges arose that Catholics were attempting to destroy the common schools of the country by this "conspiracy" that had obtained municipal funds for Catholic schools. Brownson argued that he did not oppose public schools or secular education for non-Catholics; that was their business. Catholics opposed the system only when it was intended for Catholics and when it taxed Catholics for its support. For Catholics, education was a Church function. Secular education and religious training could never be separated for they had to be harmonized as one dialectic whole. Brownson charged that the advocates of secular education were attempting to destroy the Church by ruining her children. He pro-osed the division of public schools into two classes based on the European system: one for Catholics, the other for non-atholics; that is, a system of denominational schools. The ystem could stand as it was for non-Catholics, or they could call t or do with it whatever they wanted. For Catholics, the state

[153]O. A. Brownson, "Our Established Church," Catholic World, X (August, 1869), 580.

should appropriate them their proportion of the tax fund and
reserve a way for itself to check that the money has been used in
the way designated, and that Catholic schools met the minimum
requirements of the State in providing secular education. If this
system was not satisfactory, Brownson suggested that the state
exempt Catholics from paying the school tax for public schools and
allow them to establish and maintain schools under the supervision
of their Church. Either way, Brownson maintained, would satisfy
Catholics; one or the other must be done because the present system
was "grossly unjust and in direct violation of the equal rights
guaranteed /‾Catholics_7 by the constitution."[154]

This controversy continued into the spring of 1870. The
Reverend Thomas Preston had become a spokesman for the Catholic
position, giving lectures and distributing pamphlets on the school
question. One member of the hierarchy, however, felt Preston had
provided a "very feeble statement" on the Catholic position, one
more likely to "injure rather than benefit the cause." At the same
time he praised a writer in the New York Tablet

> who manifests a thorough knowledge and grasp of the
> subject in all its strongest points. He could do
> the subject justice / and_/ he would render a great
> / and_/ much needed service at this moment if he
> would present the Catholic views and grounds upon
> the School Question to take the place of Rev. Mr.
> Preston's pamphlet for general circulation.[155]

---

[154]Ibid., p. 586.
[155]Bishop Thomas L. Grace to D. & J. Sadlier, March 23,
1870, OABP, UNDA.

The proprietors of the _Tablet_ gave the Prelate's letter to Orestes
Brownson. At practically the same time, the _New York Times_
attempted to defeat the Catholic position by citing Preston as an
authority. Brownson responded with "The Truth About the School
Question."[156]

Brownson accused the _Times_ of being unfair, "lacking candor,"
and for being "disingenuous" in citing authorities. The _Times_ had
reinserted the question of the Bible, charging that Catholics
demanded its exclusion from the public schools. Brownson brushed
aside these remarks, for Catholics had long since dropped the Bible
as an issue. Furthermore, Catholics did not seek to destroy the
public school system but demanded "that the system be so amended
as to be just to all classes, and unjust to no one . . . . We
have no desire to destroy or even to impair the efficiency of the
system, but to perfect it."[157] For the perfection of the system,
Brownson argued, meant dividing the school funds _pro rata_ to produce
what Protestants just now "so earnestly insist on: the religious
education of all the children of the State," Protestant children
in Protestantism, and Catholic children in Catholicity. Not only
did Protestant public schools receive school funds, but Protestant
colleges and academies also obtained money from the Literary Fund.
Catholics demanded equal rights and justice, not charity. Protes-
ants, not Catholics, had been receiving special favors. Protestant

---

[156]The Brownson Papers contain this incomplete draft of the
rticle Brownson wrote immediately after receiving Grace's letter.
[157]O. A. Brownson, "The Truth About the School Question,"
ABP, UNDA.

understanding of equal rights and religious liberty was mere "hypocritical pretence," for all the liberties were on one side.[158]

Brownson took up another argument at about the same time in
the April issue of Catholic World. In "The School Question,"[159]
he asserted that the origins of the American school were un-
deniably religious and certainly not secular. The school system
"was simply a system of parochial schools." Even though the
religion of the Congregationalists and Presbyterians was defective
and false, "the principle on which the schools were founded was
sound." The system had worked well, and violated no conscience
because "the character of the school, as well as the religion
taught in it, was determined by the inhabitants of the school
district."[160] Furthermore, the school taxed only those whose
children attended.

> The Schools were originally founded by a religious
> people for a religious end, not by seculars for a
> purely secular end. The people . . . did not dream

[158]Ibid. See O.A.B. to Mrs. James Sadlier, c. February 24,
1870, OABP, UNDA. Also Fr. Preston expressed his thanks to the
writer who helped bail him out. See Fr. Thomas S. Preston to
Editor of the Tablet, April 27, 1870, OABP, UNDA.

[159]O. A. Brownson, "The School Question," Catholic World,
XI (April, 1870), 91-106. Although the article was unsigned, see
the following letters that verify authorship: Fr. A. F. Hewit to
O.A.B., January 23, 1870, O.A.B. to Fr. A. F. Hewit, February 3,
1870, Fr. A. F. Hewit to O.A.B., February 20, 1870, and Fr. A. F.
Hewit to O.A.B., March 3, 1870, OABP UNDA; and Sarah Healy
Brownson to H.F. Brownson, March 31, 1870, HFB Collection, UNDA.
The * Note on p. 106 was added by Hewit; he extended Brownson's
remarks to include colleges and universities. This essay is also
published in Henry F. Brownson, ed., The Works of Orestes A.
Brownson, XIII (Detroit: H. F. Brownson, 1887), pp. 241-262.

[160]"The School Question," pp. 92-93.

of divorcing secular education from religion. The
schools were intended to give both religious and
secular education in their natural union, and there
was no thought of the feasibility of separating
what God had joined together. The Bible was read
as a class-book, the catechism was taught as a
regular school exercise, and the pastor of the
parish visited the schools and instructed them in
religion as often as he saw proper. Indeed, he was,
it might be said, <u>ex officio</u> the superintendent of
the parish schools.[161]

Hence, American schools in their colonial origins included

religion in the curriculum, violated no conscience, and levied

taxes only upon those in attendance. Viewed in this fashion,

the present system needed overhauling, for in its attempts to

eliminate sectarianism by reducing instruction to what was called

our common Christianity," the schools became either secular (un-

American) or Protestant (violating Catholic conscience, and hence,

n-American). Taxing Catholics for schools they did not and could

ot use in good conscience was also contrary to American constitu-

ional guarantees.

Brownson insisted that Catholics were not attempting to

orce their religion upon others; that would be just as unconstitu-

ional as the current system that failed to recognize the rights of

atholic conscience. "Their rights are equal to ours, and ours

re equal to theirs; and neither does nor can, in the eyes of the

ate, override the other."[162] Brownson saw but one solution to

e problem. He rejected the proposal that the Bible and religion

excluded; that would only make the public schools "nurseries

---

[161]<u>Ibid</u>., p. 93.
[162]<u>Ibid</u>., p. 95.

of infidelity and irreligion." He dismissed any attempt to make
the schools voluntary because such a step would break up the whole
system of free public schools, and render universal education
necessary to sustain American institutions impractical or unlikely.
He favored for all children free public schools financed by the
state. The best and only solution was dividing the school fund
pro rata between Protestants and Catholics. Such a system,
Brownson believed, would provide "a religious education, so necessary to society as well as to the soul," for all children "without
the slightest lesion to any one's conscience or interference with
. . . religious freedom . . . guaranteed by our constitution."[163]
The American founders never called for any division of school funds
because there was no need at that time. But with society becoming
more religiously heterogeneous, the only practical way to maintain
religious liberty was to divide the school fund.

Brownson answered two possible objections to such a plan.
First of all, the New York Tribune warned of its impracticality
in small towns and sparsely settled districts where separate
schools might be too great an expense. Brownson believed this
objection would likely diminish with time as population rose. Or,
each religion could receive their pro rata share and make up the
difference of the amount needed by either Catholic or Protestant
charity. Even though most of these rural districts were largely
Protestant, Catholic children would face less danger in such mixed
schools because they would not be exposed to all the evils of

---

[163]Ibid., p. 99.

cities and large towns. Secondly, the charge was made that if
Catholics received school funds, what was to stop the "Israelites"
and Protestant denominations from seeking and obtaining funds?
Brownson's criteria boiled down to a matter of conscience. "If
. . . any denomination . . . can in good faith demand separate
schools on the plea of conscience, we say at once let it have
them."[164] In matters of religion and education, Brownson held
conscience supreme. "Conscience is accountable to no civil
tribunal. All secular authority and all secular considerations
whatever must yield to conscience. In questions of conscience
the law of God governs."[165] Brownson did not perceive the utter
impracticality of such a suggestion. Evil, cruelty or other
wrong-doing could just as easily be defended in the name of
conscience, just as Nazis attempted to vindicate their slaughters
of millions of Jews.

Brownson called upon Protestants not to fight Catholics but
to join them in battling the public enemy. In establishing and
maintaining separate denominational schools,

> it would also remove some restraint from Protestant
> schools, and allow them more freedom in insisting
> on whatever is doctrinal and positive in their
> religion than they now exercise. The two classes
> of schools, though operating separately, would aid
> each other in stemming the tide of infidelity

---

[164]Ibid., p. 101. Brownson believed that most Protestant
denominations, however, would have difficulty obtaining funds on
the basis of conscience; after all, most of them were unified in
support of the public schools as they now existed. But, if the
case arose, he would grant the funds.

[165]Ibidem.

and immorality, now setting in with such fearful
rapidity, and apparently resistless force, threatening
the very existence of our republic. The division
would operate in favor of religion, both in a Catholic
sense and in a Protestant sense, and therefore tend
to purify and preserve American society. It would
restore the schools to their original intention,
and make them, what they should be, religious
schools.[166]

Brownson, however, had barked up the wrong tree on this issue.

The 1869 bill that had provided Catholics with only a small part

of their pro rata share had proven politically damaging to Boss

Tweed. He reluctantly allowed legislation to pass that prohibited

such aid after the close of the 1870-1871 school year. Opposition

had arisen from Albany Argus, New York Observer, Christian Advo-

cate, New York Times, and Putnam's and such notables as Peter

Cooper, Henry Ward Beecher, and William Dodge. A state Council

of Political Reform, composed largely of Protestant ministers and

laymen, helped defeat Tweed's measure.[167] Hence, the bill that

Hecker hoped would "pave the way for denominational schools" on a

"broad and unsectarian" basis demanding "no exclusive privileges

for Catholics," a bill that involved the future success of the

Church in America,[168] was defeated.

---

[166] Ibid., p. 105.

[167] See Pratt, pp. 197-199. Section 10 was defeated in 1870;
but because school budgets had already been prepared and to save
face for Tweed, appropriations were granted anyway. In April,
1871, Section 10 was killed.

[168] Fr. Isaac Hecker to O.A.B., March 18, 1869, OABP, UNDA.

Brownson now turned his efforts toward national educational
issues. Senator Henry Wilson of Massachusetts, in efforts to re-
unite and improve the country following the Civil War, proposed in
January, 1871 a national system of unification and education that
included a "thorough and practical education of the people." He
recommended that all support the Hoar bill before congress that
would establish a national system of education. However, in his
closing remarks, he pointed out the "priestridden" educational
system of France as a lesson for America to avoid; instead he
pointed to the systems of Germany and Prussia as models.[169] Again
Archbishop McCloskey was alarmed, spoke with Hecker, who in turn
asked Brownson to write an article to appear in the April issue.
Brownson responded with what Hecker called "one of the most finished
/ essays_/ that ever came from your pen."[170]

In "Unification and Education,"[171] Brownson denounced Wilson's
plan as revolutionary and unlawful, aimed at usurping state powers
by concentrating all powers of government in the federal government.
In addition, the proposal violated the rights of parents and
annihilated religious liberty by imposing universal and uniform
compulsory education.[172] Catholics were not opposed to universal

---

[169]See Henry Wilson, "New Departure of the Republican Party,"
Atlantic Monthly, XXVII (January, 1871), 104-120.

[170]See Isaac Hecker to O.A.B., January 28, 1871 and April 3,
1871, OABP UNDA; and O.A.B. to Isaac Hecker, January 30, 1871, and
February ?, 1871, Paulist Archives.

[171]O. A. Brownson, "Unification and Education," Catholic World,
XIII (April, 1871), 1-14.

[172]Brownson viewed this plan in the context of the usurping
of powers by the federal government during reconstruction.

or compulsory schooling, Brownson added, but demanded it for

spiritual and religious ends. Only the Church could provide such

instruction through Catholic schools. Brownson warned of the

implied dangers in Wilson's scheme:

> It is precisely education by the Catholic Church that
> Mr. Wilson and his party do not want, do not believe in,
> and wish to prevent us from having even for our own
> children. It is therefore they demand a system of uni-
> versal and uniform compulsory education by the authority
> and under the direction of the general government, which
> shall effect and maintain the national unification pro-
> posed, by compelling all the children of the land to be
> trained in national schools, under Evangelical control
> and management. The end and aim of the New Departure
> . . . is to suppress Catholic education, gradually
> extinguish Catholicity in the country, and to form one
> homogeneous American people after the New England Evan-
> gelical type. Of this there can be no reasonable
> doubt.[173]

Brownson charged that the Evangelicals were alarmed at the growth

of Catholicity in the country and were attempting to change the

constitution, suppress religious liberty, and take the education

of children out of the hands of their parents, thus hoping to

destroy the Church at its roots.

Brownson repeated his call for tax-supported, universal,

compulsory, free, religious education directed by each denomination.

He rejected the voluntary principle and the secular or godless

school as well, and very neatly threw the argument to Wilson:

> Mr. Wilson proposed for our admiration and imita-
> tion the Prussian system of public schools . . . . But,
> what the Evangelical senator does not tell us, the
> Prussian system is strictly the denominational system,
> and each denomination is free and expected to educate

[173]"Unification and Education," pp. 6-7.

in its own schools its own children, under the direction
of its pastors and teachers, in its own religion. The
Prussian system recognizes the fact that different com-
munions do exist among the Prussian people, and does not
aim to suppress them or at unification by state authority. It meets the fact as it is, without seeking to
alter it. Give us the Prussian system of denominational
schools, and we shall be satisfied, even if education
is made compulsory.[174]

The state should set up minimum standards for secular studies, and

insist that all schools receiving funds live up to these guidelines.

In this way, secular and religious education would be imparted in

the right way. Although this was the system Brownson advocated,

he saw little or no hope of its adoption. Evangelicals, Unitarians,

humanitarians, and other "religious and philanthropic busy-bodies"

who fancied themselves as Atlas holding up the world and securing

the rights of everybody, would never allow Catholic rights to be

exercised. "The denominational system would defeat their darling

hope, their pet project, and require them to live and let live."[175]

If the implications of Wilson's plan were to destroy the

Church, an explicit attempt was offered by Judge E. P. Hurlbut. In

A Secular View of Religion in the State, and of the Bible in the

Public Schools (Albany, 1870), Hurlbut proposed a constitutional

amendment to Article I that read:

But Congress may enact such laws as it shall deem
necessary to control or prevent the establishment
or continuance of any foreign hierarchical power in
this country founded on principles or dogmas antagon-
istic to republican institutions.[176]

---

[174]Ibid., p. 12. Brownson was willing to accept this school
system as a Catholic; however, as an American citizen, he still
believed the federal government was usurping a state function.

[175]Ibid., p. 13.

[176]Quoted in O. A. Brownson, "The Secular Not Supreme,"
Catholic World, XIII (August, 1871), p. 690.

Nothing more needed to be said. Wherever Brownson looked, he saw enemies of the Church. He felt society had become corrupted by Protestantism, paganism, and secularism.

> This corruption, especially since the late civil war is hardly less, perhaps even greater among the easy classes, than that of ancient Sodom and Gomorrha. From the crown of the head to the sole of the foot, there is no soundness in us. We are one mass of rottenness.[177]

The corruption of American government under Grant, the hollowness of the financial system, government revenue officers spying, the irreverence and impudence of young America, immodesty, lack of respect for parents, marriages on the rocks, an increasing number of abortions--all pointed without exaggeration to the sickness of American society. To continue with Protestantism or secularism or paganism meant the cultivation and perpetuation of "our moral and social ruin."[178] No remedy could come from nature; the only melioration possible was of Divine origin. Only religion could support private and public virtue, and the Catholic Church was the only Christian religion capable of training children properly in accordance with the principles of life and the destiny of man and society. "Obviously then the Church is the only competent educator, and only a thorough Catholic education has or can have any value for men or nations."[179] Brownson, who had once viewed American civilization as the greatest to have yet appeared, became increasingly cynical of American Society.

---

[177]O. A. Brownson, "Education and the Republic," BrQR, XXIII (January, 1874), 42.
[178]Ibid., p. 43.
[179]Ibid., p. 44.

Society was not only corrupt but was decidedly anti-Catholic
as well. Public schools attempted to wrench the faith away from
Catholic children; legislatures were cutting off aid to Catholic
educational and charitable institutions; national education proposals implied the suppression of Catholic schools; and Bismarck's
work of suppressing the Church in Germany--all caused Brownson
alarm. In addition,

> the Protestant leaders, the Wilsons, the Dodges, the
> Pomeroys, the Colfaxes, the Bellowses, the American
> and Foreign Christian Union, the Evangelical Alliance,
> the Young Men's Christian Union, American Bible and
> Tract societies, the Home and Foreign Missionary
> Society, the Union League, Freemasons, Odd Fellows,
> the Internationale, and the "thousand and one" other
> associations, leagues, and unions, some open, some
> secret, some hostile to all religion, some holding
> on to the Christian name, but all deadly enemies of
> the Church, are prepared, and busy at work.[180]

Indeed, the Church did seem to be not only in an infidel world but
besieged by countless enemies as well. If anything, Brownson's
support for Catholic schools became even more entrenched during the
last few years of his life; they were "the only Christian schools
in the country, and . . . the education they give is the only
education that can in the slightest degree contribute to the safety
of the republic."[181]

During the final three years of the revived Review, Brownson
urged Catholics to improve the character of Catholic schools and
to increase their number. One of the first needs of all schools

---

[180]O. A. Brownson, "Whose is the Child?," BrQR, XXII (July,
1873), 299.

[181]"Education and the Republic," p. 54.

was suitable books. Brownson complained that texts were not as intellectual as they should be, and that Catholic publishers were following the modern trend of taxing the mind as little as possible. Children needed to be brought up under a system that required mental effort and hard study. "We object to the whole modern theory of education, and we throw into the fire the whole of the literature of youth."[182] School books for Catholic children were "too childish," did not exercise the mind, and were not sufficiently Catholic. The lessons did not quicken the mind, create a craving for knowledge, or cultivate and refine taste; and the books needed better literary style. Throughout the system, superficiality reigned supreme.

> We wish the mind of the child to be taxed, and taxed severely. It is only in grappling with difficulties and overcoming them that his mind grows and becomes strong and healthy. We detest all these modern inventions and royal roads to learning. They are ruining the intellect of the age.[183]

Although he protested the course of all modern textbooks, Brownson never thought much good would come; it was "as idle as throwing straws against the wind."[184] Brownson did hope, however, that Catholics would study the Bible and Bible history more in school."[185]

---

[182]O. A. Brownson, "Literary Notices and Criticisms," BrQR, XXIII (October, 1874), 567. Brownson harshly reviewed The Young Catholic's Illustrated School Series, published by the Catholic Publication Society. Yet, he called it the best he had seen. The next year, however, he preferred a series put out by Benziger Brothers.

[183]O. A. Brownson, "Literary Notices and Criticisms," BrQR, XXIV (April, 1875), 293.

[184]Ibidem.

[185]Ibid., pp. 290-291.

Besides improving the quality of schools, Brownson urged the
multiplication of Catholic schools. He still argued for separate
denominational schools, protested not only double taxation--but
triple taxation as well.[186] But he had resigned himself to the
reality that Catholics would have to pay for their own schools.
The conscience of the minority had no chance of a fair hearing.
Only Catholics would benefit from a pro rata division of the school
funds, "for non-Catholics really had no religion to teach in connection with secular instruction."[187] The Catholic minority was
powerless against "fanatics, bigots and hypocrites" who had been
elected to office in 1872. Catholics would have to rely on their
own resources in establishing and maintaining schools for their
children.

Brownson, who had always questioned and doubted the ability of
schooling to effect much good or evil, cautioned Catholics not to
hastily conclude that the mere establishment of Catholic schools
was sufficient to cure the evils of society or to produce a
Catholic society. In "Education and the Republic" (1874), Brownson
analyzed the role of "education in relation to the stability of
the Republic, to public and private virtue, and the moral and
social well-being of the people."[188] The perfectibility of man

---

[186]Besides paying taxes for public schools, and supporting
Catholic schools, Catholic school buildings and property were also
taxable. See O. A. Brownson, "The Public School System," BrQR,
XIV (October, 1875), 532.

[187]O. A. Brownson, "Literary Notices and Criticisms," BrQR,
XII (January, 1873), 139.

[188]"Education and the Republic," p. 37.

was a Christian doctrine that could only be effected by the supernatural infusion of grace; hence, only Catholicity could provide a
good and salutary education capable of helping man individually,
socially, and politically. Although Brownson rejected public
school education because of its Protestant or secular nature, he
refused to blame public schools for the evils in society. Rather,
the evils of society pervaded the community upon which the public
schools were based. At most, public schools were "only the
exponents of the false principles and ideas" of a corrupt society.
Furthermore, "education itself has no reforming or progressive
power."[189] This law, Brownson advised, held true for Catholic
schools and communities as well, for only the smallest part of
education received actually was acquired in the school-room. The
family, the streets, social intercourse, the thought and manner of
the country all affected the educational process. Catholic children
breathed the same atmosphere as non-Catholic children. Hence, the
education of adults and adult society was essential, for their
intelligence, habits, manners, and Catholicity (or lack of it) could
either enhance or neutralize the efforts of the school. Of itself,
the school could accomplish but little. Catholic schooling,
although certainly necessary for the preservation of Catholic
faith, was not sufficient "to save our daily deteriorating republic.
Nothing will save it but the conversion of the people to Catholicity."[190]

---

[189]Ibid., p. 52.
[190]Ibid., p. 54.

Even though Catholic schools alone were not sufficient to
insure the preservation of Catholic faith, they were necessary. In
the very last issue of his Review, Brownson urged the Catholic
community to unite, to waive petty differences, and to labor
perseveringly to gain Catholic rights and to get the majority to
adjust the public school system, by voting only for those candidates who promised to make amends for the monstrous injustices to
Catholics.[191] Brownson also feared that unless Catholics united
vigorously and organized well-directed efforts in fighting for
their rights, a day might come when even their right to maintain
schools might be prohibited.[192] The school question was indeed the
great question for Catholics and for the country. The preservation of the faith of Catholic children, with a thorough Catholic
education, was an essential interest of both religion and the
state.

Catholics had justice and right on their side; not only was
the country founded by Catholics but the original system of
schooling in colonial America was religious. The non-Catholic
majority had violated the constitution and republican freedom of
conscience; Catholics sought only "to restore that freedom, and
secure respect for the constitution." Reverting to metaphor,
Brownson remarked: "It does not become the thief to complain that
he is wronged, outraged, when the owner of the goods he has stolen

[191]Brownson here was accepting the ideas of Bishop Richard
Gilmour of Cleveland. In 1873, Brownson had rejected Gilmour's
recommendation for political action.

[192]"The Public School System," p. 537.

demands, in a legal and peaceful way, their restoration."[193]
Catholics must not allow false charges and clamors to distract
them from their purpose. He hoped that "Catholic Unions"[194]
growing and spreading throughout America would create and sustain
Catholic unity and direct a concerted effort in defense and promotion of Catholic interests.

> We do not pretend that the struggle will be slight or
> brief, it will be severe and protracted; but the victory
> will be more than half-won, nay, will be assured, the
> moment we have got our whole Catholic population united
> and acting in concert to gain our rights, and make
> civil equality of all religious denominations a truth.
> We may count with confidence on the blessing of the
> divine Head of the Church: for we shall be engaged in
> his work, and laboring to promote the glory of the
> kingdom.[195]

Soon after this last issue appeared, one priest wrote Brownson:
"You leave us now when the school question has but commenced to
command the attention it deserves."[196] Less than two months after
Brownson wrote his last essay on schooling, Rome issued the

---

[193] Ibid., p. 538. Brownson highly praised a speech given by
Hon. Edmund F. Dunne, Chief-Justice of the Supreme Court of
Arizona, entitled Our Public Schools: Are they free for all, or
are they not? (San Francisco: Cosmopolitan Printing Co., 1875).
Dunne was overjoyed that Brownson considered his first lecture
ever as one of the best treatments he had ever read on the school
question. Appropriately, Dunne acknowledged his admiration for
Brownson and his indebtedness. He, too, had never attended school;
furthermore, he credited Brownson's writings with providing him
most of his learning and views on government. See E. F. Dunne to
O.A.B., November 29, 1875, OABP UNDA.

[194] See Isaac Hecker to O.A.B., January 8, 1872, OABP UNDA in
which Hecker noted the importance of Catholic Unions, which he
hoped would provide a daily newspaper, a university, and a Catholic
Congress.

[195] "The Public School System," p. 538.

[196] Fr. P. F. Quigley to O.A.B., November 4, 1875, OABP, UNDA.

"Instruction of the Congregagion de Propaganda Fide Concerning Catholic Children Attending American Public Schools."[197] He was already dead eight years before the convocation of the Third Plenary Council of Baltimore (1884). Nor obviously did he actively take part in "the school controversy" of the 1890's; some of his friends, however, were engaged in it. Might not these key figures have re-enacted the same basic questions that had concerned Brownson?

In assessing Brownson's views on the question of schooling, it would be easy to point to a major change he underwent during the 860's and 1870's. On the surface he seems to have drastically modified his position in giving whole-hearted support to the Catholic school movement. Although his public statement was written in 1862, his Review stopped two years later. His private decisions (involving his son) and his unsigned articles (in Catholic World and New York Tablet) were generally unknown to most Catholics. When he resumed the Review in 1873 he wrote:

> Up to this time, hardly a Catholic organ in the
> country has even attempted any vindication of my
> Catholic reputation; and for the public at large the
> cloud that hung over me in 1864 hangs, I apprehend,
> over me still, so far as I am not forgotten, or
> thought of as already dead and buried.[198]

Because his words of 1862 had been forgotten, and because he had been absent from public notice, Brownson felt compelled to vindicate his name (as he promised his dying wife he would). His essays schooling during the last three years could easily be interpreted

---

[197]November 24, 1875.

[198]O. A. Brownson, "Introduction to the Last Series," BrQR, II (January, 1873), 1.

as reactionary, and that Brownson had broken radically with his previous thoughts, reversed direction, and merely obeyed the Syllabus against his former better judgment. However, such was not the case.

That a change took place it is senseless to deny; but this modification constituted no radical departure from his earlier views on schooling. If anything, his later views point to his consistency and to his gradual loss of optimism concerning America. Careful examination reveals that Brownson had always advocated religious education--before his conversion, during the 1840's and 1850's, and in the 1860's and 1870's. In his early period, he had opposed Horace Mann's system of non-denominational Christianity and believed it would end in "nothingness." When he urged Catholics to attend public schools in the 1850's, he still advocated religious training--in the home and Church. In 1854, there was no contest between Catholic schools and public schools; rather, it was between public schools and the streets. In 1858 and 1859, the question was over public schools and deficient Catholic schools. Brownson had always preferred good Catholic schools; when they were not available, public schools would provide secular education with parents and priests providing religious instruction. His decision to completely support Catholic schools in 1862--a big step indeed-- meant that he now advocated the union of secular and religious studies in the school, something he had always desired anyway. When he did depart from it, to borrow Bishop Fitzpatrick's words, the public schools in Boston in the 1850's were the best he could do, "but not the best he could wish."

His opposition to a national system of education was nothing new either. As early as the 1830's he had objected to state systems, except of course to provide funds. Educational matters were best and rightfully left in the hands of local authorities and those who had children in attendance. He had also argued at that time that only those who used the school should be taxed for its support. In the 1850's, Brownson had opposed taxing Catholics for schools which they could not use in good conscience; he also maintained that the ideal system of schools was the separate denominational pattern that existed in Europe. Moreover, it was in the 1850's when Brownson stated that the school question lay in the hands of the hierarchy. If they deemed certain schools unsafe, Catholics, including Brownson, must obey.

Brownson's acceptance of the Catholic school movement did not prevent him from still calling for reform--just as he had done during the 1850's. He still insisted Catholic schools meet the same academic standards expected of secular public schools. Nor did Brownson's own lack of schooling prevent him from realizing the ever increasing importance of common schools for others. He rejected the voluntary system in favor of compulsory attendance, essential for the preservation and advancement of both Church and state. And despite his support of Catholic schools, Brownson never categorically condemned common schools or blamed them for the evils so prevalent in society. He still believed schools were susceptible to societal influences and were more likely to reflect society than to reform it. At the same time, his advising Catholics not to expect too much from Catholic schools, alone and of themselves, was

consistent with his lifelong belief dating back as far as his
Winnisimmet Address of 1837. Schools were necessary, but certainly
not sufficient to create and sustain a Catholic nation or raise
up an army of scholars.

The basic change, then, that Brownson underwent in the 1860's
and 1870's was neither radical or reactionary. It was consistent
with his earlier thoughts and seemed but the natural outgrowth of
them at a time when he was growing increasingly pessimistic about
America's future. His objections to the values of American society
intensified; religion was needed more than ever to combat and offset the prevailing evil tendencies; religious education had always
been necessary, and now, the family and Church needed assistance
from the school also--just as the Founding Fathers had conducted
their schools in Colonial America.

Perhaps the biggest change is in Brownson's image. His later
writings, as well as his very early ones, are certainly not as
well known as those between 1854 and 1862. Somehow, he seems to
come off these pages at best as a reluctant supporter of Catholic
schools; and at worst, as a thorn in the side of the Catholic
school movement. This present picture provides his early views
and background, puts those essays of the 1850's into clearer perspective and also expands upon his remarks of 1862 and follows
their logical path into the 1870's.

Yet, the trail may lead even beyond. Brownson's essay on
"The School Question" for the Catholic World (April, 1870) has
been cited as a significant writing in the buildup to the school

controversy of the 1890's.[199]   Inadvertently and understandably

(since it was anonymous) Fr. Isaac Hecker, the editor, has been

credited with the authorship. Also, during Brownson's last years,

his closest friend among the hierarchy was Michael Corrigan.

Several times Corrigan asked his good friend, Bernard McQuaid, for

statistics of appropriations of state funds for schools and

charitable institutions so that Brownson could use them in his

essays. Being praised by McCloskey and Grace, and favorably

reviewing Gilmour's Pastoral--all these things strongly suggest

that Brownson was much more important (and perhaps crucial) a

thinker on the school question than has previously been believed,

especially as a conservative spokesman in the forefront of the

Catholic school movement.

---

[199]See Daniel F. Reilly, The School Controversy (Washington,
D.C.: The Catholic University of America Press, 1943), pp. 34-35.

CHAPTER IV

COLLEGES AND HIGHER EDUCATION

Prior to his conversion to Catholicism, Orestes Brownson
extended many of his critical comments about schooling to include
collegiate learning as well. Basing his conclusions upon his own
sense of the importance of books, Orestes Brownson tried to dispel
a popular notion that equated college attendance with the achievement of real education.

> Men who have not passed through the schools are said to
> be uneducated; but no man, who has free access to books,
> and is a diligent reader of them, can with any justice
> be said to want education. We should like to know
> what is learned in the university which cannot be learned
> from books? It is rare that your professors can advance
> on their textbooks, or that they know as much of the
> sciences they undertake to teach as the student may
> find in his manuals. Whoever knows how to read, and
> has the proper books within his reach, may attain, for
> aught we can see, to all the scientific and literary
> eminence he could, were he to graduate at the first
> university in the land.[1]

Basically Brownson contended that the content presented in college
courses, at least in the 1840's, could be learned just as well
without attending college, if one were an avid reader.[2]

However, he did not object to colleges merely because the
content could be readily acquired by reading. He protested the

----

[1]"The School Library," op. cit., p. 29.

[2]Brownson's own development certainly influences his views on
this matter.

subject matter itself, in what it stressed or implied, and in what it overlooked or ignored. Two and one-half years before Brownson delivered The Scholar's Mission, he wrote that "education has no higher or holier vocation than that of fitting its subjects to be stern, uncompromising, and indefatigable Reformers."[3] But because colleges and "higher seminaries" were founded by and for the wealthy, under the control of the wealthy, and taught by aristocratic or conservative professors, young men were "not educated to regard the well-being of Humanity, to be Reformers, the champions and servants of the people; but they are educated to get their living out of the people."[4] Colleges failed to imbue their students with unquenchable zeal, burning desire, or distinterested love in the cause of human progress.

Another essential fault with colleges, like all other institutional agencies of education, was that they did not draw forth the true end of man nor did they stress the proper end of knowledge. The belief prevailed that education and knowledge were acquired for self-benefit and betterment, for rising above the people; the usefulness and practicality of education were measured by what job, trade, or profession it enabled one to obtain. Brownson, on the other hand, believed that God's mission for America demanded that every educated person make "the good of all the end of each

[3]O. A. Brownson, "Conversations with a Radical," BoQR, IV January, 1841), 13.

[4]Ibid., p. 14. The Scholar's Mission, it will be recalled, as addressed to collegiate audiences and called for the same type f dedication to ameliorating the human condition.

one's labour."[5] Usefulness meant being useful to the world, not merely to oneself.

But the concept of usefulness to oneself and professional preparation seemed to dominate institutions of higher learning. Brownson objected to this orientation because it merely provided training for jobs and did not embrace man's whole nature. Just as he had objected to Horace Mann's curricular proposals and philosophy of education and criticized Normal Schools on the same grounds, so too he denounced trade schools for farmers and mechanics and professional schools for lawyers and doctors. All of them, Brownson argued, viewed trades and professions as ends rather than as means. Schools and colleges produced trained mechanics and put men on farms, but did they educate men with goals of improving the morals of men and society? Medical and law schools were no better, and perhaps even worse. Physicians, if properly educated, could be social reformers, but their education had not taught them to work on alleviating the true causes of suffering, disease, and poverty; rather, it taught them only cures for the symptoms. The law profession trained its members to sacrifice the spirit of the law to the letter, justice to technicalities. Lawyers seemed "Blind to moral distinctions, and equally ready to uphold the wrong as the right."[6] This type of education, which Brownson called "specific," or education for a trade or profession, did not aid in helping mankind to accomplish its mission. Such training was

---

[5]"Means and End of Knowledge," op. cit.

[6]See "Social Evils and Their Remedies," op. cit. for the objections above.

anti-social, unprogressive, and detrimental to human advancement. Colleges had stressed various forms of specific, vocational training, and regarded such training as an end in itself; moreover, they had overlooked and ignored what Brownson considered the true ends of education. Accordingly, Brownson called for reform and improvement in American institutions of higher learning. He argued the "necessity of $\underline{/}\,a\,\underline{/}$ liberal education,"[7] an education for Humanity.

In the summer of 1843, Brownson had delivered The Scholar's Mission at Dartmouth College and at Vermont University. His purpose was "to make the scholar perceive and feel his duty to the people, and to stimulate him to its faithful and energetic performance, at whatever hazard to himself, to his own ease, wealth, or reputation."[8] The scholar, of necessity, elevated himself above the people in order to assist and direct the progress of humanity, and not to live off the people. But complaints abounded that

---

[7]O. A. Brownson, "Necessity of Liberal Education," BrQR, I April, 1844) 194-208. This essay was occasioned by a letter Brownson received from Theophilus Fisk, dated December 23, 1843. Fisk included a copy of a speech, "The Bearings of College Education on the Welfare of the Whole Community," delivered by Rev. George Junkin, President of Miami University, Oxford, Ohio. Fisk was furious over the "anti-Republican tendency" at all American colleges, comparing them to the systems of Oxford and Cambridge, calculated to produce an educated aristocracy. He objected that the educated did not work for the elevation of the masses. Fisk felt that Junkin was advocating an English rather than an American system. Fisk asked Brownson to analyze the whole question. Brownson did, but at the same time, believed that Junkin was partly correct, and Fisk, in his extreme democratic views, partly wrong. Letter is contained in OABP, UNDA.

[8]"Necessity of Liberal Education," p. 195; this essay may openly be viewed as a sequel to The Scholar's Mission.

scholars transcended the "common mind." Popular opinion favored
the unlettered mass over the lettered few. All agreed that scholars
must work as educators or servants of the people. But too many
believed that the scholar's job was to defer to the people, not
to contradict, or to run against their judgments, convictions
or tastes. If scholars sought only their own good, or if they
deferred to the masses, the human race would stand still. Brownson
did not mean to denigrate the "common mind" at the expense of the
lettered few;

> we simply contend that the amount of knowledge attained
> to by the common mind, is not all the knowledge neces-
> sary to the well-being of the whole community. To
> carry the race forward, to improve the condition of
> the mass, requires profounder, more comprehensive views
> of truth, moral and political, scientific and reli-
> gious, than the common mind has as yet attained to,
> and to which it cannot attain without thorough mental
> and moral discipline.[9]

The "common mind" needed improvement, and scholars must be the
ones to do it. Efforts would not be futile, for all were capable
of being cultivated; all had the capacity for progress. Only by
educating the "common mind" could it be prepared to comprehend
the great problems of life; hence, the need for liberal studies
at the college level.

> There cannot be education without educators. There
> must be some in advance of the mass, to be in some way,
> directly or indirectly, the educators of the mass, or
> the mass cannot be educated. Colleges and universi-
> ties would seem, then, to be essential as the condition
> of educating the educators; at least, there should be

---

[9]Ibid., p. 201.

some means provided for the education of the few above
that of the mass; for if none rise above the level of
the mass, there will be none to quicken and direct the
common mind, which, in that case, instead of being
progressive, must remain stationary.[10]

Brownson realized that objections would be raised against his

ideas. Was he not calling for an educated aristocracy, and

insisting on an educated class? The welfare of the community,

Brownson explained, demanded an educated class. But this class

would not be an aristocracy; instead, it would be the servant of

the people. And Brownson did insist on an educated class, but not

on a class to be educated. "The education determines the class,

not the class the education."[11] This, of course, could only be

accomplished by the expansion of colleges and universities. If

colleges were neglected, and all efforts put into common schools,

an aristocracy would be created at once. For common schools only

provided a little elementary instruction, and could not meet the

demands of a finished education. Higher and more thorough educa-

tion would then be only possible for the rich; in that way, class

would determine education, and not education the class. Brownson

proposed that

the true interest of republics is to found, and liber-
ally endow, colleges and universities, so as to bring
the highest education within the reach of individuals
from the humblest classes . . . . Demolish these
institutions, and the evil would fall very lightly
on the wealthy, but a crushing weight on the gifted
sons of the poor.[12]

---

[10]Ibid., p. 204.
[11]Ibid., p. 205.
[12]Ibid., pp. 205-206.

Colleges and universities seemed essential to the creation of an educated class, and this class in turn, must be devoted to ameliorating man's moral, religious, mental, and social condition.

Thus, although colleges and universities needed much reforming within themselves, Brownson considered them as integral parts in the education and elevation of mankind. His critical comments about the condition of American colleges and his vision of the scholar's role in directing thought and action were written during the years just prior to his conversion to Catholicism. These early remarks should be kept in mind in assessing his views on Catholic higher education.

The state of Catholic colleges during the Pre-Civil War days was not a bright one. Colleges were costly and most Catholics could not afford to attend them. But their purposes were noble. In 1792, Bishop John Carroll spoke of Georgetown College as an institution which aimed "to instruct all, who resort to them, in useful learning, and those of our own religion, in its principles and duties." He continued:

> I know and lament, that the expense will be too great for many families, and that their children must be deprived of the immediate benefit of this institution; but, indirectly, they will receive it; at least, it may be reasonably expected, that some after being educated at George-Town, and having returned into their own neighborhood, will become, in their turn, the instructors of the youths who cannot be sent from home.[13]

---

[13]"Pastoral Letter (1792)," p. 7.

The purpose of the Catholic college was quite similar to its Protestant counterpart--the development of religious and lay leaders
of the faith who, in turn, would spread the benefits of their
education to others. By 1840, the Bishops stated that although
much had been done respecting the colleges,

> yet much remains to be done by their multiplication,
> and we exhort you for the sake of your children, your
> country and your religion, to come to our aid for the
> purpose of making the effort thus to provide for the
> literary, moral and religious education of one sex as
> well as the other.[14]

Indeed, the Church realized that colleges could stand improvement.

What were the colleges--Catholic as well as Protestant, and
private--like prior to the Civil War? Historians of American
higher education generally conclude that colleges were gradually
shifting emphasis from a goal of educating leaders to one of more
democratic proportions. The institutions were generally more
concerned with moral development and piety, rather than intellectual achievement. There was a rapid proliferation of small
colleges under religious and denominational sponsorship. Along
with the westward movement came local pride and boosterism and a
democratic spirit with a lowering of academic standards. One final
characteristic was the extremely high mortality rate. Eighty-one
percent (412 of 516) of the colleges founded prior to 1860 did not
remain permanent institutions.[15]

---

[14]"Pastoral Letter (1840)," p. 95.

[15]Donald Tewksbury, The Founding of American Colleges and
Universities Before the Civil War, With Particular Reference to
the Religious Influence Bearing Upon the College Movement (New
York: Teachers College, Columbia University, 1932) is the seminal

Historians of Catholic higher education agree on the purposes

of Catholic colleges:

> The specific aims of the Catholic colleges, apart from
> their predominantly religious purpose, were the same
> as those of the ordinary liberal arts colleges of
> America at the time. The Catholic colleges endeavored
> by means of a religious training, mental discipline,
> and liberal culture, to produce the complete Christian
> character.[16]

The mortality rate of Catholic colleges was equally high. Only

ten of the forty-two colleges (less than 25%) founded before 1850

became permanent, with most closing within a few years.[17] Edward

---

work in the field; Richard Hofstadter and Walter P. Metzger, The
Development of Academic Freedom in the United States (New York:
Columbia University Press, 1955) see this age as "The Great
Retrogression"; R. Freeman Butts, The College Charts Its Course:
Historical Conceptions and Current Proposals (New York: McGraw-
Hill Book Company, 1939) is optimistic in his estimation of the
reform, experimentation, progress and important innovations in
higher education prior to 1860; Fredrick Rudolph, The American
College and University: A History (New York: Alfred A. Knopf,
1962) sees a Jacksonian reflection in the colleges; Theodore Rawson
Crane, ed., The Colleges and the Public, 1787-1862 (New York:
Teachers College, Columbia University, 1963) is similar to Rudolph
and attempts to reconcile the two divergent opinions of Butts and
Hofstadter-Metzger. For the mortality statistics, see Tewksbury,
p. 28.

[16]Sebastian A. Erbacher, Catholic Higher Education for Men in
the United States, 1850-1866 (Washington, D.C.: The Catholic
University of America, 1931), p. 65. This position is endorsed by
the only historian of Catholic higher education, Edward J. Power,
A History of Catholic Higher Education in the United States
(Milwaukee: The Bruce Publishing Company, 1958), pp. 34-35. See
also Francis P. Cassidy, The Catholic Colleges: Foundations and
Development in the United States 1677-1850 (Washington, D.C.: The
Catholic University of America, 1924). Power has updated and
expanded his work in Catholic Higher Education in America, A
History (New York, 1972). See also a three part series of articles,
"Formative Years of Catholic Colleges Founded before 1850," Records
of the American Catholic Historical Society of Philadelphia, LXV-
LXVI (March, December, 1854, March, 1855), 24-39, 240-250, 19-34.

[17]Edward J. Power, A History of Catholic Higher Education in
the United States, p. 34.

Power points out that Catholic education developed from the top

down. A wide gap existed between elementary schools and colleges.

Secondary schools were few in number and did not provide the neces-

sary link between elementary and collegiate instruction. "Colleges

were more often than not forced to provide the basic as well as

the more advanced education"[18] for students. The curriculum of

the Catholic college before the Civil War "was more often secondary

than collegiate and sometimes more elementary than secondary."[19]

The Catholic clergy and hierarchy could nevertheless express happi-

ness at the very existence of these institutions, and yet be dis-

appointed that not more had been achieved.[20]

---

[18]Ibid., p. 51. As late as 1877, some Catholic colleges
offered courses in rudiments. Around 1900, of the 20,000 students
enrolled in Catholic colleges, 4,000 were pursuing what we would
today consider collegiate courses. Another 12,000 were pursuing
preparatory studies, while the remaining 4,000 were enrolled in
professional studies. In other words 60% of Catholic college
students were actually enrolled in secondary courses. It was not
until the twentieth century that any serious reform was undertaken
to separate the college from the high school. See Philip Gleason,
"The Reorganization of Catholic Higher Education, 1900-1925" (Unpublished paper delivered at a conference on Saint Mary's College
in the Seventies: Its Christian Dimension, April 6, 1974). For
the development of elementary and secondary schools see the following: James A. Burns, The Principles, Origin and Establishment of
the Catholic School System in the United States (New York:
Benziger Brothers, 1908) and The Growth and Development of the
Catholic School System in the United States (New York: Benziger
Brothers, 1912); James A. Burns and Bernard J. Kohlbrenner, A
History of Catholic Education in the United States (New York:
Benziger Brothers, 1937); Edmund J. Goebel, A Study of Catholic
Secondary Education During the Colonial Period Up to the First
Plenary Council of Baltimore, 1852 (New York: Benziger Brothers,
1937); and Harold A. Buetow, Of Singular Benefit: The Story of
Catholic Education in the United States (New York: The Macmillan
Company, 1970).

[19]Ibid., p. 53; Power provides a good analysis of the development of curriculum and method on pp. 49-78.

[20]Ibid., pp. 34-35. For an enlightening discussion of the
social, institutional, and ideological adjustments that Catholics
faced in higher education see Philip Gleason, "American Catholic

During his first years as a Catholic, Brownson uttered sentiments similar to those of the bishops. He ably defended Catholic
colleges, especially those run by the Jesuits, against charges made
by the Reverend William S. Potts of St. Louis. Potts, a Presbyterian, had delivered a sermon entitled "Dangers of Jesuit Instruction" in September, 1845. He asserted that graduates of Catholic
colleges were not qualified to enter the junior class at Princeton,
Yale, or any respectable Protestant college. Brownson refuted the
statement, claiming that Jesuit education was as thorough, as
extensive, and of as high an order as the best Protestant institutions; however, "university education in this country, whether by
Catholics or Protestants, $\overline{/}$ was $\overline{/}$, . . . far from being what it
should be."[21] Americans, Brownson believed, were unwilling to
"spend the time necessary to become thorough scholars; consequently
the whole scholarship of the country, with a few individual exceptions, is limited and superficial."[22] Regardless of these limita-
tions, the Jesuit colleges were "admirably adapted to the present
wants of the Catholic population." If none of the colleges had
achieved intellectual greatness, at least Catholic colleges
trained students "in the way they should go," caring for their
moral and religious character. "Science, literature, the most

Higher Education: A Historical Perspective," in Robert Hassenger,
ed., The Shape of Catholic Higher Education (Chicago: University
of Chicago Press, 1967), pp. 15-53; Gleason also discusses the
weakness in the Catholic "system" that forced the colleges to
incorporate high school and preparatory studies, pp. 30-43.

   [21]O. A. Brownson, "Dangers of Jesuit Instruction," BrQR, III
(January, 1846), 86.

   [22]Ibid., pp. 86-87.

varied and profound scholastic attainments, are worse than useless, where coupled with heresy, infidelity, or impiety."[23]   At the same time, Brownson cited Catholic female academies under the direction of the Ursulines, Sisters of Charity, Visitation, and Sacred Heart orders for producing excellence of character in young ladies, both Catholic and Protestant.[24]

Despite the present inadequacies of Catholic colleges, Brownson believed the Jesuits would soon achieve the same high status in this

---

[23]Ibid., p. 87. Brownson had enrolled four of his sons in Jesuit colleges. Orestes Jr. attended St. Xavier (Cincinnati) briefly, and then enrolled at Holy Cross in 1846 where he joined his three brothers, John, William, and Henry. That Brownson realized the academic short-comings of Holy Cross is clear. First of all, nearly 7½ years separated the oldest, Orestes, from the youngest, Henry. In 1846, Orestes was 18, and Henry 11. Besides the obvious difficulty of disciplinary rules and instruction for such different age groups, Brownson's sons wrote several letters complaining about occurrences at Holy Cross. Orestes complained "I have seen injustice with the Jesuits" (OAB Jr. to OAB, June 17, 1846, OABP, UNDA). William apparently received a thrashing so bad that Orestes Jr. feared he might lose use of his arm because it was stiff (OAB Jr. to OAB, November 17, 1847, OABP, UNDA). John complained about a poor philosophy professor, a rationalist, who would not allow John to use his reason, but suddenly, relying on faith and revelation, accused John of heresy and blasphemy (John H. Brownson to OAB, April 19, 1847, OABP, UNDA). See also OAB to Fr. Cummings, October 22, 1849, OABP, UNDA. Orestes complained about a new math teacher. "During the first half of this term, I studied mathematics hard and had got far ahead of the rest, but a new teacher came we were all put in the same class and now after two months and a half, I have not yet with the Class reached the point I was at when I started" (OAB Jr. to OAB, March 1, 1848, OABP, UNDA). The policy of corporal punishment, however, apparently was abated in 1848. Henry wrote his mother: "They have given up whipping the boys mostly and have adopted the method of giving lines for punishment. I had ten lines once which was much easier than a flogging" (Henry F. Brownson to Mrs. O. A. Brownson, March , 1848, OABP, UNDA).

[24]So much better were Catholic academies, Brownson claimed, that many Protestants sent their daughters. In Cincinnati, Protestant efforts to initiate an academy for girls failed due to lack of support--Protestants were attending the Catholic academy. Protestants attended St. Xavier College also. While Orestes Jr.

country as they had in Europe. He called their system of education "the most perfect and the wisest ever devised by the genius of man."[25] Its most distinguishing feature was that it rendered all physical and intellectual education "subordinate to the moral and religious culture of the mind."[26] Its dual goals were to make Christians, and then scholars and men. Throughout the remainder of his life, Brownson's remarks on higher education aimed at improving deficiencies in Catholic colleges and their graduates-- as men, as Christians, and as scholars.

In an address before the Philomathian Society[27] of Mount Saint Mary's College (Md.) in 1853, Brownson emphasized the importance

---

was there, Brownson received a letter from Fr. Elet remarking that there had been six recent converts. See Fr. Elet to OAB, May 13, 1846, OABP, UNDA.

[25]O. A. Brownson, "Influence of the Jesuits on Religion and Civilization," BrQR, III (April, 1846), 189.

[26]Ibidem.

[27]The existence of such societies on college campuses added another educational dimension, similar to the self-help and mutual improvement adult societies that were springing up throughout the country. See Chapter Nine for a discussion of non-collegiate adult organizations. Brownson encountered many such societies during his life. The Philomathian Society of Pennsylvania College at Gettysburg elected him an honorary member in 1841; the Thalian Society at Milledgville in 1843; the University Institute of the University of Vermont in 1843; the Few Society of Emory College in 1844; the Reading Room Society of St. Mary's College in 1845; the Philodemic Society of Georgetown College in 1845; the Philo-demic Society of St. Louis University in 1851; a Literary Society at Mercersburg in 1851; the Philopedian Society of St. Joseph's College (Ohio) in 1856; and the Philolegian Society of St. Mary's College of the Mountains (date unknown) also elected Brownson as an honorary member. In addition, the Seton Hall Seminarians named their organization the Brownson Literary Association in 1873. Notre Dame's St. Aloysius Literary Association also requested Brownson to lecture. At Notre Dame, where Brownson is buried, an Orestes Brownson Society exists to this day.

of "liberal studies in relation to the wants of a free state." In
terms reminiscent of The Scholar's Mission delivered ten years
before, he urged his audience to labor to form the popular mind,
and to serve as guides and leaders of the people.

> Understand well that this is your mission, and dare dis-
> charge it, fearlessly, bravely, heroically, whether you
> have the multitude with you, or have, as most likely
> will be the case, the multitude against you. Be brave,
> courageous, chivalrous knights, in defence of truth and
> justice, so shall you be without fear and without
> reproach; so shall you serve your country, avert, it
> may be, the dangers which threaten it, gain a name,
> which 'posterity will not willingly let die', and what
> is infinitely better, everlasting life and eternal
> glory in heaven.[28]

Brownson's charge to the graduates of 1853 was quite similar
to the one he gave to those of 1843. His views had not changed one
bit. He still insisted on inequality of rank, and opposed any
attempts to "level" society, either upwards or downwards, as
contrary to the laws of God and nature. "The strength and glory
of a nation depend not on the vulgar, the commonality, the low
born, the servile, or the simple; but on its freemen, its gentlemen, its nobility,"[29] on those who have received a liberal education. He stressed the needs of nations for leaders, just as an
army needed generals. This nobility or aristocracy of intellect
was not possessed for the beholder, but rather it was a sacred
trust. American society--with its "bankers, sharpers, brokers,

---

[28] O. A. Brownson, An Oration on Liberal Studies (Baltimore:
edian & O'Brien, 1853), pp. 5, 24.
[29] Ibid., p. 8.

stock-jobbers, traders, speculators, attornies, pettifoggers, and
in general worshippers of mammon"[30]--was loaded with people who
possessed selfish views of their positions. The country needed
more leaders who would serve rather than use the people.

The quality of leadership emanated from above, from the top
downwards. The higher classes needed to direct and guide the
lower and ignorant classes.

> The whole order of Providence is that the higher should
> guide and govern the lower, and that whatever is wise
> and good cometh from above, and operates from high to
> low, never as the age presumptuously teaches from low
> to high.[31]

Brownson hoped that such leadership would come from the graduates
of Catholic colleges. Also he warned against two movements
occurring almost simultaneously. On the one hand, many were
placing all their hopes in the common schools; on the other hand,
others believed all should receive a liberal college education.
Brownson found both conceptions ill-suited to American progress.

Common schools, with their watered-down curriculum, were either
sectarian or godless and failed to provide necessary religious
education. Even in religious (Catholic or common) schools, not
much should be expected, at least in terms of securing the nation.
Common school education just could not provide ample enlightenment
for a people, or "make them wise and virtuous, competent to
/ administer_7 all the complicated affairs of civil and social

---

[30]Ibid., p. 15.
[31]Ibid., p. 16.

life."[32] Nor were all fit to attend college. The natural inequal-

ity in the various stations of life made a liberal education for

all incompatible with the simple facts of human existence.

> Give it were possible, to the whole community the educa-
> tion, the culture, the refinement and elevated manners
> and tastes of the few, and without which a nation remains
> uncivilized, the great business of life would come to a
> stand-still, and your nation would be like an army with-
> out privates, or a ship without common sailors. On the
> other hand to reduce all education and all culture to
> the level of your common schools, is to have no officers,
> none qualified to take the command and fill the higher
> offices of civilized society.[33]

Hence, Brownson denied the overemphasized importance of common

schools and insisted that all good things came from above, not

from below. His remarks on sending too many to college seem more

pertinent today than then, especially with the number of unemployed

and underemployed graduates increasing yearly. Also, many jobs

that are available call for certain skills and training, require-

ments which colleges cannot provide and which are better met

elsewhere.

A society advanced and flourished when its upper classes,

whether titled or untitled, were properly trained with the princi-

ples, virtues, habits and tastes essential for its well-being; the

few lifted the many.

---

[32]Ibid., p. 21.

[33]Ibid., p. 22. Brownson cited the recent Mexican War and the
contributions of West Point graduates. "We shall not very soon see
again ignorant civilians chosen in preference to trained soldiers,
to command our troops. The great bulk of every community has
depended and always will depend on the leadership in all things
of the few."

Liberal studies are the studies of the few, they are
the studies of freemen, that is, of gentlemen, and their
office is to qualify them to be wise and prudent, just
and noble, able guides and leaders, that is, the faithful
and competent servants of the community. It is not
because you have better blood than others, it is not
that society exists for you, for you all nature blooms,
and for you the people live and labor, that you are
to pursue liberal studies, and acquire the knowledge,
the tastes and accomplishments of gentlemen, but that
you may exert a wise and salutary influence on the great
body of the nation. You are for the nation, not the
nation for you; you are to sustain it, not it you.
Your liberal education is a trust which you hold from
God for . . . serving $\diagup$ the people $\diagup$.[34]

The graduates of Catholic colleges Brownson now urged to fulfill

The Scholar's Mission. The goals he set in 1853 were no different

from his earlier objectives.

However, envisioning an end result and achieving it are two

different entities. Graduates of Catholic colleges did not often

attain this high standard. Accordingly, in the period from 1857-

1861 Brownson's Quarterly Review published several essays devoted

to reforming the entire structure of Catholic education, including

the colleges.[35] Brownson's major statement on this issue appeared

---

[34]Ibid., p. 23.

[35]Most of these essays were not written by Brownson, although
they did reflect the same basic sentiments and arguments. I will
only discuss Brownson's writings, although it should be understood
that the question of higher education was widely discussed at this
time. See the following articles: F. G., "Public Instruction,"
BrQR, XIV (July, 1857), 357-388; F.G., "Our Colleges," BrQR, XV
(April, 1858), 209-244; W.J. B$\diagup$arry$\diagup$, "Ecclesiastical Seminaries,"
XVI (October, 1859) 456-472; J.W. C$\diagup$ummings$\diagup$, "Vocations to the
Priesthood," BrQR, XVII (October, 1860), 497-515; W.J. B$\diagup$arry$\diagup$,
"Dr. Arnold and Catholic Education," BrQR, XVII (July, 1860), 302-
329; J.W. C$\diagup$ummings$\diagup$, "Seminaries and Seminarians," BrQR, XVIII
(January, 1861), 97-117. The essays pertaining to seminary educa-
tion will be discussed in Chapter Six, along with Brownson's
writings on the training of candidates for the priesthood.

in the form of a dialogue, "Conversations of Our Club,"[36] in late
1858, the same period in which he was most critical of deficient
parochial schools.

Brownson perceived that the American bishops were devoting
most of their efforts to the establishment of parochial schools.
He preferred, instead, to see them build up Catholic colleges,
academies, and seminaries. The Catholic schools were not able to
reach all Catholic children, and to those they did reach, could
not offer the same advantages of the common school. "The education of the whole mass of the children in common schools /‾or
parochial schools_7, may be a necessity of modern times, especially
in a democratic country, but it can never, however thorough,
suffice for the wants of the Church or of society."[37] Brownson
believed the first need of the Church was "a numerous and well-
educated clergy."[38] The establishment of seminaries in every
diocese was preferable to the proliferation of simple parochial
schools.

Brownson believed the overemphasis on parochial schools reinforced the exaggerated democratic notion of educating the mass
of privates and neglecting the education of officers. Certainly
education was more diffused than in the past, but "the higher and
more thorough education of the few is relatively more neglected,

---

[36]See O. A. Brownson, "Conversations of Our Club," BrQR, XV
October, 1858), 425-466. The Conversations began with the January
number of 1858, and ran for seven straight issues through July,
859. Actually, pp. 425-444 dealt with parochial schools, and pp.
44-466 analyzed higher education.

[37]Ibid., pp. 444.

[38]Ibidem. Chapter Six analyzes the educational role of the
hurch, including the education of priests.

and inferior in the cultivation and discipline of the mind, and in the formation of character."[39]   Just as the people needed a clergy to care for religious needs, they also needed leaders in secular matters as well, whether it be lawyers, surgeons or statesmen. "After the seminary, . . . the next most important thing is the college and university for training and preparing . . . lay or temporal chiefs."[40]

The first step in bettering the existing colleges must be the separation of the college from the seminary. The collegiate portion did not receive proper attention, Brownson remarked, because the college had been viewed as a feeder for ecclesiastical seminaries and religious orders. Unfortunately, the colleges failed in both respects--they produced neither the caliber of lay graduates nor the number of seminary candidates. The Church ought to rely strictly on seminaries to fill its spiritual wants. Furthermore, the Church was under no obligation to found colleges for seculars; all it had to do was to see to it that the colleges worked in subordination and subserviency to the spiritual interests of the Church. Paradoxically, Brownson did not say how the colleges might come into being without the aid of the Church in establishing and maintaining them.

"The primary object of the college or university, save the faculty of theology, should be to meet the secular wants of secular society, whether the professors are priests, religious, or seculars."[41]   Fortunately, Brownson believed this work of

---

[39]Ibid.
[40]Ibid., p. 446.
[41]Ibid., p. 447.

separating the seminary from the college was in progress and would
be completed before long. Another benefit from such an arrangement
would be the employment of educated laymen as teachers in the
colleges. This would not only provide an open field for lay
participation in their religion, but also free a number of priests
for other work in the pastoral care of Catholics or on missions to
Catholics and non-Catholics.[42]

Secondly, Catholic colleges aimed too low, and were well
below European institutions and other American colleges like
Harvard, Yale, Dartmouth and Columbia in secular education.
Whereas Brownson had defended Catholic colleges against Protestant
charges twelve years earlier, he now was addressing a Catholic
audience and calling for reform. One can defend his cohorts
against an enemy, and then discuss with those same allies ways for
improving a sub-par or mediocre situation. His critical comments
must be seen in the spirit of this "period of fermentation" and
as an attempt to improve Catholic colleges, not to destroy them.
Brownson attributed the defects mainly to the immigrant nature of
the population, especially to the oppression and injustice that
many of them had faced before coming to this country. He did not
blame the immigrants, but rather their oppressors for the current
state. Oppression resulted in producing a timidity, a feeling of
inferiority, a certain deference to non-Catholic public opinion.
Brownson wanted Catholics to "shake off this deference to non-
Catholic public opinion, to rise above this sense of inferiority,

---

[42]Ibid., pp. 449-451.

and to assume . . . their rightful position as freemen, as God's noblemen on earth."[43] This could only be done, of course, by a more thorough education than existed at present.

The third step involved internal reorganization. Pupils were received at too young an age; government and discipline for an eight year old could not be adapted to nineteen year olds. The preparatory school merged with the college, as did the grammar school; the college itself combined with the university. In fact, it seemed as though only one school existed. Brownson proposed the creation of and adherence to four distinct grades of schools: 1) the common school, divided into primary and secondary; 2) the high school or academy; 3) the college; and 4) the university. Brownson believed that state-established common schools would suffice for general instruction (with religious instruction coming from the home and the Church) for the majority of Catholic children. The next three levels would have to be provided by Catholics themselves. High schools would feed colleges, which in turn would feed the university. Parents who sought more education for their children would advance them beyond the common schools and high schools; only those who wanted a complete liberal education would take university courses (four years) after taking the Baccalaureate (four years). Brownson realized the plan might reduce the number of college students and even the number of institutions calling themselves colleges. Yet such changes and modifications would remove the reasonable objections raised against Catholic colleges

[43]*Ibid.*, p. 455.

and elevate the college to a position of respectability.[44]

These three steps--the separation of college from seminary,
the elevation of educational aims, and the structural reorganization
of the educational system--formed the basis of significant educational change and growth for Catholics. Many of these changes were
taking place when Brownson wrote "Conversations"; yet rather than
allow things to merely take their course, he decided to add an
impetus to the movement. Although Brownson was a layman, he felt
it within proper limits to discuss Catholic higher education for
seculars. Whether colleges or academies were run by religious or
laity, the secular education of these colleges was a secular
concern and public opinion had a right to be enlightened about it.
Once the Catholic public became informed, necessary changes would
be hastened and facilitated.[45]

---

[44]Ibid., pp. 457-459.

[45]Ibid., pp. 455-466; Brownson had also defended girls'
academies against Protestant charges a dozen years before; now
he was directing his thoughts to Catholics. Brownson advocated
changes within girls' academies as well claiming the curriculum
covered many areas in too superficial a manner, and taught nothing
thoroughly, "unless a few light and showy accomplishments." The
intellectual side was neglected, and the education seemed "to
forget that girls have intellect, and that intellect in wives
and mothers is not a superfluity." Brownson hoped the Sisters
would place more emphasis on developing the understanding of
their pupils, for young ladies no less than men needed strong
intellects and a rational education. He reasserted one of his
early views: "I have great respect for the female mind, and
I measure the civilization of a country by the cultivation and
intelligence of its women." Also, see Mrs. McNally to O.A.B.,
December 25, 1857 (enclosed is a letter from Sr. M. Eulalia
Pearce to Mrs. McNally, November 37, 1857), OABP, UNDA; Mathilde
Victor to O.A.B., August 22, 1859, OABP, UNDA; and O. A. Brownson,
"The Woman Question," Catholic World, IX (May, 1869), 155-157.

One problem in this area was that the colleges had failed to quicken the intellects of its men and boys. Part of this problem arose because there were boys at college. Not enough schools of intermediate level existed, and in other cases, some boys went straight to college without even the common or parochial school. In fact, many graduates were still young boys who left college "when the passions begin to unfold, and /‾when_7 he commences the dangerous period of transition from the boy to the man."[46] Hence, the boy graduated at the worst possible moment, before he was prepared to handle the "battle with the world, the flesh, and the devil." The separation of the preparatory department from the college, and acceptance of students for college at an older age could remedy this situation. Otherwise, as too often happened, the graduate would succumb. Also, the young student--a boy of fourteen--certainly could not understand essential philosophical questions or become a thorough scholar.

Besides the intellectual aspects, Brownson believed the disciplinary system of colleges needed revision. Colleges nursed their students, doing things for them, but seldom allowed boys to think and act for themselves. Colleges needed to adapt to American republican standards and help form the qualities of self-help, self-reliance, and self-government in their students. Instead of fostering independence and strength, colleges produced weak and dependent students. Brownson believed all colleges, Catholic and non-Catholic, suffered from this same defect which made "the

---

[46]Ibid., p. 460.

maintenance of the college authority the great thing to which,
if need be, all else must be sacrificed."[47] Such a system prevented young men from taking their proper rank and exerting their
proper influence in American society; instead, they lost their
independence, frankness, and ingenuousness, and became "shy,
artful, deceitful, and hypocritical."[48]

Brownson's remarks were certainly critical; he was not pleased
with the results of Catholic colleges. Nonetheless, he believed
both the colleges and academies would be improved by their facul-
ties, as fast and as prudently as possible. Unlike his suggestions
for Catholic attendance at common schools, Brownson did not recommend that Catholics attend Protestant or secular colleges. He was
willing to accept common schools for secular studies (where
Catholic schools were non-existent or deficient), but the college
(the most important level) was indispensable for Catholic progress
and success. Hence, he aimed his remarks at reforming Catholic
colleges.

One other item attracted Brownson's attention: the need for
an American Catholic University.[49] During the 1850's, he claimed

---

[47]Ibid., p. 461; Brownson praised Mount Saint Mary's the
following year for possessing an American character. See O. A.
Brownson, "Literary Notices and Criticisms," BrQR, XVI (July,
1859), 412.

[48]Ibid., p. 462.

[49]Brownson briefly cited desirability of a Catholic University
n 1853 in An Oration of Liberal Studies, p. 21. In 1854, the
atholic University of Ireland at Dublin opened its doors to twenty
tudents, thus becoming the first Catholic University in the English
peaking world. Brownson urged all Catholics to support the
niversity under its fine head, John Henry Newman, and to send
heir children there until Americans had their own Catholic
niversity. Newman had invited Brownson to teach as "lecturer
xtraordinary." Although Newman realized Brownson wanted to teach

Americans needed a Catholic University in order "to acquire the

commanding position in the modern world which is our right."[50] The

university demanded a larger and more liberal plan[51] than the

college, and embraced a wider circle of studies and aimed more at

the intellectual development of a class of scholars who would be

not only free, vigorous and original thinkers, but also well-reared

in Catholic tradition and doctrine, and able to compete success-

fully against non-Catholic scholars as well. The world was no

longer a Catholic place; moral and ascetic discipline would not

---

theology or philosophy of history, he was not able to offer those
courses to a layman. Instead, he offered Brownson the chair of
geography, and told him he could analyze its physical, moral,
political, and philosophical implications and speculations. After
Brownson's essay on "Native Americanism" in July, 1854, Newman was
forced to withdraw the offer and asked Brownson to postpone the
visit until the Irish matter abated. Archbishop Paul Cullen, a
major force in establishing the university, most likely was the
chief instigator against Brownson. Cullen referred to this matter
in a letter to Cardinal Barnabo in 1861 when he wrote to Rome
complaining of Brownson's writings on the temporal power of the
pope. The postponement, in the end, proved to be a cancellation,
as Brownson never did teach at Dublin. See the following letters
in OABP, UNDA: J.H. Newman to O.A.B., December 15, 1853, June 6,
1854, August 23, 1854, and September 27, 1854; and John D. Acton
to O.A.B., May 13, 1854. Fr. Sorin also extended two offers to
Brownson to teach at the University of Notre Dame. Brownson turned
down the first in early 1863 due to the poor pay and rigorous
working hours--6:00 a.m. until 10:00 p.m. After his wife died in
1872, Brownson again turned down Sorin's offer to make Notre Dame
his home. Brownson did, however, present several lectures to
Seton Hall students in the 1870's at the request of Fr. Michael
Corrigan.

[50]O. A. Brownson, "Present Catholic Dangers," BrQR, XIV
(July, 1857), 362.

[51]O. A. Brownson, "Literary Notices and Criticisms," BrQR,
XVI (October, 1859), 552, 554-555. Brownson apparently never read,
or at least there is no record of it, Newman's lectures of 1852
that were published in February, 1853 entitled Discourses on the
Scope and Nature of University Education Addressed to the Catholics
of London. This review in 1859 was of Lectures and Essays on
University Subjects, which contained occasional lectures Newman
had addressed to members of the Catholic University. It was first
published in 1858, but Brownson stated: "Since we have read this

suffice. More attention needed to be paid to secular learning in philosophy, literature, and science. Just as the Jesuits had risen and revived Catholic learning throughout Europe after the Reformation, so too Brownson hoped the time was at hand to reapply these same principles in nineteenth century America by means of a Catholic University.[52]

During the Civil War and the succeeding years, Brownson published no major essays on higher education. Finally, he revived the question in October, 1874. He felt it his duty as a Catholic publicist not to lavish undeserved praise on Catholic colleges, but rather

> to point out their defects, and to urge the need of a higher and more thorough education than they now give, and thus stimulate the Catholic public to furnish from their abundance the means needed to obtain it.[53]

His primary objection was that Catholic colleges had not provided sufficient and sound instruction in theology and philosophy that enabled its graduates "to keep and defend their faith against the false sciences and miserable sophistry of this shallow but

---

volume by Dr. Newman, we have a deeper interest and greater confidence in the ultimate success of the University" (p. 552). Ironically, the year was 1859, and Newman had already resigned in 1858.

[52]Ibid., pp. 362-364. Brownson often felt Catholic parents needed enlightenment. If a University was to succeed, parents must leave their sons in college longer. Most withdrew at age sixteen or eighteen, and did not remain long enough to become scholars. By allowing their sons to remain another four or six years, only then would it be possible to have "the educated and highly-cultivated body of young men the interests of our religion and of our Catholic population demand" (p. 365). See also O. A. Brownson, "Catholic Polemics," BrQR, XVIII (July, 1861), 355-378.

[53]O. A. Brownson, "Letter to the Editor," BrQR, XXIII (October, 1874), 540.

pretentious age."[54] The philosophy in Catholic colleges was inadequate to combat the pantheism and atheism so prevalent in
society. Even "Jesuit philosophy," though better than any taught
outside of Catholic colleges, was nonetheless unable to meet and
refute the errors Catholics faced, or to save religion and
society.[55] Moreover, Catholic colleges had failed to produce
enough scholars, in fact, very few compared with England and
Ireland.[56]

In the final year of the Quarterly Review, Brownson wrote his
last essay on Catholic higher education.[57] He included two
letters--one from a college president, the other from a professor--
that cited the main weaknesses of Catholic higher education:
insufficient intellectual training and improper instruction in
sound Catholic philosophy. Brownson added that besides deficiencies in mental and moral culture, he also noticed weaknesses in
literary attainments and general knowledge. Even worse, many
graduates had become infidels, or nominal Catholics, with very
few taking active parts in the leadership of Catholic movements
and societies.

---

[54]Ibid., pp. 538-539.

[55]Ibid., pp. 542-543. See also O. A. Brownson, "Father Hill's
Philosophy," BrQR, XXIV (April, 1875), 260-280 and "Hill's
Elements of Philosophy," BrQR, XXIV (October, 1875), 490-515.
Similarly, another writer published three articles entitled "The
Necessity of Philosophy As a Basis of Higher Education," Catholic
World, XV (1872).

[56]O. A. Brownson, "Literary Notices and Criticisms," BrQR,
XXIV (October, 1875), 571.

[57]O. A. Brownson, "Our Colleges," BrQR, XXIV (April, 1875),
246-260.

Whence the failure, or only limited success of Catholic colleges?[58] Brownson believed the colleges were too bent on inculcating piety and religious practices, rather than intellectual stimulation and religious principles. Undoubtedly, he felt, Catholics had been influenced by Protestantism and its emphasis on religion of the heart. Catholicism itself was intellectual, rational, and even super-rational; it did move the heart, will and affections, but by instructing the understanding. In addition, Catholics in America required a more thorough understanding of the Catholic faith, for, unlike the situation in old Catholic countries, Catholics represented only a small minority in a society whose public opinion and power were on the side of their enemies. Moreover, Brownson still complained that eight-year olds were being admitted to some colleges, and that most of the graduates averaged seventeen to eighteen years of age. Certainly these young boys could not grasp philosophy or attain a mastery of languages at such an age.[59]

Brownson's remedy was again a four-level structure. The base was no longer the common school, but the parochial school, then the preparatory school, college, and at the head, the university. Religious orders, like the Jesuits, Lazarists, Christian Brothers were to take charge of the preparatory and college departments, while the university should be directed by the bishops or even the pope. It would be established on a broader basis than any

---

[58] Ibid., pp. 251-252.
[59] Ibid., pp. 252-254.

religious order could provide, and would enlist the most competent

professors available, whether members of religious orders or

laymen.[60] Only by improving this total institutional framework

could Catholic formal education influence the Catholic population,

elevate its intellectual, literary, and cultural tastes, and

create an environment where Catholic thought could influence

political and social decisions and actions.

That Catholic colleges were not all they should and could be,

Brownson did not deny. But he refused to label them utter failures

as some were doing.

> As unsuccessful as our Catholic colleges have been, they
> have not been more so than the non-Catholic colleges
> of the country, although they have labored under many
> disadvantages. Catholic schools and colleges are exotics,
> not the natural production of the country, and they are
> of very recent introduction; and established Catholic
> education has hardly yet been naturalized in any of
> the States. The country regards even the Church herself
> as a foreigner in our midst, as she would be if she
> were not catholic, and therefore at home in all nations,
> wherever she has an altar on which to offer the Holy
> Sacrifice. All things considered, we think it becomes
> us to be grateful for what our colleges have done,
> rather to complain of them for not having done more.
>   We discover, or think we discover, great defects
> in them. We think too much time is given to the Greek
> and Roman classics, and that the education given has
> a heathen rather than a Christian basis. Christianity
> is included in their curriculum, we grant, but it does
> not seem to us to be made its principle and groundwork.
> It is taught as supplementary to the classics; and too
> often the young men when they leave college lay it aside
> and retain only the classical heathenism, in which they
> were thoroughly grounded. We think the education
> should be more intellectual, and a more thorough course
> of philosophy should be taught, and a philosophy that
> is less heathen and more Christian, and more in
> accordance with the principles of things, more real,
> and dealing less in abstractions. But we must trust

---

[60]Ibid., pp. 254-255.

mainly to time to remedy these defects. We have had
to meet new social conditions, new wants, and to
adjust old systems to new circumstances, and with our
limited means, it was not to be expected that we could
reach perfection at a single bound.[61]

This final essay by Brownson on higher education reflected
the conservative turn he had taken since the mid 1860's. Parochial
schools became a part of his plan; he wanted more religious instruction as well as intellectual content; he wanted Catholics better
prepared to battle and refute the age, rather than join it; and
it seemed he was more thankful than critical concerning Catholic
institutional progress, even with its faults. Yet, his thankful-
ness did not prevent him from urging reform. He never rested
contently, claiming all was well. He gave his support to Catholic
colleges, as well as his advice. That some if not most of this
advice was critical, yet constructive, only adds to his reputation
as a true reformer, fulfilling his mission as a scholar.

Brownson's desire for an American Catholic University was
not fulfilled in his own lifetime. His dreams of an army of
Catholic scholars leading and directing American thought did not
occur either. But at least posterity could look at his efforts
and positively state that Orestes Brownson had helped point the
way to the improvement of Catholic higher education.

[61]Ibid., pp. 259-260.

CHAPTER V

THE FAMILY AS EDUCATOR

The American family had undergone historical change. During
the colonial period, the family was considered the prime agency of
education and socialization. The maxim of "honor thy father and
thy mother and thy superiors" was indicative of the hierarchical,
patriarchical family structure. Church and school were subservient
to the family. Yet legislation indicates that even then the family
was losing part of its authority in the American environment.[1]

During the late 1700's and early 1800's, children played an
even more enhanced role as democratic notions of individualism
and laissez-fairism made their way into the government, the economy,
the church, and the family. The hierarchical structure of the
family was undermined, and American child-rearing manuals encouraged parents to allow their children to form individual habits
and attitudes of mind. American children were more independent
and more socially precocious than their European counterparts.
Observers of the day remarked on the lessening of children's
politeness and deference toward adults. Children were more apt
than ever before to challenge statements of parents. The legal
rights of fathers became even more limited in judicial cases over

---

[1]Robert H. Bremner, Children and Youth in America: A Documentary History, 3 Vols. (Cambridge, Mass.: Harvard University
Press, 1970), I, pp. 27-42.

the custody of children.[2] Alexis de Tocqueville, in his observa-

tions of American society, remarked that

> in our time the several members of a family stand upon
> an entirely new footing towards each other; that the
> distance which formerly separated a father from his
> sons has been lessened; and that paternal authority,
> if not destroyed, is at least impaired . . . . In
> America the family, in the Roman and aristocratic
> signification of the word, does not exist.[3]

What de Tocqueville noted about American families became a

cause of concern to Orestes Brownson. The establishment of a

"Rights of Children's Society" had been proposed by what Brownson

called a "class of radicals among us who think it a gross outrage

upon natural rights that children should be required to obey their

parents."[4] In addition, Brownson believed that agitation of the

woman's rights question--husband-wife relationship, easier divorce,

and work equality--would further undermine the family structure,

deprive it of its rights, and cripple it in the performance of its

duties and obligations.[5]

---

[2]Ibid., pp. 131-144, 343-346.

[3]Democracy in America, trans. Henry Reeve, ed. Phillips
Bradley, II (New York: Alfred A. Knopf, 1945), p. 192; first pub-
ished in 1835 after de Toqueville had traveled in the United
States in 1831-1832.

[4]O. A. Brownson, "Spiridion. Par George Sand (Madame
Dudevant)," BoQR, V (April, 1842), p. 241. This essay was basically
a review of French literature, and included an analysis of content
and themes in the work of George Sand.

[5]Ibid., pp. 240-246. In The Convert Brownson later stated
that he found it remarkable how most reformers invariably find
fault with Christian marriage. Brownson believed, though, that
women do not admire men who cast off their manhood or are uncon-
scious of the rights and prerogatives of the stronger sex. Women
admire just as little those strong-minded women who strive to
excel in masculine virtues. "I have never been persuaded that it
argues well for a people when its women are men, and its men women.
Yet I trust I have always honored and always shall honor woman. I

Reading his words today, many would call Brownson a male
chauvinist. He believed the world of work was man's sphere of
activity, the duties of home woman's sphere. However, he did not
relegate woman's role to a position of inferiority. "In her own
sphere, as a wife, and a mother, in the quiet affections and
duties of home, which after all is the more important and the more
elevated sphere, we readily own woman's equality, and even her
superiority."[6] Woman, then, Brownson considered superior, for
she performed the most important functions as mother and wife.
These functions were not merely cooking and housekeeping; they
involved, most importantly, the education of children.

When Brownson discussed education and called for universal
schooling, he emphasized the education of both sexes:

> Woman's is the more important sex, and if but one
> half of our race can be educated, let it be woman,
> instead of man. Woman forms our character . . . .
> Her rank determines that of our race. If she be high
> minded and virtuous with a soul thirsting for that
> which is lofty, true and disinterested, so is it with
> the race. If she be light and vain, with her heart
> set on trifles, fond alone of pleasure--alas! for
> the community where she is so, it is ruined![7]

---

raise no question as to woman's equality or inequality with man,
for comparisons cannot be made between things not of the same
kind. Woman's sphere and office in life are as high, as holy, as
important as man's, but different, and the glory of both man and
woman is for each to act well the part assigned to each by Almighty
God." (pp. 215-216)

[6]Ibid., p. 240.

[7]Dedham Address, p. 22; see also Ibid., p. 244; and "Social
Evils and their Remedies," op. cit. The entire question of the
family as an educational agency (for good, of course) presupposes
the idea that adult family members were themselves educated.
Subsequent sections of this dissertation will discuss those
agencies responsible for the education of adults.

Woman, then, was the prime educator because education was, according to Brownson, character formation. He did not believe that woman alone was responsible for character formation; he wanted to see men as strong fathers in a patriarchical family structure. He believed that fathers should teach by example, and especially practice the habit and virtue of temperance. By following the good example of parents, children would also become temperate. But if parents were drunkards, they train "up their children to be nuisances to society, and a curse to themselves."[8]

Besides setting good example, parents had a direct obligation to teach their children.

> Go, teach your children virtue; go, imbue them with a love of goodness; 'train them up in the way they should go'; set them example worthy to be followed; by your kindness, your gentleness, your piety, your usefulness, arm them against crime, and fix their habits on the side of moral excellence.[9]

The idea of parents training their children for moral excellence was, basically, the same type of education that Brownson had received as a child. After he converted to Catholicism, Brownson

---

[8]O. A. Brownson, An Address on Intemperance, Delivered in Walpole, N. H. February 26, 1833 (Keene, H.H., 1833), p. 6. Recall that Brownson, in his diary, had also noted the dangers of drunkenness ten years earlier. Also, Brownson delivered many speeches, lectures and addresses on the evils of drinking to various lyceums, institutes and temperance societies.

[9]O. A. Brownson, An Address, Prepared at the Request of Guy . Clark, with the Intention of Having it Delivered to the Assembly on the Day of his Execution, Feb. 3, 1832 (Ithaca, 1832), p. 5 (italics Brownson's). In this speech on the day of Clark's hanging, Brownson argued that the best deterrent to crime was not by hanging a man as an example to deter others, but by educating children for moral excellence.

continued to advocate the necessity of moral education and the importance of the family's role in providing the right sort of education. The Catholic Church itself had long recognized these same educational needs.

The American hierarchy, from Bishop John Carroll's Pastoral Letter of 1792 up to the Fifth Provincial Council in 1843, repeatedly exhorted the clergy and laity upon the importance of a Christian upbringing. Parents were reminded of their primary obligation in the Christian education of their children. Christian education "can, in general, be far better attained under the parent's roof" emphasized the Pastoral Letter of 1829.[10] In the Pastoral Letter of 1843, parental obligations were again stressed as primary. "Parents are strictly bound, like faithful Abraham, to teach their children the truths which God has revealed; and if they suffer them to be led astray, the souls of the children will be required at their hands."[11] It is clear that in 1843, the Bishops considered the family as the primary educator of children.

However, recently arrived immigrant population created a Catholic community that was unsettled and still in the process of formation. The primary educator, the family, posed even more problems. Reports abounded of drunkards, illegitimate children, paupers, criminals, street beggars, vagrants, and pilferers among immigrant families. The low percentage of school attendance and

[10]"Pastoral Letter to the Laity (1829)," in Hugh J. Nolan, Pastoral Letters of the American Hierarchy 1792-1970 (Huntington, Indiana: Our Sunday Visitor, 1971), p. 25; all future references to any of the Pastoral Letters in this chapter will be taken from Nolan.

[11]"Pastoral Letter (1843)," p. 109.

fear of rowdies running the streets caused further alarm. Charges were made that immigrant parents, dissolute in their morals and filthy in their habits, would surely bring up children in their footsteps.[12] Not only did parents neglect to instruct their children, but many also chose not to send them to schools. The obvious problems stood clear: How could such parents educate for good? How could schools educate the Catholic population when so few children attended? Could schools accomplish much within this lower class community when families and neighborhoods failed to provide proper atmosphere, attitudes and values?

Brownson's most penetrating answers to these questions appeared in his review of Mrs. J. Sadlier's novel, The Blakes and Flanagans: A Tale Illustrative of Irish Life in the United States.[13] He praised the work not only as a piece of fiction, but more importantly for its high moral aim, "intended to impress upon the minds and hearts of parents the necessity of securing a Catholic education for their children."[14] Brownson noted that the Church considered the religious education of the young more important than anything else. But, as important as it was, the

[12]See Bremner, op. cit., pp. 398-434 for numerous documents supporting these contentions.

[13]O. A. Brownson, "The Blakes and Flanagans," BrQR, XIII (April, 1856), 195-212. Brownson became good friends with the Sadlier family, and eventually wrote for their New York Tablet

[14]Ibid., p. 199. Brownson did, however, object to Mrs. Sadlier's decision to single out the Irish. Brownson preferred that no distinctions be made over nationality. The question was not between Catholics and Americans, but between Catholic and non-Catholic society. "The interests, the wants, the trials, and the dangers of Catholics here are the same whatever their original nationality. The children of all . . . are alike exposed to the corrupting influences of a non-Catholic society" (p. 197).

religious education of Catholic children was not always practically
possible.

The vast multitude of immigrants pouring into the country
(before American Catholics had the time or means to properly
receive them), their poverty and their meager education, combined
with a scarcity of churches, priests, and teachers, created a situation where the administration of the sacramental system became an
absolute necessity and absorbed nearly all the time and efforts of
Catholic leaders. How could suitable provision be made for the
young without a hierarchy, priests, churches and fixed congregations? By the mid 1850's, Brownson believed the situation had
changed. He boasted of the institutional growth of the Church--
1,190 Churches, 7 archbishops and 35 bishops, 1761 priests, 33
Theological Seminaries, 5 preparatory seminaries, 26 incorporated
and 9 unincorporated colleges (more than any Protestant sect), 137
female academies, plus numerous convents, nunneries, hospitals,
and orphan asylums. Citing these Catholic accomplishments,
Brownson believed Catholics could no longer make excuses; the time
to act was at hand, especially with the swelling numbers of immigrants still entering the country.

What compounded matters was that many of these Catholic
parents were themselves uneducated and unable to provide proper
religious training for their children. This large number of unlettered peasants, small mechanics, servant girls, and common
laborers had not received sufficient intellectual, moral or
religious training in their native lands; here they would have to
exhaust themselves to obtain the bare necessities of physical

existence.[15] In Ireland, with a settled Catholic population, a child could "grow up wild" and still grow up a Catholic, because the tone and atmosphere of Irish society was Catholic. But in the United States, neglect a child and "he is equally sure to grow up a Protestant, or an unbeliever."[16] Catholic education for the young was a necessity to be secured at all costs.

Brownson agreed with Mrs. Sadlier that "one of the first and most necessary measures for the protection of our children is the establishment of Catholic day schools . . . . But we cannot agree with Mrs. Sadlier that they are themselves sufficient to secure our children."[17] Mrs. Sadlier had attempted to present a cause-effect relationship between Catholic school attendance and growing up to be a good Catholic. To illustrate her case, she showed Tim Flanagan sending his children to a Catholic school, and Miles Blake sending his to a public school. The Flanagans grew up good Catholics, and the Blakes bad Catholics. However, Brownson noted that Mrs. Sadlier failed to control for one major factor besides the school: home influences.

Miles Blake, a "sorry sort of Catholic," devoid of "any earnest conviction or living faith," failed to teach his son Harry his religion, or to love and practice it. He never warned his children of the dangers to which their religion was exposed. Instead he taught Harry to hate Yankee boys and encouraged him to fist fight. Soon, the boy realized he too was a Yankee, and grew to lose respect for his father, his religion, and his father's

_____

[15]Ibid., pp. 201-202; see also The Convert, pp. 418-424.
[16]"The Blakes and Flanagans," p. 202.
[17]Ibidem.

original country. Tim Flanagan, Blake's brother-in-law, was a
"sensible man," who loved his religion, and understood the dangers
to which his children were exposed. He taught his children to love
and practice their religion, and to honor it by their virtues and
their correct and winning deportment.

> With such a father and his judicious training, Ned
> Flanagan would have passed through the public schools
> even, with comparative safety. The home influences
> would have counteracted to a great extent the unfavor-
> able influences of the school room. The Catholic
> school, being as it was a very excellent school--not
> as such as some we have seen--was unquestionably an
> advantage, but even without it, Ned Flanagan would
> never have been a Harry Blake; nor with it would Harry
> Blake have been a Ned Flanagan. More depends on home
> and the family than on the school, and when parents
> are sufficiently interested and disposed themselves to
> train their children right at home, there is less
> danger than Mrs. Sadlier would have us believe in our
> public schools, bad as they are.[18]

This essay of 1856, when viewed along with his essays on schools
during that same period, can also be viewed as an attempt to allay
Catholic fears about losing the faith by attending common schools.
Brownson wanted it understood, though, that he disliked common
schools and was sympathetic to Catholic schools. "All we wish to
do here is, to guard against expecting from our day-schools what
they of themselves alone will not and cannot give, and against
attributing to the public schools what is really the fault of
Catholic parents."[19] Thus, Catholic parents by faithfully
performing their duties of home education, through good judgment,

---

[18]Ibid., pp. 203-204.
[19]Ibid., p. 204.

piety and intelligence, were the primary educators of the rising

generations of Catholics. Also, good Catholic parents were essen-

tial for assisting the school in its attempts to educate children.

Brownson seemed confident, in the mid 1850's, that good parents, by

honest effort, could adequately raise up their children to be firm

and dedicated Catholics.

However, during the shattering days of the Civil War, Brownson

wrote:

> The right sort of education is, in our age, especially
> in our country, a difficult thing, because the old
> notions of parental authority and filial obedience have
> been set aside as obsolete, and parents oftener obey
> their children than children their parents. But still
> it is the great thing, and can never be safely neglected.
> We, however, shall never make much progress in it till
> we get back to religion, and learn that Christianity
> is the supreme law, and the only true philosophy of
> life, whether private or public life, whether the life
> of individuals or of nations.[20]

Brownson wondered, though, just how did a nation get back to

religion. America had "taken the leap over Niagara Falls," and

only the intervention of Divine Providence seemed capable of

restoring and preserving true national greatness. The adult genera-

tion had lost its capacity to correctly rear up its children.

Society had become perverted, had lost faith in God, lacked confi-

dence in truth in the "unseen and Eternal." Instead, materialism

and its evils reigned throughout the land. Brownson lamented:

> Now, how can a society, so fallen and debased,
> bring up children as they should be brought up, since
> no parents, however just their own views, wise and

---

[20]O. A. Brownson, "Literary Notices and Criticisms," BrQR,
(January, 1863), 121.

judicious their treatment of their children, can wholly
protect them from the evil influence of their times.
The spirit of society will infect them more or less,
let us do the best we can. That spirit is in the
atmosphere, and is inhaled with every breath. There
is no human protection against it.[21]

America's only source of salvation lay in a return to faith and

religion.

The educational role played by the family had grown increas-

ingly more difficult; it was well-nigh impossible for the family

to perform the task alone. The family seemed to be losing its

effectiveness at a time when it was needed more than ever.

Brownson's acceptance of the Catholic school movement in 1862

becomes more readily understood. He now believed that the educa-

tional responsibilities of the family, which he had expected to be

fulfilled, in many cases were not being carried on; and even where

they were being carried on, the family needed more assistance.

Besides calling upon the Church and school to educate all Catholic

children, Brownson still considered the family crucial. For these

reasons, Brownson addressed himself to the issue of the importance

of the family itself, its structure and its functions.

Brownson's most complete statement on the family came in

October, 1875. In "The Family, Christian and Pagan," he viewed the

family as the primary social unit. It was "not only the basis of

society, but society itself; and as is the family, so is society."[22]

Logically, then, Brownson concluded that

[21]Ibid., p. 122.

[22]O. A. Brownson, "The Family, Christian and Pagan," BrQR,
XXIV (October, 1875), 469.

> if society is constituted by the family, the family is
> constituted by marriage, and marriage demands sanctity,
> unity, and indissolubility: three things which it
> lacked in the pagan world, and which it lacks also in
> the modern world, in proportion as the modern world
> ceases to be Catholic.[23]

Any social corruption, Brownson maintained, originated in the family

and eventually the corruption in the family would bring about the

ruin of society.   All efforts must be made, therefore, to preserve

the family and to keep it strong and Catholic.

Brownson traced the role of the family back to ancient Rome

and concluded that the decline of religion, and the subsequent

toleration of divorce and repudiation of marriage vows, led to

ultimate decline in everything else--the family, state, education,

and society itself.   True Christian or Catholic social order main-

tained the family until the Reformation, when Protestant ideas

proceeded to weaken and destroy the family by sanctioning divorce.

What resulted was a destruction of filial respect, love, and

obedience, thus rendering family government impracticable.

Democratic family notions destroyed mutual love and respect and

produced insubordination between the parents themselves as well

as children and parents, and disrespect and disobedience to duly

constituted religious and civil authority.   By thus rejecting the

Church, society attempted to resolve its problems by following

nature.   Because man was finite and imperfect, such a remedy could

never work.   Man needed elevation to the supernatural; this could

be accomplished only by restoring the purity and integrity of the

---

[23]Ibidem.

family and by returning to the Catholic idea of marriage: sanctity, unity, and indissolubility. Only by union with the supernatural through the Sacraments could society elevate and reform itself. Thus, Brownson insisted, as he always did, "that it is only by a return and filial submission to the Church that the wounds of modern society can be healed,"[24] for without the Church, the family would decay.

One threat to the family, Brownson warned, was the women's rights movement. Brownson praised womanhood, but reminded everyone that God had assigned specific roles for women. It was not man who designated certain roles for women, but God himself, and it was woman's duty to perform those duties. Brownson viewed the women's rights movement as a direct threat to the Christian family. Not only did most reformers advocate the abolition of marriage, but they denied the spiritual nature of the family and marriage. Furthermore, rights' advocates favored contraception and abortion. The destruction of authority, obedience and respect was inevitable; both the family and society faced destruction.[25] "The life of a nation is gone when the purity and the sanctity, the sacredness and inviolability of the family, are no longer maintained, and children are counted a nuisance instead of a blessing."[26] The

---

[24]Ibid., p. 489.

[25]Brownson addressed these issues several times. See the following by O. A. Brownson: "Miss Fuller and Reformers," BrQR, II (April, 1845), 249-257; "The Woman Question," Catholic World, IX (May, 1869), 145-157; "The Papacy and the Republic," BrQR, XXII (January, 1873), 22-25; "The Woman Question," BrQR, XXII (October, 1873), 508-529; and "The Family, Christian and Pagan," op. cit.

[26]"The Papacy and the Republic," p. 25.

preservation of the Christian family became paramount in such a
society, for it alone was capable of educating its children and
providing a Catholic atmosphere for proper development.

Throughout his entire life Brownson stressed the importance of
home education. He called on parents to procure good reading
material for their children;[27] he advised them to educate their
children in a religious manner,[28] and published another article
stressing the importance of domestic education.[29] It almost seems
that the older and more pessimistic Brownson got, the more he
emphasized the importance of home training and influence, the
spiritual nature of marriage, and the rights and duties of parents.
In the very last year of his Review, he reiterated his earlier
stand. "No matter how competent and excellent are the educators
employed /‾in schools‾/, they can effect little if the children
receive a bad or no home-education."[30]

Brownson's final remarks on the family, written exactly one
hundred years ago, could be submitted for publication with little
or no revision in any newspaper, journal, or magazine today. The
most significant study comparing the effects of Catholic and public
schools upon Catholic children concludes as Brownson did over a
century ago: the family--whether Blakes or Flanagans--is more
important a factor in the education of children than the school

---

[27]Brownson reviewed The Redbreast, The Forget-me-not, and
nselmo, all by the German Christopher von Schmid. See "Literary
otices and Criticisms," BrQR, V (July, 1848), 410-411.

[28]"The Blakes and Flanagans," op. cit.

[29]See Jeremiah W. Cummings, "Domestic Education," BrQR, XV
(October, 1858), 523-543.

[30]See Brownson's review of Bishop Dupanloup's The Child in
Literary Notices and Criticisms," BrQR, XXIV (July, 1875), 438.

is, especially in terms of values, attitudes, beliefs, and character formation.[31] At the same time, familial discipline and parental
authority have continually eroded; parents seem to obey their
children. The corruption of society--whether seen in political
scandals, lowering of sexual mores, or the drug or drink culture--
make it even more difficult for parents to raise children.
Increased divorce, legalized abortion, women's liberation, abolition of marriage--all appear today in much greater proportions
than in Brownson's day. Social workers and police who work with
juvenile offenders invariably (with few exceptions) lay the blame
of wayward youths upon defective home education and environment.
And just as Brownson attempted to get parents more involved with
the domestic training of their children, rather than delegating
all responsibility to the school, so today the Church since Vatican
II has stressed the importance of responsible parenthood in the
Christian upbringing of children.

---

[31]Andrew M. Greeley and Peter H. Rossi, The Education of
Catholic Americans (Aldine Publishing Company, 1966).

CHAPTER VI

THE CHURCH AS EDUCATOR

Brownson's conception of the need for the church to lead

society did not arise during his Catholic period, nor was the

pessimism of his old age merely the result of calamities such as

the Civil War. He may have intensified his pleas for religious

elevation toward the end of his life, but he had always viewed

the ministry as performing an educational function, and had long

noted the religious weakness of the country.

> The Christian ministry was instituted expressly for
> the education of the people; and it is in the preachers
> of Christianity comprehending and embracing the whole
> scope of their office as educators of the people, I
> find among the chief powers competent to effect the
> peaceful regeneration of society.[1]

By the "regeneration of society," Brownson meant spiritual and

social amelioration and progress. Education formed the base of

his scheme of progress, and the Church, through its ministers,

was among the most important agents in the work of regeneration.

In Brownson's semi-autobiographical, semi-fictional account

of Charles Elwood, or the Infidel Converted, he cited several

reasons why society desperately needed regeneration: the reli-

gious world was all but dead; the church had practically lost all

---

[1]"Social Evils and their Remedies," op. cit. See also O. A.
Brownson, New Views of Christianity, Society, and the Church
(Boston: James Munroe & Company, 1836), pp. 115-116.

sense of its mission; men were indifferent to their duties as
religious and social beings; and the world of materialism seemed
to engross the minds and hearts of the community. Something was
needed to awaken man's conscience, to rescue him from selfishness
and worldly-mindedness, to make him conscious of his higher and
better nature and destiny.[2] Brownson's answer, of course, was in
a clergy with strong and bold minds, able to communicate with
people and to effect action and reform. The ability of mind to
act upon mind, and of mind to act upon matter, was basic to all
progress in society and in individuals.

> One mind acts upon another in quickening its
> powers and directing its forces. Many minds thus
> become quickened, become aware of what is needed to
> be done, and by their combined action and force they
> attack outward circumstances and bring them into
> harmony with our moral and spiritual nature.[3]

Brownson regarded the clergy as primarily responsible for steering
mankind to work for social and religious progress.[4]

---

[2]O. A. Brownson, Charles Elwood, or the Infidel Converted
(London: Chapman Brothers, 1840), pp. 25-26. (Originally written
in 1834, but withheld from publication by Brownson for six years.)

[3]See "Means of Effecting a Reform," op. cit.

[4]In his own work as a minister, Brownson had engaged in two
such projects already discussed: the Unitarian Committee for the
Diffusion of Christian Truth, and the formation of his own Society
for Christian Union and Progress. Besides what he actually did
in these functions, Brownson wrote and spoke on the specific role
of the Church and its ministry to effect reform. Brownson's
friend, Isaac B. Peirce, after reading Brownson's article in the
Christian Examiner and General Review, XX (May, 1836), p. 158,
wrote: "I agree with you that the people must be educated, and
the clergy must do it." Peirce wished Brownson well in his Boston
venture, the Society for Christian Union and Progress.
    Brownson had given credit to William Ellery Channing for
influencing his religious beliefs. Channing, then, in the early
1830's, pushed Brownson's mind to accept Christianity as a principle of reform--a reform intended to improve individuals, the

The clergy must, first of all, perform the traditional and commonly supposed role of working for the salvation of souls. The Church had always taught men and women to be moral and religious, and had presented hell as the alternative for the wicked. The Church had also played a role in the teaching of reading, writing, grammar, theology, philosophy, history, geography, geology, and many other things. All of these things Brownson considered good, proper and indispensable for the progress of man and society; yet more work was needed:

> But it does not enlighten. It does not prepare our sons and daughters to meliorate the condition of Humanity. All has reference to things as they are, not to the modifying of what is unpropitious in outward circumstances, of altering the social organization or of bringing the outward condition of man into harmony with his nature.[5]

This, then, was the second, and most important, role for the clergy to perform: working for social improvement in this life. Brownson realized that this function ran contrary to current belief. Many felt that the pulpit was not the proper place to discuss man's political and social state. Brownson, at least during the late 1830's and early 1840's, however, called for such a pulpit. He was not disposed to abolish religion, the Church, or its ministers-- all were basically good and moral, yet the whole institution

---

community, and the whole fabric of society. As one clergyman to another, Channing told Brownson that all clergy must feel obligated "to labour unceasingly for the intellectual and moral redemption of the large class of ignorant, poor, / and / depressed." See Dr. Channing to O.A.B., January 11, 1834, OABP, UNDA.

[5]"Means of Effecting a Reform."

needed to redirect its emphasis.[6]

Brownson felt that the pulpit often forgot that individual character was influenced by social settings and institutions which were unjust and in opposition to the individual. After all, the true mission of society, Brownson asserted, was to assist the development of the individual. When society, by institutions and laws, impeded instead of aided this progress, "the pulpit is desecrated only by silence,"[7] not by rebuking social injustice.

> It is beginning to be discovered that men are not all evil; that the vices of individual character are, in no inconsiderable degree, the consequences of social vices, and social institutions. If this be so, it must be vain to expect a very general improvement of private character, without reforming the social principles, which have influenced private character, and prevent improvement.[8]

Brownson used the term "influenced" rather than "determined" in describing the impact of social surroundings upon man's action. After all, man was free and not all of his vices could be attributed to society. But man was not pure will; obstructions within society did influence and affect man's decisions. Prevalent social principles were unfavorable to man's spiritual culture, and the clergy must work to ameliorate such conditions.

---

[6]Brownson no doubt was influenced here by the economic setback of 1837 and its consequences. Much of his thought at this time emphasized social justice for the laboring classes and the redistribution of the fruits of labor. He mentioned these items in "Means of Effecting a Reform" and "Social Evils and their Remedies." See his published writings in BoQR during the 1840-1842 period.

[7]"Social Evils and their Remedies."

[8]Ibidem.

One major difficulty faced by the clergy was their own education. They had been trained to regard man's individual salvation
and man's relation with God. Brownson remarked that the clergy
had been ineffective in promoting man's true end, and even had
become obstacles in his religious development. Instead of only
preaching the duty of citizens to the state, the clergy must teach
the prior rights of citizens, and the obligation of the state to
its citizens. They must speak out against unjust laws and social
oppressions. "Let them, in short, embrace in all its extent the
idea of social progress; and I can conceive of nothing, that would
give a mightier impulse to private and social improvement."[9] The
role Brownson assigned for the clergy was similar to the mission
of the scholar; furthermore, the work he had been doing as a
minister, especially in Boston, certainly influenced his views
concerning the educational role of the clergy.

Social improvement was inextricably linked to politics.
Brownson's scheme, therefore, viewed the clergy as capable of
influencing political decisions. "The true science of politics is
simply the application of the principles of Christianity to the
social relations of man."[10] Brownson believed that the gospel
announced glad tidings to the poor, stressed human equality before
God, denounced oppression, and promised the regeneration of society
as its end. In this sense, Christianity, with the aid of the
Church and its ministers, served as a vehicle of social progress.

[9] Ibidem.
[10] Ibidem.

Brownson realized his proposal might cause embarrassment, and even sacrifice and suffering. Society just was not prepared to accept such a ministry. But, just as the scholar was years ahead of his contemporaries, so too ministers needed to possess honesty and boldness, and to act from the deepest conviction in uncovering the present state of society for what it was, and for laboring to bring about the type of society that ought to be.

The minister, then, must obligate himself to address the intellect and heart of men and to convince them that the moral and intellectual forces the Church collected would be directed to accomplishing this end.[11] Brownson's remedy called for setting man's mind to work in the right direction. It would discover the causes of human vices and woes, and immediately work for the solution and improvement. "The great instrument after all is mind. Mind is the only real power in the universe."[12] If mind was the great instrument of social progress, the clergy, as Brownson perceived them, certainly played a major role in bringing about intellectual, social, moral, and religious progress.

These views that Brownson maintained prior to his conversion undoubtedly carried over to his Catholic period. He asserted that the Church's primary goal was to instruct and educate Catholics in matters of faith and morals. Bishops and priests must see to it that parents were "thoroughly grounded in the principles of Catholicity, and thoroughly emancipated in their intelligence,

---

[11]"Means of Effecting a Reform."

[12]Ibidem.

habits, and manners from paganism."[13] Just as he had advocated
some forty years earlier, Brownson believed the new generation was
to be educated by the old. Unless adults and parents were educated properly, they would neutralize the best training available
in schools and colleges. By educating adults, the community became
educated; hence, the spiritual growth of children facilitated.
Only by properly educating adults could children be secured in
their faith and morals. Obviously, then, it was only a thorough
Catholic education, such as only the Catholic Church can give,
"rendered efficient by her sacraments," that secured the eternal
salvation of the soul, and sustained the republic.[14]

Brownson proposed several ways for the Church to educate.
First of all, sermons provided a basic educational structure
between priest and those present at Mass. Sermons should deal
with dogmatic truth, instructing Catholics about their daily moral
and religious duties. Sermons should "bring home to our own
hearts, our consciences, and our convictions, everyday truths, and
stir us up from the depth of our souls to practice our ordinary
duties."[15] Besides teaching moral duty, sermons should also aim
to assert and explain Catholic dogma. Brownson praised the efforts
made by the Paulists, who had presented nearly all the great

[13]O. A. Brownson, "Education and the Republic," BrQR, XXIII
January, 1874), 52.

[14]Ibid., p. 53-54.

[15]O. A. Brownson, "Sermons by the Paulists," BrQR, XX (April,
863), 161-162; in this essay, Brownson heartily endorsed the
ublication Sermons preached at the Church of St. Paul the
postle, New York, during the year 1862 (New York: Sadlier & Co.,
862), pp. 393.

Catholic mysteries in their book of sermons--Trinity, Incarnation,

Redemption, Original Sin, Grace, Sacraments, Church, Penance, Holy

Eucharist, Mass, Real Presence, Virgin Mary, Saints, Purgatory,

Indulgences, etc. In sum, Brownson viewed sermons as vehicles of

moral suasion and as an intellectual basis for spiritual truth.

Secondly, Brownson urged the Church to start a new translation

of the Bible and to get Catholics reading it.[16] Biblical scholar-

ship, Brownson felt, fell naturally into the hands of the Catholic

Church which had always encouraged the reverential and pious study

and meditation of the "Book of books."[17] The Church must annotate

and explain, must make intelligible the meaning of the Bible and

thus provide the necessary instruction that must accompany the

Scriptures.[18] Also, a new translation must be "good, faithful, and

elegant," more readable than the Latinized Douay version. Brownson

preferred the rich language of the King James Version and called

for a translation using it as a basis, but correcting it "according

to the readings of the Vulgate, and avoiding its mistranslations

and its few grammatical and literary errors."[19] What Brownson

hoped to accomplish by such a translation was to supplant the King

---

[16]Brownson was gratified at the appearance of Introduction
Historique et Critique aux Livres du Noveau Testament (1861), a
two volume translation and annotation of the New Testament.

[17]See O. A. Brownson, "Reading and Study of the Scripture,"
BrQR, XVIII (October, 1861), 492-509.

[18]Brownson believed that Christian and Evangelical sects, not
merely Catholics, actually questioned the validity of allowing
the Bible to speak for itself. Why else did Protestants have
Sunday Schools, catechisms, commentaries, theological seminaries,
professors of theology, preachers and teachers, but to prepare
their co-religionists for reading and understanding the Bible.
See Ibid., p. 499.

[19]Ibid., p. 504; Brownson believed the King James Version was
created at a time when the English language had reached its

James Bible for the English speaking world, to get Catholics and
Protestants to agree on a common Bible, to remove many obstacles
Catholics faced in schools, and to relieve Catholics from the necessity of establishing separate schools. Finally, he considered the
Holy Scriptures "the best means of enlightening and confirming
. . . faith, of elevating . . . devotion, of purifying and
strengthening . . . piety, and giving robustness and vigor to
. . . religious life."[20] For all these reasons, then, Brownson
urged the Church to produce a new translation of the Bible and to
encourage more widespread reading and study on the part of
Catholics.

Thirdly, Brownson repeatedly argued the case for missions
and retreats on two grounds: 1) the salvation of Catholics; and
2) the conversion of non-Catholics. Saving Catholic souls, for
Brownson, was the primary function of missions. A pastor's
responsibility included care of the faithful of the parish and
their children and the re-conversion of lax Catholics.[21] One of
the best means of accomplishing these ends was the creation of
movable missions and missionaries.[22] Throughout the country

---

eak. The Rheims New Testament of 1582, and the Douay New Testament of 1609 were produced by exiled Englishmen, more in tune with
Latin and French, than with English. Brownson also criticized
Archbishop Kenrick's edition of the Bible; even though it was an
improvement, it still fell "far short of what an English Translation of the Holy Scriptures should be."

[20]Ibid., p. 509.

[21]O. A. Brownson, "Aspirations of Nature," BrQR, XIV (October,
1857), 495.

[22]See O. A. Brownson, "Revivals and Retreats," BrQR, XV (July,
1858), 303-306 in which he traces the history of formal Catholic
missions dating back to the Dominican and Franciscan Orders of the
13th century, and informally, back to Apostolic times.

missions had met with remarkable success, Brownson noted. Religious enthusiasm was heightened by the Catholic program of mass, sermons, courses of instruction, lectures, and confessions. The number of Church attendants and communion recipients skyrocketed.[23]

Brownson regarded missions as adjuncts to the work performed by pastors in quickening the faith, conscience and piety of parishioners, and fostering the habits of prayer, and regular attendance at Mass. Furthermore, missions attempted to produce permanent changes by helping to eliminate Catholic faults:

> the conversion of bad Catholics, the proper training of Catholic children, the correction of the vice of intemperance, and other immoralities, . . . and the introduction of morality, good order, sobriety, and economy, into what are now haunts of drunkenness, dens of vice, and petty crimes.[24]

Eliminating faults was indispensable for Catholic progress. By elevating the Catholic adult population, children would receive a better home environment and education; moreover, the development of a Catholic atmosphere in society would be enhanced. With the ever-increasing secularization of American life, "the reliance must be on the missionary rather than the schoolmaster"[25] for securing a truly Catholic atmosphere.

---

[23]Ibid., p. 308. Brownson had been in continuous touch with Isaac Hecker who reported the progress of all Paulist missionary efforts. See letters from Hecker to Brownson dated 1851?, May 15, 1851, September 5, 1851; January 6, 1852; September 14, 1854; February, 1855; March 27, 1855; April 7, 1855; August 7, 1855; September 1, 1857; November 27, 1857, OABP, UNDA.

[24]"Aspirations of Nature," p. 495; see also O. A. Brownson, "Weninger's Protestantism and Infidelity," BrQR, XIX (April, 1862), 253-259.

[25]O. A. Brownson, "The Papacy and the Republic," op. cit., p. 28.

Brownson also viewed the uplifting of the Catholic populace

as a primary means of converting non-Catholics. Lower class

actions and morals could never induce Protestants to accept member-

ship in the Catholic Church. The good example displayed by

Catholics

> would do more for the conversion of non-Catholics than
> all the books and reviews we can write, all the journals
> we can edit, or efforts we can make expressly for their
> conversion, for it would prove to them what they now
> doubt, the practical moral efficiency of our religion.[26]

Besides good example, Brownson felt that Catholics were

obligated to do everything possible to convert all Americans to

Catholicism, since Catholicism was the true religion, the only

religion capable of effecting and sustaining American growth and

progress. The chief means of bringing about the conversion of

America was the mission. Brownson cited the work of his long

time friends, the Paulists, and the Redemptorists, and a group of

Jesuits headed by the Reverend Francis X. Weninger, as examples

for future efforts. What seemed to Brownson to be a logical,

necessary, common sense approach to Catholicizing America, in

reality turned out to be a difficult task.

For several reasons, Brownson remarked, Church authorities

hesitated to launch an all-out missionary effort to convert

America. With a shortage of priests, all available clergy were

needed to work with the Catholic population. The luxury of

---

[26]"Aspirations of Nature," p. 495.

having too many priests, or even enough, did not exist.[27]   Also,

the bishops seemed to doubt the possibility of making converts

among Americans, were reluctant to sanction certain apologetical

approaches, and finally, the foreign-dominated hierarchy seemed

content to maintain the Church along European, national lines and

did not care to bring native Americans into the fold.

Brownson called for the hierarchy to change their attitude

toward converting non-Catholics. Throughout the 1850's and 1860's,

Brownson received glowing reports of the successes of the

Redemptorists, Jesuits, and Paulists in conducting missions

primarily for Catholics;[28] he saw no reason why such success could

not be met in converting non-Catholics. As early as 1851, Fr.

Isaac Hecker wrote Brownson of success in converting some non-

Catholics. In 1857, Hecker attempted to make arrangements for an

American House of his congregation to be missionaries to America.[29]

In the same year, a priest in Georgia wrote Brownson asking for a

reading list, and remarked that Protestants had occasionally

---

[27]Throughout his Catholic period, Brownson realized the need
for more vocations to the religious life, of both men and women.
And in the final year of his Review, he wrote: "When and where
these vocations are numerous, there is life, there is hope. All
Christians, it seems to us, should pray our Lord that these vocations may be multiplied. In no way can we labor more effectually
for the diffusion of our faith, and the conversion of our country.
O. A. Brownson, "Literary Notices and Criticisms," BrQR, XXIV
(July, 1875), 413.

[28]See 23 above.

[29]Hecker was turned down, his vows were relaxed and he was
dismissed from the Redemptorists by the General of the Congregation. Hecker was unable to get a hearing in Rome before the
decision was made. See O.A.B. to Hecker, August 5, 1857, Paulist
Archives; Hecker to O.A.B., September 1, 1857, OABP, UNDA; O.A.B.
to Hecker, September 29, 1857, Paulist Archives. Later, Hecker's
requests were approved, and a new Congregation, the Paulists, was
formed.

requested him to preach.

> The more I travel the more do I find that Protestants
> are anxious to hear an explanation of Catholic
> doctrine . . . . I find so much honesty and sincer-
> ity among many of our Georgians . . . . Many of them
> are disgusted with the eternal calumnies against
> Catholicism which form the principle theme for a
> horde of brainless preachers. Though these calumnies
> have been refuted a thousand times by you and others,
> yet the refutation of them is to our Georgia Protes-
> tants a dead letter, for they never see what you and
> others write.[30]

The fact that Protestants did not get to read Catholic arguments,

but seemed willing to listen to them, reinforced Brownson's notion

that missions could solve this problem and effect the conversion

of America.

If missions were to be successful, though, they must be con-

ducted under a new framework. Brownson advised Hecker that the

'old controversialists" had their own method and tended to suspect

and distrust any new approaches. Brownson saw the need to refute

old errors in new ways. He especially approved of Hecker's way,

as presented in Hecker's Questions of the Soul and Aspirations of

ature, and in Weninger's Protestantism and Infidelity: an Appeal

o candid Americans. These new methods involved approaches to the

heart as well as to the head. Traditional methods--exclusively

ntellectual, logical, and fault finding--were the worst ones.[31]

nstead, methods that appealed to religious feelings, man's heart

---

[30]Fr. James Hasson to O.A.B., October 14, 1857, OABP, UNDA.
asson also referred to the shortage of priests. He was the only
atholic priest within 100 miles of Macon, Georgia.

[31]Brownson placed himself in this category. See O.A.B. to
r. (Augustine F.) Hewit, March 17, 1856, OABP, UNDA.

and conscience, that showed dogmas and mysteries of the Catholic
faith answering the requirements of reason, and that emphasized
the Sacraments filling the wants of the heart--these were the
appropriate methods for converting America.[32] Almost in the same
way that Brownson had earlier criticized the extremes of both
Catholicity and Protestantism, now he advocated apologetical
methods that combined arguments appealing to both the head as well
as the heart. Yet new methods were not enough. Brownson saw
another major difficulty in presenting Catholicism to the American
people. A large number of Bishops had a "settled conviction that
nothing can be done for their conversion. They are not missionaries."[33] Moreover, the hierarchy, along with priests and laity,
were too national, too Irish, and wanted to keep the Church that
way. But Brownson had always objected to nationalism within the
Church; the Church was catholic, not Irish, not French, not German,
not even American; it was universal, for all mankind, including
Americans. Brownson expressed disappointment when Hecker's plans
for an American order of Redemptorists was rejected; for he agreed
with Hecker that it was the mission of America to become a Catholic
nation, and that missionary efforts could effect the conversion
of non-Catholics.

Brownson's optimism over America's conversion continued into
the early 1860's. Still believing it was a Catholic duty to
convert America, he felt that "the time was never more favorable

---

[32]See Hecker to Brownson letter of September 14, 1854; March
27, 1855; and April 7, 1855, OABP, UNDA.

[33]O.A.B. to Hecker, June ?, 1855, Paulist Archives.

than now."[34] The calamities of the Civil War, distress throughout
the country, failure of Americans' hopes and plans,

> have disposed the great body of the American people
> to thoughtfulness, shaken their confidence in most of
> the radicalisms in religion, politics, and morals, so
> rife a few years ago, made them more ready to listen
> to the wisdom of past ages /⁻the Catholic Church⁻7,
> and to be told that the true future must have its root
> in what has been, and be simply its evolution and
> development.[35]

Progress was achieved not by radical revolution but by gradual
evolution. Brownson had always tempered his optimist about missionary efforts; both Hecker and Weninger, Brownson asserted, regarded
American's conversion as a much easier, simpler affair than he
did.[36]

The old expression "by their fruits ye shall know them" contained much meaning for Brownson. In America many Catholic
"fruits" were basically faults; hence Protestants received improper
notions of what Catholicism actually was. Until Catholics cleaned
up their own backyard first, little chance existed that they would
attract Protestants into the garden of salvation.[37] In the late
1860's, Brownson was less optimistic that Protestants were at all
willing to join the Church. As anxious as he was for the conversion of the country, after years of observation and experience,
Brownson concluded that

---

[34]O. A. Brownson, "Weninger's Protestantism and Infidelity,"
BrQR, XIX (April, 1862), 245.
[35]Ibidem.
[36]See O.A.B. to Hecker, September 29, 1857, Paulist Archives.
[37]See "Weninger's Protestantism and Infidelity," pp. 252-263.

it is to be effected, or not at all, by the gradual
/‾e‾/xpression, growing influence, and untiring zeal
of our old Catholic population. No direct efforts
intended to operate specially on American non-Catholics
will effect much. The American people . . . will
never become Catholics through any systematic efforts
we may make for their conversion.[38]

By 1870, Brownson, old, conservative, and pessimistic, told

Hecker that the Church had made little impression on the American

population. He regarded Catholicism and democracy as incompatible

with one another.[39] He seemed to despair of Catholic missionary

efforts to convert non-Catholics. In each of the last three

volumes of his Review, however, Brownson called for more vocations

to the priesthood, more missions and missionaries, and still

insisted that America would be converted. He concluded an essay,

"Education and the Republic," by reasserting his belief that

American progress would be achieved by education, though, only if

the people were converted to Catholicism. This conversion was to

occur not by missionary efforts to non-Catholics; "our reliance

for its conversion is on missions and the missionary orders, who

strengthen the faithful, quicken their zeal, and recall them to

their duties."[40] Brownson's skepticism of missionary appeals to

non-Catholics during the late 1860's and 1870's merely is another

reflection of his increasing pessimism regarding American society.

Also, it indicates another sign of his withdrawal from the secular

---

[38]O.A.B. to James Sadlier, April 2, 1867, OABP, UNDA.

[39]O.A.B. to Hecker, August 2, 1870, Paulist Archives.

[40]O. A. Brownson, "Education and the Republic," BrQR, XXIII
(January, 1874), 54. See also "Literary Notices and Criticisms,"
BrQR, XXIV (July, 1875), 409-413 and "The Papacy and the Republic,"
BrQR, XXII (January, 1873), 27-28.

society and his concerted effort to build up all things of Catholic origin--whether it be reforming schools and colleges, strengthening the family, or directing missionary efforts at Catholics. Catholicizing America became a job of Catholicizing Catholics first, who in turn by their example, influence, and zeal, would bring about a Catholic America.

Obviously, much of Brownson's scheme relied on the success of educating Catholic adults, who in turn would instruct their children. However much faith and confidence he professed concerning the benefits of good home education, Brownson was well aware that many parents were not providing sound Christian education. The 1840's had brought 700,000 more immigrant Catholics to America, most of whom were beset with problems.

> Owing to the poverty of a large class of our people, their little acquaintance in their own country with the dangers of town life, and their neglect or inability, from various causes, to educate their children as they should be at home, there is in all our cities an undue proportion of Catholic children, orphans, or worse than orphans, that crowd our streets and grow up rowdies.[41]

Where parents failed to provide home education, even worse, where they did not even furnish a home, it was the responsibility of the Church to establish oprhanages for the preservation of Catholic youth. Brownson believed that a child belonged to God, his parents, and the state, in that order. The Church, as God's representative, worked in conjunction with the family in the moral

---

[41]O. A. Brownson, "Literary Notices and Criticism," BrQR, III (January, 1851), 122.

and religious education of children; the state Brownson relegated to a tertiary role.

However, modern political philosophy had adopted the view that the child belonged to the state; hence, the state became involved in the maintenance and education of orphans. Besides the state, Protestant philanthropy aided homeless children. Neither group, though, cooperated with either the Catholic clergy or religious nuns in looking after the faith and morals of Catholic children; instead, state and Protestant institutions and charities merely provided "for the body at the expense of /̲Catholic̲7̲ souls."[42] The major hindrance to Catholic efforts in providing orphanages was money; accordingly Brownson urged public authorities, private associations, and liberal individuals "to aid our clergy in training up these children in the religion of their parents, that is, to relieve the Catholic poor as Catholics"[43] by building Catholic orphanages and by allowing priests and nuns to visit public institutions and instruct Catholic youth. Without Catholic religious instruction, Catholic youths would certainly be the pests of society, for only the Catholic Church was able to produce moral and spiritual attitudes conducive to individual and social progress. Protestant charities were "emissaries of Satan, the prime conspirators against the souls of poor boys."[44] Catholic

---

[42]Ibid., p. 124.

[43]Ibidem.

[44]Ibid., p. 123; see also O. A. Brownson, "Sick Calls," BrQR, IX (January, 1852), 130-131.

charity not only uplifted man's bodily condition, but supplied his spiritual wants as well.

Neither the state nor Protestant charities paid any attention to Brownson's suggestions.[45] It is doubtful whether Brownson ever really thought that they would. He could only hope that Catholic institutional growth would be able to rescue increasing numbers of Catholic children, otherwise lost to Protestantism or infidelity. Catholic immigration continued to increase--985,000 in the 1850's and 741,000 in the 1860's--and problems of poverty and ignorance, a shortage of priests and churches, all hindered the Church's efforts.[46] The Church, though, increasingly realized these same dangers to Catholic youth. In the Second Plenary Council of 1866, the Prelates called it a "melancholy fact" and were forced to make

---

[45]For another related manner, see Fr. Pierre De Smet to O.A.B., June 2, 1852, OABP, UNDA in which De Smet complained about government Indian missionary policies. Protestant missionaries were receiving all the good public land for missionary work, even though Catholics were more effective civilizers and educators of Indians. In several cases, De Smet claimed, Indian requests for Catholic missionaries in their schools had been rejected.

[46]See "Spes" to O.A.B., November 11, 1862, OABP, UNDA in which the author charged that clerical ambivalence, if not antipathy, toward initiative on the part of the laity, prevented the work of salvation. He cited a case involving the establishment by Sunday school teachers from various eastern cities of an organization aimed at preventing the state from snatching Catholic children away from parents and placing them in Protestant institutions to be fed, clothed, and proselytized. A convention was called in 1855, with several clergy invited, one of whom presided as chairman. After discussing various opinions on the feasibility of the organization and the present dangers of losing more children to Protestantism, the clergy caucused and finally rejected the enterprise. Thus, a movement, that allegedly would have involved five thousand Sunday School teachers, to secure Catholic orphans in New York, Brooklyn, Jersey City, and Newark, was squelched, never to meet again. Even worse, no substitute plan was adopted.

"humiliating avowal" that a very large portion of the idle and vicious youth were children of Catholic parents. Despite the efforts made in establishing orphanages, still more needed to be done. The Pastoral urged the formation of Catholic Protectories and Industrial Schools to correct the "waywardness of youth," and to plant "good seed."[47] Brownson continued his concern over what he called Catholic "street Arabs," and called for intensified efforts by parents and priests to secure good home education, and where possible, to establish orphanages, asylums, protectories, reformatories, Sunday schools and parish schools in order to secure Catholic upbringing and education for these children.[48]

All the educational functions of the Church, in establishing and directing orphanages, in teaching and elevating Catholics, in sending missionaries to Catholics and non-Catholics, presupposed one basic necessity: an educated clergy. Brownson's schemes, hopes, and dreams for the Church's success were based on the availability of a sufficiently large clergy, an enlightened clergy, and eventually, a clergy composed mainly of native Americans, who would perform sacerdotal duties in advancing God's cause.

The Church had long realized its educational responsibilities and problems. The shortage of priests and the need for vocations was expressed by the Bishops in the Pastoral Letters of 1792, 1829, 1833, 1837, and 1840. The First Plenary Council of 1852

[47]"Pastoral Letter (1866)," contained in McCluskey, pp. 84-85.

[48]See O. A. Brownson, "Catholic Popular Literature," BrQR, XXII (April, 1873), 186-187 and O. A. Brownson, "Maria Monk's Daughter," BrQR, XXIV (January, 1875), 70-74.

stated that "the education of candidates for the ministry is one
of our most urgent wants."[49]   With the population rapidly expanding,
the religious needs of the laity called for even more ministers
of God. Not only did the Church seek to increase the number of
clergy, but their quality as well. The First Provincial Council
of 1829 addressed a "Pastoral Letter to the Clergy" to remind them
that they were the "Light of the World"; and that they should seek
sacerdotal perfection in discharging their duties. Meditation,
prayer, Scripture reading and the study of theology and church
history would help uplift the members of the clergy. As ambassa-
dors of Christ it was their duty to zealously perform the duties
of the sacramental ministry and the liturgy. It was a clerical
duty to instruct youth and to encourage others (parents and
teachers) who also devoted themselves to the instruction of
children.[50]

The education of priests, according to John Tracy Ellis,
suffered from many defects at this time. Seminaries were often
small and feeble foundations, drained the Church's meager personnel
and financial resources, and offered a static curriculum.[51]

---

[49]"Pastoral Letter (1852)," p. 137.

[50]"Pastoral Letter to the Clergy (1829)," pp. 34-47.

[51]John Tracy Ellis, "Short History of Seminary Education," in
James Michael Lee and Louis J. Putz, eds., Seminary Education in a
Time of Change (Notre Dame, Ind.: Fides Publishers, 1965), pp.
3-68; see also Lloyd Paul McDonald, "The Seminary Movement in the
United States 1784-1833" (Unpublished Doctoral dissertation, The
Catholic University of America, 1927); and William S. Morris, The
Seminary Movement in the United States: Projects, Foundations, and
Early Development 1833-1866 (Washington: Catholic University of
America Press, 1932); John Tracy Ellis, The Catholic Priest in the
United States: Historical Investigations (Collegeville, Minnesota:
Saint John's University Press, 1971).

Facilities in the United States were such that many seminarians
found it necessary and more practical to study abroad. The
Bishops realized that if the Church was to take root in the United
States, it was indispensable to develop a native clergy.

Brownson basically agreed with the Bishops' call for more
priests, better priests, and native priests. Certainly the effort
of striving for improvement was commendable; anything that
approached Brownson's ideal was praise-worthy. Although Brownson
himself considered the Catholic clergy better prepared than
Protestant ministers, especially in logical training, theological
sciences, and erudition,[52] nevertheless they were below what they
should be.

One development that Brownson greeted with applause was the
opening of the American College at Rome, on December 8, 1859 under
the auspices of Pope Pius IX. Rome offered neutral ground, where
candidates to the priesthood would acquire a full conviction of the
unity and Catholicity of the Church; narrow or national prejudices
would be minimized, if not totally eliminated. Rome provided a
cosmopolitan character, free from national peculiarities; thus,
seminarians would not be influenced by the competing forces of the
Irish, French, and German elements in American seminaries, which
tended to create rivalries and bitter feelings between nationalities. At Rome, all could be united; no one triumphed, and no one
was humiliated. Brownson wanted a universal Church and objected
to an American Church:

---

[52]The Convert, p. 426.

> The only way to guard against an ultimate injurious
> and destructive Americanism is to substitute in our
> ecclesiastical education the Roman cosmopolitan, which
> can offend nobody, and which leaves the people free
> in every country to be Catholics, not Gentiles.[53]

Not only did Brownson object to ethnic rivalries within the United States, but also cast doubt on America also, showing a definite preference for universal Catholicism.

In addition, Brownson believed Rome to the the best place to train missionaries; the whole world was represented there and a man could be trained to perform any duty in any country. Also, Rome offered true teaching of the ceremonies and liturgy of the Church, where no national or slovenly influences could infiltrate. Roman education also produced respect for the Holy See, furthering the cause of Church unity and binding both priests and laity to the center of Catholicism. For all these reasons, then, Brownson endorsed the American College at Rome, and preferred it to any institution in the United States. He realized that many Americans hesitated to give financial support to the Roman institution; many wanted a major seminary established in the United States. Brownson advised them:

> We are as solicitous for the grand seminary at home as
> they are, but we do not think the time for it has yet
> come; and, moreover, we do not want a national clergy
> in their sense. We do not want the Church national,
> either in a native or a foreign sense.[54]

---

[53]O. A. Brownson, "American College at Rome," BrQR, XVII (April, 1860), 255.

[54]Ibid., p. 259; several years before this statement, Brownson wrote the now infamous letter to Montalembert in which he called the Irish politicians "the most noisy, brawling, and corrupt," and as a body the Irish "are the most drunken, fighting, thieving,

Brownson wanted an intelligent, cosmopolitan clergy; their birth-
place did not matter. "We look to what the man is, not to where
he was born."[55]

Brownson's final recommendation of the college at Rome was
significant. He envisioned that the American College would hasten
the day and prepare the way for a grand seminary in this country
that would be worthy of both the country and the Church. By
bringing cosmopolitan priests to this country, by instilling the
same conception of the Church in the laity, America would thus be
prepared for a national seminary that would exemplify Roman and
universal Catholicism, rather than narrow and national misconceptions of the Church.

Brownson's remarks concerning the American College at Rome
illustrated his belief in gradual, evolutionary progress. The
College was building the seeds of a better clergy, and hence laity
and Church, in America. Yet hope for the future did not remove
present difficulties. American seminaries were deficient and most
priests received their education in them. Just as Brownson called
for reform in many areas--schools, colleges, domestic education,
orphanages--so he saw the need for the reformation of seminary
education. However, because of the many recent controversies in

---

lying and lascivious class of our population." However, the little
mentioned fact is that Brownson laid this blame on the oppressions
to which the Irish had been subjected. He also stated: "The
Irish people would do well, be a noble people, if they had only a
tolerably decent clergy. The Irish clergy here are for the most
part poorly educated, ignorant, and lazy . . . . No care is taken
of the morals of the people." See O.A.B. to Montalembert,
December 25, 1855, OABP, UNDA.

[55]Ibid., p. 260.

which he had become involved,[56] because of the suspicions enter-

tained concerning his status as a Catholic,[57] and because the

advice of a mere layman might not be appreciated by the hierarchy,

Brownson hesitated to publish his views on this sensitive issue.

Instead, he hand-picked two priests, William J. Barry and Jeremiah

W. Cummings, to discuss this topic in his Review.[58]

Barry, after tracing the history of ecclesiastical seminaries,

called on the Church to better prepare its candidates for the

priesthood. Convinced that the Church had taken firm root in the

United States, he believed the hierarchy could give seminarians

"long and thorough course of instruction, necessary to make

polished scholars."[59] With an increase in the present number of

clergy, and numerous colleges, and at least thirty-three seminaries,

along with some preparatory seminaries, the American hierarchy

---

[56]Brownson was in "hot water" on several counts. His articles
on Native Americanism, the Know-Nothings, the temporal power of the
Popes and Catholic education had created bitter controversy between Brownson and the hierarchy, clergy, and press. He had lost
his "seal of approval" of the hierarchy for his Review, and was
eventually deposed to Rome in 1861.

[57]The more "liberal" Brownson got, the stronger the rumors
that he would leave the Church. See a letter from Archbishop
Purcell to Bishop Blanc, October 27, 1859, Archdiocese of New
Orleans Papers, UNDA.

[58]See William J. Barry, "Ecclesiastical Seminaries," BrQR,
XVI (October, 1859), 456-472; Jeremiah W. Cummings, "Vocations to
the Priesthood," BrQR, XVII (October, 1860), 497-515, and "Seminaries and Seminarians," BrQR, XVIII (January, 1861) 97-117. Barry
himself taught at Mt. St. Mary's of the West, the provincial
seminary in Cincinnati.

[59]William J. Barry, "Ecclesiastical Seminaries," p. 466. The
essay is initialed W.I.B. (p. 472), but correspondence corroborates
that Barry wrote it. His initials, of course, are W.J.B.; typo-
graphical errors did happen, especially when printers attempted to
read Brownson's handwriting. In all probability, Brownson
inserted the initials at end of Barry's essay.

could now provide longer and more extensive ecclesiastical studies.
Barry proposed a system of seminary education with four gradations:
1) a preparatory seminary in each diocese; 2) a theological
seminary in each diocese; 3) a provincial or metropolitan seminary;
4) a national seminary in the United States, and an American
college in Rome. Besides establishing seminaries and elevating
the standards of ecclesiastical training, Barry stated that no
longer could the Church rely on European missionaries to fill
clerical ranks; instead he urged the Church and its hierarchy,
through the aid of parents, teachers, priests, and professors, to
seek out and encourage American candidates for the priesthood.

Cummings picked up where Barry left off. He cited the
Catholic Almanac of 1860 and remarked that none of the seven
archbishops, only twelve of the forty-eight bishops, and scarcely
fifteen percent of the priests were born in this country. He
called for the seeking out of vocations and the creation of a
native clergy, necessary for both instructing Catholics and for
converting non-Catholics. America was no longer receiving first
rate clerics from Europe; such men were not being forced out of
their countries by calamities like the French revolution or the
Irish famine. The American Church must find and educate her own
priests. Native priests, in turn, stood a better chance of converting non-Catholic Americans. Cummings quoted Latin texts from the
Council of Trent, Pope Benedict XIV's _Epistola commonitoria ad
omnes Episcopos_ and _De Synodo Dioecesana_, the Provincial Council
of Baltimore (1833), and the First Plenary Council of Baltimore
(1852). All encouraged the formation of native clergies best

suited to the wants of religion in a particular country. "The
means have been clearly pointed out. What doubt or fear prevents
their practical adoption?"[60]

In the very next issue of Brownson's Quarterly Review,
Cummings felt compelled to amplify and explain his arguments. What
he had quoted in Latin, in the previous essay, he now translated
into English to make an even deeper impression that the Church,
including the American hierarchy, had advocated the necessity of
early and thorough seminary training, the preference for a native
clergy, and the establishment of more seminaries. He clarified
one point: by establishing a native clergy, he did not mean to
exclude foreigners on the ground of nativism.

> We are anxious only to have a trained clergy, that is
> to say, a body of ecclesiastics the majority of whom,
> from early youth, have been educated for the particu-
> lar kind of work which they are expected to do after
> being ordained.[61]

Cummings concluded by praising many of the devoted and dedicated
foreign clergy in this country; yet, he felt compelled to publicize
this new movement for the advancement of the priesthood and Church
in America.[62]

---

[60]"Vocations to the Priesthood," p. 512.

[61]"Seminaries and Seminarians," p. 104.

[62]He bluntly asked "Is it better to have candidates for the
priesthood who understand the peculiar wants of their place of
mission, or candidates who do not understand them? Is it better
to have persons trained for their peculiar work from early boyhood,
or persons who take up that work after being trained for another
entirely different? Is it better to have young ministers whose
thoughts, habits, and feelings are already in harmony with those
of the class they wish to attract to the Church, or such as are
entirely different from them in these important particulars?" (p.
103).

What Brownson wanted to say, but felt he could not, was said by Barry and Cummings. Brownson's hope to avoid controversy and ill-feelings by having priests advocate seminary reform was but a dream. Barry's article, and another that he published in 1860 on Catholic colleges,[63] brought him clerical criticism. He decided to write no longer in essay form for fear that further irritation of the issue might defeat his purpose. Instead, he planned to write a romantic novel, secretly, in which he would depict "ecclesiastical perfection, by setting up a higher standard than we have in the United States, of intellectualism and ascetism."[64] Barry asked Brownson to keep his remarks about the state of the clergy "confidential."

If Barry was chided by the American hierarchy, Cummings' critics came from as far away as Rome. When Cardinal Barnabo wrote Cummings and instructed him to counsel Brownson over his essay on the temporal power of the Pope, he also advised Cummings that although his own article on "Vocations to the Priesthood" was in harmony with papal promulgations of 1845 concerning the formation of an indigenous clergy, nevertheless the matter should not be discussed by a simple priest. Cummings received an admonition so similar to many Brownson had received: "Something that in itself is good and desirable is not always expedient in practice."[65]

[63]See William J. Barry, "Dr. Arnold, and Catholic Education," BrQR, XVII (July, 1860), 302-329.

[64]William J. Barry to O.A.B., April 11, 1861, OABP, UNDA; see also William J. Barry to O.A.B., October 5, 1860, OABP, UNDA.

[65]Cardinal A. Barnabo to Fr. Cummings, December 15, 1860, Archives of the Sacred Congregation de Propaganda Fide.

Furthermore, the papal instruction had been addressed to the
Bishops and it was up to them to decide on a course of action.
Also, Barnabo advised Cummings of the dangers of hurting the
feelings of foreign born clergy in America. Little did Barnabo
know that Cummings had already written another article for the
next issue.[66] The dispute ended in March, 1861 when Barnabo told
Cummings that he was glad about the priest's docility and cooperation in suspending any further articles on vocations, even though
Barnabo knew the essays were written with good intentions.[67]
Brownson did not lose his respect for Rome as a result of Barnabo's
decision. The voice of authority had spoken, and for all practical
purposes, it did so in a tone much more conciliatory than the
American hierarchy's. In fact, Brownson and Cummings were only
cautioned and never condemned or placed on the Index. That in
itself seemed like a victory, and certainly a fairer hearing and
a more lenient verdict than would have been accorded in America.

Brownson, like Barry and Cummings, deeply desired reform in
the recruitment and education of seminarians and progress in the
establishment of a native clergy. In the years following Barnabo's
instructions to Cummings, no more "seminary" articles appeared in
the pages of Brownson's Quarterly Review. One thing Brownson did
not possess, and that was obdurance or recalcitrance toward Church
authority when properly exercised and designated. Brownson was
obedient, and after the appearance of the Syllabus of Errors in

---

[66]See Fr. Cummings to O.A.B., November 29, 1860, OABP, UNDA.

[67]Cardinal A. Barnabo to Fr. Cummings, March 7, 1861, Archives
of the Sacred Congregagion de Propaganda Fide.

1864, he was even more cooperative with hierarchical designs and
instructions. In the final three years of his Review he did not
discuss seminaries, the quality of education, of the development of
a native clergy.[68] Instead, he placed all his hopes on the ability
of the Church and its missionaries and priests to both elevate and
instruct the Catholic population and to bring about the conversion
of the American people.

---

[68]In fact, as early as 1857 Brownson had remarked: "As we
understand it, the uniform policy of the Church has been, in all
ages and countries, to provide for each country, at the earliest
practicable moment, a native clergy, and such, we are assured, is
the policy, as far as practicable under the circumstances, pursued
by our own venerable hierarchy. It has never entered into our
head or our heart, we own, to question the wisdom of that policy,
or to arraign the Church at the bar of public opinion for having
uniformly pursued it." See O. A. Brownson, "Archbishop Hughes on
the Catholic Press," BrQR, XIV (January, 1857), 121.

CHAPTER VII

THE PRESS AS EDUCATOR

More than a dozen years before his entry into the Catholic
Church, Brownson noted the educational importance of the press.
In a Fourth of July Address delivered in 1831, he pointed out the
new zeal and energy that had recently been aroused and exerted on
behalf of popular education. Happy he was to announce that "the
Press, that mighty engine, is enlisting on the side of the progressive movement."[1] Although not much had been accomplished to date,
and part of the press even had caused Brownson some regrets, he
looked forward to a time when it would exert a positive influence
on the education of the people.

By the press, Brownson meant the periodicals, newspapers,
magazines, reviews and journals. Between 1831 and 1838, Brownson
observed a remarkable increase in the circulation of periodicals.
More people were reading; hence, more minds were acting upon other
minds. So great were the possibilities for education--mind acting
upon mind--that Brownson believed "the press in modern times has
become a power, a sort of 'fourth estate,' and the most efficient
gent in our possession for acting on the opinions of the people."[2]

---

[1]"Ovid Address," p. 15; see also "Social Evils and their Reme-
ies," op. cit.; "Means of Effecting a Reform," op. cit. In all
three, Brownson clearly states that he considered the press to be
ne of many educational agencies.
[2]"Education of the People," p. 428. In early 1844, a post
ffice bill that threatened the spread of periodical literature

He saw the press as a powerful agent of education, reaching an
ever-increasing number of people. Brownson based his hopes on the
great potential of the press, on the idea of what it could be,
what it ought to be, rather than what it actually was.

Yet the periodical press, especially the religious periodical
press, suffered from the same defects as the Church and clergy--an
inability to enlighten readers on the means to regenerate and to
change man's social condition. The press, like the clergy, was
moral in intent but did not seek to bring the outward world in
harmony with the destiny of human nature and society. This situation stemmed in part from the nature of the press itself. It often
only reflected public opinion; yet Brownson believed the press
capable of doing more.

> It has the capacity to be a leader of public
> opinion, in some degree to originate it, to correct
> and elevate it. How great this capacity is, it is
> impossible to say. We have no means of measuring it.
> But that it exists, cannot be doubted. The great
> value of the press, as an educator of the people,
> depends almost entirely on the proper unfolding and
> exercise of this capacity. The mischief, or ineffi-
> ciency of the press, hitherto, has consisted in its

and might even cause it to diminish was introduced into Congress.
Brownson wrote to John C. Calhoun on February 5 objecting to the
proposal. The bill would reduce the cost of individual letters,
but would seriously injure the publishers of periodicals by raising
the cost of mailing by 33% (newspapers were excluded from this).
The bill seemed to consider periodical literature a luxury.
Brownson noted: "Yet works of the class of which mine belong are
the ones most needed in the community, and the most difficult to
sustain. The higher the order of literature most needs the encouragement, and in our country can least bear being taxed." O.A.B. to
John C. Calhoun, February 5, 1844, OABP UNDA. It is easy to
attribute a self-interest to Brownson's motives here; all true
indeed. But, it should also be noted Brownson's more general
concern for the dissemination of all periodical literature as a
means of achieving American progress.

attempt to follow, rather than lead, public opinion.
Editors have inquired WHAT IS, rather than, WHAT OUGHT
TO BE?[3]

Brownson regarded the main weakness of the press to be a lack
of freedom and independence, for without these qualities, it would
never rise above an inefficient educational level. Freedom of the
press was not restricted in this country by government as it was
in monarchical Austria or Prussia. But a restraint, perhaps even
more powerful, public opinion, was in operation. When a man disagreed with an editor, he stopped his subscription. The publisher
soon realized he had to either limit or destroy his independence
or else echo popular sentiments to remain in business. Publish
or perish, to publishers, meant sell or starve. All too often,
Brownson believed, editors and publishers chose not to utter any
new or leading ideas.[4] Consequently, the press could accomplish
little in the cause of advancing progress.

One should not find it surprising, then, that Orestes Brownson
himself embarked upon an independent journalistic career in 1838.
He offered no apology for adding another periodical to the number
that already existed. In "Introductory Remarks" to the Boston
Quarterly Review, he stated: "I undertake the present publication,
with a deep feeling of responsibleness, and with the hope of
contributing something to the moral pleasure and social progress
of my countrymen."[5] He felt compelled in this endeavor by an

[3]Ibid., p. 429.
[4]Ibid., p. 430.
[5]O. A. Brownson, "Introductory Remarks," BoQR, I (January,
1838), 1.

inner voice, to undertake the work.

Citing the many intellectual and moral doubts and perplexities he had encountered during his lifetime, Brownson stated that all of them were part of his struggle to answer the basic question: What was the Destiny of Man and Society? His answer he felt compelled to disseminate; he hoped to urge others to seek the same solutions. In the midst of society he found himself a solitary thinker and different from the majority around him. In trying to circulate his views, he felt constrained, even though practically everything he had submitted for publication in periodicals (with one or two insignificant exceptions) had been published. He felt editorial censorship, correction, or even approval hindered him from putting down what he might otherwise have written. Brownson's solution to the problem of literary independence and freedom was the establishment of his own journal. "I undertake this Review, then, for myself; not because I am certain that the public wants it, but because I want it."[6]

Now he was able to say whatever he wanted, however he wanted, and whenever he wanted. Whether or not the public wanted his Review, he felt they needed it. He therefore came forth to execute his mission: to contribute to the progress of mankind by bringing independence to the press and by evoking thought.

> I would discourse freely on what seem to me to be
> great topics, and state clearly and forcibly what I
> deem important truths;--push inquiry into all subjects
> of general interest, awaken a love of investigation,

[6]Ibid., p. 4.

and create a habit of looking into even the most
delicate and exciting matters, without passion and
without fear. This is all.[7]

Brownson, then, hoped to stimulate inquiry and thought by his
endeavors in the periodical press.

The *Boston Quarterly Review* lasted five years. In his closing
remarks of October, 1842 Brownson summarized not only his own
goals but the objectives he believed all periodicals must reach:
"to be true to the great Idea which has possessed him almost from
the cradle--that of man's moral, intellectual, and physical
amelioration, on earth."[8] In 1843, Brownson joined pens with
John L. O'Sullivan's popular *Democratic Review*. The marriage was
short-lived for within the year Brownson felt editorially constrained and decided to revive his new *Brownson's Quarterly Review*.
But even during partnership with O'Sullivan, Brownson undoubtedly
appreciated a letter from one of his readers. "I admire your
straight forward way in which you tell the truth to the people."
The letter continued: "A friend of mine tells me you always give
him 'matter for thought, and irresistibly compel him to think.'
That is good service to any man of good understanding."[9] Just as
Brownson stimulated thought, he believed the entire press could
engage in the same process.

Brownson believed the American people were more receptive to
the discussion of ideas than imagined by the press. He cited his

[7]*Ibid.*, pp. 5-6.
[8]O. A. Brownson, "End of the Volume," *BoQR*, V (October, 1842),
14.
[9]James Kennard to O.A.B., September 8, 1843, OABP, UNDA.

own efforts as proof. What reputation Brownson had, he secured
by means of the independence, freedom, and boldness with which he
directed the Review. Not even loss of reputation was an obstacle,
for Brownson had himself felt indebted to the Review for his
reputation.

> Let the American press but assert its freedom, and
> enter freely and fully into all the great questions
> we have raised, and it will do not a little to advance
> the education of the people. It must be free; it must
> address itself to the mind of the community, and labour
> incessantly to quicken thought, and direct it to the
> solution of the problem of human destiny. It must . . .
> seek . . . to throw what light it can on all questions
> of interest to man or society, to elicit discussions
> and induce people to find out the truth for them-
> selves.[10]

In this way the community became educated by the free action of
mind on mind.

The periodical press served one more important function in
bringing mind to act on mind: it served as a means for educating
people by paving the way for the development of literature.
Brownson acknowledged that the widespread circulation of the
periodical press was doubtless the cause of the meagreness of
American "book" literature. The periodical press was a ready
channel for thinkers who wanted to communicate their thoughts to
the public. It answered the most urgent wants of people by
discussing subjects of immediate interest. In some ways, the
press superseded the necessity of writing books. Therefore, there
was less demand for more elaborate works--at least for the moment.

---

[10]"Education of the People," pp. 433-434.

In the end however, the periodical press would increase the demand
for literature "by calling forth the ability and giving the pre-
liminary information necessary for understanding and relishing
books."[11] Periodical literature provided a general view of all
matters, and prepared for a special view of any matter. The
periodical press will "end in creating a taste for literature; in
preparing a literature; in leading directly to its creation; and
so long as we sustain it, we can by no means be said to be doing
nothing for literature."[12]

Just as Brownson himself had long recognized the power of
the press, the Catholic Church similarly stressed its importance.
At first, it seemed necessary for the Church to employ the press
in self-defense. Because of many attacks on the Catholic faith,
the Bishops in the Pastoral Letters of 1829, 1833, 1837, 1840 (and
even more so in the Plenary Councils of 1866 and 1884) attempted
to strengthen the position and effectiveness of the Catholic press.
"The Power of the press is one of the most striking features of
modern society,"[13] remarked the Bishops. The Protestant press and
the secular press had employed the printed page in a massive
campaign against American Catholicism. In 1822 the United States
Catholic Miscellany had been established in Charleston and became
the first strictly Catholic religious journal.[14] The Catholic

---

[11]O. A. Brownson, "American Literature," BoQR, II (January,
1839), 18.

[12]Ibidem.

[13]"Pastoral Letter (1866)," pp. 152-153.

[14]There had been a dozen or so "Catholic" journals and papers
prior to this; however, they were mostly Irish national journals.
See Paul J. Foik, Pioneer Catholic Journalism (New York: The

<u>Press</u> of Hartford and the <u>Jesuit</u> <u>or</u> <u>Catholic</u> <u>Sentinel</u> (later <u>The</u>
<u>Pilot</u>) of Boston appeared in 1829. The function of these papers
was two-fold: to combat false charges and misrepresentations of
Catholic teaching; and to instruct and enlighten the Catholic
populace. More often, these early efforts by the Catholic Press
became important voices in the Catholic struggle for civil and
religious liberty. Between 1829 and 1833, at least a dozen new
papers had started publication. By 1840, another fourteen newspapers and magazines had begun to publish for the Catholic cause.[15]
However, they were not able to stem the tide of anti-Catholic
feeling. The Philadelphia Riots and the political organizing of
Catholic opponents in the 1840's and 1850's testify to this fact.

Certainly the Catholic Church considered the press a very
powerful weapon in the formation and instruction of proper religious attitudes, beliefs, and principles. Yet it was obvious that
stronger voices were still needed to assist the Church in com-
batting anti-Catholicism and at the same time to "explain our
doctrines, to protect our feelings, and to increase our devotion."[16]

United States Catholic Historical Society, 1930), pp. ix-75 for
an analysis of these national journals.

[15]Foik, <u>op</u>. <u>cit</u>., p. 213. Foik provides a chronological list
of Catholic periodicals up to 1840. Many of these papers, however,
were quite mediocre.

[16]"Pastoral Letter (1833)," p. 52. See also two important
works on the Catholic press at this time: Robert Gorman, <u>Catholic</u>
<u>Apologetical</u> <u>Literature</u> <u>in</u> <u>the</u> <u>United</u> <u>States</u> <u>1784-1858</u> (Washington:
The Catholic University of America Press, 1939); and Robert
Francis Hueston, "The Catholic Press and Nativism, 1840-1860"
(Unpublished doctoral dissertation, University of Notre Dame,
1972).

One prelate believed a stronger voice had been found. About one month after Brownson's conversion, Martin John Spalding of Louisville wrote: "I really view your accession to our ranks as an era in our Catholic history; and I have no doubt that your future career will be such as to mark it as an era; I trust to see you the instrument in the hands of God for doing immense good in this country."[17] Spalding realized the need for a Catholic quarterly, and had "no doubt" that Brownson's would meet the demand of "high tone, of Romish principles, /¯and_/ of the proper spirit."[18] Other prelates had similar hopes; in New York, John Hughes and George McCloskey had asked Isaac Hecker to feel Brownson out on the prospects of starting an American Catholic review in their diocese.[19] Another priest suggested a merger of Brownson's Quarterly Review with The Catholic Expositor of New York.[20] Brownson, though, decided to remain in Boston, and, with the encouragement of Bishop Fenwick, and the later Bishop Fitzpatrick, to continue his Review as a Catholic quarterly.

In his first four years as a Catholic reviewer, Brownson spoke little on the role of the press. Occasionally, he commended the United States Catholic Magazine for its exposition and defense of Church doctrine, and criticized anti-Catholic writers for

---

[17]M. J. Spalding to O.A.B., November 21, 1844, OABP, UNDA (italics Spalding's).

[18]Ibidem.

[19]See Isaac Hecker to O.A.B., August 17, 1844 and September 5, 1844, OABP, UNDA. These offers were made even before Brownson's Baptism on October 20, 1844.

[20]Fr. Charles Pise had suggested this to Hughes, who felt it deserved consideration. See John D. Smith to O.A.B., November 28, 1844, OABP, UNDA.

presenting false evidence to their readers.[21] It was not until

1849 that Brownson launched a major essay on the function of the

press.

In tones reminiscent of The Scholar's Mission, Brownson argued

the need for teachers and masters to elevate the people; otherwise,

they were "as helpless . . . as a flock of sheep without a

shepherd."[22] The press in particular must not succumb to leveling

tendencies, for like it or not, "the few lead, the many are led."[23]

Brownson explained:

> We speak not in contempt of the people, or in
> disregard of their claims. God has made it our duty,
> for his sake, bound us by our allegiance to him, to
> love the people, to devote ourselves to their service,
> to live for them, and, if need be, to die for them.
> There is nothing too good for them. Scholars, philoso-
> phers, teachers, magistrates, all are for them, are
> bound to live and labor for their temporal and
> spiritual well-being; and they neglect the duties of
> their state, if they do not. That they often do not
> is but too lamentably true.[24]

Within the Catholic Church, the dearth of clergymen compounded the

difficulty of elevating the population. As a result, Brownson

viewed "Journalism, as our only practicable medium of reaching

that public which most needs to be addressed."[25]

---

[21]See O. A. Brownson, "Catholic Magazine and Ourselves,"
BrQR, II (April, 1845), 258-262, and O. A. Brownson, The Investi-
gator and Advocate of Independence in "Literary Notices," BrQR,
IV (January, 1847), 134-135.

[22]O. A. Brownson, "The Catholic Press," BrQR, VI (January,
1849), 2.

[23]Ibid., p. 3.

[24]Ibidem.

[25]Ibid., p. 10.

To be truly Catholic, editors of the press, although not part of the hierarchy, must subject themselves to legitimate superiors and confine themselves within proper limits. In this fashion the press would diffuse Christian doctrine, defend the rights of the Church and freedom of religion, and preserve the social order and the rights of man. And yet, Brownson spoke of an ideal; in reality, the press faced many difficulties. Despite improvement in its quality, the press suffered from a lack of priests, insufficient preparation of lay editors, and a clientele mostly foreign and limited in education. Too often, the press had to devote its pages to news of the old countries. At times it merely touched upon matters concerned with the rights and duties of Catholic citizens here, and was forced to repel attacks made against the Catholic religion.[26] This was all the press had been able to do up to 1849; however, Brownson saw a different future for the press.

Convinced that American greatness could only be achieved through Catholicism, Brownson believed the press had a special duty--to save America. The press needed to assume a higher tone and to enlarge the scope of its discussions. It must be a vehicle for disseminating correct principles to the Catholic population and enabling them to understand the relationship of their religion to the great questions of the day in politics and social reforms. To save America, the press must prescribe "our public as well as private morals,"[27] especially in the battle against socialism

---

[26]Ibid., pp. 11-13.
[27]Ibid., p. 14.

and its destructiveness of Church, state, family and property.
Yet, in opposing modern tendencies, the press faced unpopularity.
Despite the seeming inverse proportion between worth and popularity
in journals, Brownson urged the Catholic press to "take a high
stand, be conducted with energy and ability, on true Catholic
principles, and we will not believe that Catholics will suffer it
to languish."[28] Catholic institutional growth had produced an
ever-rising intellectual level among the laity. Brownson called
on Catholics to support the press, out of duty, to the fullest
extent possible.

Brownson envisioned a three-fold structure and approach for
the press.

> We want a quarterly review, for the more elaborate and
> scientific discussion of the great questions which come
> up; we want also a monthly magazine, for that class of
> readers who have not the leisure to master the elaborate
> discussions of the quarterly--supposing the quarterly
> to be properly conducted--and who yet want something
> more solid and of more permanent interest than the
> weekly journal; we want the weekly journals in all
> parts of the country, for the whole body of the Catholic
> community, to keep them informed of what is passing at
> home and abroad, and to direct them in forming their
> judgments of passing events. These three classes of
> publications, each in its sphere, are all wanted, and
> one as much as another.[29]

All the time, though, the press must keep in mind that it was performing the work of God and the Church. It must not follow the
people but lead them by forming public opinion, correcting evil

---

[28]Ibid., p. 18.

[29]Ibid., pp. 18-19. (Italics mine.) Certainly other editors
had reason to feel slighted. Despite the final sentence of the
quote, the overall impression was that the quarterly review, i.e.,
Brownson's, headed the list in importance.

tendencies, and rejecting unsound doctrines.

Besides calling for an elevation of the tone of the press, Brownson hoped to eliminate editorial rivalries. All devoted themselves to God's cause, each in their own sphere. Unanimity for the mutual good of all was essential on matters of faith and morals. On other matters, if Catholics had to dissent from one another, Brownson urged them to reason the conflict down, not to cry it down. "We have enemies enough elsewhere, without making enemies of one another."[30] Because Catholic editors had embarked on the same cause of working for God, they should have a mutual understanding that if they must occasionally rebuke one another, they "should do it in a truly fraternal spirit so as to lead to the correction of the error, without any loss of mutual good feeling and affection."[31]

Working for the same cause, no editor should feel jealous, unwanted, or unneeded. God needed all to work for the Catholic cause; hence, no editor should interfere with another but instead, each should be serviceable to one another. In this bulwark of unity, the power and efficiency of the press would aid the Church as an auxiliary to her modes of instruction.[32]

---

[30]Ibid., p. 21.

[31]Ibidem.

[32]Ibid., pp. 22-24; Brownson did criticize a portion of the Irish "Catholic" press for taking their political and social principles, not from the Church, but from the socialistic and radical tendencies of the age. Even these papers, though, if elevated to conform with Catholic doctrine and thought, could also do "valiant battle" in behalf of the Church against her enemies.

So impressed were the hierarchy by Brownson's <u>Review</u> and by this blueprint for the press, that later in the same year after the Provincial Council at Baltimore, Bishop Francis P. Kenrick of Philadelphia induced the hierarchy to endorse a letter of approbation and encouragement to Brownson. Signed by twenty-five prelates, the letter became a permanent fixture on the cover of <u>Brownson's Quarterly Review</u>.[33]

Having received the hierarchical stamp of approval, Brownson appeared to be at the top of his class. Earlier, in 1847, Brownson attempted to smooth over a controversy between Bishop Hughes' organ, the New York <u>Freeman's Journal</u>, and the editor of the Boston <u>Pilot</u>. He wrote Hughes that "it is better to reform the <u>Pilot</u> than to kill it. You can kill it if you continue."[34] Hughes was not offended by the letter, apparently, because in the following year he offered Brownson the editorship of the struggling <u>Freeman's Journal</u>. J. M. Capes also asked Brownson for advice in starting a new English periodical, <u>The Rambler</u>.[35] English speaking Canadians asked his advice about establishing a Catholic journal in Montreal.[36] The editors of the Baltimore <u>Catholic Mirror</u> asked Brownson to become a weekly or bi-weekly contributor

[33]Francis Patrick Kenrick to O.A.B., May 13, 1849, OABP, UNDA. Brownson published the letter in the July issue of <u>BrQR</u>, VI (1849), 411-412.

[34]O.A.B. to Bishop John Hughes, January 19, 1847, New York Archdiocesan Archives.

[35]See Fr. James R. Bayley to O.A.B., March 27, 1848, OABP, UNDA; O.A.B. to Fr. James R. Bayley, April 3, 1848, New York Archdiocesan Archives; J. M. Capes to O.A.B., October 18, 1847, OABP, UNDA.

[36]George Edward Clerk to O.A.B., July 3, 1850, OABP, UNDA.

to their columns.[37] Indeed, Brownson's reputation was well-established--scarcely five years a Catholic and already recognized as the leader of the Catholic press.

But even the leader faced the same problems encountered by other editors. Brownson received complaints that publishers were neither correct nor punctual in printing Catholic periodicals, that agents who sold the Review were very late in getting copies to subscribers, especially in New York and Washington where he could obtain more subscriptions if he had good agents. Insufficient customers and defaults on payment by some who did subscribe accentuated the tight money situation of running a periodical.[38] Brownson was embarrassed over his own finances. He had lost $500 in trying to aid the Catholic Observer and another $300 on account of his agents. Bishop Kenrick, in early 1850, sent him a contribution to sustain the review and to encourage him to continue.[39]

Financially, the Review was able to survive until the hardships of the Civil War. Brownson lost about two-thirds of his subscribers at this time, about half as a direct result of his

---

[37]Hedian and O'Brien to O.A.B., December 29, 1850, OABP, UNDA.

[38]See McGarhan to O.A.B., May 28, 1848, OABP UNDA; James A. cMaster to O.A.B., July 16, 1848, OABP, UNDA; and Fr. Jeremiah W. ummings to O.A.B., June 8, 1849, OABP, UNDA. That finances were ad can be seen further in a confidential letter to Brownson. The nited States Catholic Magazine of Baltimore was threatened with xtinction in late 1848. See John Murphy to O.A.B., November 14, 948, OABP, UNDA.

[39]O.A.B. to Fr. Jeremiah W. Cummings, June 23, 1849, OABP, NDA; Bishop F. P. Kenrick to O.A.B., July 7, 1849, and January 28, 950, OABP, UNDA. In 1852, Fr. John McCaffrey tried to get the ierarchy to establish a fund to support and sustain the Review; owever, Bishop Eccleston vetoed it. See Fr. John McCaffrey to ohn B. Purcell, March 9, 1852, Archdiocese of Cincinnati Papers, JDA.

stand in support of the national government, and the other half as a result of losing his subscribers in England and Ireland. Even loyal subscribers had difficulty in paying. One man, and his sister, each owed three years, or a total of $18. The moneyless man offered to pay Brownson a gallon of whiskey for every $1.25 owed; or if that wasn't enough, he offered forty gallons just to keep his subscription to the Review.[40]

Brownson considered financial difficulties--non-payment of bills, not enough subscribers, and less than energetic agents--as secondary; the major problem of the Catholic press was the quality of the press itself. From the early 1850's until his death, Brownson repeatedly found himself engaged, and at times embroiled, in intra-Catholic disputes. He expected harsh treatment from the non-Catholic press and received it. But it was Catholic controversy that concerned and upset him the most. His 1849 blueprint for the Catholic press he found to be an ideal; as usual, the realities contradicted the dream.

Brownson wrote only three more major essays on the role of the Catholic press--in 1857, 1866, and 1875. But interspersed throughout his writings, in literary notices and editorials, are a steady flow of comments concerning the press. Between 1850 and 1856, Brownson praised a German paper, the New-Yorker Sion, for emphasizing the right of religion to influence the direction of political actions. He congratulated Le Correspondant and The Rambler for reviving Catholic thought and faith and for aiding

---

[40]See incomplete letter, O.A.B. to ?, 186?, OABP, UNDA; for the whiskey bartering proposition, see E. A. Graves to O.A.B., January 3, 1862, OABP UNDA. Graves resided in Lebanon, Kentucky.

God's glorious cause in Europe. He remarked of himself that he
conducted his review for God, not for himself or any other man.[41]
These scattered remarks, of course, further revealed his criteria
for what good journalism ought to be. At the same time that he
praised a portion of the Catholic press, he objected to a few
journals that lacked refinement, courtesy, fairness and candor
toward opponents. Overall, he believed the merits outweighed the
defects of the press; furthermore, even the bad points could be
corrected.

> The best way to correct the faults of the press is for
> those who are aware of them and are annoyed by them to
> set an example free from them. The Catholic journal-
> ists must learn to bear with one another, treat one
> another with kindness and courtesy, and to be always
> ready to maintain each other's rights and to defend
> in an honorable way each other's honor.[42]

Brownson's hope to elevate Catholic journalism, and his
confidence that it could be done, were tested severely from 1854
until the cessation of the Review in 1864. The appearance of
"Native Americanism," "Schools and Education," and "The Temporal
Power of the Pope" created a flurry of criticism.[43] The

---

[41]See O. A. Brownson, "Literary Notices and Criticisms,"
BrQR, VII (April, 1850), 270; O. A. Brownson, "Literary Notices and
Criticisms," BrQR, XIII (July, 1856), 399-402; O. A. Brownson,
"Literary Notices and Criticisms," BrQR, X (January, 1853), 136.

[42]O. A. Brownson, "Literary Notices and Criticisms," BrQR,
I (October, 1854), 534.

[43]See Celts and Saxons, Nativism and Naturalization: A Complete Refutation of the Nativism of Dr. Orestes A. Brownson (Boston:
Thomas Sweeney, 1854). This eighty-eight page book, edited by
Bishop O'Connor of Pittsburgh, was a collection of editorials and
comments by virtually the entire Catholic press of America. The
book also contained a refutation of "Mr. Brownson's Extravagant
Theory of the (so called) Temporal Powers of the Popes" which had
appeared in April, pp. 187-218.

objections raised against Brownson seemed to repudiate every

journalistic principle he espoused.

> The true policy, we suppose, is, in all open questions,
> for us to express our dissent from opinions we dis-
> approve, to assign our reasons, but to do it with
> courtesy, without passion, without vituperation, and
> in a calm, serene, and respectful tone, although in
> a firm and manly manner.[44]

However, the criticism levelled at Brownson was strident, voci-

ferous, unjust, and un-Catholic. Brownson called the indignation

"a low blow" aimed at destroying free thought and discussion of

issues that were not themselves a matter of faith or morals.

Undoubtedly feeling persecuted by the lower levels of the press,

Brownson reprinted a letter of apostolic benediction he had

received from Pope Pius IX, in testimony of his writings in the

Review.[45]

Despite all the opposition, he remained convinced that his

path was the right one. He re-emphasized his position, the ideal

position for journalists: "We have never taken the sentiments or

wishes of the multitude as our guide; we have never courted popu-

larity; and it has always been our aim to lead public opinion,

not to follow it."[46] Although the "passing squall" of 1854 was

no indication, Brownson believed that eventually fair play, sense

and love of justice, and respect for free discussion on open

questions would prevail in the body of American Catholics.

---

[44]See 42 above.

[45]Pope Pius IX to O.A.B., April 29, 1854, OABP, UNDA, reprinted in O. A. Brownson, "End of the Eleventh Volume," BrQR,
XI (October, 1854), 538-539.

[46]"End of the Eleventh Volume," p. 540.

In 1857, Brownson reiterated the rights and duties of
journalists on open matters and on issues of faith and morals. He
defended himself against the criticisms of Archbishop Hughes and
others, and denied that he had sought to cause divisiveness within
the Catholic community.[47] Furthermore, he stressed the importance
of a unified field of Catholic journalists. Brownson, citing La
Civilta Cattolica, argued that the modern press dated from the
onset of the French Revolution and aimed specifically at over-
turning Catholicism; hence, Protestant journals attempted for the
first time in history to act "directly on society, and $\sqrt{\ }$ to
effect $\underline{7}$ by the formation and force of public opinion great political, social, moral, or religious ends."[48] Since the press was so
powerful an agent for working on the public mind, Brownson urged
the Church to turn the press into an instrument for her own good.
Catholics must use the press "as a means of neutralizing the
effects of the non-Catholic press, and of promoting what may be
called the external interests of religion."[49] In addition,
Brownson viewed the press as a means of converting non-Catholics,
which was "always God's work."[50]

Later, in the same year, Brownson called upon the Church
to meet the demands of intelligence and to command by her intrinsic
excellenece the intellect and thought of the day by guiding the
free development of intellect through the press. However,

---

[47] O. A. Brownson, "Archbishop Hughes on the Catholic Press,"
rQR, XIV (January, 1857), 114-141.

[48] Ibid., pp. 114-115.

[49] Ibid., p. 115.

[50] Ibid., p. 127.

Brownson's confidence appears to have abated somewhat.

> We hardly recollect in the nearly thirteen years of our
> Catholic life an instance in which an able and intel-
> ligent Catholic writer has been met by his Catholic
> opponents with fairness and candor, or his opinion
> discussed on its merits with courtesy or common civil-
> ity. Our domestic controversies speak but ill for our
> civilization, our liberality, and our conscientious-
> ness. Our so-called Catholic press, in regard to our
> disputes among ourselves, where differences are allow-
> able, stands far below that of any other country, and
> indicates a lower moral tone, and an inferior intellec-
> tual culture. For the honor of American Catholic
> journalism . . . we must labor to elevate the charac-
> ter of our journals, demand of them a higher and a
> more dignified tone, and insist that their conductors
> devote more time and thought to their preparation,
> take larger and more comprehensive views of men and
> things, exhibit more mental cultivation, more liberal-
> ity of thought and feeling, and give some evidence of
> the ability of Catholics to lead and advance the
> civilization of the country. We want the men who
> conduct our Catholic press to be living men, highly-
> cultivated men, up to the highest level of their age,--
> men who are filled with the spirit of our holy reli-
> gion, and will take their rule from the morality,
> gentleness, courtesy, and chivalry of the Gospel, not
> from petty passions, envyings and jealousies, or from
> a low and corrupt secular press, that disregards
> principle, mocks at conscience, seeks only success,
> and counts success lawful by whatever means obtained.[51]

The disappointment he expressed continued into the 1860's; in

almost every volume of the Review, Brownson felt compelled to

caution, warn, castigate or advise other editors.

Brownson accused other editors of a host of mistakes: they

had not criticized his real views on certain issues but rather had

misconstrued his intended meaning and had failed to understand his

position; they had refuted him with popular prejudice, not with

logic and sound argument; they had spoken as if they represented

---

[51]O. A. Brownson, "Present Catholic Dangers," BrQR, XIV
(July, 1857), 367.

official Church doctrine and by dragging bishops' names into arguments unfairly; and they had failed to read all his essays on an issue to comprehend his overall view, but instead read only a partial view on a subject.[52] Granted, most of Brownson's objections were warranted; however, he himself had carried the bishops signatures on his cover, and had printed a letter from the pope. Even he had difficulty following his own guidelines; of course, it does not imply that he was a hypocrite, but rather that he too was a human being. Perhaps it reveals that when a person is unable to convince others by his own words, he often turns to an authority for supporting evidence. And it cannot be denied that Brownson often failed to convince the rest of the press that he was correct and not they.

Even in the heated arguments between Catholics and Native Americans and Know-Nothings the Catholic press aligned itself against Brownson. Hueston demonstrates Brownson's practically solitary position in a chapter entitled "The Catholic Reaction to Know-Nothingism" (pp. 226-274). On sensitive issues, such as the power of the pope, common schools, and Native Americanism, Brownson's views were often misinterpreted, quoted out of context, and only partially read. When others accused him of holding views that he really had not held, and especially when so many editors disagreed with him all at once (in unkind terms), understandably

[52]See the following: an incomplete letter, O.A.B. to Mr. Editor, October, 1859, OABP, UNDA; O. A. Brownson, "Note," BrQR, VI (July, 1859), 414-416; O. A. Brownson, "Literary Notices and Criticisms," BrQR, XVII (October, 1860), 538-540; O. A. Brownson, "The End of the Volume," BrQR, XVIII (October, 1861), 547-548; O. A. Brownson, "Explanations to Catholics," BrQR, XXI (October, 1864) 470-489.

he had difficulty "turning the other cheek" or responding with
complete dignity at all times. That he generally did reply in a
respectful manner is probably due to his painstaking efforts in
writing replies. The Brownson Papers often reveal several partial
drafts of his responses; if he became angry, he seldom wrote in
haste. He usually calmed down and tempered his rebuttals.

On the positive side, Brownson attempted to set an example
for other editors. Truth, not popularity, was the goal. He hoped
journalistic wrangling would cease so that editors could get down
to fulfilling their duties to God, Church, and country. The press
must elevate the views, tone, literature, science, and general
education of Catholics throughout the world. In addition, Brownson
believed the press must not only work to preserve the faith of
Catholics, but try to extend it to those who did not as yet have
it. Especially during the Civil War, Brownson displayed an
intense loyalty to the Union with an adjoining desire to demonstrate
the harmony between Catholic dogma and modern American life. He
openly courted non-Catholics whose conversion, he hoped, would
augment national, domestic, and individual progress, and secure
for the Catholic Church a leading role for the future direction
of American life and thought.[53]

The liberal, optimistic attitude toward Protestants that
Brownson displayed in the early 1860's, and his generally critical
view of Catholic journalism, abated after the cessation of the

[53]See "The End of the Volume," BrQR, XVIII (October, 1861),
547-548; O. A. Brownson, "Literary Notices and Criticisms," BrQR,
XIX (January, 1862), 132-134; O. A. Brownson, "Our New Programme,"
BrQR, XXI (January, 1864), 1-12.

Review in 1864. The Quarterly folded for numerous reasons. On

the surface, the Review was $1200 in debt, owing to a loss of

Southern subscriptions, the failure of subscribers in Ireland and

England to pay their bills, and an increase in the cost of paper.[54]

Below the surface, though, lay the real reasons for the demise of

the Review. Never was Brownson able to unite the Catholic press

to work uniformly and in conjunction with one another; when unity

did exist, it was usually directed against rather than with

Brownson.[55] Even more importantly, from the late 1850's until

about 1862, key members of the American hierarchy, namely Hughes,

Purcell, Spalding, and Kenrick increasingly disapproved of

Brownson's writings; Luers and Elder wrote letters filled with

complaints and advice to Brownson; Archbishop Cullen of Ireland

complained directly to Rome, as did Kenrick and Timon. James F.

Wood, Bishop of Philadelphia, denounced the Review in the Catholic

Herald and Visitor. Indeed, hierarchical objections were the main

blow to Brownson's Quarterly Review.[56] For even though Brownson's

[54]Fr. Jeremiah W. Cummings to O.A.B., November 5, 1864, OABP,
NDA; L. Kehoe to O.A.B., May 22, 1863, OABP, UNDA; C. A. Alvord to
O.A.B., December 11, 1863, OABP, UNDA.

[55]One notable exception comes to mind. In 1858, Patrick
Donohoe, proprietor of the Boston Pilot, did unite with Brownson,
even selling joint subscriptions to the Review and Pilot for $5.
Donohoe told Brownson: "Let the hatchet be forever buried about
former affairs"; and "Let us work hard this and the ensuing years
to get the Review where it ought to be." See P. Donohoe to O.A.B.,
January 3, 1858 and January 5, 1858, OABP, UNDA. Even this
marriage proved but temporary. See Fr. Edward Putnam to O.A.B.,
January 19, 1860, OABP, UNDA. Apparently, Brownson's essay on
schools and Barry's on seminaries caused the rift.

[56]As early as 1855, Brownson had agreed to remove the letter
of approbation which he had received in 1849 from the American
hierarchy. It appears that Purcell was the main instigator behind
the prelates' disavowal of BrQR. Correspondence reveals a bevy of
letters emanating from Purcell to practically every Bishop in

writings were not condemned by the Roman Congregation of the Index,

Brownson never recovered his former stature. Perhaps John Hughes,

more than anyone else, helped perpetuate hierarchical animosity

against supporting Brownson's Review.

Hughes wrote Barnabo on September 30, 1861 suggesting that

Barnabo not carry on a dispute with Brownson; however, the reasons

he gave were quite different from what he told Brownson on October

3, when he assured Brownson that he had told Rome that he never

doubted Brownson's orthodoxy.[57] Actually Hughes told Barnabo that

the Review was on the decline, having few readers, and having no

influence even among Catholics. Hughes felt any open attack on

Brownson would only serve to revive interest in the Review. He

America, with return letters all revealing a displeasure over
Brownson. See the Archdiocese of Cincinnati Papers, UNDA for
countless examples. After that, Brownson's support continually
eroded, reaching its peak between 1860-1862. Numerous letters were
exchanged between the hierarchy; considered together, they seem
like a landslide burying their target. See the following letters
in OABP, UNDA: George Hilton to O.A.B., January 13, 1860; Hilton
liked to inform Brownson of Cincinnati affairs, and often mentioned
Purcell's adverse comments about Brownson; O.A.B. to Fr. J.
McMullen, October 20, 1860; Fr. Smarius to O.A.B., November 5, 1860;
P. Pendergast to O.A.B., November 27, 1860; Bishop John Luers to
O.A.B., November 29, 1860; Fr. Gresselin to O.A.B., December 7,
1860; Bishop W. H. Elder to O.A.B., December 18, 1860; O.A.B. to
Bishop W. H. Elder, December 29, 1860; O.A.B. to Fr. Cummings,
January 11, 1861; Fr. Cummings to O.A.B., January 25, 1861; George
McCloskey to O.A.B., April 10, 1861; Fr. Cummings to O.A.B., July
19, 1861; Bishop W. H. Elder to O.A.B., July 26, 1861; Fr. Cummings
to O.A.B., October 9, 1861; O.A.B. to Bishop J. F. Wood, May 2,
1862; George Hilton to O.A.B., November 3, 1862; also see the
following in ASC de PF: Cardinal Barnabo to Fr. W. McCloskey,
December 19, 1860; Archb. Paul Cullen to Barnabo, Feburary 18,
1861; Barnabo to Cullen, March 13, 1861; Barnabo to Cummings, June
25, 1861; Barnabo to Cummings, August 31, 1861; Barnabo to Cummings,
September 2, 1861; Barnabo to Cullen, November 14, 1861; and see
Archb. Kenrick to Cullen, December 25, 1861, Cullen Papers, Kildare,
Ireland.

[57]See Archb. John Hughes to O.A.B., October 3, 1861, OABP,
UNDA.

accused Brownson of making the acquaintance of several young

priests, who, as a group, criticized the Church and the Supreme

Pontiff. Hughes compared the group to the Lamennais school and

suggested that Brownson might apostatize as Forbes had done.[58]

In another letter, Hughes described Brownson as one always ready to

make apologies and then turn around and continue the same offen-

sive conduct.[59] Shortly afterwards, Barnabo, apparently following

Hughes' advice, decided to avoid controversy with Brownson.[60]

If Hughes had tried to deceive Brownson, he failed. Brownson

believed that Hughes was trying to incite the Irish against him by

appealing to their pro-slavery sentiments, and thus get them to

excoriate Brownson's _Review_. Brownson wrote his friend Montalembert

the following:

> The Archbishop is a man whose word can not be relied
> on, and he remembers to speak the truth only when
> truth best serves his purpose. I know him well; but
> he is old, broken in body, and ___?___ in mind, and
> though he is determined to ruin me, I pray God to help
> me from harboring any uncharitable or vindictive
> feeling towards him. It will take half a century to
> repair the evils he has done /‾and‾/ is doing to the
> cause of Catholicity in this country.[61]

Brownson, though not condemned by Rome, did agree not to write on

the temporal power of the pope; and by 1864, because of conflicts

---

[58]Archb. John Hughes to Cardinal Barnabo, September 30,
1861, ASC de PF.

[59]Archb. John Hughes to Cardinal Barnabo, October 12, 1861,
SC de PF.

[60]Cardinal Barnabo to Archb. John Hughes, November 15, 1861,
SC de PF.

[61]O.A.B. to Montalembert, April 11, 1862, OABP, UNDA.

with the American hierarchy, he had stopped writing on theological
issues altogether. He became fed up, and learned "it was my duty
not to insist publicly on opinions however sound."[62] When the
Review folded,[63] Brownson left the field a defeated man.

Yet, no sooner had the Review closed than Catholics gave an
annuity to Brownson to sustain him until he died. Furthermore,
if Brownson felt unwanted, it must have been gratifying to receive
offers to write for the Catholic World, Ave Maria, New York Tablet,
The Rambler, and The Home and Foreign Review. Almost as soon as
he had left the field, he rejoined it once again. Soon, too, he
addressed the issue of the Catholic press. The changes Brownson
had undergone after 1864 were evidenced in his writings on the
role of the press also.

Writing for the Catholic World in 1866, Brownson believed the
press so powerful that he called it more than a "fourth estate,"
because it had usurped the functions of all the others. It had
become "the most powerful influence, whether for good or for evil,
that man wields or can wield."[64] He called on the Church to enlist
the press to advance truth, maintain order, intelligence, morality,
and civilization. Believing that America sustained more journals
than any other country--hence the population had acquired a taste

---

[62]See an incomplete draft, O.A.B. to ?, 1866?, OABP, UNDA.

[63]Brownson did remark, however, that his Review died because
he had supported Fremont for the Presidency in 1864. His Review
had already lost the support of the hierarchy; it was on its last
leg, and concentrated on politics in 1864. The Fremont issue was
merely the final blow.

[64]O. A. Brownson, "Use and Abuse of Reading," Catholic World,
III (July, 1866), 463.

for reading--the Catholic press needed to elevate itself and meet the demand by producing good literature. He compared the situation to a hungry person--"when wholesome food is not to be had, people will feed on unwholesome food, and die of that which they have taken to sustain life."[65] He saw a twofold solution: 1) to appeal to Christian conscience not to read bad literature; and 2) to demand as a matter of conscience that Catholics support and sustain Catholic publications; otherwise, journals would fold as a result of the difficulties of publishing and selling Catholic books and journals to an unresponsive secular society. Brownson viewed the creation and sustenance of Catholic books as a measure needed to arrest the downward tendency so prevalent in society, and to provide good reading for Catholics, especially for children when they have finished school (or else the good influences of Catholic schools would be negated). The dissemination of the Catholic faith could save America and the press was needed to help spread it.

One thing conspicuously absent from Brownson's remarks, in the last years of his life, was any major reference to intra-Catholic squabbles and battles. The real struggle was between Catholicism and an infidel world. What was needed, according to Brownson, was strong, conservative editors living and writing in accordance with the Syllabus, who would condemn errors, expose false principles, and erect a barrier to the destructiveness of American society, by juxtaposing positive Catholic principles to false, pernicious ones.[66]

---

[65]Ibid., p. 470.

[66]O. A. Brownson, "Introduction to the Last Series," BrQR, XII (January, 1873), 1-8.

Having declared war on the "pagan element" of society,
Brownson wanted the press to assist the Bishops and clergy in
educating and protecting Catholics. Although he briefly mentioned
some of the same inadequacies within the Catholic press that he
had noted earlier, Brownson remarked that nonetheless he had
notices "a great improvement . . . during the last ten years."[67]
Accordingly, he urged the press to undertake the work of instructing
and elevating the Catholic public, and of encouraging the creation
of a "high-toned, solid Catholic literature."[68] Furthermore, as
Brownson closed his Review for 1874, he added that another aim of
the Catholic press should be "to aid in forming able and well-
trained reviewers among our younger clergy and educated young
laymen."[69]

In the last issue of the final volume, Brownson's leading
article was entitled "Protestant Journalism." He cited the
Protestant roots of modern journalism and called on Catholics to
neutralize the evil tendencies. Knowing it was his last issue,
Brownson attempted to improve certain features of the Catholic
press: better trained and educated laymen; the creation of a
reading public; stronger Catholic support of their journals.
Because of the overwhelming power of the Protestant press, at best
the Catholic press would be able to protect the religion of

[67]O. A. Brownson, "Answer to Objections," BrQR, XXIII (October,
1874), 456.

[68]Ibid., p. 457.

[69]O. A. Brownson, "The Review for 1875," BrQR, XXIII (October,
1874), 571. Brownson's age and health had been taxing him of late.
To get him through another year with the Review, he accepted the
help of several other writers.

Catholics. Brownson seemed to have given up any hope that it would be instrumental in the direct conversion of America. Quite simply, Catholic journals never reached the non-Catholic reading audience.[70]

The Catholic press, in directing its energies to the Catholic population, must stress the importance of religion and subordinate politics to religious principles.

> The great difficulty a Catholic reviewer encounters is in convincing Catholic laymen and journalists that Catholic means Catholic . . . . If religion is catholic, it is supreme and universal, the supreme law in every department of life, extending to every species of human activity. Whether we eat or drink, whether we sleep or wake, whatever we do, we are to do it for the glory of God. The goods of this life, whether national or political, social or economical, are never secured, or, if secured, cease to be goods, by being made the direct object or end of our activity: - "Seek, first, the kingdom of God and his justice, and all these things shall be added unto you."[71]

Brownson concluded his journalistic career by asking his readers to remember him in their prayers as one who never courted popularity, but one who loved his Church and his fellow Catholics.[72]

Brownson's final essays on the press reflected his more conservative views since the 1860's. He still made criticisms and offered advice in the spirit of reform, yet his tone was refined and supportive rather than harsh and self-defensive. He no longer

---

[70]O. A. Brownson, "Protestant Journalism," BrQR, XXIV (October, 1875), 441-469.

[71]Ibid., p. 467.

[72]O. A. Brownson, "Valedictory," BrQR, XXIV (October, 1875), 578-580.

was battling his Catholic cohorts, but the evil adversaries of
Satan in American society.

That Brownson received little love in return from most of his
contemporaries, especially from Catholic editors, cannot be denied.
Criticism directed at Brownson continued right up to the last issue
of Brownson's Quarterly Review.[73] Despite all this criticism,
despite the erosion of hierarchical support, Brownson contributed
significantly to Catholic growth and progress in America. As he
himself stated throughout his career, Brownson wrote for the educated and addressed his essays to the scholars.

Viewed from this perspective, Brownson's influence and importance can be judged by the impact on his contemporaries. Many
Catholic colleges purchased subscriptions to the Review, with some
having a scramble for it when it arrived. History teachers learned
from it as did their students. A professor at St. Thomas Seminary
learned his philosophy and theology from the Review, and another
at St. Louis used Brownson's essays on government, civil liberty,
law, and ethics as required readings in his course and urged
Brownson to combine them into a textbook. Many of the subscribers
were priests, and one acknowledged "cribbing" his sermons from the
Review. One Bishop hoped to obtain two back issues of the Review
to make two complete sets—one for his college's library, and the
other to be sold for a "handsome profit" to build up the library's
holdings. Many considered Brownson the greatest thinker of his

---

[73]The Boston Pilot was an especially harsh critic of the last
three volumes of BrQR; and when Brownson was writing for the Tablet,
James A. McMaster often criticized Brownson in the Freeman's
Journal. Of course, the secular press continued its rebukes also.

ne, an intellectual giant, a man beyond his age destined to be

emembered by posterity. Letters to and about Brownson abound with

uch praise; none, however, capture the real Brownson and his

.ight as well as the future Archbishop John Ireland:

> I consider it a shame for any man who pretends to have
> some theological or literary qualifications not to be
> a constant reader of the review, and I do blush that
> there should be in our country so many soi-disant
> catholic writers, or rather I should say scribblers,
> who are bent on opposing you. True, I can explain
> this opposition; they are ignorant; they have just
> tastes, summis labiis, a few branches of science, and
> thinking they know all, because they never know what
> is to be known, they boldly set down as an error what-
> ever is unintelligible to them.
>   In this remote corner of the world, we heartily
> wish you success, Dear Sir; be of good spirits; you
> have on your side truth and justice, and truth and
> justice will never be confounded. You will be always
> appreciated by all earnest enquirers of truth; and
> you will always have the testimony of a good conscience,
> that you have strenuously labored for the good of
> religion.[74]

reland described exactly what Brownson had hoped to accomplish--

he fulfillment of The Scholar's Mission.

---

[74]Fr. John Ireland to O. A. B., December 21, 1863, OABP, UNDA.

CHAPTER VIII

LITERATURE AS EDUCATION

Literature

"I place no value on literature for its own sake, and never make it an end to be sought. It deserves attention only as a means of individual and social growth."[1] In his address on The Scholar's Mission, Brownson stated that the end of literature, or any art for that matter, was "never the production of a work of art, however grand in conception, successful in execution, or exquisite in finish; but the realization of a good to which art is subsidiary."[2] The good that Brownson referred to was the moral, religious, intellectual, and social betterment of the human race.

Since social progress was achieved through education, and education involved the action of mind upon mind, literature became a significant agent in the education of people. Literature was mind producing new thought in every field of endeavor. The world proceeded as mind advanced. How did a person get acquainted with the progress of mind? By reading,[3] for mind met mind and thought proceeded to action.

---

[1] O. A. Brownson, "Introduction," BoQR, III (January, 1840), 19.
[2] The Scholar's Mission, p. 9.
[3] See O. A. Brownson, "Lecture on Reading," unpublished manuscript of speech given sometime before Brownson's conversion to Catholicism, OABP, UNDA.

Although books could be helpful in getting mind to think, reason and reflect, they alone were not sufficient. Brownson himself, his son tells us, read a book by analyzing it thoroughly, chapter by chapter, by writing notes summarizing what each chapter or section was intended to explain or prove, and by recording his own judgment as to whether or not the author had succeeded.[4] In this way, books for Brownson served as catalysts for thought, reason and reflection.

Mind meeting mind was necessary; just as much importance, though, lay in the quality of the content and the values presented in books. Literature, if its purpose was to better mankind, had to be the right sort. Brownson estimated the worth of a book by the degree to which it conformed to his notions of individual and social progress.

"All we ask of the artist, and this we do ask of him, is that he create with a moral purpose, with reference to a moral effect."[5] Since literature must be addressed to man's whole nature, it must be addressed to his soul. Since the moral sense constituted an integral part of the soul, any work of art to be acceptable must satisfy man's moral sense. The aim of art and of literature, Brownson maintained, must be directed at enlarging man's ideals, giving him glimpses of a more elevated and pure existence, exalting his sentiments, purifying his affections, creating in him longings for what he had not, and making him consecrate himself

[4]Henry F. Brownson, Brownson's Early Life. 1803-1844 (Detroit: H. F. Brownson, 1898), p. 86.

[5]"Bulwer's Novels," op. cit., p. 268.

"to the glorious work of regenerating the world."[6] This is what
Brownson meant by "moral sense." Literature must display a faith
in man and in virtue; it must point out individual and social
maladies, and then promote the welfare of mankind and its efforts
to advance society.

Brownson considered literature "one of the mightiest powers of
our times,"[7] capable of developing energies of the soul, enlarging
man's views, and advancing the civilization of mankind. America,
however, had not yet produced such a literature. Brownson attributed
the paucity of this genre of literature to several factors: America
was a young nation, at least politically; it had been dependent for
a long time upon England and its language, laws, customs, fashions,
methods, sentiments, and opinions; it regarded English modes as
superior to American; it attempted to model its literature after
England; it lacked confidence in itself; and writers were slow in
adopting democratic principles and doubted the institutions of the
American experience.[8] Internal development, not literature, was a
nation's first want. Literature, therefore, had not been in great
demand by Americans. "Literature springs up only in those epochs
when there is great work to be performed for the human race, when
there are great moral, philosophical, or social problems up for
solution, and when all minds and hearts are busy with them."[9]

---

[6]Ibid., p. 271.

[7]O. A. Brownson, "American Literature," BoQR, III (January,
1840), 58; see also O. A. Brownson, Oration, Delivered at Washington
Hall, July 5, 1841 (G. Washington Dixon, 1841), pp. 5-8. The overall theme of the speech was that all political reform should have
its foundation in religion.

[8]Ibid., pp. 59-64.

[9]Ibid., p. 67.

Brownson drew a correlation between social fermentation, change or revolution, and the appearance of great national literature. Church history, and all of Hebrew, Greek, Roman, German, French, Italian, and English history, in periods of upheaval, produced literature. So too, American literature would develop. Brownson believed the American struggle would soon be a contest of man versus money, or Christian and democratic principles versus those systems which spawned individual and social inequality. Americans would then engage in a great work of "solving some great problem, or making some great moral, religious, philosophical or social principle prevail."[10] When Americans became devoted to such noble ends and great principles; when they worked for freedom, truth, justice, and love; when they fully comprehended the great mission that God had in mind for them; then would Americans produce a great literature.

This literature would strengthen man's mind and heart and make him mentally and morally strong. Books must supply man with a knowledge of duty, morality, and religion; they related to first principles and made man think instead of merely remember. Literature awakened man's good feelings, pure affections, and confirmed his good resolutions. It would make him conscious that he was a being of thought, reason, and virtue; literature would provide man with the seeds of the highest mental and moral greatness.[11]

---

[10]Ibid., p. 77.

[11]"Lecture on Reading," op. cit. Brownson recommended to his audience that they read biographies of great men, such as those contained in Plutarch or Franklin. Also, he recommended works which thought highly of man's fellow beings, and showed man his duty toward other humans, and caused man to reflect on the shortness of life and his duties toward God.

Perhaps nobody worked harder at developing an American Catholic literature than Orestes Brownson once he entered the Church.[12] From his first Catholic number in 1845 until the last in 1875, Brownson repeatedly labored for the development and sustenance of Catholic literature. Following his conversion, Brownson wrote: "Literature is nothing but the exponent of the life of a people, the extension of its sentiments, convictions, aims and ideals."[13] Hence, Catholic literature reflected the life of Catholics, while Protestant literature reflected the life of Protestants. One was essentially different from the other. However, both types reflected human existence; accordingly both must have as their aim assisting man to fulfill his destiny. Viewed in this fashion, literature was not a question of primary importance to Brownson. In itself, literature was neither good nor evil; it became one or the other according to its

[12]The importance of literature also occupied the deliberations of the Catholic hierarchy. Acknowledging tne press as "a powerful engine for good or for evil," the Bishops also sought to foster a growing body of Catholic literature. In 1837 the Bishops reported that some "publishers have put forth a number of books containing a correct exposition of our doctrines and the defense of our tenets," and had formed themselves "into a society for the production and dissemination of books useful to the cause of truth and of virtue." By 1840, the Bishops were encouraged and happy at the "existence of a spirit to sustain the efforts recently made to supply our schools, and our families with some books" that would "remove the dis-colourings of fiction, and vindicate the truth of History," while rescuing from "unmerited censure a portion of our illustrious dead, without doing violence to the feelings of even our opponents." The Bishops also encouraged those capable to undertake the task of creating suitable Catholic reading for young children. For all practical purposes, though, a Catholic literature remained in its incipient stage. See "Pastoral Letter (1837)," pp. 81-82; "Pastoral Letter (1840)," p. 94, in Nolan, op. cit.

[13]O. A. Brownson, "Modern Idolatry," BrQR, II (July, 1845), 381.

quality and the purpose it was made to serve. Brownson objected to
any notion that literature existed for its own sake. It was a
means to man's end as a religious being.[14]

Brownson belonged to a class of reviewers who judged subjects,
doctrines, principles, and tendencies of books, rather than books
as mere literary productions. He was a moralist; "/_o_/ur theology
determines our ethics, and our ethics determines our aesthetics."[15]
Brownson considered theology the queen of the sciences, whose practical application to life and all its activities was essential. As a
critic, then, "we are always obliged, whether we are reviewing a
work of science or art, to review it under its relation to
Catholicity, and to judge it by its bearing on Catholic doctrine
and morals."[16] Brownson adhered to these critical religious
principles in his reviews of fiction and non-fiction.[17]

[14]O. A. Brownson, "American Literature," BrQR, IV (July, 1847),
pp. 386-397.

[15]O. A. Brownson, "Dana's Poems and Prose Writings," BrQR,
VII (October, 1850), 466.

[16]Ibidem. On this point, Brownson was accused of being narrow,
illiberal, and bigoted, certainly unfair to non-Catholic writers,
and as we shall see, to Catholic writers also. As a literary critic
he went so far as to say that "only Catholic Americans are in a
position to assert and maintain American literary independence."
In several reviews, Brownson seems to say of non-Catholic writers
"Not bad, about the best a non-Catholic could write" or "any
heathen or pagan couldn't have said it better."

[17]Brownson believed "the primary object of poetry is, not to
instruct, but to move and please. It addresses the sentiments,
affections, imagination, rather than the understanding." O. A.
Brownson, "Novel-Writing and Novel-Reading," BrQR, V (January,
1848), 54. Hence, poetry will not be examined in this chapter,
since its purpose was not to educate. For additional remarks on
poetry, see O. A. Brownson, "Synthetic Philosophy," Democratic
Review (December, 1842; January and March, 1843); "R. W. Emerson's
Poems," BrQR, IV (April, 1847), 262-276; "The Vision of Sir
Launfal," BrQR, VI (April, 1849), 265-274; "Dana's Poems and Prose
Writings," BrQR, VII (October, 1850, 466-490; "Wordsworth's Poeti-
cal Works," BrQR, XII (October, 1855), 525-538.

In the first Catholic number of 1845, Brownson defended the
Church's Index, arguing that all religions practiced at least an
informal regulation of reading matter. In the case of Catholics,
the Church published its list and maintained the index as a matter
of discipline, guarding "the faithful against the destructive
effects of the licentiousness of the press."[18] Furthermore, he
argued that throughout the centuries the Church had always fostered
and preserved learning and literature. As the Church would continue its work to promote literature, so too would Brownson. He
would write but also serve as critic and reviewer, pointing out
the evils of modern literature and working to uplift Catholic
efforts. In much of his work, though, Brownson found himself a
rigid and severe critic, demanding a truly Catholic and Christian
literature; for him Catholic literature meant much more than a book
written by a Catholic.[19] He hoped his comments, however stern,
might serve as an aid in the formation of a true Catholic literature.

Fiction

Although he considered fiction less important than non-fiction,
nevertheless he found it the most worrisome. He offered his
advice to aspiring novelists, urging them to pray, meditate, and

---

[18]O. A. Brownson, "Literary Policy of the Church of Rome,"
BrQR, II (January, 1845), 4.

[19]Many of Brownson's criticisms in the ensuing pages sound
quite similar to current criticism of Afro-American literature by
the Black intelligentsia. The charge of "white man with black
skin" is comparable to Brownson's reminders that many Catholics
were still tainted by the pervading atmosphere of Protestant
America.

study Catholic philosophy and American institutions. Such a
preparation was essential for the development of a popular, national
literature

> which, though natural, is pure and innocent; though
> secular and free, is inoffensive to Catholic truth and
> virtue; and which, though not doing much directly to
> advance us in spiritual life, shall yet tend to culti-
> vate, refine, and humanize barbarous nature, and to
> remove those obstacles to the introduction and progress
> of Catholic civilization, which are interposed by
> ignorance, rude manners, rough feelings, wild and
> ferocious passion. The office of popular literature
> is not precisely to spiritualize but to civilize a
> people; and, as we look here for the highest develop-
> ment of modern civilization, we demand of our American
> Catholic the highest and purest secular literature.[20]

Setting a standard for novelists to follow may have been easy for
Brownson, but the task of the novelist to meet the criteria was
indeed difficult. No one realized this more clearly than Brownson
himself.

Just as America herself had not developed a national literature, neither could American Catholics expect a popular literature.
The Catholic population was unsettled and had not defined itself
yet; the clergy, of necessity, devoted themselves to pastoral
functions; finally, Catholic colleges had not yet produced enough
capable lay leaders, though this situation would change in a
matter of time.[21] Furthermore, Catholic writers of fiction did

---

[20]O. A. Brownson, "Catholicity and Literature," BrQR, XIII
(January, 1856), 70.
[21]O. A. Brownson, "Thornberry Abbey: A Tale of the Times,"
BrQR, III (October, 1846), 534-544. Brownson noted a general,
world-wide deterioration, and blamed it on the "want of force and
constancy of will, which itself is owing to the neglect of severe
studies, the want of true philosophical discipline, and of high
and noble aims;" see O. A. Brownson, "Catholic Secular Literature,"
BrQR, VI (July, 1849), 367.

not appeal to Catholics; the devout either had no taste for fiction

or had scruples about reading novels; those who were neither devout

nor scrupulous wanted novels more "highly spiced." Catholics

generally regarded Catholic writers as inferior (and no doubt they

were), except in works of faith and piety; hence, Catholics read

non-Catholic authors. Also, a Catholic author did not appeal to

the general, non-Catholic public, especially if he paraded

Catholicity before his readers. To succeed, writers relied on

appealing to foreign nationalities, drifting even more apart from

an American Catholic literature,[22] and selling to a limited

audience. What resulted was a case of Catholic fiction being a

very unprofitable business for both publishers and authors.

Publishers raised their prices to insure some return for their

investment, while authors received little financial remuneration.

Publishers attempted to make their books attractive by adding

extravagant bindings, enlarging the print, and thus increasing the

cost of paper, and limiting the number of purchasers.[23] Business

---

[22]O. A. Brownson, "Literary Notices and Criticisms," BrQR, XVI (July, 1859), 410.

[23]See the following letter Brownson received in 1854 complaining of such high costs: James Boyle to O.A.B., January 24, 1854, OABP, UNDA. See also, Patrick Donohoe to O.A.B., November 24, 1857, OABP UNDA, in which Donohoe, a publisher, complains to Brownson that he is unable to advance any money to a Mr. Stuart for his book Joan of Arc. Donohoe was facing very hard times, barely able to keep his head above water. Another author, C.E.T. Clarke, author of Lizzie Maitland, complained to Brownson that she had not received any money from her publisher, and that writing Catholic stories was so much bother and so little profit. She earned more money writing short stories for Harper's. See C.E.T. Clarke to O.A.B., October 18, 1860, OABP, UNDA. In the case of Mrs. Clarke, she needed the money desperately, herself an invalid for three years and her husband not well either. She also complained that American publishers would rather republish European works because in the absence of copyright laws publishers would not have to pay

agents suffered too; Lawrence Kehoe, an agent for Brownson, the

Catholic World, and other publications, lamented in 1865:

> My expenses are great and I have but little faith in
> Catholic Publications. I have spent 8 years--the best
> years of my life, at such business, and what have I got?
> Nothing. I am poorer now than when I went into it.[24]

Until Catholics were enlightened and increased not only their

demand for books, but also their ability to purchase them, financial

considerations would continue to hinder the writing, publishing,

and selling of Catholic literature.

More important than financial difficulties was the art of

writing fiction itself. The longer Brownson lived and the more

novels he read, the more he disliked them. If he considered litera-

ture merely of secondary importance, he placed the novel at the

bottom of the list of worthwhile literature. His antipathy toward

novels reached its peak in 1875 when he stated "we are strongly

opposed to all novels."[25] In reality, though, he had long opposed

novels, but because the novel was the most popular form of reading,

Brownson continually devoted his columns to improving the Catholic

novel in order to offset the evil effects arising from modern

secular literature.

One objection Brownson raised was that certain authors failed

to depict Catholicism properly. In reviewing Mora Carmody: or

Woman's Influence, Brownson advised Catholic writers to find a

---

any money to authors; see C.E.T. Clarke to O.A.B., November 26, 1860,
JABP, UNDA. In an undated letter, Peter F. Cunningham to O.A.B.,
JABP, UNDA, Cunningham, a publisher, asked Brownson to find out Mrs.
Clarke's lowest terms, and whether she would accept copies of the
book as payment.

[24]Lawrence Kehoe to O.A.B., February 15, 1865, OABP, UNDA.

[25]O. A. Brownson, "Women's Novels," BrQR, XXIV (July, 1875), 373.

better way to dispose of heroines "without sending them to a
convent."[26] In this case, the religious vow had not been freely
made but resulted from embarrassment or disappointment in love.
Entering a monastery or convent on the rebound was not proper
motivation for Catholics nor was it desirable to leave such an
impression on Protestant minds.[27]

Brownson also objected to several literary efforts made by
recent converts. He criticized John D. Bryant's Pauline Seward
for drawing too much of its spirit and tendency from the age and
country rather than from the Church. Love portrayed was merely
profane and certainly not the ideal of Christian perfection that
the Church demanded. Even worse, Brownson noted passages in which
Bryant expressly or implicitly denied the infallibility and
sanctity of the Church. In all probability, Brownson explained,
the author had not even realized his anti-Catholic statements.[28]

Like Bryant, Lady Georgiana Fullerton, another recent convert,
entered the Catholic literary scene with Grantley Manor, A Tale.
Although the novel had been praised by the Freeman's Journal,

---

[26]O. A. Brownson, "Literary Notices and Criticisms," BrQR,
II (January, 1845), 135.

[27]As an aside on the topic of motivation, Brownson also
criticized Hawthorne's The Scarlet Letter on the grounds that
Hawthorne did not choose a suitable topic, that his characters
only felt a sense of regret and not true remorse for their crimes,
that they never repented their crime, that their "love" was really
illicit and criminal and not as laudable as Hawthorne depicted it.
Brownson charged Hawthorne with not understanding that man sins
against God, not against himself. Finally, Hawthorne's characters
did not find interior peace, so characteristic of true penance.

[28]O. A. Brownson, "Novel-writing and Novel-reading," BrQR, V
(January, 1848), 48-71.

Brownson found several disturbing items. He objected to Lady

Fullerton's use, or rather misuse of Catholic theology, in which

she unknowingly praised in her Catholic characters things which

the Church abominated or forbade. Also, in trying not to be offen-

sive to former Protestant friends, she had watered down Catholic

principles to resemble Protestant ones, and thus, deprecated good

Catholics and demeaned the Church. Brownson also urged her to

write more about Catholic characters, and always within a Catholic

setting.[29]

In the case of these and other writers, Brownson offered

solemn strictures. No matter what the intentions of the author

may have been, he or she was responsible for presenting truth to

readers. An author must know whether or not his content contra-

dicted Church doctrine. Too often, Brownson complained, converts

with much zeal and a little knowledge had hurriedly dashed off a

publication that displeased or embarrassed the Church. He advised

them that "if we do not know Catholic faith and theology well

enough not to compromise either, our business is to hold our

peace."[30] Errors were serious and would only hurt the Church and

religion. For this reason, those who chose to write novels needed

to be thoroughly instructed in Catholic faith and theology, and

needed to meditate and frequent the sacraments. The production of

---

[29]O. A. Brownson, "Grantley Manor, or Popular Literature,"
BrQR, V (October, 1848), 482-506. See also, O. A. Brownson,
"Catholic Popular Literature," BrQR, XXII (April, 1873), 189-205,
in which Brownson again objects to converts who write in apolo-
gizing or conceding tones to their non-Catholic friends.

[30]"Novel-writing and Novel-reading," p. 70.

a false and corrupting "Catholic" literature would cause more harm
than the combined efforts of the entire anti-Catholic press. True
Catholic literature must provide ideals for Catholics, not concessions to non-Catholics. It must form Catholic minds, not by
following or exaggerating popular errors and sentiments but by
placing before its readers Catholic principles, ideals, and
doctrines.[31]

Certain novelists thought that a Catholic novel had to explain
and defend the Church on theological and dogmatic matters. Usually,
they resorted to love stories, with a dash or two of theological
disputation and instruction. Brownson objected to this kind of
literature also. In the first place, reviews, journals, and newspapers were the proper sphere for presenting polemical and controversial remarks. Novelists needed to refrain from flaunting
theological arguments in the face of their readers. Secondly,
readers who wanted to learn dogma turned to reviews, works of piety
ascetism and not to novels. Thirdly, fiction readers did not
pursue novels for dogma either; they sought entertainment. Mixing

---

[31]"Grantley Manor, or Popular Literature," pp. 502-506. Lady
Fullerton took Brownson's advice to heart and in the ensuing years
Brownson came to regard her as one of the best Catholic novelists.
Bryant, however, was upset over certain of Brownson's remarks. In
John D. Bryant to O.A.B., February 4, 1848, OABP, UNDA, Bryant
wrote: "Mr. Brownson will stand corrected in the following important point. -All those texts of Ancient Scripture, which forbid the
yoking of oxen and asses, do not, as Mr. B. supposes, refer to
religious novels. They are prophetic, and refer exclusively to the
press and a certain Editor. The press is the powerful ox signified.
The Editor is the ass, and the texts, thus interpreted, mean,
"Thou shalt not yoke (or rather hitch) this Editor to the press,
otherwise mischief will ensue as the one is not competent to work
with, or upon, the other."

profane, sentimental love stories with theological instruction
resulted in failure, for the combination pleased no readers at
all.[32] Such a novel that attempted to connect dogma with love and
marriage Brownson called "a literary monstrosity which is equally
indefensible under the relation of religion and that of art."[33]
Although authors intended such works as antidotes to the impure
and corrupting sensational and sentimental novels that flooded the
market, Brownson doubted any beneficial results would accrue.

> In the first place, serious-minded people, who will read
> the graver part, the controversy, the exposition and
> defense of Catholic doctrine and morals, find the story,
> the love and marriage portion, an annoyance of which
> they would prefer to be relieved; and those who read
> for the story are equally annoyed by the graver part,
> and usually skip without reading it. The fact is, the
> reading of either part indisposes one to read the other
> part. The state of mind produced by reading the one
> part is quite different from that necessary to relish
> the other. The parts do not cohere and produce unity
> of impression. In the second place, the romance part
> of these novels seldom differs except in degree from
> the objectionable popular novels . . . . We think,
> therefore, that these religious novels, in so far as
> they are novels at all, only create in their readers
> a taste for the highly-spiced and poisonous litera-
> ture they are intended to counteract or supersede.[34]

Besides cautioning against novels that contained ill-formed
notions of Catholicism and others that tried to join romance and
dogma, Brownson disliked novels (usually written by women), that

---

[32]Brownson restated this over and over again. See the following as samples: "Religious Novels" (1847), 116, 128; "Novel-
writing and Novel-reading" (1848), 48-71; "Catholicity and Literature" (1856), 62-81; "Religious Novels (1873), 53-69.
[33]"Religious Novels" (1873), p. 59.
[34]Ibid., pp. 59-60.

considered human love above God's law, that effeminized society,
and that tended to destroy the family. The modern tendency in
literature considered love an infallible indicator of God's will.
Love legitimated marriage, and where no love existed, the family
dissolved. Furthermore, most writers were women who depicted their
own sex with "cruelty."[35] Brownson believed authors ought to depict
ideal Christian perfection; instead they painted woman devoid of
her charms and lovable qualities, and as heartless, despotic,
intriguing, capricious, and indifferent to ruin and misery. Man's
chivalric nature was also obliterated, for woman was no longer
capable of inspiring such sentiment and respect from man.

Just as womanhood was denigrated, so too was manhood shabbily
depicted. Brownson believed that no matter how cruelly women
depicted one another, nonetheless women always turned out superior
to men. Woman ran the household, while man lost his firmness and
strength of character; woman led, while man followed. As much as
Brownson disliked Puritanism, it did maintain man as head of the
family who played a positive role in rearing children. In modern
literature, children received all their values from women, and
thus reflected both maternal weakness and the absence of paternal
authority. Children grew up overly sentimental and effeminate.
"The mother's influence softens, weakens, and enervates, when not
tempered and hardened by the influence of the father."[36] Mothers

[35]"Religious Novels" (1873), p. 61. Brownson here speaks of
his ideal of womanhood so essential for family stability and the
education of children.

[36]"Women's Novels," p. 372.

were not always qualified to train sons up to be strong, energetic, and self-reliant men, capable of carrying on in a rough life and distinguishing themselves as upright, bold, and honest Catholic citizens. As the backbone of society, the family needed positive pictures of itself.

> The object of the Catholic novelist, or cultivator
> of light literature, is not or should not be to paint
> actual life, or life as we actually find it, but to
> idealize it, and raise it, as far as possible to the
> Christian standard, not indeed by direct didactic dis-
> courses or sermonizing, which is out of place in a
> novel; but by the silent influence of the pictures
> presented, and the spirit that animates them.[37]

What Brownson wanted to see and what he actually saw were quite distinct. After reading sentimental novels for nearly thirty years, Brownson seemed to despair that women writers could produce a popular and true Catholic literature. Instead, he urged them to write history or biography where they could exert an influence for good.[38]

Yet, as much as he disapproved of novels, Brownson realized their necessity in an age when people were reading them. If most of his remarks seemed negative, he did praise several novels during his years as a Catholic reviewer. He liked works of the German, Canon Christopher von Schmid, Lady Georgiana Fullerton, Mrs. James Sadlier, Jedediah V. Huntington and the productions of Dunigan's

---

[37]"Religious Novels" (1873), pp. 65-66.

[38]Ibid., p. 67. Brownson's daughter, Sarah, wrote a biography of Demetrius Gallitzin which he praised. Some disgruntled critics charged that he had relaxed his standards and shown favoritism toward his daughter's work.

Home Library. Overall, though, he found little in the Catholic
novel of much worth.[39]

Although Brownson geared most of his comments on literature
to adults, he also reviewed (and usually unfavorably) literature
for children. Prior to his conversion, and after it, Brownson
found fault with most children's books. "We wish the greater part
of books sent out for children were burnt up, or so completely
destroyed that no trace of them should be left." He objected to
the false notions of religion, philosophy and education presented
by these books. They turned the mind outward to contemplate the
material and animal kingdoms. This could only lead to sensualism,
materialism, atheism and scepticism. Furthermore, such books
attempted to teach by pouring outward experiences onto the mind.
Real learning took place by enabling the child to draw forth from
himself the facts of his own spiritual nature. The real merit of
books "is to be measured by their power of revealing the mind to
itself, of making the child a thinking, reasoning and reasonable
being." Books devoid of religion, guided by a false philosophy,
and tied to an incorrect approach to learning dominated children's
literature. Certainly no social progress could be expected from

---

[39]Another writer in the Catholic World noted this same weakness in American Catholic novels. See "Use and Abuse of the
Novel," Catholic World, XVI (1872), 240-254. On page 247, the
author defined the modern sensational novel as: "A complexity of
improbabilities woven around a crowd of nonentities, interspersed
with fashionable filth, and relieved by sleek-coated beastiness;
meaning nothing, and good for less."

such books.[40] One of the few authors he recommended, though, was
Canon von Schmid.

The novel, or light literature, then, Brownson viewed as a
civilizing or humanizing means to man's religious end in life. He
did not expect it to spiritualize man, or to present theological
or dogmatic truths; but he did expect fiction to idealize life
through its Christian tone and spirit. At best perhaps, Brownson
hoped Catholic fiction could offset the evil influences of popular
literature that permeated the American literary scene, especially
since most readers preferred the novel to non-fiction. His views
as a novel critic closely resembled his attitudes toward American
society. In the early stages, he urged the creation of a moral
"American" literature; following his conversion, he seems to have
merely substituted "Catholic" for "American." Although he had
generally disliked the novel all along, his antipathy reached its
peak in those pessimistic years following the Civil War. After so
many years of reading, he finally concluded that novels were just
as corrupt as American society. Living in corruption was one
thing, but no longer did he want to read its exponents--novels.

Non-Fiction

If the Catholic novel was meant to provide moral enjoyment
and entertainment for the less serious reader, non-fiction appealed
to more serious Catholics. Brownson was much more optimistic over
the progress and prospects of Catholic efforts in non-fiction.

---

[40]O. A. Brownson, "Children's Books," contained in a scrapbook
of clippings that Brownson kept while he was editor of the Boston
Reformer in 1836, OABP, UNDA. See also, "Lecture on Reading,"
op. cit. For his remarks on Canon von Schmid, see Chapter 5, ftn.
7.

Doctrinal, polemical, controversial, biographical, historical, and
ascetic works were more abundant, of higher quality, and sold
better. Oddly though, Brownson rarely directed a full-length essay
devoted to the purpose and creation of Catholic non-fiction. In
his dialectical fashion, Brownson tried to offset extremes;
certainly the poor quality of Catholic fiction was the reason that
he devoted so many complete articles to improving that genre. And
for all the time he devoted to bettering the novel

> we should be glad to see the novel less frequently
> resorted to, because of its fatal facility of composi-
> tion, and its inevitable tendency to enfeeble the mind
> both of the writer and of the reader. We should like
> much to see the departments of history and biography,
> especially of emiment Catholics, enlarged. Both history
> and biography furnish more startling incidents, and
> produce a deeper and intenser interest, than any
> possible work of fiction; and what is more to the
> purpose, they cannot be prepared and well written with-
> out labor and pains, or read without stimulating
> thought, awakening noble aspirations, or strengthening
> the mind and adding to its stock of knowledge.[41]

The light literature of fiction could never be as important as non-
fiction which not only provided knowledge and strengthened mind,
but also elevated man's thoughts and aspirations.

Just as the Catholic novelist contended against and attempted
to offset the evils in pernicious novels, so too the historian and
biographer faced similar difficulties. Brownson believed that much
of the writing that passed for "history" was merely speculation.
"History is not a speculative science; it deals exclusively with
facts, and is simply a record of events which have succeeded one

[41]O. A. Brownson, "Catholic Popular Literature," BrQR, XXII
(April, 1873), 205.

another in time."[42] Facts and events were not isolated; and they did have to be arranged and explained by the historian. However, Brownson believed modern writers were fitting the facts to the theory, and were not drawing out the theory from the facts. "History" became a tool for philosophical, theological, metaphysical, ethical or political theories of the universe, of God, of man, and of society. Hence,

> facts encountered which contradict their theories are passed over in silence, denied, distorted, or explained away; facts which are needed to explain and establish them, if not encountered, are invented; and facts which have no apparent bearing on them one way or the other are discarded as unimportant and without historical significance.[43]

What such writers recorded as history was merely what to them history ought to be.

But because a work of history presented itself as fact, it was a more powerful weapon on the mind than the novel--for good or for evil. Unfortunately, especially from a Catholic point of view, modern historians had misrepresented much of the Catholic past.

> Of all the devices for disseminating falsehood, corrupting youth, and destroying all true intellectual and moral life, this of making history the vehicle of communicating the theological, metaphysical, ethical, and political theories of the author is the most ingenious and the most effective. The novel or romance did very well, but it was in bad odor with the graver part of the community, and often went no farther than to corrupt the heart and disturb the senses. More could be accomplished under the grave mask of the historian than under the light and fantastic mask of

---

[42]O. A. Brownson, "Bancroft's History of the United States," BrQR, IX (October, 1852), 422.

[43]Ibid., p. 423.

the novelist or romancer. Hence our histories are
nearly all written with a view of inculcating, often
without the design of being suspected, some crude
and in general mischievous theory on religion,
philosophy, or politics. The author professes to
give you facts, so interwoven with them that none
but a disciplined mind can separate them; he insinu-
ates into the ingenuous and unsuspecting reader his
false and pernicious speculative theories.[44]

This ability of historians to misrepresent truth under the guise of

fact was especially disturbing to Brownson for practically every

popular history that circulated among Catholics, especially in the

United States and England, had been written by "unbelievers,

heretics, Gallicans, or lukewarm Catholics." Furthermore,

Catholics' appreciation of their own history and religion diminished

when Catholic writers conceded as true many of the unfounded

charges leveled against the Church or Catholic personages.

Brownson saw a wide open field for qualified Catholics in the

production of works of non-fiction. "Never was there a nobler

work, never did a more honorable or glorious career open to the

ingenuous youth."[45] Just as Brownson considered himself a scholar

doing God's work, so too he looked for more aspirants.

---

[44]Ibid., pp. 425-426.

[45]O. A. Brownson, "Literary Notices and Criticisms," BrQR, IX
(April, 1852), 282. The relations between the most noted Catholic
historian of the period, John Gilmary Shea, and Brownson were
always strained. Brownson had criticized the first edition of
de Courci's work (and Shea translator), and had objected to some
historical inaccuracies in a school text prepared by Shea.
Also, Brownson had not noticed one of Shea's first works until a
couple of years after its publication. Brownson praised Shea's
History of the Catholic Missions Among the Indian Tribes of the
United States, 1829-1854, but his four volume work did not appear
until after Brownson's death. Their misunderstandings and dis-
agreements were never straightened out.

Young men, we look to you to enlist in the grand army
of the living God, and to march forth with brave hearts
to the battle against ignorance, superstition, heresy,
infidelity, irreligion, the implacable enemies of the
Church, and always in arms against the Lord and his
Christ.[46]

Unless Catholics labored to write history and biography, misrepre-

sentations would be passed down as the facts of history, picturing

Catholics and their religion less creditable than they really were.

History of the wrong sort would operate to weaken faith, diminish

charity, and dampen Catholic zeal.

As important as Brownson considered history and biography,

he seldom devoted articles on their development. Actually,

though, practically every issue of Brownson's Quarterly Review

devoted several pages to "Literary Notices and Criticisms." In

these pages Brownson commented on the ever increasing volume of

Catholic literature that was being produced. He cited dozens of

works, such as the following: Thomas D'Arcy McGee, Historical

Sketch of O'Connell and his Friends, with a Glance at the Future

Destiny of Ireland; A History of the Irish Settlers in North

America, from the Earliest Period to the Census of 1850; A History

of the Attempts to establish the Protestant Reformation in Ireland,

and the Successful Resistance of the Irish People from 1540-1830;

The Catholic History of North America; Alban Butler, Lives of the

Saints; M. Collet, Life of St. Vincent de Paul, Founder of the

Mission and of the Sisters of Charity; Charles C. Pise, Saint

Ignatius and His First Companions; John Lingard, A History of

England, from the First Invasion by the Romans to the Commencement

---

[46]Ibidem.

of the Reign of William The Third (13 vols.); Pierre de Smet,
Oregon Missions and Travels over the Rocky Mountains in 1845-46;
Chevalier Artaud de Montor, Histoire des Souverains Pontifes
Romains; Count de Montalembert, The Life of St. Elizabeth, of
Hungary, Duchess of Thuringin and The Monks of the West, from St.
Benedict to St. Bernard; John Gilmary Shea, History of the Catholic
Missions Among the Indian Tribes of the United States, 1829-1854
and Henry de Courcy (and Shea trans.), The Catholic Church in the
United States; Martin John Spalding, History of the Reformation;
Cardinal Wiseman, Fabiola; or the Church of the Catacombs; Cardinal
Newman, Callista: a Sketch of the Third Century; P. E. Moriarity,
The Life of St. Augustine, Bishop, Confessor, and Doctor of the
Church; Richard H. Clarke, Lives of the deceased Bishops of the
Catholic Church in the United States; Sarah M. Brownson, The Life
of Demetrius Augustine Gallitzin, Prince and Priest; Richard
Simpson, Life of Edmund Campion. Brownson cited many works not of
American origin because the Church was catholic, her message
universal, and true accounts of history and biography provided
themes common to the entire Church. He hoped books of this sort,
that maintained fidelity to historical facts, would present
Catholics with a truer picture of the past, help clear up many
misrepresentations and calumnies that prevailed in popular
histories. True Catholic history provided knowledge, strengthened
the mind, and increased respect and reverence for the Church,
thus securing the ties of serious readers to the Church.[47]

---

[47]Many of Brownson's remarks are quite similar to current
complaints by racial and ethnic minorities about distorted history
books and their effects on self-respect and group identity.
Consider Brownson's words in light of recent Black, Chicano,

Besides clearing up historical inaccuracies, Catholics needed
to be able to defend the Church against Protestants and anti-
Catholics. They had to know the grounds upon which their claims
were based and had to refute any arguments denying the authenticity
and universality of the Church. They had to meet non-Catholics
squarely; hence, polemical, controversial and apologetical literature was needed. In an age of religious controversy, Brownson was
again able to cite several worthwhile Catholic works: Francis
Patrick Kenrick, The Primacy of the Apostolic See Vindicated and A
Vindication of the Catholic Church, in a Series of Letters addressed
to the Rt. Rev. John Henry Hopkins, Protestant Episcopal Bishop of
Vermont; Martin John Spalding, Lectures on the Evidences of
Catholicity and Miscellanea; James Bossuet, History of the Varia-
tions of the Protestant Churches; Robert Manning, The Shortest
Way to end Disputes About Religion; Henry Major, Reasons for
Acknowledging the Authority of the Holy See of Rome; F. M. Pittar,
A Protestant converted to Catholicity by her Bible and Prayer book;
J. G. Penny, The Exercise of Faith Impossible except in the
Catholic Church; J. Balmez, Protestantism and Catholicity compared

---

Indian, Polish, Hungarian, and Italian identity and power movements.
Besides encouraging Catholic publications to correct misrepresentations of Catholic history, Brownson also criticized non-Catholic
publications for their selection of writers to cover Catholic
topics. He criticized Dr. Worcester's Dictionary for its poor
definition of Catholic terms, and George Ripley's Cyclopedia for
selecting Protestant writers to handle articles on the Catholic
Church. Nevertheless, Brownson refused to write on philosophy for
the latter, after he had seen the first three volumes. See a
letter from Worcester's publishers, Swen, Brewer & Tileston to
O.A.B., April 23, 1860, OABP, UNDA, and for Ripley's response to
Brownson's objections, see George Ripley to O.A.B., August 5,
1858, QABP, UNDA.

in their effects on the Civilization of Europe; Milner's End of
Religious Controversy; Dr. Levi Silliman Ives, The Trials of a Mind
in its Progress to Catholicism; a letter to his Old Friends;
Cardinal Newman, Loss and Gain; or the Story of a Convert; Isaac
Hecker, Questions of the Soul and Aspirations of Nature; Francis X.
Weninger, Protestantism and Infidelity; Rt. Rev. Dr. Shiel, The
Bible Against Protestantism and for Catholicity; Ambrose Manahan,
Triumph of the Church in the Early Ages; and Brownson's own Spirit
Rapper and The Convert.

Besides works of controversy, Brownson also believed it essential that Catholics produce spiritual works, including not only
new and improved translations and commentaries on the Bible, but
also works of devotion, of dogmatic and moral instruction, of piety
and ascetism. He did not feel that nineteenth century productions
were as pure or rigorous as those of the Middle Ages, but he
certainly could not complain about their paucity. Hundreds and
probably thousands of such works were sent him by publishers either
for review or notice. The pages of Brownson's Quarterly Review
were filled with remarks, listings, or advertisements of spiritual
books, whether current productions or re-publications or new
translations of the Church fathers or saints. If novels provided
for moral entertainment, if history and biography presented
knowledge and stimulated the mind, if works of controversy enabled
Catholics to defend their faith and Church, strictly religious works
were meant to spiritually uplift the soul, to stimulate meditation,

and to direct Catholics to lead holy, devout, and moral lives.[48]

Brownson himself certainly contributed many historical and

controversial articles in the pages of the Quarterly Review. He

even attempted religious fiction with "Edward Morton" in 1845,[49]

and when he wrote for Ave Maria most of his contributions were

dedicated to the devotion of the Blessed Mother.[50] Merely pro-

viding Catholic schools did not guarantee that graduates would be

able to keep the faith. Besides the other formal and informal

agencies literature too could serve several educational purposes.

For light readers as well as the serious minded, Catholic fiction

and non-fiction provided a moral antidote against the corrupting

influences of secular novels, corrected erroneous history and

biography, and instructed Catholics with knowledge and truth,

pointed out moral duty, and directed Catholics in the way they

should go.[51]

---

[48]Literally, hundreds of titles appear in BrQR; a few representative samples include The Pious Guide to Prayer and Devotion; The Way of Salvation, or Meditations for every Day in the Year; The Flowers of Piety; The Practice of Christian and Religious Perfection; The Golden Manual, being a Guide to Catholic Devotion Public and Private; and Familiar Instruction in the Faith and Morality of the Catholic Church, adapted to the Use both of Children and Adults.

[49]See O. A. Brownson, "Edward Morton," BrQR, II (January, 1845), 98-129; it was probably fortunate that Brownson did not write much fiction if this story is any indication.

[50]See Orestes A. Brownson, Saint-Worship--The Worship of Mary, ed. by Thomas R. Ryan (Patterson, New Jersey: St. Anthony Guild Press, 1963).

[51]Yet, financial considerations still limited non-fictional works at this time. Another writer in the Catholic World proposed the establishment of some 2400 local Catholic libraries throughout the nation. Each group would get fifty people to contribute $2 each, thus enabling each group to purchase about 150 volumes for circulation. This would create a demand for literature, urge more people to write, and bring down the cost of publications. See "On

When Brownson revived the <u>Review</u> in 1873, he assessed Catholic
literary progress. He granted that the list of accomplishments was
not overwhelming; nonetheless, he was able to count several
meritorious works of non-fiction. Even more encouraging to Brownson
was the change he noted; in his editorial role, books just seemed
to keep coming his way. He estimated that the number of Catholic
volumes being written and published had increased ten-fold between
1864 and 1873.

> This proves that our Catholic books are in demand, that
> our community is a reading community, and are encouraging
> their own literature. This is a wholesome symptom, and
> proves that our Catholic Schools are doing this work.[52]

Brownson had merely noted Catholic progress, and called the
accomplishments a "wholesome symptom." Yet, a symptom was not the
realization or attainment of perfection.

Brownson qualified his apparent over-optimism of 1873 during
his final year as a reviewer. If American Catholics had progressed,
they had not gone far enough; if Catholic schools had given literature an impetus, they still had not produced sufficient intellectual
powers among the laity. American Catholics continued to remain
behind Catholic Europe in literary attainments, especially in
secular and popular literature. Brownson looked to the schools,
especially colleges and universities. Just as he had stated in

Catholic Libraries," <u>Catholic World</u>, XIV (1871), 707-715. This
author recommended for purchase many of the same works Brownson
had suggested, and added the works of D'Aubignes and, of course,
Brownson.

[52]O. A. Brownson, "Literary Notices and Criticisms," <u>BrQR</u>,
XXII (July, 1873), 432.

1847 that a Catholic literature would not spring up in America until scholarship was pursued even beyond the college years, and then allowed to filter down to the masses, so again in his last number of October, 1875, Brownson called on the hundred or so colleges and their graduates to demonstrate to the world that American Catholics were capable of producing and sustaining a literature. He asked:

> Do we ever reflect that we owe our intellect and literary ability, if we have any, to God? Do we never feel that we owe something to our country, and are bound to do our best to enlighten it, and to consult its literary honor and glory?[53]

As he had done his best, he now called on other capable Catholics to fulfill "the scholar's mission."

Because of the intimate relationship between literature and the press, one must regard Brownson's comments of each in light of the other. His request not to read bad literature (in the previous chapter) certainly applies to his denunciations of the novel during the post-Civil War period. His demand that Catholics support their press must also be extended to include book literature. He did not change his criteria for evaluating the worth of books, but he did take a more conservative stand in his last years. He gradually withdrew himself from things American, and resorted to all things Catholic.

It is not the purpose of this chapter to evaluate Brownson as a literary critic per se; rather, it is an attempt to assess

---

[53]O. A. Brownson, "Literary Notices and Criticisms," BrQR, XXIV (October, 1875), 571.

Brownson's views of literature as an agency of education--
civilizing, humanizing, instructing, moralizing, and spiritualizing
the Catholic population. Considering the position of the Church
and its despised status as a minority in nineteenth-century America,
Brownson's remarks are analogous to the current power and identity
movements of various racial and ethnic groups within American
society. His admonitions to Catholic novelists to make their
works breathe a Catholic atmosphere and tone are quite similar to
modern calls for "blackness." What minority group today is not
"re-writing" its history, digging up the past, clarifying misconceptions, building up heroes and tearing down myths (and in some
cases replacing old myths with new ones)? Whether it be Black,
Indian, Chicano, Italian, Polish, Hungarian, Jew, Greek, or woman,
a minority consciousness awakens and attempts to paint positive
pictures of itself, to have its rights recognized by the dominant
(and often hostile) majority, to develop group pride and solidarity,
to shed feelings of inferiority, and to build a people capable of
doing things for themselves. Viewed in this light, Brownson's
views of the educational importance of literature represent a
perennial, and perhaps profound, contribution to the education of
Catholic Americans.

CHAPTER IX

LYCEUMS AND ADULT SOCIETIES AS EDUCATORS

i

PRE-CATHOLIC PERIOD

In a Fourth of July Address delivered in 1831, Brownson
pointed out a recent development in behalf of education. "A new
energy has lately been given to the cause of popular instruction,
by the establishment of Lyceums in our populous cities, and in many
of our villages."[1] In another address, he cited not only the
associations called Lyceums, but also the popular lectures as
contributing to the education of the people and to the work of
social renovation.[2]

This "town meeting of the mind,"[3] Brownson felt, was destined
to contribute significantly to the education of the people. "It
possesses a capacity, which, when fully developed, will make it an
institution of immense power."[4] The Lyceum had sprung up from the
feeling of the age and the country that greater exertions needed
to be made in behalf of educating the people. The Lyceum was but

---

[1]Qvid Address, p. 15. The Lyceum had started just five years
before this in 1826.

[2]"Social Evils and their Remedies," op. cit.

[3]See Carl Bode, The American Lyceum, Town Meeting of the Mind
(New York: Oxford University Press, 1956) for the widespread
growth of the lyceum since its founding in 1826 by Josiah Holbrook.

[4]"Education of the People," p. 424.

in its infancy; it had not accomplished much yet, but with proper
direction, it could emerge as a central educational agency.

Brownson's major concern about the defects of Lyceums and popular lectures was that hitherto they had discussed topics too
remotely connected with man's life. The Lyceum had dealt with
facts, mostly of physical science, rather than with moral and
intellectual philosophy. Facts certainly gratified man's curiosity
and filled his memory but man had deeper wants. Ideas and ever-
lasting principles appealed to man's inner and more enduring needs,
and awakened his mind and set it to work. Only by studying religious and political ideas would man shed light on the questions of
individual and social destiny and work for human advancement.
Lyceums and lectures must involve themselves with ideas. "Whoever
has an idea is always a king and a priest. Ideas work all the
revolutions which affect the moral and political world."[5]

The Lyceum could do this, though, only if it became serious
and manly. It needed to aim higher and strike deeper, rather than
waste its strength on less important matters. All its energies
must be devoted to the solution of the problem of human destiny--
"What is my destiny, as a man? What is the destiny of society?
And how may I best fulfill my own destiny, and contribute to the
fulfillment of the destiny of society?"[6]

In addition to the content of the Lyceum and popular lectures,
Brownson felt that oratorical styles also needed improvement.[7]

---

[5]Ibid., p. 428.

[6]Ibidem.

[7]These remarks also apply to the preaching of sermons from
the pulpit.

The main weakness of speakers was that their thoughts centered on themselves and not on their audience. Orators were generally cold, restraining their emotions, gestures and natural promptings. Their manner, tones, and gestures became artificial, stiff, formal, and unvaried. The best speakers "felt" their subjects, forgot themselves, and relied on the force of truth, the majesty of theme, and the naturalness of tone. What resulted was a stream of "strong, rushing, $\lceil$ and $\rfloor$ overwhelming eloquence."[8]

In his first speeches Brownson was himself shy and perspired much. But through years of exertion and study, he gradually felt at ease, adapted his voice and manner to his content, and illustrated his expressions by appropriate gestures. In addition, he had great power in his voice which was produced by the abdominal muscles, thus enabling him to speak at length without fatigue.[9] In his own speaking, then, Brownson combined oratorical ability with what he considered an important topic aimed at elevating the populace. One newspaper wrote that Brownson's energy and ability "provoke his hearers and readers into reflection. It is a great luxury to hear him, whether his opinions are yours or not."[10] Although he had for many years been a speaker, having delivered hundreds of sermons and several Fourth of July Elections, his move to the Boston area, his establishment of the Society for

[8]Henry F. Brownson, Brownson's Early Life, pp. 89-90.

[9]Ibid., p. 89.

[10]Unidentified newspaper, undated (although definitely prior to is conversion to Catholicism; probably 1843 or 1844), in N.Y. ublic Library. A photostat copy of this is contained in the ABP, UNDA.

Christian Union and Progress, and his editorship of the <u>Boston</u>

<u>Quarterly Review</u> brought him into public notice. Accordingly, the

luxury of hearing Brownson increased during the early 1840's, as

he received many additional requests for speaking engagements. He

was becoming known at a time that witnessed the proliferation of

adult, self-help societies. Prior to his Catholic period, he was

a well-known speaker in the eastern states from Maine to Baltimore.

He spoke at colleges and universities, lyceums, literary institutes

and associations, labor organizations, mechanics institutes,

library associations, state conventions, and Democratic party

organizations.[11] His topics ranged from improving education to

elevating labor. His aim was to lecture in a proper oratorical

style, to present moral and intellectual ideas, to cause people

to think, and above all, to contribute to moral, religious,

intellectual, and social improvement of mankind.

ii

CATHOLIC ADULT SOCIETIES

Prior to Brownson's conversion he had associated himself with

several adult, mutual-benefit societies--as a learning member and

---

[11]In the Brownson Papers are numerous letters to verify these
pre-Catholic engagements. Among known places, Brownson spoke
several times each year in New York and Philadelphia. In many
places, like Providence and Baltimore he was invited back year
after year. He spoke at Lyceums in New York, Concord, Milton,
Lynn, Haverhill, Lexington. At the collegiate level he appeared
at Brown, Vermont, Dartmouth, Wesleyan, and Waterville. He lectured in Ovid, Dedham, Ipswich, Deerfield, Greenfield, Nantucket,
Brooklyn, Chelsea, Portland, Beverly, Woonsocket. He also
addressed the Jefferson Society of Reformed Drinkers, New Haven
Young Men's Institute, Hamilton Literary Association, Mechanics'
Institute of New York, Mercantile Library Association of New York,

as a guest lecturer. All such activities revealed the on-going

process of education, from the cradle to the grave. Certainly,

Brownson believed education took place beyond the school years and

outside the school room. In fact, these adult societies were

essential for the elevation of adult population by creating a

climate for intellectual and moral advancement. Especially

important, Brownson believed, was the creation of similar societies

for Catholic adults whose surrounding environment was over-

whelmingly Protestant.

Even if Catholic children received a good home education, and

attended parochial schools or Catholic colleges, no guarantee

existed that they would be secure in their religious beliefs and

practices after school days. The principal reason, Brownson

asserted, was because no Catholic society at large and no Catholic

public opinion exerted an influence to encourage, protect, and

sustain these young adults. Instead, they found a society hostile

to their religion. The Church, especially the clergy, needed to

take a deep interest in them, to consult them, and to engage them

in the service of religion.

> The way to retain our young men, collegebred or not,
> is to place a generous confidence in them, to devise
> ways and means by which they can take an active part
> in promoting Catholic interests. We lose them by
> giving them nothing to do, and leaving them to run away
> with the notion that they are regarded as of no impor-
> tance, are counted for nothing, and must seek their
> friends outside of the Catholic body.[12]

Andover Library Association, the Calvert Institute of Baltimore,
and the Catholic Young Friends Society of Boston. Many of the
letters informed Brownson of other invited speakers: Bancroft,
Emerson, Dana, Phillips, Everett, and Seward.

[12]"The Blakes and the Flanagans," p. 206.

Yet, even as he complained, Brownson saw nascent Catholic societies taking shape and remedying the situations he had noted. By the mid-1850's, Catholic Institutes had sprung up in Albany, Cincinnati, St. Louis, New Orleans and other places. Young Catholics' and Friends' Societies existed in Boston, Baltimore, Washington, Portland, Syracuse, Newark, Brooklyn and in some parishes in New York. Brownson saw several advantages to be reaped from these societies.

First of all, these organizations served as educational agencies, complimenting the education derived from the home, school, and church. The Catholic Institutes were associations seeking the intellectual and literary improvement of the members, and, directly or indirectly, the advancement of Catholic interests. They involved young men with their religion and created a Catholic public opinion. The Institutes brought in talented lecturers from all parts of the country, and encouraged local talent to step forward on the platform. Generally, the societies were run by laity, with clerical support and approval. The clergy, Brownson felt, should have the power to suppress any society deemed unfavorable to religion. Overall though, very few cases existed where these societies had transcended their liberties.[13]

Secondly, Young Catholics' and Friends' Societies, established to protect and instruct poor Catholic children, enabled members to engage in Catholic work, helped them develop a Catholic spirit, provided them with spiritual uplifting and renewal, deepened their love of religion, strengthened their attachment to the Catholic

---

[13]Ibid., pp. 206-208.

body, and secured graces for them to resist non-Catholic societal influences.[14]

Besides benefitting the members, the Young Catholics' and Friends' Societies were intended to aid poor Catholic children by assisting and cooperating with the clergy in the gathering together of children and in giving them spiritual instruction. Enough clergy just did not exist; Brownson believed the extension and perfection of the YCFS could substantially aid the Church's work. With the ever-growing institutional structure of the Church, the Church had spread to almost every area where it could reach.

> We have a laity able and willing, if called upon, to
> do all that the laity can do to assist the clergy in
> the religious instruction of the children who cannot
> receive a proper religious education from their parents.
> Alone, the clergy, we admit, cannot do all that needs
> to be done; that is, they cannot do it with their own
> hands. But they can in this matter multiply themselves
> a thousand-fold, by calling to their aid the young men
> and women of their parish, employing them to find out
> the children and to bring them to catechism, and under
> the direction of the pastor, teach them the catechism
> itself. Some may have it for their mission simply
> to teach Christian doctrine, others to look after the
> children of parents unable or too careless to send
> their children; other still may have it for theirs to
> raise funds to clothe decently the children of the
> destitute. In this way the whole congregation may be
> engaged as a committee of safety for the rising genera-
> tion. The parish might be divided for this purpose
> into districts, and special persons appointed to look
> after the children of particular district, and thus
> every Catholic child would be known, looked after,
> and protected. Not a child would be lost or tampered
> with, without the whole congregation knowing it, and,
> if necessary, rushing to its rescue, and the soul of
> any one child is worth more than all this would cost.
> The thing is practicable enough, and is no more than
> some Protestant sects are doing to steal our children
> from us. Can we not be as active and as vigilant as
> the enemies of our religion, and do as much to save
> them as they do to destroy them? The thing is already
> done in many places, and it needs only to have atten-
> tion called to it, in order, after a little time, to

---

[14]Ibid., p. 208.

have it done everywhere. It is nothing new, it is
no suggestion of ours, and we are doing nothing but
simply urging the extension of that which already
exists.[15]

In sum, then, Brownson believed that these societies provided
for the adult education of their members and created a sense of
belonging, involvement and attachment to the Church. They provided
a Catholic public with common ends and goals and shared experiences.
Finally they could serve as a valuable aid to the clergy in the
education of Catholic youth, especially those surrounded by poverty,
unfortunate home situations, and Protestant philanthropic efforts
attempting to "rescue" Catholic youth and bring them up Protestant.
Furthermore, Brownson noted that he was not the originator of
these plans.

In the early stages of these Catholic societies, at least one
member of the clergy envisioned that Catholic Institutes would
achieve great accomplishments. The Reverend Martin John Spalding
of Louisville privately proposed[16] the establishment of a national
organization, the Catholic Institute, with its center at Baltimore
and the Archbishop its head. Each diocese, would initiate an
Institute, with the bishop presiding as president, and in turn,
appointing a lay or clerical vice-president to take active charge
of the organization in conjunction with a committee of two or three.
Every clergyman in each diocese would automatically become an
honorary member, and was expected to establish an institute branch

---

[15]Ibid., pp. 209-209.

[16]See Rev. Martin J. Spalding to Bishop J. B. Purcell,
January 30, 1846, Archdiocese of Cincinnati Papers, UNDA.

in his parish. Each member would pay $1.00 in dues annually. The
proposed Institute would have four objectives: 1) to publish and
circulate religious tracts, cheap books, and school books; 2) to
support the local and general Catholic press; 3) to establish
circulating libraries in each parish and city in the United States;
and 4) to distribute books and tracts gratuitously among Protestants.

All this of course would be accomplished with the funds
collected through membership dues. Spalding suggested that one-
fifth of the money go to the central Institute at Baltimore (which
would repay the parishes with books and tracts for their libraries
or for distribution); one-fifth to the parent Institute of each
diocese (to purchase books and tracts, and to aid the poorer
congregations); one-fifth for subscriptions to the local papers
and other Catholic periodicals (some to be placed in libraries for
Catholic use and some distributed to Protestants); the remaining
two-fifths to be used for local purposes such as library acquisi-
tions.

Spalding made these proposals because he believed Catholics
lacked an organization that could thoroughly and efficiently carry
out the more ambitious programs of the Protestant denominations.
He wanted to establish the machinery of a vast book-concern, tract
distribution, and a system of itinerant lectures that would "exert
a powerful influence from one end of the Union to the other."[17]

---

[17]Ibidem. Spalding wanted Purcell to think the proposal over
before the Council of 1846. Spalding, however, was not very confident that much would come out of Baltimore. "The great desideratum
would be an active and efficient Central Committee at Baltimore,
which would be made to work, . . . Can any thing-I'll not say

Perhaps his proposals were too premature; at any rate, neither the
Councils of 1846 nor of 1849 considered the plan. Catholic
societies, like the YCFS and the Catholic Institutes, were to remain
local or diocesan affairs. Although no national organization
evolved, the idea spread throughout the 1850's and 1860's as evidenced by the ever-increasing existence and growth of these and
other parish and diocesan organizations throughout America.[18] The
hierarchy itself in the Pastoral Letter of 1866 mentioned the ever-
increasing participation of the laity in such organizations as the
St. Vincent de Paul Society and the Young Men's Catholic Associations. Many of these societies were composed of adults and young
adults, laity and clergy, and had as their goals the religious,
social, and intellectual advancement of their members. They
usually maintained libraries and rooms for discussions and social
gatherings. They also resembled the American Lyceum movement by
sponsoring courses of lectures by prominent Catholic leaders.

iii

CATHOLIC LECTURES

The lecture season generally ran from late fall to early
spring, sometimes ending as late as May. Societies set up either
a series of individual or double lectures by eight to ten speakers,
often selecting the same night of each succeeding week. Some
societies secured anywhere from four to six speakers, with each

---

good-but active and enterprising come out of Baltimore? I would
like to try."

[18]Spalding himself often lectured to these organizations:
however, he seems to have lost much of his enthusiasm, at least

speaker presenting a course of lectures spanning four evenings in
a week, or two or three lectures per week over a two-week stretch.
In this latter arrangement, usually only the top names, like a
Brownson, would be engaged for several successive lectures. A
typical course of lectures Brownson gave was described in an
article that Brownson had glued in his "Scrapbook of Newspaper
Clippings." The course consisted of five lectures: "The American
Mission"; "Protestantism and Liberty"; "Papacy and Liberty";
"Infallibility"; and "The Spirit of the Age." The pattern was
natural: show America's mission; explain why Protestantism was
insufficient and even detrimental; and illustrate how Catholicism
alone was capable of carrying America onward to greater achieve-
ments.

Not all speaking engagements were well planned in advance;
most, of course, were, but in many instances one community, hearing
of the availability of a person who might be passing through en
route to another lecture, would engage that person to speak. All
in all, the extent and popularity of Catholic adult societies,
including their lecture programs, appears to have been widespread.
An examination of one man's path on the lecture circuit reveals
not only his popularity, his ups and downs, but also the degree
to which Catholics participated in this form of adult education.
This analysis is limited basically to Brownson's path, relying on

---

concerning the lecture segment. In 1855, while preparing for
lectures in Chicago, New Orleans, and Cincinnati, he wrote Purcell
the following: "These lectures are pretty much of a bore, and
besides encouraging Catholics, especially young men-which is itself
a benefit-do little good." See M. J. Spalding to J. B. Purcell,
October 18, 1855, Archdiocese of Cincinnati Archives, UNDA.

correspondence indicating invitations to lecture, the name of the

sponsoring organization, the financial terms (when stated), the

size of the audience, and the names of other prominent speakers as

they are mentioned. This section is not intended as a history of

the adult societies and their lecture courses; rather it will show

Brownson's connection with them.[19]

Catholic societies providing potential lecture audiences

existed in Boston, Baltimore, Philadelphia and Pittsburgh at the

time of Brownson's conversion to the Catholic Church. Even prior

to his conversion he lectured before the Calvert Institute and

the YCFS of Baltimore, presenting to the latter an address on

their third anniversary. The YCFS of Boston, in its eighth year

of operation, asked Brownson to lecture during the winter of

1843-44,[20] almost a year before he entered the Church. In

Philadelphia, the clergy announced from the pulpit that Brownson

was to speak in early 1845, and the Bishop there requested Brownson

to give a course of lectures on literature and political philosophy

that spring. During the summer of the same year, the Catholic

[19]Hopefully, it will raise more questions than it answers
about the nature and extent of these organizations. I suspect
that a thorough examination of the early Catholic newspapers,
parish histories, and other correspondence, will provide material
for at least one book, if not more. Also, it should be noted, the
analysis of Brownson's role will reveal only what can be gathered
from his correspondence. Without doubt, many letters no longer
exist; in all probability he received more invitations to lectures
than are present here. I do present though what I know to be
minimally true. I say this because several letters refer to other
invitations extended to him which he apparently never received,
misplaced, discarded, or forgot about.

[20]Normally, one lecture season constituted one year's (or
season's) limit. Hence, it seems that the Boston YCFS was started
during the winter of 1836-37. A Table will be provided in this
chapter that will document the sources of these invitations, etc.

Institute of Pittsburgh engaged him to lecture.[21]   In 1846, Brownson
addressed Catholic audiences in Utica, New York City and Albany.
By 1856, societies in Buffalo, Worcester, Cincinnati, Montreal,
Toronto, Portland (Maine), St. Louis, Chicago, Milwaukee, Mobile,
New Orleans, Savannah, Charleston, Milford, Roxbury, Hartford,
Washington, New Haven, Cleveland, Louisville, Newark, Detroit,
Syracuse, Norfolk, Newburgh, and Bangor had all invited Brownson
to lecture. And before he died in 1876 he also received invita-
tions from societies in Zanesville (Ohio), Cumberland, Salem (Mass.),
Pittston, Brooklyn, Williamsburg, Kingston, Rondout (N.Y.),
Titusville (Pa.), Jersey City, Lansingburg (N.Y.), and Saugerties
(N.Y.).

Brownson spoke in some of the smaller places perhaps once or
twice, but in many of the larger cities he was asked back repeatedly.
He was invited to address Catholics in Boston at least twelve
times, those in Baltimore seven, Philadelphia eight, New York
twelve, Albany five, Cincinnati four, Chicago eight, St. Louis
seven, Detroit four, with at least two visits to the Southern
cities as well as to Milwaukee, Cleveland, Buffalo, and Louisville.
Canadian Catholics in Montreal asked Brownson for at least seven
visits to their city. The colleges too asked Brownson to speak;
Notre Dame's invitations numbered at least three, with other
requests from St. John's College (Fordham), St. Joseph's (Phila.),
Loyola College of Baltimore,and Seton Hall.

---

[21]It seems that Cincinnati had "a sort of Institute" at this
time also. See Martin J. Spalding to John B. Purcell, January 30,
1846, Archdiocese of Cincinnati Papers, UNDA.

Besides his appearances before Catholic societies, Brownson continued to receive speaking invitations from the general public, from lyceums and institutes.[22] The tables following this chapter contain a listing of known invitations that Brownson received for lectures to Catholic and non-Catholic sponsoring groups.[23]

1843-1849

Several generalizations can be made from Table 1: 1) In the case of Baltimore, Philadelphia, Pittsburgh, Buffalo, and Cincinnati, bishops played a major part in securing Brownson as a lecturer, and even strongly suggested his topics; 2) Brownson often gave more than one lecture per visit; 3) he was still on good terms with these bishops, with the Irish, and with James A. McMaster, editor of the Freeman's Journal; 4) he was still respected in some non-Catholic circles; 5) his topics attempted to refute modern tendencies, to defend the rights of Catholics, and to show the need for Catholic principles in conducting social and political matters; 6) Brownson's engagements were primarily in the East--New England, New York, Pennsylvania, and Baltimore; the Cincinnati offer was the only western engagement offered him; and 7) not enough is known about the fees Brownson received during this period, except

---

[22]Not all the letters clearly identify the sponsors of the lectures. In some cases, Brownson was familiar with his correspondents who probably didn't need to identify their organization or group. It is quite conceivable that other letters he received were from Catholic groups. Rather than designating the groups as Catholic, the Table in this chapter will merely list the dates and places. Those invitations which positively reflect a Catholic sponsor will be designated as such.

[23]The tables, followed by discussion and explanation, are arranged chronologically and grouped into segments of several years each for purposes of analysis, development, and comparison of Catholic societies with themselves and with the non-Catholic American lyceum.

that the $25 from the Bangor Lyceum in 1847 was above the typical

fee of the mid-1840's which was $10-$15; also, the $106.50 fee

obtained in New York in 1848, whether for one, two, or three

lectures, was also well above the Lyceum fee schedule.[24]

1849-1854

Table II, covering the period from 1849-1854, reflects the

growth of Catholic societies not only in the East but in the South,

Midwest, and even in Canada. The large eastern cities maintained

their organizations, while places like Milford, Roxbury, Portland,

Hartford, New Haven and Kingston developed either a YCFS or a

Catholic Institute. Portland even erected a new hall to accommo-

date an audience of one thousand. In the South, Bishop Michael

Portier was instrumental in getting Brownson and other Catholic

speakers to visit Mobile, New Orleans, Savannah and Charleston.

In the Midwest, St. Louis had developed perhaps the best Catholic

Institute of the day. Under the auspices of Archbishop Peter

Kenrick and a committee on lectures headed by Alexander Garesche,

its program attempted to present anywhere from twelve to twenty-

four lectures per season. The object of the Institute was to dis-

sipate Protestant prejudice, dispel erroneous notions of the Church,

and awake Catholic fervor in defense of the Church. Also they

hoped to erect a Catholic Institute Hall where all Catholic

---

[24]See Carl Bode, The American Lyceum: Town Meeting of the
Mind (New York: Oxford University Press, 1956), pp. 189-191.
Bode reports that Concord paid $10 during the mid-1840's, while
Salem paid $15. Exceptions of course existed; Louis Agassiz
received $250 for six lectures, while Daniel Webster received $100
for his "History of the Constitution of the United States." Henry
David Thoreau received $20 during the course for 1848-49.

benevolent societies could meet, combine libraries, and hold
fairs, suppers and lectures.

Several lecture patterns or circuits began to emerge; once a
lecture date was confirmed in any section of the country, several
other engagements were practically assured. Thus, by 1854,
Brownson lectured on several different circuits. One centered in
the East, and included Boston, New York, Philadelphia, Baltimore,
and Washington.[25] Another centered in the Midwest, involving St.
Louis, Cincinnati, Louisville, and occasionally Notre Dame,
Cleveland and Pittsburgh. Another in the South included tne major
cities of Mobile, New Orleans, Savannah, Charleston, and later,
Norfolk.

One other circuit had emerged following 1850--the Montreal
lectures.[26] James Sadlier, husband of the authoress and himself

---

[25]That this circuit existed can be seen in a letter from
George F. Haskins to O.A.B., December 17, 1857, OABP, UNDA, in which
Haskins asked Brownson for some contacts in arranging a series of
fund raising lectures on "Public and Private Reformatories."
Haskins hoped to lecture in Boston, New York, Philadelphia, "etc."
Haskins had lectured mostly in New England prior to that time.

[26]The Montreal Catholic Institute was founded in 1850, with
Toronto following in August, 1852. By November, another twelve
Institutes had been formed in Upper Canada. The Institute in
Toronto sprung up in order to get a unified Catholic effort on
securing equal rights on the school question. Dr. de Charbonnel,
Catholic Bishop of Toronto, engaged himself in a dispute with the
Superintendent of Education, Dr. E. Ryerson, a Methodist minister.
The Institutes of Upper Canada were independent of each other, yet
did have ecclesiastical approval and clerical participation. The
Quebec Institute (Montreal) originated as an offshoot of the St.
Vincent de Paul Society in the parish of St. Roeh. The latter
Institute subscribed to several newspapers, and contained about
600 volumes in its library. Its objects included the instruction
of Catholics (under the guidance of the Church), and the defense
of their political rights by employing news rooms, libraries, and
lectures. The Canadian Institutes appear to have been more politically active than American Institutes. See Fr. E. J. Horan to
O.A.B., December 14, 1852, OABP, UNDA. The letter contains another

a Catholic editor and publisher, was asked by the Bishop of
Montreal to secure Brownson for some lectures. Brownson's
lectures were well-attended and usually caused a flurry of religious controversy in Canada. The Canadians hoped the lectures
would not only strengthen Catholics but also decrease Protestant
animosity and even persuade some to convert to Catholicism. When
Brownson selected a topic for his first appearance in Montreal,
Sadlier wrote and advised him that the Bishop wanted him to change
the title to attract Protestants. However, the Bishop still wanted
Brownson to deliver tne same lecture![27] The following year he gave
at least four to six lectures; and by the 1852 season, Sadlier
could write "The Protestants begin to grumble a little at your
coming. They have never forgiven you for your last course of
lectures. I tell them you intend finishing them now completely."[28]
The American controversialist apparently met the same success in
Canada that he had achieved on the American circuit.

In regard to the American circuit, it would appear that
besides Brownson, the most popular speakers of the day included
Bishop Hughes, Fr. Cummings, James McMaster, Thomas d'Arcy McGee,

letter from G. M. Muir to Fr. Horan, November 27, 1852 which
describes the origins of the Canadian Institutes.

[27]See James Sadlier to O.A.B., March 15, 1850, OABP, UNDA.

[28]James Sadlier to O.A.B., March 28, 1852, OABP, UNDA. It
also is evident that Brownson caused the same type of controversy
while in St. Louis. His invitation for the 1853-54 season specifically requested he lecture on non-theological topics. Religious
controversy was in the air in St. Louis, as the Rev. Rice and the
Rev. Dewey were giving lectures throughout the city. Kenrick
apparently decided not to further antagonize Protestants. Also,
Kenrick may have distrusted Brownson's theology (or any layman's,
for that matter).

Fr. Roddan (of the Boston <u>Pilot</u>), and Martin John Spalding. The fees Brownson received appear to have been extremely high, at least in comparison to the Lyceum. Granted, many of the invitations did not disclose the terms; in those that did, however, the low fees appear to be $50 plus expenses and $58 plus expenses. For highs, Brownson received $100 plus expenses per lecture in Baltimore, and $400 plus expenses for four lectures in St. Louis.[29] There were exceptions though; St. John's Orphan Asylum in Philadelphia lost money during the 1849-50 season on a course of lectures by a Mr. Buckingham. In this case, Brownson was asked to postpone his visit until more auspicious times. Overall, the financial failures of lecture courses appeared to be few. By the mid-1850's, most Catholic societies were able to support attractively courses of lectures, engaging the prominent names of the day.

1854-1859

Table III covering the period from 1854-1859, reflects the spread of Catholic societies to other major cities. In the South, Charleston appeared to have the best organized group, with a new Catholic Institute evolving in New Orleans, and the Reverend John Barry taking the initiative and risk of inviting Brownson to Savannah where no Catholic society existed yet. In the East, societies sprang up in Newark, Newburgh, Albany, Utica, Syracuse, Buffalo. The New York cities formed a natural network, with an invitation from one often spurring engagements from the others.

[29] Bode estimates the Lyceum paid $15-$25 at this time, with few exceptions. See pp. 190-191.

In the Midwest, Chicago, Milwaukee and Detroit initiated Catholic Institutes. One city noticeably absent from the list during this period was Montreal, where Irish Catholics became irritated by Brownson's remarks and refused to invite him back to their city.[30]

The fees paid during this period were again above the Lyceum figures. Brownson's lowest recorded salary was $47 for one lecture in New York, still double the normal Lyceum rate. Several lectures brought him $50 apiece, but generally speaking, $100-$150 per lecture plus expenses was not uncommon for Brownson. The newly established Institute in Chicago guaranteed Brownson, McMaster, and McGee at least $150 per lecture. Milwaukee paid $200 minimum for three lectures;[31] Cincinnati paid $160 (number of lectures unknown). In Baltimore, George Miles offered Brownson $150, expenses, and the door take! Nothing however, came close to Brownson's lecture at the Academy of Music in New York where approximately 5,376 Catholics attended; it resulted in a fee paid to Brownson of $1,018.65 for a single lecture!

This New York lecture highlighted Brownson's 1857-58 campaign. One important thing stands out during this campaign--it seems that

---

[30]See George E. Clerk to O.A.B., August 28, 1856, OABP, UNDA. In 1859, the Boston YCFS withdrew an invitation to Brownson for a lecture because of his alleged downgrading of the Irish race. In sympathy, another speaker in the course, Thomas Quinn, refused to give his lecture because the YCFS had rescinded Brownson's invitation. See E. A. Palmer and D. Moore to O.A.B., November 25, 1859 and Thomas Quinn to O.A.B., December 11, 1859, OABP, UNDA.

[31]Bode states that Chicago and Milwaukee Lyceums after 1855 started paying higher fees $75, $100, $135, and even offered Beecher $250. The reason behind the sudden increase was to attract eastern lecturers. The same probably holds true in Brownson's case--yet he received similar fees in the East also.

Brownson initiated the circuit himself by writing to several
Bishops requesting lectures. After Brownson set up his own
itinerary, then several other invitations also came his way. The
result may well be called a "Grand Tour," for it took him to Boston,
Philadelphia, Pittsburgh, Cincinnati, Zanesville, Louisville,
Cumberland, St. Louis, and ended up in New York.

1859-1864

Table IV indicates that Brownson remained in the East during
the 1859-60 season. The high fees paid during the previous years
seemed to dwindle to $50 plus expenses.[32] During the Civil War
the lecture circuit diminished throughout the nation. Just as
William D. Kelley told Brownson that Philadelphians had curtailed
their lectures during the 1862-63 season and were hoping to start
up for 1863-64,[33] so too most communities cut short their courses
during the confrontation. Of the invitations he did receive
though, more than half concerned national rather than Catholic
topics, and Brownson probably discussed national issues even before
Catholic audiences. Unionists read and praised the Review during
the Civil War, and Brownson's popularity before non-Catholic
audiences certainly accounted for invitations to lecture in Boston,
Albany, Washington, Wilmington, Lynn, Cincinnati, Chicago, Peoria,
Ottawa, and Detroit.[34] He spoke on the same platform with Horace

[32]This was still above the $20-$30 range of most Lyceum fees.
Wendell Phillips received $50 and Beecher $100 at this time. See
Bode, p. 191.
[33]William D. Kelley to O.A.B., June 7, 1863, OABP, UNDA.
[34]Brownson's address in Detroit was entitled "The Union and
the War." The Detroit Public Library contains a front page newspaper clipping of January 23, 1863 describing the lecture. Brownson was quoted as saying: "War is business now. It should be

Greeley, Bayard Taylor and Gerritt Smith to name a few. It would '
appear that Brownson received fees of about $100 plus expenses in
Boston and Chicago. Little can be said about the Catholic lectures
at this time, except that they were drastically curtailed and the
few that did exist seemed connected with fund raising efforts.

1865-1875

Table V indicates that during the post-Civil War period,
Brownson basically limited himself to Eastern speaking engagements.
Also, nearly every lecture after the War involved Catholic societies
and topics. Only a few letters indicated fees, which generally
ran about $100. Gout and old age made it very difficult for him
even to attend Mass, and with a busy writing schedule besides,
Brownson was seldom able to lecture on the circuit. Perhaps this
was understood throughout the country, for when dissolution
threatened Brownson's Quarterly Review in 1874, the Detroit Catholic
Union immediately asked Brownson to lecture. Brownson asked his
son Henry to explain to the sponsors that he had decided to continue the Review for one more year, and hence, would not be able
to venture to Detroit.[35]

In the following year, no sooner had the Review closed than
invitations arrived from the West once again. The Union Catholic

conducted on military principles, not on political principles or
humanitarian principles, but on war principles. This consists in
inflicting the greatest possible damage in the least possible time
upon the enemy, with the least possible injury to ourselves." The
article noted that Brownson's address was interrupted frequently
by applause.

[35]See Wm. B. Moran and C. J. O'Flynn to O.A.B., August 3,
1874, OABP, UNDA, and O.A.B. to Henry F. Brownson, August 18,
1874, Henry F. Brownson Papers, UNDA.

Library Association and the St. Vincent de Paul Society of Chicago
wanted two lectures, and were willing to set up engagements in
Milwaukee and St. Louis. One week later, the Catholic Central
Association of Cleveland also requested a lecture. Its president,
T. H. Graham, expressed regrets over the termination of the Review,
but added: "We trust however we are not to loose $/$ sic $/$ your
services in the staunch advocacy and defense of the truth.
Catholics in this country need able, fearless champions now more,
it would seem, than ever before."[36] In arranging the course of
lectures for the winter, Graham hoped Brownson would come to
Cleveland because "no layman in America will be more acceptable or
welcome among us."[37] Brownson certainly must have felt gratified
at the personal praise, and undoubtedly agreed that the Church,
now more than ever, needed strong voices to carry on the Catholic
cause.

Brownson's voice, like his pen, was no longer to defend the
Catholic Church; he died less than six months later, on April 17,
1876. Yet, he must have felt encouraged that the Catholic laity
were progressing, as evidenced both by the growth of numerous
societies and their interest in and support of Catholic lectures.
He also must have been flattered to have societies named after
him, even during his lifetime. As early as 1851 members of
St. Joseph's parish in New York had formed a Brownson Literary
Association, for the purpose of improving their mental and moral
knowledge, and through a system of debates, bettering their

[36]T. H. Graham to O.A.B., October 22, 1875, OABP, UNDA.
[37]Ibidem.

elocution as well.[38] In Providence, a Brownson Literary Institute
with one hundred members existed in 1859.[39]

In addition, Brownson was awarded honorary membership in many
societies, including the YCFS of Washington, St. Augustine's Reading
Room Society of Philadelphia, the State Historical Society of
Wisconsin, St. Charles Institute of Brooklyn, Catholic Library
Association of New York, the Young Men's Catholic Institute of
Jersey City, and the Union County Historical Society of Elizabeth,
New Jersey.[40]

Ten years after Brownson's death, two major honors were
accorded him. The University of Notre Dame requested to exhume
Brownson's body from Detroit and to place it in a specially built
Brownson Memorial Chapel in its Sacred Heart Church. Secondly,
the Catholic Young Men's National Union, prompted by a suggestion
of Bishop Gilmour of Cleveland, established a Brownson Memorial
Committee to collect money to build a monument to his memory in
New York's Central Park. Fifty-four laymen composed the committee,
headed by M. J. Harson. A Board of Episcopal Trustees, composed
of Cardinal Gibbons, Bishops Corrigan, Williams, Gilmour and
McQuaid, and Monsignor Doane, along with treasurer Rev. J. H.
Mitchell of Brooklyn, supported and assisted the collection.

---

[38]John I. Olone to O.A.B., May 2, 1851, OABP, UNDA. The Association held yearly celebrations. See John Rafferty to O.A.B.,
January 21, 1861 and January 31, 1862, OABP, UNDA in which Brownson
was invited to attend the 11th and 12th Anniversary celebrations at
the Bleeker Building in New York. Ironically, Olone, in asking
permission to name the society after Brownson, spelled his name
"Bronson."

[39]Thomas Quinn to O.A.B., November 26, 1859, OABP, UNDA.

[40]See the following letters in the OABP, UNDA: John Carroll
Brent to O.A.B., August 18, 1853; Wm. A. Turner to O.A.B., September 14, 1854; Lyman C. Draper to O.A.B., November 8, 1854; Edw. S.

Doane, first president of the CYMNU, hoped the monument would
help to perpetuate the memory of the man and to show that his
valiant labors and struggles for the Church would not be forgotten.

It was especially significant that a lay society paid tribute
to Brownson. In his "Orestes A. Brownson--Address to the Catholics
of America," M. J. Harson reminded potential donors that many
Brownson articles were aimed at elevating the young Catholic laity
of America. Harson concluded by quoting Brownson:

> These Catholic young men who now feel that they have
> no place and find no outlet for their activity, are
> the future, the men who are to take our places and
> carry on the work committed to us. We must inspire
> them with faith in the future and encourage them to
> live for it. Instead of snubbing them for their in-
> experience, quizzing them for their zeal, dampening
> their hopes, pouring cold water on their enthusiasm,
> brushing the flower from their young hearts, or
> freezing up the well springs of their life, we must
> renew our own life and freshness in theirs, encourage
> them with our confidence and sympathy, raise them up
> if they fall, soothe them when they fail, and cheer
> them on always to new and nobler efforts . . . .
> Bear with them, tread lightly on their involuntary
> errors, forgive the ebullitions of a zeal not always
> according to knowledge, and they will not refuse to
> listen to the councils of age and experience. They
> will take advice and will amply repay us by making
> themselves felt in the country, by elevating the
> standard of intelligence, raising the tone of moral
> feeling, and directing public and private activity to
> just and noble ends.[41]

Young to O.A.B., December 18, 1854; Wm. F. Bugie to O.A.B., July
29, 1857; D. McAghan to O.A.B., Feburary 25, 1865; Geo. E. Sibbley
to O.A.B., June 1, 1860.

[41]Quoted in M.J. Harson, "Orestes A. Brownson--Address to the
Catholics of America, by the Brownson Memorial Committee of the
Catholic Young Men's National Union," Feburary 15, 1887. Harson had
sent out letters the previous year to establish the committee it-
self. The letter is dated November 8, 1886. See OABP, UNDA. One
should also note that in 1889, Brownson's son, Henry, became one of
the outstanding leaders in the Lay Catholic Congress Movement. See
Marie Bernadette Kriner, "Henry Francis Brownson As A Lay Catholic
Leader" (Unpublished master's dissertation, University of Notre
Dame, 1944), pp. 13-56.

This organization, the Catholic Young Men's National Union, seemed but the natural outgrowth of the many adult educational societies that sprang up during the nineteenth century. The Catholic Institutes, Young Catholics' and Friends' Societies, and other parish and diocesan societies, had all hoped to encourage lay participation in Catholic and American affairs. They provided a Catholic gathering ground for college graduates and other adults, so necessary in a hostile, Protestant environment. In addition, these societies enhanced the moral and intellectual dimensions of their members by supporting a variety of programs that included lectures, debates, and discussions, setting up libraries and reading rooms, and organizing social functions such as picnics, fairs, and suppers. Furthermore, lay activities such as these involved Catholic adults in Church affairs and strengthened their ties to the Church and to God. Most importantly, this elevation of the Catholic populace, besides being good in itself, enabled adults and society to bring up children "in the way they should go"--for the honor and glory of God.

In the very last issue of the Quarterly Review, Brownson expressed hope that Catholic Unions would sustain Catholic unity and direct concerted efforts in behalf of Catholic interests. Apparently, his call for an active laity had not gone unheeded. The Catholic laity themselves had adopted his own words aimed at elevating intelligence and morals, and at directing such knowledge to practical application in man's personal, religious, intellectual, social, and political endeavors; it was merely "the scholar's mission."

TABLE I

Brownson Lecture Invitations 1843-1849 Seasons*

Date of Letter	Society (or Sender)	City	Details, Remarks, Fees, etc.
Oct. 19, 1843	Calvert Institute	Baltimore	Will pay all expenses
Nov. 13, 1843	YCFS	Boston	8th Course, constitution enclosed
Nov. 15, 1843	YCFS	Baltimore	3rd Anniversary, sent constitution
Jan. 2, 1845 & Mar. 5, 1845	(Wm. A. Stokes)	Philadelphia Philadelphia	Bishop Kenrick wanted a course of Lectures on literature and political philosophy
June 13, 1845	Catholic Institute	Pittsburgh	O.A.B. to be guest of Bishop O'Connor
Nov. 30, 1845	People Lyceum	Portsmouth	
Dec. 16, 1845	YCFS	?	
Jan. 5, 1846	YCFS	Baltimore	O.A.B. to give lecture, then a course
Jan. 6, 1846	(John Warland)	Manchester, N.H.	
Jan. 12, 1846	YCFS Baltimore	Philadelphia	O.A.B. to go to Philadelphia after Baltimore
Jan. 17, 1846	(A.B. Johnson)	Utica, N.Y.	Mentions recent O.A.B. lecture in Utica
Feb. 21, 1846	(Bp. John McCloskey)	New York	Hundreds of tickets sold to O.A.B. lecture
June 11, 1846	Norwich University		Calvinist respect Brownson
Mar. 2, 1846	Young Friends of Ireland		O.A.B. main guest for St. Patrick's Day
Oct. 29, 1846	Gt. Falls Institute	Gt. Falls	Thursday, Nov. 12
Nov. 2, 1846	Woburn Lyceum	?	Any Wednesday
Dec. 14 & 16, 1846	(Francis Manahan)	Utica	O.A.B. to lecture on Jan. 12 after speech in Troy
Dec. 16, 1846 Feb. 4, 1847	(Bp. John McCloskey)	New York	Hughes wants O.A.B. to lecture on "The Revolutionary Spirit of the Age"
Dec. 16, 1846	(J. Mullahy)	?	Refers to recent O.A.B. lecture to YCFS on "The Protestant Reformation"
Dec. 22, 1846	Young Men's Assoc.	Troy	Invited to stay with H.W. Strong
Mar. 2, 1847	Young Friends of Ireland		Forced to cancel St. Patrick's Day dinner and O.A.B.'s role as guest--"improper to celebrate...by a dinner, when our kindred are perishing from hunger."
July 9, 1847	Bangor Lyceum	Maine	$25; Emerson to lecture on same program
Jan. 5, 1848	(James A. McMaster)	New York	O.A.B. to prepare 2 or 3 lectures on "Fourierism and why it can't work"
Jan. 22, 1848	(O.A.B. to Fr. J.W. Cummings)	New York	O.A.B. wants to deliver either 1 or 3 lectures on "The Necessity, means, and prospects of the political and social regeneration of Europe"
Jan. 24, 1848	(Fr. Joseph Stokes)	Utica	Want O.A.B. on way to or from Buffalo
Mar. 4, 1848 & Apr. 12, 1848	(Fr. Francis Guth)	Buffalo	Bp. Timon wants 3 lectures beginning on Thursday, Apr. 24
Mar. 12, 1848 & Apr. 14, 1848	(Fr. Cummings)	New York	Sent O.A.B. at least $106.50 for lecture(s) at Tabernacle
Sept. 8, 1848	(Fr. John Boyce)	Worcester	Heard O.A.B. to lecture there in Oct.
Jan. 20, 1849 & Jan. 25 & 29, 1849	(J.A. McMaster) (Fr. Cummings)	New York	O.A.B. lecture Feb. 14 on "Religious Liberty"
Jan. 25, 1849	St. Peter's Benevolent Society Anniversary	Cincinnati	Bp. Purcell asks O.A.B. to be orator for 2 lectures to benefit destitute female orphans; wants a topic to attract Catholics and non-Catholics; trip could open up Cinci. and the West to Brownson and secure more subscriptions to BrQR

*Source OABP, UNDA unless otherwise indicated. It should be mentioned that Brownson received at least 26 other lecture invitations during 1843-44 from lyceums, associations, and colleges. These have been mentioned previously and are not included in Table I, which stresses the Catholic groups that extended invitations to him.

TABLE II

Brownson Lecture Invitations 1849-1854 Seasons*

Date of Letter	Society (or Sender)	City	Details, Remarks, Fees, etc.
Oct. 22, 1849	Library Association	Phila.	Fee: Brownson willing to lecture for just expenses if organization is non-profit or charitable; whatever they offer otherwise
Nov. 25, 1849	Mechanics Assoc.	Newport, R.I.	People sensitive at mention of Catholic religion
Dec. 5, 1849	(James McMaster)	New York	OAB to open lecture series on Jan. 3, and close before Lent. $50 or more per lecture
Jan. 18, 1850	(James Fullerton)	Phila.	Lecture schedule in a state of confusion; St. John's Orphan Asylum lost money on course by Mr. Buckingham; better to postpone OAB's lecture. Mentions Bp. Hughes lecturing also
Mar. 15, 1850	(J. Sadlier)	Montreal	Bp. of Montreal requested Brownson to change the title of address to attract Protestants, but to give the same address
Apr. 12, 1850	(A. LaRocque)	Montreal	Want two more lectures
Sept. 24, 1850	(J. Sadlier)	Montreal	Want more lectures this fall or winter
Sept. 31, 1850	Catholic Institute	New York	Requests lecture; others are Cummings, McMaster, Roddan, Manahan, Hughes
Nov. 4, 1850	Bishop and Catholics of Toronto	Toronto	Lecture after Montreal lectures
Nov. 9, 1850	(Bp. F.P. Kenrick)	Phila.	Glad OAB will give lectures there
Dec. 2, 1850	(Geo. A. Hamilton)	Little town near Boston	OAB to give two lectures on "The Church and Civilization"; to be announced in Pilot
Dec. 9, 1850	Saco (?) Lyceum	Saco (?)	On Jan. 12
Dec. 18, 1850	(Bp. F.P. Kenrick)	Phila.	OAB to give four lectures on Jan.13, 14, 15, 17; hall seats 800; Berg has been replying to Hughes--OAB should get good crowds
July 21 & Oct. 17, 1851	(J. Sadlier)	Montreal	Want four lectures on "Why I Am Not a Protestant" and "Why I am a Catholic," plus two more lectures
Oct. 28, 1851 & Nov. 19, 1851	Catholic Committee on Lectures (Archb. P.R. Kenrick)	St. Louis	Want OAB as one of three or four lecturers to give four to six lectures each for season; proceeds go to building a Catholic Institute Hall where all Catholic benevolent societies can combine libraries and hold meetings, suppers, and lectures. Fee: $400, plus expenses; topic "Catholicism and Civilization"
Dec. 12, 1851 & Dec. 13, 1851	Archb. F.P. Kenrick (George Miles)	Baltimore	Wants a few lectures; guarantees OAB at least $100 per lecture
Dec. 29, 1851	(J. Sadlier)	Montreal	Want OAB in Apr. (to begin Apr 15)
Jan. 17, 1852	YCFS	Milford	One or more lectures between Feb. 1-Mar. 17
Mar. 9, 1852	(James M. Gonahan)	Mobile	Bp. Portier requests lectures and suggests lectures in New Orleans, Savannah, and Charleston
Mar. 10, 1852	(Bp. Van de Velde)	Chicago	Wants one or two lectures
June 2, 1852	(Isaac Hecker)	New York	Hears OAB to lecture in N.Y. soon
June 28, 1852	(John O'Donnell)	Portland	Wants several lectures to open up new season on Oct. 6; totally Catholic in approach; have new hall that seats 1000
Sept. 10, 1852	(James Mitchell)	New York	Sends $58 for recent lecture; will also pay expenses
Dec. 8, 1852	Philopathian Society	Phila.	Dec. 23
Dec. 30, 1852	YCFS	Roxbury	
Jan 3, 1853	St. Augustine's Church	Phila.	Four lectures on Jan. 24, 25, 26, 28
Jan. 11, 1853	YCFS	Baltimore	Annual address this winter; $100 plus expenses
Jan. 20, 1853	Catholic Institute	Hartford	Society just getting established; will pay at least expenses, more if possible
Jan. 25, 1853	YCFS	Washington	Wants a lecture after Baltimore
Feb. 12, 1853	Catholic Institute YCFS	Buffalo New Haven	Hears OAB to lecture on 24 in Buff.; also want him in New Haven
Oct. 2, 1853	YCFS	Boston	Lecture on Russia-Turkey question about Nov. 30
Oct. 17, 1853	(Bp. Rappe)	Cleveland	Lecture, plus stay at episcopal residence
Oct. 25, 1853	Young Men's Catholic Literary Institute	Cinci.	On way to or from St. Louis
Nov. 15, 1853	(Bp. Spalding)	Louisville	Wants several lectures
Nov. 23, 1853	St. Bridget's Church	St. Louis	Wants 1 or more lectures to help pay for new Church
Nov. 23, 1853	Catholic Institute	St. Louis	Bishop requested several lectures on non-theological topics. Seems Brownson brewed quite a storm with Rev. Rice and Rev. Dewey during last trip there.
Mar. 20, 1854	(John O'Donnell)	Portland	On March 30
Apr. 4, 1854	(Fr. Madden)	Kingston (NY)	

Source OABP, UNDA.

TABLE III

Brownson Lecture Invitations 1854-1859 Seasons*

Date of Letter	Society (or Sender)	City	Details, Remarks, Fees, etc.
May 14, 1854	(Fr. Sorin)	Notre Dame	Wants a lecture in fall to start off _Ave Maria_, a new journal he hopes to begin
Sept. 10, 1854	YCFS	Boston ?	In November
Sept. 23, 1854	Catholic Institute	Milwaukee	Want three lectures, Oct. 31, Nov. 2, 7 for $200 minimum
Sept. 25, 1854	Catholic Institute	Chicago	Three lectures at least Nov. 10-16; Young Institute, opposed by clergy until new Bishop arrived, will pay proceeds, at least $150 per lecture; McMaster and McGee accepted same terms. Chicago Catholics are "a lecture going people"
Oct. 24, 1854	Library Association	Chelsea	On Dec. 14
Nov. 28, 1854	(D. Bryan, Jr.)	Utica	Utica Catholics want OAB this winter
Feb. 26, 1855	(Fr. Cummings)	New York	Prefers OAB to lecture after Lent--so many lectures, sermons, instructions, and addresses in the process of delivery by NY pastors
Feb. 5 & Mar. 5, 1855	Catholic Institute	New Orleans	Newly formed group want 2 or 3 lectures from OAB in April; prefer one on a literary topic; other speakers have already lectured on Immaculate Conception, Catholicity & Liberty, Religious & Civil Obligations of Catholics
Aug. 13, 1855	Young Men's Association (McQuaid)	Newark	$50 for lecture; Dr. Manahan to give Introductory address on Nov. 15
Sept. 4, 1855	Young Men's Catholic Library Society	Albany	Between Dec.-Feb.
Oct. 12, 1855	St. Joseph's College (Fr. Noon)	Philadelphia	Commencement address in July 1856; college students and professors like OAB's political, theological, and philosophical articles
Dec. 19, 1855	Catholic Institute	St. Louis	Want OAB for 2 of 15 of their lectures
Dec. 27, 1855	Catholic Institute	Detroit	In early Jan. to newly formed society
Feb. 20, 1856	(Jas. Woolworth)	Syracuse	Catholics want OAB's topic on Feb. 29 to be "The Republic and the Church"; apparently having trouble getting speakers--3 did not show up; people are edgy about it
Feb. 23, 1856	(Ch. O'Conor)	New York	Sends money for OAB's lecture at Tabernacle
Mar. 12, 1856	Young Friends of Ireland	?	Invite OAB to 13th annual St. Patrick's Day Celebration
Mar. 31, 1856	(M.T. Cosans)	New York	Sends $47 for lecture in N.Y.
Apr. 12, 1856	(Hecker)	?	Mentions 2 upcoming lectures
Apr. 26, 1856	Catholic Institute	Charleston	Want 3 or 4 lectures after May 15; refers to Protestant interest in hearing OAB
May 15, 1856	(Fr. John Barry)	Savannah	Want 1, 2, or 3 lectures; no Catholic society in Savannah yet; Barry fully responsible
Aug. 20, 1856	Catholic Institute	Chicago	2 lectures, $100 plus expenses
Aug. 28, 1856	(G.E. Clerk)	Montreal	Canadian Irish are upset with OAB; lecture prospects are dim (Brownson had apparently requested lectures there)
Oct. 30, 1856	(E.J. O'Reilly)	Newburgh (NY)	Catholics had invited OAB earlier; now, their whole program is listed
Dec. 29, 1856	YCFS	Bangor (Maine)	Want OAB, McMaster and Ives to lecture
Feb. 18 & 23, 1857	Baltimore Catholics (George Miles)	Baltimore	On May 11; $150 for lecture and expenses, plus take at door; topic--"The Church as affected by Concordats in Europe and Constitutions in the U.S." Ives to lecture on April 20
Apr. 20, 1857			
Feb. 20, 1857	Young Friends of Ireland		Invite OAB to 14th Annual Celebration of St. Patrick's Day at Apollo Room, Tues. Mar. 17
May 20, 1857	Ss. Peter & Paul Church	South Boston	Speak on naturalization
Sept. 2, 1857	Columbian Literary Association	Boston	Mentions YCFS lecture also
Dec. 6, 1857	(Bp. Wood)	Philadelphia	Bp. Neumann has accepted OAB's proposed course of lectures
Dec. 7, 1857	St. Vincent de Paul Society (Bp. O'Connor)	Pittsburgh	O'Connor accepted OAB's proposal to lecture on way to or from Louisville
Dec. 11, 1857	Young Men's Catholic Literary Institute	Cincinnati	Agreed to have OAB lecture; will give him entire proceeds from one or more lectures ($160)
Dec. 29, 1857	(Catholics)	Zanesville (Ohio)	Want OAB on way between Pitts.-Cinci.; surplus proceeds for new school (an English-German parish)
Jan. 4, 1858			
Jan. 8, 1858	Catholic Literary Assoc.	Louisville	On Jan. 28
Jan. 18, 1858	House of Studies of the Redemptorists	Cumberland	Want a visit, and will get a lecture for OAB
Jan. 24, 1858	Catholic Institute	St. Louis	Hear OAB to lecture in Cinci.; want 2 lectures at OAB's terms; don't want to denounce Protestants, but to improve the morals of Catholics
Apr. 20, 1858	(Committee)	New York	Roughly 5,376 Catholics of New York attended OAB's recent lecture at the Academy of Music; OAB receives $1,018.65! for lecture
Apr. 28, 1858	(Math. Hart)	New Haven	OAB requested to lecture; Bishop has ordered no fund raising this year
June 6, 1858	(Mrs. Brownson)	100 miles up Hudson	Mentions OAB lecturing on this day
Sept. 16, 1858	Young Men's Catholic Temperance Society	Salem	This winter; OAB to state terms and date
Sept. 24, 1858	Catholic Institute	St. Louis	Want 3 or 4 lectures; $300, plus expenses, in Jan. Refers to unpleasant connections of past visits, not caused by Cath. Institute or its friends (Religious controversy)
Dec. 23, 1858	Catholic Institute	Chicago	Heard OAB from St. Louis; also want him.
Jan. 26, 1859	Circulating Catholic Library (Math. Hart)	New Haven	Setting up a course of lectures; want OAB, Ives and Huntington

*Source OABP, UNDA

TABLE IV

Brownson Lecture Invitations 1859-1864 Seasons*

Date of Letter	Society (or Sender)	City	Details, Remarks, Fees, etc.
June 24, 1859	Loyola College Literary Society	Baltimore	A lecture
Aug. 9, 1859	YCFS	Boston	Course begins in Nov.
Oct. 19, 1859	Literary Association	Pittston (Pa.)	A mostly Protestant organization--will do good for religion if OAB lectures; $50, plus expenses
Oct. 28, 1859	(Fr. O'Brien)	New Haven	Postpone OAB's lecture 1 month
Oct. 31, 1859	St. Peter's Church	Brooklyn	Need money for new Church; plans 6 lectures, OAB to give first one; $50 plus expenses
Nov. 1, 1859	Fordham University Literary Union	New York	$25 on Nov. 21 or so
Nov. 18, 1859	(P. Lawlor)	Waterbury	$50
Nov. 29, 1859	St. Vincent de Paul Society	?	On Dec. 6, all the pastors will inform Catholics of topic
Jan. 5, 1860	Catholic Literary Society	Albany	OAB to close lectures on Jan. 25
Feb. 8, 1860	(Fr. B. O'Reilly)	Williamsburg	Lecture, plus more subscribers
Jan. 10, 1861	Young Men's Catholic Literary Association	Rondout	Mentions another lecture at Kingston
Oct. 21, 1861	Independent Course of Lectures	Albany	A.D. Mayo invites OAB to speak on "The State of the Country"
Nov. 30, 1861	National Union	Washington	On political conditions and perils; OAB to lead course on Dec. 13 or 20; lists other speakers such as Beecher, Greeley, Everett, Dickinson, Taylor, "Origin and Mainspring of the Rebellion"
Dec. 9, 1861	Wilmington Institute	Wilmington	In Jan. or Feb.
Dec. 20, 1861	Boston Emancipation League	Boston	$100 plus expenses; other speakers include Gen. Lane of Kansas, Ben Wade of Ohio, Gerrit Smith
Dec. 29, 1861	(Fr. Cummings)	Rondout, Kingston	OAB requested to fill in for the ill Cummings
Jan. 11, 1862	Lynn Lyceum	Lynn	February
Jan. 14, 1862	Young Men's Merchant's Library Association	Cincinnati	At least $50 or split gate
Dec. 24, 1862	(John A. Gurley)	Chicago	At least 2 lectures; $100 per lecture; at Metropolitan Hall, on "War and Union"
Jan. 25, 1863[a]	(OAB)	Chicago, Detroit	Tells wife he gave 3 lectures in Chicago, only 1 of which was for Catholics, and 1 in Detroit. Will lecture for Catholics in Ottawa, then in Peoria, and in Detroit again
June 7, 1863	(Wm. D. Kelley)	Philadelphia	Hopes OAB can lecture in winter; Phila. had no lectures last winter
Feb. 24, 1864	(Fr. Oram)	Titusville (Pa.)	Lecture to help pay for new Church
Mar. 7, 1864	(Fr. Garesche)	St. Louis	Asks OAB to lecture for Fair in May; object is to collect money for sick and wounded

Source OABP, UNDA

AB to Sarah Healy Brownson, Odiorne Collection, UNDA.

TABLE V

Brownson Lecture Invitations 1865-1875 Seasons*

Date of Letter	Society (or Sender)	City	Details, Remarks, Fees, etc.
Feb. 25, 1865	Young Men's Catholic Institute	Jersey City	Thanks OAB for lecture on Feb. 17 and elects him Honorary Member
Dec. 10, 1865	(OAB)	(West)	Tells Fr. Sorin he has been asked West this winter, but ill health forces him to cancel the lecture circuit
Oct. 27, 1866	(Kehoe)	Jersey City	A society headed by Mr. Farrelly (?) wants OAB to lecture
Dec. 9, 1867[a]	(OAB)	Boston	Will lecture on Dec. 20
Mar. 29, 1868	(Fr. M. Power)	Lansingburg, Saugerties	April 11 in Lansingburg, Saugerties on return home
Jan. 7, 1870	Young Men's Catholic Association	Newark	Have new hall for lecture; Feb. 22
Jan. 24, 1870[b]	Catholic Institute	Chicago	$100, plus expenses or $150 on "The Church and Liberty"
Mar. 18, 1870	Institute of St. Paul the Apostle	New York	Lecture on "Church and State" after Easter
June 16, 1870	St. John's College (Fordham)	New York	Asks OAB to deliver a toast to the graduates at Commencement on June 29
Sept. 12, 1870	(Kehoe)	?	Pays OAB $100 for recent lecture
Oct. 7, 1870 & Oct. 29, 1870	Sisters of Charity of Carney Hospital	Boston	Will pay expenses, plus whatever OAB wants; proceeds to benefit new hospital; topic is "Papal Infallibility"
Sept. 25, 1871	Seton Hall College	South Orange (N.J.)	Fr. Michael Corrigan invited OAB to give a course of lectures at Seton Hall
Nov. 8, 1871	"	"	Next lecture on Nov. 16 on "The Origin of Civil Power"
Mar. 30, 1872	Newburyport Lyceum	Newburyport	
Dec. 13, 1872	St. Mary's Church	Albany	In January
Aug. 3, 1874	Catholic Union	Detroit	This winter (OAB unable to lecture because of BrQR)
Dec. 13, 1874	Sisters of Charity	Boston	To help the hospital; Bp. of Buffalo will lecture there on Jan. 10, OAB in April on "Papal Supremacy and Civil Allegiance"
Feb. 5, 1875	Xavier Union	New York	At OAB's earliest convenience
Oct. 15, 1875	Union Catholic Library Assoc. & St. Vincent de Paul Society	Chicago	At least 2 lectures, $100; can arrange for Milwaukee and St. Louis
Oct. 22, 1875	Catholic Central Assoc.	Cleveland	This winter

*Source OABP, UNDA.

[a]OAB to Fr. Hecker, Paulist Archives.

[b]OAB to Henry F. Brownson, Henry F. Brownson Papers, UNDA.

CHAPTER X

BROWNSON IN PERSPECTIVE

Orestes Brownson--Catholic educator and publicist--became a man of ideas despite his lack of formal schooling; he was a self-educated man. At the same time, he was a man who had yearned for and struggled to find religious certitude. When he converted to Catholicism, he believed he had found the religion he needed and the one necessary to secure America's national greatness. In addition, he believed it was his scholarly duty to do everything possible to bring about the moral, religious, intellectual and social improvement of Americans, and especially of Catholics. He advocated the advancement of society through education. Yet he has not previously fared well in the Catholic educational legacy. He has been slighted on two counts: first, his real views on the school question have never been adequately presented; and secondly, his views on education went far beyond the confines of the school room, a little appreciated fact during an age that uncritically praised the common schools.

Brownson's most remembered essays on schools are those from the 1854-1862 period. His 1854 essay was misinterpreted by many then. He had only advocated public schools where no Catholic schools existed; charges that he had preferred common schools to Catholic schools were unjustified. When his earlier writings (1830-1852) on schools are considered, he can in no way be re-garded as a champion of the common school. And when he argued that public schools were not potent enough to injure the faith of Catholic children, he was merely asserting a long-standing belief in the inability of common schools to effect either good or evil. His critical comments of 1858 and 1859, though offered with a view to reform, again were labeled as a condemnation of Catholic schools. Indeed, Brownson had aroused much ire by stating his preference for common schools over deficient Catholic schools; yet he did say that he preferred good Catholic schools to the public schools. His essay of 1862 also contained heavy criticism of deficient Catholic schools, and yet he did come out, though a bit reluctantly, in favor of the Catholic school movement. The story usually ends there, with Brownson as a hostile critic or half-hearted supporter of Catholic schools.

Yet Brownson had always promised obedience to duly constituted authority. If he had doubts about the Catholic school movement in 1862, he never hesitated from then until he died. He grew more pessimistic about America and its values and came to regard public schools as dangerous to the faith of Catholic children. In addition, the Syllabus (1864) and the pronouncements of the Second Plenary Council of Baltimore (1866) helped to reinforce his attitude. If ever his beliefs were severely tested it was surely in 1869 when he agreed that the Bishop of Dubuque had rightfully exercised his authority in declaring Orestes, Jr.'s school unsuitable for Catholic children. Yet, this was a private decision, certainly unknown to most of his contemporaries. Equally unknown were his anonymous writings for the Catholic World and New York Tablet, in which Brownson played a prominent role in advancing the

Catholic position on the school question. "Our Established Church," "The Secular Not Supreme," "The Truth About the School Question," "Unification and Education," and "The School Question" represent significant contributions in advancing the Catholic cause. The last essay especially has been recognized as extremely important--yet the article has not been associated with Brownson. Call it what you will, but it is obvious that he was misinterpreted in his earlier writings and never received acknowledgement for his later ones. When one adds to this list the essays that appeared in. the Review--"Whose is the Child?," "Education and the Republic," and "The Public School System" (1873-1875), Brownson emerges as a staunch supporter (yet reformer) of the Catholic school movement.

Because of the misconceptions concerning Brownson's stand on the school question, he has been regarded as opposed or luke-warm to "Catholic education." Nothing could be further from the truth. Brownson's conception of education encompassed much more than schooling. Certainly his own background and self-education significantly influenced his views on education. Accordingly, he envisioned not only formal agencies such as schools and colleges as contributing to Catholic education, but also the informal and popular agencies of the family, Church, press, literature, and adult societies and lectures. To argue that he was at any time opposed to Catholic education misses the point. Brownson was a deeply religious man who had always advocated religious education-- if not in school, then in the other agencies, especially the family and Church. His comments and views on these other agencies were as equally significant as his contribution to the school movement.

Brownson's attempts to reform higher education came at a time
when most Americans, Catholic and non-Catholic, seemed, at least to
Brownson, to be overemphasizing the benefits of common schools. In
one sense, his efforts at improving the colleges were interpreted
to mean he was hostile to Catholic schools and "Catholic education."
Not only was this charge incorrect, but it also took something
away from his remarks on the colleges by confusing the issue.
That he was critical is of course true; yet, he hoped to build up
the colleges, not to tear them down. His call for a Catholic
University and for Catholic intellectuals and leaders mark a
contribution. John Tracy Ellis' American Catholics and the Intellectual Life (1955) has aptly pointed to Brownson as an example of
one nineteenth century Catholic who took part in and tried to uplift Catholic intellectual development. His conception of the
scholar and his mission, although extremely idealistic, is nonetheless refreshing to read today when we witness "credibility gaps,"
conflicts of interest, and outright wrong-doings performed by
"leaders" of public opinion. And Brownson's emphasis of the role
of theology and philosophy in Catholic higher education is exactly
what the University of Notre Dame's "Blueprint for a Catholic
University" specified in its most recent statement. Brownson
displayed a keen insight for the nineteenth century, and yet
remains relevant today.

Besides formal agencies of education, Brownson made incisive
comments about informal and popular agencies as well. His remarks
on the family's importance were consistent with hierarchical
promulgations; and his critiques in "The Blakes and Flanagans"

and "The Family, Christian and Pagan" are as pertinent today,
and perhaps even more so, than they were one hundred years ago.
Since Vatican II the Church has placed increased emphasis on the
role of the family in providing not only for material needs, but
for the religious formation of Christian children. We see parents
being urged (and in some cases required) to provide instruction for
Penance, and First Communion, and even sponsorship for Confirmation.
The unquestionable belief is that parents form an integral part of
"Catholic education."

The Church's role as a religious educator of children is self-
evident. Brownson's temporary acceptance of public schools for
Catholics reflects his firm belief that both the family and Church
could and would provide religious education outside of school. In
addition, he viewed the Church as responsible for the education of
adults; and when familial conditions worsened, he urged the Church
to establish orphanages and reformatories to make up for faulty
or lack of domestic education.

Brownson's critical comments (and those of Barry and Cummings)
on American seminaries came at a crucial time and were connected
with his remarks aimed at improving the colleges as well. Following
Rome's intervention, Brownson did not continue his criticisms.
Obediently, he stopped calling for reform and left the matter in
hierarchical hands. This was the only area of "Catholic education"
that Brownson ceased writing about during the 1860's and 1870's.
In all other areas, he was both a supporter and a reformer of
Catholic education.

In regard to the press and literature, Brownson arrived on the
Catholic scene immediately after the "Bible riots" and right in the
midst of rising anti-Catholic sentiments. His educational efforts
in these areas reflected his own education--the love of reading and
the learning by reading. Not only did he contribute, but also he
urged others to write for the Catholic cause--whether it be polemical, fictional, historical, biographical, moral, dogmatic or
ascetical literature. His labors were attempts to elevate
Catholics morally and intellectually, and to raise the position
of the Church to one of respectability in a hostile environment.
In this last respect is perhaps where Brownson's most significant
contribution lay--his attempts to lead, direct, and elevate a
despised minority by calling for a more enlightened press, urging
those capable to contribute, and by clearing up misrepresentations
of the past and fighting for legitimate rights, just as so many
ethnic and racial group spokesmen are doing currently in American
society.

Brownson was not the originator of Catholic adult societies--
but he urged their formation, lectured hundreds of times before
them, and urged the laity to actively involve themselves in Church
affairs (and urged the Church to encourage lay participation).
The ever-increasing number of these Catholic societies is an indication that Catholics participated in this form of popular education to a much larger extent than has been previously believed.
Besides maintaining libraries, reading rooms, discussion and debate
programs, Catholics appeared to be willing to pay their speakers
more than, or at least as much as, the parallel lyceums were

offering. Later in the century, the Catholic summer school
rivaled the Chatauqua movement, and probably died for the same
reasons--radio, movies, automobile. Brownson's encouragement of
lay participation may have "smelled" of lay trusteeism at the time,
yet today in practically every parish (since Vatican II) we witness
more lay involvement in decision-making affairs. The Church of God,
we have discovered, includes more than the pastor and his assistant; an active and intelligent laity have been found indispensable
as well.

This dissertation, then, has presented a reinterpretation of
Orestes Brownson and Catholic education. First, it concludes that
his real views on Catholic schools reveal him to be more conservative, and even instrumental, in the movement for Catholic schools
in the 1860's and 1870's. Also, in light of his earlier writings
on schools, his essays between 1854 and 1859 were badly misinterpreted. Secondly, to discuss Brownson and schools and equate the
latter with education is to miss the point. Brownson conceived of
education in the broadest possible terms. To him, Catholic education meant schools and colleges, but also the family, Church,
press, literature, adult societies and lectures. Indeed, Brownson
made significant contributions to Catholic education.

As for Brownson himself, this dissertation has considered
him in the light of a scholar with a mission to perform in life--
to labor for man's moral, religious, intellectual and social
advancement. He always emphasized the importance of religion, and
believed it was America's mission (and only hope for success) to
become a Catholic nation. The Catholicizing of America was to be

brought about by Catholic education--not just by the schools and colleges, but by the family, Church, press, literature, and adult societies. Brownson's own learning experiences--those of a self-educated man--significantly influenced his views on education, and when seen in perspective, certainly help clarify his position on public and Catholic schools. Quite understandably (yet certainly frustrating to his contemporaries) could he support Catholic attendance at common schools and still call for Catholic "education" at the same time. He always favored "Catholic education"--in not in school at least in the home, the Church, and in the popular and informal educational agencies.

The period of the late 1850's and early 1860's was a period of reform in which Brownson was highly critical of Catholic schools, colleges, seminaries, and the press. The 1860's witnessed his gradual loss of confidence in American society along with a corresponding promotion of Catholic positions and institutions. Less and less did he envision harmony between Catholicity and American institutions; hence, he withdrew--call it a siege mentality--and accepted and argued for the establishment and improvement of Catholic schools and colleges, for a stronger family unit, for a more elevated Catholic press and literature, for more adult societies, for more orphanages, reformatories, and asylums.

Yet, Brownson was lost to the public between 1865 and 1872; his conservative stand, especially on the school issue, throws a much different light on his reputation and legacy, as he penned for the New York Tablet and Catholic World significant, anonymous arguments analyzing the Catholic position. When the Catholic

Young Men's National Union honored him as America's first Catholic layman, it was no coincidence that Bishop Gilmour proposed the award, nor that other conservatives like Corrigan and McQuaid were among the episcopal committee. In his last years, these three prelates were all connected in some way with Brownson's writings on the school question. In good conscience could they pay tribute to Orestes A. Brownson for laboring for the moral, religious, intellectual and social elevation of the Catholic American; he had, in good conscience, fulfilled the scholar's mission.

Yet, where does Brownson stand in history? Except in learned circles, Brownson has been forgotten in American history. Prior to his conversion, he surely was the equal of Emerson and superior to Thoreau. He had sacrificed a great name for himself by entering the Catholic Church, and, as one friend wrote, he had departed the company of "Emerson, Holmes, Whittier and all those names the American people cherish as household words."[1] Considering the religious climate of the day, Brownson's exclusion from general American history is understandable, even though regrettable. As much as Brownson loved his country, he loved his God more. He was quite willing to forego any earthly reputation in order to save his soul and labor for the kingdom of God.

And yet, even in Catholic history Brownson does not occupy the place he rightfully deserves. Perhaps Andrew Greeley's explanation is the best. In The Catholic Experience (1967), he suggested that Orestes Brownson was basically a man of ideas

---

[1] William Seton to O.A.B., March 9, 1872, OABP, UNDA.

356

who could step back from the hustle of everyday activities and think about ultimate goals. In the mushrooming
Catholicism of the middle nineteenth century there was
precious little room for such people. There were new
dioceses to be formed, new churches to be built, new
immigrants to be cared for, new locations to be sought,
new schools to be opened. The church leaders of the
middle nineteenth century were not on a priori grounds
opposed to men with ideas, nor even suspicious of them.
But they really didn't quite know what to do with such
men.[2]

Throughout his Catholic period, Brownson received (besides

continuous and often harsh criticism) periodic unbounded praise.

Generally, these favorable comments encouraged him not to despair

in the face of such vociferous criticism; correspondents acknowl-

edged that true thinkers appreciated his efforts; and that some

day, in all likelihood after his death, Catholics would consider

him as the greatest American Catholic mind of the nineteenth

century. Consider one evaluation from the Catholic Library Magazine,

written in the heat of the nativist controversy of 1854. While

dissenting from Brownson's views, nevertheless the editor wrote:

we cannot refuse to him the credit of being the greatest
Catholic lay writer of his age, and the first of American
reviewers. We do sincerely wish that our Catholic Journalists would read his articles before they notice them,
and copy them in preference to the extracts from other
weeklies. His writings are the seed of a noble Catholic
American literature in the future, and will bear rich
fruit in educated generations, long after he is removed
from the scenes of his invaluable labors. We cannot
sufficiently admire the calm, and even grandeur of his
views--the power of his logic, and the sincerity of his
Faith. He is no half-informed and boastful intellect--
but possesses the child-like humility of solid and
cultivated genius. --He is as willing to acknowledge his
own short-comings as to rebuke those of others. He must

[2]Andrew Greeley, The Catholic Experience (New York: Image
Books, 1969, ed.), pp. 149-150.

be regarded by every unprejudiced mind as a blessing to
the struggling Catholicity of our age.[3]

And when Brownson's views during 1859 caused another flurry, the

German immigrant priest, the Reverend F. Lukas Wimmer, compared

his plight to that of the prophets, and urged him not to despair

just because so many disagreed with him:

> The reason now why these are so badly satisfied with
> your respective views, cannot be another one than
> this: that they do not stand upright, like you, but
> so, as if one holds his head through his own two legs
> in order to look at the world; no wonder with them,
> if they say those things stand below, which you see
> to be above.[4]

Shortly before he died, a doctor from upstate New York wrote

Brownson.

> You are the greatest thinker of our age, or perhaps,
> of any age. Thousands in this country, and in Europe,
> are indebted to you for valuable information on the
> most important of all subjects--the Knowledge of the
> "Truth as it is in Christ Jesus."[5]

One of those indebted to him wrote to his son thirteen years after

Brownson's death.

> I do not say that your Father was the greatest man that
> ever lived, for I never knew all men; but I do wish to
> say that for me personally, for my mental training, if
> I have any, and for a faith that I think has not an
> objective flaw, he was the greatest man. Why, Sir, he
> was the giant of mental giants.[6]

[3]Contained in OABP, UNDA.
[4]Fr. F. Lukas Wimmer to O.A.B., October 6, 1859, OABP, UNDA.
[5]Thomas J. Berger, M.D. to O.A.B., January 8, 1873, OABP, UNDA.
[6]Fr. W. O'Rourke to Henry F. Brownson, May /?/, 1889, HFB Collection, UNDA.

Yet, one hundred years later, Brownson still does not occupy
the place in Catholic history that he deserves, although this does
seem to be changing with the increasing interest and re-examination
of Brownson in practically every field of thought. In addition to
his son's three-volume biography,[7] other biographies by Schlesinger,
Whalen, and Maynard,[8] and a two-volume biography[9] that hopefully
will appear for his centennial, have helped and will help bring
about a reinterpretation of Brownson. More recent works dealing
with specific aspects of his thought include the following: Per
Sveino, Orestes A. Brownson's Road to Catholicism (op. cit., 1970);
Germain Faddoul, "The Harmonizing of Faith and Reason in Brownson's
pre-Catholic Experience" (Unpublished doctoral dissertation,
University of Notre Dame, 1963); Americo D. Lapati, Orestes A.
Brownson (New York: Twayne Publishers, 1965); Leonard Gilhooley,
Contradiction and Dilemma: Orestes Brownson and the American Idea
(op. cit., 1972); Hugh Marshall's two works: "Orestes Brownson and
the American Civil War" (Unpublished doctoral dissertation, The
Catholic University of America, 1962) and Orestes Brownson and the
American Republic; An Historical Perspective (Washington: Catholic

---

[7]Henry Francis Brownson, Orestes A. Brownson's . . . Life . . .
(Detroit, Michigan: H.F. Brownson, 1898-1900). Volume I covers
his early life from 1803-1844; II his middle life from 1845-1855;
and III his latter life from 1856-1876.

[8]Arthur M. Schlesinger, Jr., Orestes A. Brownson; A Pilgrim's
Progress (New York: Octagon Books, 1939); Doran Whalen, Granite
For God's House (New York: Sheed & Ward, 1941); and Theodore
Maynard, Orestes Brownson, Yankee, Radical, Catholic (New York:
The Macmillan Company, 1943).

[9]Fr. Thomas R. Ryan, C.P.P.S., the long time student of Brownson, is putting the finishing touches on his work at the time of
this writing.

University of America Press, 1971); James William McGrath, "The
Catholicism of Orestes A. Brownson" (1961, op. cit.); Gregory D.
Kenny, "An Historical Theological Study of Orestes Brownson's Thought
on the Church and the Progress of Civil Society" (Unpublished
doctoral dissertation, Catholic University of America, 1966);
Spencer Clare Bennett, "Orestes Brownson: On Civil Religion.
Conflicts in the Evolution of a Concept of National Faith" (Unpublished doctoral thesis, Case Western Reserve University, 1973);
and Richard M. Leliaert, "Orestes A. Brownson (1803-1876) Theological Perspectives on His Search for the Meaning of God, Christology,
and the Development of Doctrine" (Unpublished doctoral thesis,
Graduate Theological Union, 1974). From this brief sampling,
Brownson's interest and importance in so many fields--theology,
philosophy, government, the relation of Church and state, the
American mission--is readily apparent. Also, the University of
Notre Dame has prepared a twenty-reel microfilm edition of Brownson's unpublished correspondence and drafts.

It is hoped that this dissertation presents a more comprehensive picture of Brownson's educational role and views. Brownson
conceived of education in the broadest terms possible, encompassing
all influences that affected man from the cradle to the grave; he
had little regard for the common notion of education which equated
education with schooling. He was a man who exemplifies what
Bernard Bailyn described in his seminal work, Education in the
Forming of American Society. Brownson was one who thought of
education "not only as formal pedagogy but as the entire process
by which a culture transmits itself across the generations"; and

at times, he saw "schools and universities fade into relative
insignificance next to other social agencies"; finally, he viewed
"education in its elaborate, intricate involvement with the rest
of society."[10] The Brownson depicted by Bailyn's words equated
education with enculturation or socialization.

Yet, Lawrence Cremin found Bailyn's definition "so inclusive
as to define nothing for the educational historian to study except
'history in general,' a concept . . . which should not in any case
be mistaken for the history of education."[11] Cremin limited his
concept, and viewed education "as the deliberate, systematic, and
sustained effort to transmit or evoke knowledge, attitudes, values,
skills, and sensibilities."[12] In narrowing his conception, Cremin
analyzed tne formal and informal agencies that had actually shaped
American "thought, character, and sensibility" throughout its
history. He included besides schools and colleges, the family,
church, libraries (and literature), publishers, benevolent societies,
youth groups, newspapers, and lyceums. Orestes Brownson obviously
had these same things in mind; in all probability Cremin never had
Brownson in mind, although Brownson's life, education, and views on
education certainly provide a nineteenth century example that
clearly reinforces Cremin's revisionist interpretation of American
educational history.

---

[10]Bernard Bailyn, Education in the Forming of American
Society (New York: Vintage Books, 1960), p. 14.
[11]Lawrence A. Cremin, American Education: The Colonial
Experience 1607-1783 (New York: Harper & Row, 1970), p. xiii.
[12]Ibidem.

Orestes Brownson played a much more important role in the
education of Catholics than has previously been acknowledged by
the historians of "Catholic education." James A. Burns, The
Catholic School System in the United States: Its Principles,
Origin and Establishment (1908) and The Growth and Development
of the Catholic School System in the United States (1912);[13]
James A. Burns and Bernard J. Kohlbrenner, A History of Catholic
Education in the United States (1937);[14] and Harold A. Buetow, Of
Singular Benefit: The Story of Catholic Education in the United
States (1970)[15]--have concentrated on schooling and practically
ignored Brownson altogether. Edward J. Power's The Educational
Views and Attitudes of Orestes A. Brownson (1951-52)[16] concentrated
on the schools as well. Brownson just does not fit into such an
interpretation. Furthermore, just as the revisionist school of
Bailyn and Cremin has re-defined and re-interpreted the American
educational past, this dissertation gives credence to Vincent P.
Lannie's recent assertions and hypotheses that the history of

[13]James A. Burns, The Catholic School System in the United
States: Its Principles, Origin, and Establishment (New York:
Benziger Brothers, 1908) and The Growth and Development of the
Catholic School System in the United States (New York: Benziger
Brothers, 1912).

[14]James A. Burns and Bernard J. Kohlbrenner, A History of
Catholic Education in the United States (New York: Benziger
Brothers, 1937).

[15]Harold A. Buetow, Of Singular Benefit: The Story of
Catholic Education in the United States (New York: Macmillan
Company, 1970).

[16]Edward J. Power, "The Educational Views and Attitudes of
Orestes A. Brownson," The Records of the American Catholic Historical Society of Philadelphia, LXII-LXIII (June, September, December
1951, June 1952), 72-94, 142-171, 221-252, 110-128.

Catholic education needs re-focusing and re-writing as well.[17]

Lannie traces the major themes of Catholic educational history and argues that since the mission of the Church was the religious education of all Catholics, it naturally follows that not all education took place in Catholic schools where never more than 50% of Catholic children were ever enrolled. Adults and public school children as well needed religious instruction. Hence, Sunday schools, sermons, child-rearing and devotional literature, orphanages and protectories, the press and literature, and parish societies all played a role in the education of nineteenth century Catholics. What Lannie calls the "complete educational package" as the new criterion for studying Catholic educational history is nowhere better illustrated than in the scholarly mission of Orestes A. Brownson--Catholic educator.

---

[17]See Vincent P. Lannie, "Church and School Triumphant: The Historiography of Catholic Education in America" (Unpublished monograph, 1975).

BIBLIOGRAPHY

BIBLIOGRAPHIC ESSAY ON PRIMARY SOURCES

Unpublished Materials

The University of Notre Dame Archives houses the Orestes
Augustus Brownson Papers, which were donated to Notre Dame in 1900
by his son and literary heir, Henry Francis Brownson, after Henry
had prepared his twenty-volume edition of Brownson's Works (1882-
1887) and his three-volume biography (1898-1900). In 1965, the
National Historical Publications Commission sponsored the micro-
filming of the collection and published a guide for its use. The
Guide to the Microfilm Edition of the Orestes Augustus Brownson
Papers, prepared under the direction of Reverend Thomas T. McAvoy
and Professor Lawrence J. Bradley, provides basic biographical
and bibliographical information on Brownson, as well as a descrip-
tion of the entire collection and an alphabetical and chronological list of correspondents from 1823-1876. The collection contains
Brownson's correspondence, drafts for his published writings,
manuscripts of unpublished writings, sermons, and lectures, as well
as photostat and magnaprint copies of correspondence from other
collections.

Pre-Catholic Period

Among the Brownson correspondence prior to his conversion, the most significant letters are those received from Isaac B. Peirce, revealing religious and intellectual matters; from Anne C. Lynch regarding the spirit of reform and her commentary on the Boston Quarterly Review. Other correspondents, whose letters are not as great numerically, provide important information for this study: William Ellery Channing, George Bancroft, Ralph Waldo Emerson, Henry David Thoreau, Victor Cousin, James Walker, Bernard Whitman, Ezra Stiles Gannett, Edward Everett, Leonard Everett, Elizabeth Peabody, John C. Calhoun, R. B. Rhett, William D. Kelley, Richard Owen, A. H. Everett, John L. O'Sullivan, Theodore Parker, Isaac Hecker, Horace Greeley, Theophilus Fisk, Albert Brisbane, Margaret Fuller, John H. Hopkins. For a contrast between Brownson and his twin sister, see the Daphne Augusta Ludington letters. All of these early letters may also be found on rolls one and two of the microfilm edition.

Correspondence from other collections that proved valuable were Brownson's letters to his wife, Sarah Healy Brownson, found in the Odiorne Collection, UNDA; photostats of his letters to Isaac Hecker in the Paulist Archives; those to Victor Cousin found in the Bibliotheque de M. Victor Cousin, Sorbonne, Paris; correspondence with Ralph Waldo Emerson in the Harvard College Library; a xerox copy of a letter to George Bancroft from the George Bancroft Papers, Cornell University, as well as several others contained in the Massachusetts Historical Society; a photostat of a letter to Parke Godwin from the New York Public Library; and

transcripts of a letter to French, Crane, and Tucker in the Canton
Historical Society, as well as one to William D. Kelley from the
University of Virginia Library. Most of these items are on roll
nine of the microfilm.

Manuscripts of the pre-Catholic period that proved helpful
were Brownson's "Notebook of Reflections" (1823-1825); "Letters to
an Unbeliever" (1832); "Notebook of Clippings" (1836) of articles
he wrote while editor of the Boston Reformer, including essays on
manual labor schools and children's books; an essay, "Social Evils
and Their Remedies" (1842), and the following lectures: "A
Lecture Before the Trades Union," "Lecture on Reading," "Means
and End of Knowledge," "Means of Effecting a Reform," "Man's Obligation to labor for a Reform," and "The True Method of Social
Progress." Approximately sixteen sermons are also bound in the
collection. All items in this paragraph are also on roll ten of
the microfilm edition.

Catholic Period

Among the thousands of letters in the Brownson collection
during his Catholic period, the following letters from members of
the hierarchy proved most helpful: Francis Patrick Kenrick, John
Hughes, John B. Purcell, Peter Richard Kenrick, Michael O'Connor,
Martin John Spalding, John Henry Newman, John B. Fitzpatrick,
William Henry Elder, John McCloskey, John H. Luers, James R.
Bayley, John Ireland, Thomas L. Grace, Michael A. Corrigan. Other
religious whose letters are important include: Sister M. Eulalia
Pearce, Jeremiah W. Cummings, John McCaffrey, William J. Barry,
Edward Sorin, John P. Roddan, Augustine F. Hewit, Francis X.

Weninger, Joseph M. Finotti, George McCloskey, C. Gresslin, C. A. Walworth, F. Lukas Wimmer, Mother Mary Angela Gillespie, George H. Doane, Thomas S. Preston, A. J. Thebaud, William Faulkner Browne. The many Isaac Hecker letters are undoubtedly the most useful. Other important correspondents include: W. A. Stokes, John D. Bryant, Sarah F. Stearns, James A. McMaster, George H. Miles, Count de Montalembert, Jedediah V. Huntington, James and Mary Anne Sadlier, Patrick Donohoe, Alexander Garesche, Richard A. Bakewell, John D. Acton, Dr. Henry S. Hewit, George Hilton, Richard H. Clarke, Mrs. C.E.T. Clarke, George E. Clerk, Lawrence Kehoe, William Seton, J. F. Meline, Madeleine Vinton Goddard (Dahlgren), Ellen E. Sherman, Richard Simpson, Charles Sumner, George Bancroft, L. St. John Eckel, William J. Onahan, Edmund F. Dunne. In addition, letters from his wife, and children provide valuable information. These items are all contained on rolls two through eight of the microfilm edition.

Correspondence from other collections that provide invaluable assistance are Brownson's letters (1860-1875) to his son Henry, contained in the Henry F. Brownson Collection, UNDA; other family letters by and about Brownson are in the Odiorne Collection. His letters to Hughes, Bayley and John McCloskey are in the New York Archdiocesan Archives; those to Hecker in the Paulist Archives. See the Archives of the Sacred Congregation de Propaganda Fide for the Barnabo-Cummings-Cullen controversy over Brownson in 1860-1861. Brownson's letters to Montalembert are contained in the Archives du Chateau d'Ecotay and the Archives du Chateau de la Roche-en-Breny; those to Richard Simpson are in the Downside Abbey Archives, near Bath, England. Letters to the Sadliers are contained in the

Sadlier Family Collection, UNDA. For matters relating to the Civil
War and Reconstruction see Brownson's letters to Charles Sumner
in the Harvard College Library. Some Brownson-Sorin letters are
contained in the Provincial Archives of the Congregation of the
Holy Cross, Indiana Province, South Bend, Indiana. Other helpful
letters are in the James A. McMaster Papers; Richard H. Clarke
Papers; Diocese of Hartford Papers; Seton Papers, Newark; Archdiocese of Cincinnati Papers; Archdiocese of New Orleans Papers;
Reverend Daniel F. Hudson, C.S.C., Papers; and the James F.
Edwards Papers--all at the UNDA. All of these letters or photostat
or xerox copies are in the Brownson Collection, and are found on
roll nine of the microfilm edition.

The most significant manuscripts of the Catholic period
include "The Truth About the School Question," a draft of an
article for the New York Tablet; twenty-eight pages of partial
drafts on "education"; two pages on "schools." In addition,
there is a "Scrapbook of Newspaper Clippings about Orestes A.
Brownson" (1838-1857), which includes several letters written
by Brownson to various editors. The collection also contains
magnaprints of clippings from the New York Daily Times and New
York Times (1854-1867) concerning Brownson. Finally, the collection contains a photograph of an 1863 portrait of Brownson by
George P. A. Healy, along with a brief account of his life. These
items are also found on rolls eight, and sixteen through nineteen
of the microfilm edition.

Published Materials

Pre-Catholic Period

In addition to the correspondence and a handful of umpublished manuscripts, this dissertation has relied almost exclusively on Brownson's published writings. His earliest articles appeared in the Gospel Advocate and Impartial Investigator (1829), the Genesee Republican and Herald of Reform (1829), Free Enquirer (1829), The Philanthropist (1831-32), Christian Register (1833), Unitarian (1833) and the Christian Examiner (1833-36). In the last journal, see "Education of the People," XX (1836), 153-169. Several clippings from the Boston Reformer (1836) proved helpful in regard to manual labor schools. During this early period, Brownson's popularity as a speaker is evident from the yearly publications of his addresses. See the following: An Address, on the Fifty-fifth Anniversary of American Independence. By Rev. O. A. Brownson, Delivered at Ovid, Seneca Co., N.Y. July 4, 1831 (Ithaca: S.S. Chatterton, 1831); An Address, Prepared at the Request of Guy C. Clark, with the Intention of Having it Delivered to the Assembly on the Day of his Execution, Feb. 3, 1832 (Ithaca: S.S. Chatterton, 1832); An Address on Intemperance, Delivered in Walpole, N.H., Feburary 26, 1833 (Keane, N.H.: J. & J.W. Prentiss, 1833); An Address, Delivered at Dedham, on the Fifty-Eighth Anniversary of American Independence, July 4, 1834 (Dedham: H. Mann, 1834); A Sermon, Delivered to the Young People of the First Congregational Society in Canton, on Sunday, May 24, 1835 (Dedham: H. Mann, 1835).

In addition to these helpful sources, Brownson's most significant essay on education in this early period is An Address on
Popular Education Delivered in Winnisimmet Village, on Sunday
Evening July 23, 1837 (Boston: Press of John Putnam, 1837). A
xerox copy of this address was obtained from the Harvard University
Library. In Brownson's Early Life 1803-1844, Henry F. Brownson
refers to this address, but incorrectly cites its source as a
Chelsea address in 1838. There is no record of its printing at
that time. In all likelihood, Brownson may have repeated the
substance of the Winnisimmet lecture the following year.

Brownson's first book was New Views of Christianity, Society
and the Church (Boston: James Munroe and Company, 1836), followed
by Charles Elwood, or the Infidel Converted (1840). Other writings
of his pre-Catholic period were those in the Boston Quarterly
Review (1838-1842), United States Magazine and Democratic Review
(1843), and Christian World (1843). A lecture, An Oration on the
Scholar's Mission (Burlington, Vt.: V. Harrington, 1843) proved
extremely valuable and served as the springboard for this dissertation.

Catholic Period

Brownson's major periodical writings during his Catholic
period appear in his own Brownson's Quarterly Review (1844-1864;
1873-1875). During the eight-year interlude (1865-1872) his essays
appeared in Catholic World, New York Tablet, and Ave Maria. His
full-length books include: The Spirit-Rapper; an Autobiography
(Boston: Little, Brown and Company, 1854); The Convert; or,
Leaves from My Experience (New York: E. Dunigan & Brother, 1857);

The American Republic; Its Constitution, Tendencies, and Destiny
(New York: P. O'Shea, 1865); and Conversations on Liberalism and
the Church (New York: D. & J. Sadlier & Co., 1869). An important
lecture of this period is An Oration on Liberal Studies, Delivered
before the Philomathian Society of Mount Saint Mary's College, Md.,
June 29, 1853 (Baltimore: Hedian & O'Brien, 1853). See also a
collection of his writings in Essays and Reviews, Chiefly on
Theology, Politics, and Socialism (New York, Montreal: D. & J.
Sadlier & Co., c. 1852).

Besides the original editions of his published writings,
several collections have been printed posthumously. The most
famous, of course, is Henry F. Brownson (ed.), The Works of
Orestes A. Brownson, 20 vols. (Detroit: Thorndike Nourse, 1882-
1887). The contents are arranged as follows: Volumes 1-2,
Philosophy; 3, Philosophy of Religion; 4, Religion and Society;
5-8, Controversy; 9, Scientific Theories; 10-13, Civilization; 14,
Development and Morals; 15-18, Politics; 19, Literary Criticisms;
20, Explanations and Index. Since these writings have been edited
by his son, Brownson's original editions are always preferred to
the Works. In addition, it is frustrating to read monographs
with citations to the Works, for often authors neglect to mention
the title of the essay, the publication in which it first appeared,
and the original date. If the Works must be used in the absence
of original publications, proper documentation is a necessity.
One other drawback to the Works is that they do not contain any
of the "Literary Notices and Criticisms" of BrQR which proved so
valuable for this study.

Henry Brownson also edited the following writings of his
father: The Two Brothers; or Why Are You a Protestant (Detroit:
H. F. Brownson, 1888); Uncle Jack and His Nephew; or, Conversations
of an Old Fogy with a Young American (Detroit: H. F. Brownson,
1888); Essays on Modern Popular Literature (Detroit: H. F.
Brownson, 1888); Literary, Scientific, and Political Views of
Orestes A. Brownson (New York, Cincinnati: Benziger Brothers, c.
1893). Other collections include: D. J. Scannell O'Neill (ed.),
Watchwords from Dr. Brownson (Techny, Ill.: Society of the Divine
Word, 1910); David Battle (ed.), Gems of Composition and Criticism,
Compiled from the Writings of the Late Dr. Orestes A. Brownson
(Huntington, Ind.: Our Sunday Visitor, 1923); Perry Miller (ed.),
The Transcendentalists; An Anthology (Cambridge: Harvard University
Press, 1950); Russell Kirk (ed.), Orestes Brownson: Selected
Essays (Chicago: Henry Regnery Co., 1955); Alvan S. Ryan (ed.),
The Brownson Reader (New York: P. J. Kenedy & Sons, 1955); and
Thomas R. Ryan (ed.), Saint Worship /̄and̄/ The Worship of Mary
(Paterson, New Jersey: St. Anthony Guild Press, 1963).

One final item of significance is O. A. Brownson, Jr., Our
Public Schools and their Just Claims (Dubuque, Iowa: Barns &
Ryan, 1869). A xerox copy of this address was obtained from the
Harvard University Library.

SECONDARY SOURCES

Books

Bailyn, Bernard. Education in the Forming of American Society. New
    York: Vintage Books, 1960.

Baumgartner, Appolinaris W. Catholic Journalism; A Study of its
    Development in the United States, 1789-1930. New York:
    Columbia University Press, 1931.

Billington, Ray Allen. The Protestant Crusade, 1800-1860. New
    York: The Macmillan Company, 1938.

Bode, Carl. The American Lyceum, Town Meeting of the Mind. New
    York: Oxford University Press, 1956.

Bremner, Robert H. Children and Youth in America: A Documentary
    History. 3 Vols. Cambridge, Massachusetts: Harvard
    University Press, 1970.

Brooks, Van Wyck. The Flowering of New England, 1815-1865. New
    York: E. P. Dutton & Co., 1936.

Brownson, Henry F. Brownson's Early Life 1803-1844. Detroit:
    H. F. Brownson, 1898.

_____. Brownson's Middle Life 1845-1855. Detroit: H. F.
    Brownson, 1899.

_____. Brownson's Latter Life 1856-1876. Detroit: H. F.
    Brownson, 1900.

Buetow, Harold A. Of Singular Benefit: The Story of Catholic
    Education in the United States. New York: The Macmillan
    Company, 1970.

Burns, James A. The Principles, Origin and Establishment of the
    Catholic School System in the United States. New York:
    Benziger Brothers, 1908.

_____. The Growth and Development of the Catholic School
    System in the United States. New York: Benziger Brothers,
    1912.

Burns, James A. and Bernard J. Kohlbrenner. A History of Catholic
    Education in the United States. New York: Benziger Brothers,
    1937.

Butts, R. Freeman. The College Charts Its Course: Historical
    Conceptions and Current Proposals. New York: McGraw-Hill
    Book Company, 1939.

Cassidy, Francis P. The Catholic Colleges: Foundations and Development in the United States 1677-1850. Washington: The Catholic University of America, 1924.

Celts and Saxons, Nativism and Naturalization: A Complete Refutation of the Nativism of Dr. Orestes A. Brownson. Edited by Bishop Michael O'Connor. Boston: Thomas Sweeney, 1854.

Commager, Henry Stelle. The Era of Reform, 1830-1860. Princeton: D. Van Nostrand Company, 1960.

Corrigan, Sister M. Felicia. Some Social Principles of Orestes A. Brownson. Washington: The Catholic University of America Press, 1939.

Crane, Theodore Rawson. The Colleges and the Public, 1787-1862. New York: Teachers College, Columbia University, 1963.

Cremin, Lawrence A. American Education: The Colonial Experience 1607-1783. New York: Harper & Row, 1970.

_____ (ed.). The Republic and the School. Horace Mann on Education of Free Men. New York: Teachers College Press, Columbia University, 1957.

Curti, Merle. The Growth of American Thought. New York: Harper & Row, 1943.

De Tocqueville, Alexis. Democracy in America. Translated by Henry Reeve. Edited by Phillips Bradley. New York: Alfred A. Knopf, 1945.

Dunne, Edmund F. Our Public Schools: Are they free for all, or are they not? San Francisco: Cosmopolitan Printing Co., 1875.

Ellis, John Tracy. American Catholicism. 2nd ed. Chicago: University of Chicago Press, 1969.

_____. American Catholics and the Intellectual Life. Chicago: The Heritage Foundation, 1956.

_____. The Catholic Priest in the United States: Historical Investigations. Collegeville, Minnesota: Saint John's University Press, 1971.

_____. Catholics in Colonial America. Baltimore: Helicon, 1965.

Erbacher, Sebastian A. Catholic Higher Education for Men in the United States, 1850-1866. Washington: The Catholic University of America, 1931.

Farrell, Bertin. <u>Orestes Brownson's Approach to the Problem of God: a Critical Examination in the Light of the Principles of St. Thomas Aquinas.</u> Washington: The Catholic University of America Press, 1950.

Fell, Sister Marie Leonore. <u>The Foundations of Nativism in American Textbooks.</u> Washington: The Catholic University of America Press, 1941.

Foik, Paul J. <u>Pioneer Catholic Journalism.</u> New York: The United States Catholic Historical Society, 1930.

Gabriel, Ralph H. <u>The Course of American Democratic Thought.</u> New York: The Ronald Press Company, 1940.

Gilhooley, Leonard. <u>Contradiction and Dilemma: Orestes Brownson and the American Idea.</u> New York: Fordham University Press, 1972.

Gleason, Philip (ed.). <u>Catholicism in America.</u> New York: Harper & Row, 1970.

Goebel, Edmund J. <u>A Study of Catholic Secondary Education During the Colonial Period Up to the First Plenary Council of Baltimore, 1852.</u> New York: Benziger Brothers, 1937.

Gordon, Milton. <u>Assimilation in American Life.</u> New York: Oxford University Press, 1964.

Gorman, Robert. <u>Catholic Apologetical Literature in the United States 1784-1858.</u> Washington: The Catholic University of America Press, 1939.

Greeley, Andres. <u>The Catholic Experience.</u> New York: Image Books, 1969.

Greeley, Andrew M. and Peter H. Rossi. <u>The Education of Catholic Americans.</u> Chicago: Aldine Publishing Company, 1966.

Handlin, Oscar. <u>Immigration as a Factor in American History.</u> Englewood Cliffs, N.J.: Prentice-Hall, Inc., 1959.

Hassard, John R. <u>Life of the Most Reverend John Hughes, D.D., First Archbishop of New York.</u> New York: D. Appleton and Company, 1865.

Higham, John. <u>Strangers in the Land: Patterns of American Nativism 1860-1925.</u> 2nd ed. New York: Atheneum, 1967.

Hofstadter, Richard and Walter P. Metzger. <u>The Development of Academic Freedom in the United States.</u> New York: Columbia University Press, 1955.

Holden, Vincent F. The Early Years of Isaac Thomas Hecker, 1819-
      1844. Washington: The Catholic University of America Press,
      1939.

_____. The Yankee Paul: Isaac Thomas Hecker. Milwaukee:
      Bruce Publishing Company, 1958.

Hudson, Wilthrop S. American Protestantism. Chicago: The
      University of Chicago Press, 1961.

Hutchison, William R. The Transcendentalist Ministers: Church
      Reform in the New England Renaissance. New Haven: Yale
      University Press, 1959.

Kennedy, William Bean. The Shaping of Protestant Education. New
      York: Association Press, 1966.

Kirk, Russell. The Conservative Mind, from Burke to Eliot. 2nd
      ed. revised. Chicago: Henry Regnery Co., 1960.

Lannie, Vincent P. Public Money and Parochial Education: Bishop
      Hughes, Governor Seward, and the New York School Controversy.
      Cleveland: The Press of Case Western Reserve University, 1968.

Lapati, Americo D. Orestes A. Brownson. New York: Twayne
      Publishers, 1965.

Lewis, R. W. The American Adam: Innocence, Tragedy, and Tradition
      in the Nineteenth Century. Chicago: University of Chicago
      Press, 1955.

Lord, Robert H., John E. Sexton, and Edward T. Harrington. History
      of the Archdiocese of Boston. 3 vols. New York: Sheed and
      Ward, 1944.

Lynn, Robert W. Protestant Strategies in Education. New York:
      Association Press, 1964.

Lynn, Robert W. and Elliott Wright. The Big Little School, Sunday
      Child of American Protestantism. New York: Harper & Row,
      1971.

Malone, G. K. The True Church: A Study in the Apologetics of
      Orestes Augustus Brownson. Mundelein, Illinois: Saint Mary
      of the Lake Seminary, 1957.

Marshall, Hugh. Orestes Brownson and the American Republic; An
      Historical Perspective. Washington: Catholic University of
      America Press, 1971

Maynard, Theodore. Orestes Brownson Yankee, Radical, Catholic.
      New York: The Macmillan Company, 1943.

_____. The Story of American Catholicism. New York: The
      Macmillan Company, 1941.

McAvoy, Thomas T. A History of the Catholic Church in the United States. Notre Dame, Ind.: University of Notre Dame Press, 1969.

McCluskey, Neil G. (ed.). Catholic Education in America, A Documentary History. New York: Teachers College, Columbia University, 1964.

Metzger, Charles H. Catholics and the American Revolution. Chicago: Loyola University Press, 1962.

Michel, Virgil G. The Critical Principles of Orestes A. Brownson. Washington: St. Mary's Industrial School Press, 1918.

Miller, John C. Crises in Freedom: The Alien and Sedition Acts. Boston: Little, Brown, 1951.

Morris, William S. The Seminary Movement in the United States: Projects, Foundations, and Early Development 1833-1866. Washington: Catholic University of America Press, 1932.

Mott, Frank Luther. American Journalism; a History 1690-1960. 3rd ed. New York: The Macmillan Company, 1962.

Nolan, Hugh J. The Most Reverend Francis Patrick Kenrick, Third Bishop of Philadelphia, 1830-1851. Washington: Catholic University of America Press, 1948.

_____ (ed.). Pastoral Letters of the American Hierarchy 1792-1970. Huntington, Indiana: Our Sunday Visitor, 1971.

Nuesse, C. J. The Social Thought of American Catholics 1634-1829. Westminster, Maryland: The Newman Book Shop, 1945.

O'Brien, John A. Giants of the Faith. New York: Image Books, Doubleday & Company, 1960, 245-299.

O'Callaghan, Jeremiah. Atheism of Brownson's Review. Burlington, Vermont, 1852.

Potter, George. To the Golden Door: The Story of the Irish in Ireland and America. Boston: Little, Brown & Co., 1960.

Power, Edward J. A History of Catholic Higher Education in the United States. Milwaukee: The Bruce Publishing Company, 1958.

Pratt, John W. Religion, Politics, and Diversity: The Church-State Theme in New York History. Ithaca, New York: Cornell University Press, 1967.

Raemers, Sydney A. America's Foremost Philosopher. Washington: St. Anselm's Priory, 1931.

Ray, Sister Mary Augustina. American Opinion of Roman Catholicism in the Eighteenth Century. New York: Columbia University Press, 1936.

Reilly, Daniel F. The School Controversy. Washington: The Catholic University of America Press, 1943.

Roemer, Lawrence. Brownson on Democracy and the Trend Toward Socialism. New York: Philosophical Library, 1958.

Rudolph, Frederick. The American College and University: A History. New York: Alfred A. Knopf, 1962.

Ryan, Thomas R. The Sailor's Snug Harbor, Studies in Brownson's Thought. Westminster, Maryland: The Newman Book Shop, 1952.

Sargent, Daniel. Four Independents. New York: Sheed & Ward, 1935.

Schlesinger, Arthur M. Jr. The Age of Jackson. Boston: Little, Brown & Co., 1945.

_____. Orestes Brownson: A Pilgrim's Progress. New York: Octagon Books, 1939.

Shea, John Gilmary. The Hierarchy of the Catholic Church in the United States. New York: The Office of Catholic Publications, 1886.

_____. History of the Catholic Church in the United States. 4 vols. New York: J. G. Shea, 1886-92.

Smith, Timothy L. Revivalism and Social Reform in Mid-nineteenth Century America. New York: Abingdon Press, 1957.

Sveino, Per. Orestes A. Brownson's Road to Catholicism. Oslo and New York: Universitetsforlaget and Humanities Press, 1970.

Tewksbury, Donald. The Founding of American Colleges and Universities Before the Civil War, With Particular Reference to the Religious Influence Bearing Upon the College Movement. New York: Teachers College, Columbia University, 1932.

Thomas, Abel C. Civilization and Roman Catholicism: A Review of O. A. Brownson's Four Lectures. Philadelphia, 1851.

Tyler, Alice Felt. Freedom's Ferment: Phases of American Social History from the Colonial Period to the Outbreak of the Civil War. The University of Minnesota Press, 1944.

Whalen, Doran. Granite For God's House. New York: Sheed & Ward, 1941.

_____. The Influence of Orestes Augustus Brownson. South Bend, Indiana: Chimes Press, 1936.

Articles

Abell, Aaron. "Brownson's American Republic: The Political Testament of a Reluctant Democrat," Records of the American Catholic Historical Society of Philadelphia, LVI (1955), 118-127.

Bernard, Leon. "Orestes Brownson, Montalembert, and Modern Civilization," Historical Records and Studies, XLII (1954), 23-49.

Bestor, Arthur E. Jr. "Horace Mann, Elizabeth P. Peabody, and Orestes A. Brownson, An Unpublished Letter, with Commentary," Proceedings of the Middle States Association of History and Social Science Teachers. New York: Teachers College, Columbia University, 1940-41, 47-53.

Bidwell, Charles. "The Moral Significance of the Common School: A Sociological Study of Common Patterns of School Control and Moral Education in Massachusetts and New York, 1837-1840," History of Education Quarterly, VI (1966), 50-91.

Blau, J. "Kant in America: Brownson's Critique of the Critique of Pure Reason," The Journal of Philosophy, LI (1954), 874-880.

Burton, K. "A Man of Our Day," Commonweal, XXVIII (1938), 719-721.

Caponigri, Robert. "Brownson and Emerson: Nature and History," The New England Quarterly, XVIII (September, 1945), 368-390.

Conroy, Paul R. "The Role of the American Constitution in the Political Philosophy of Orestes A. Brownson," The Catholic Historical Review, XXV (October, 1939), 271-286.

Cook, Thomas I. and Arnaud B. Leavelle. "Orestes A. Brownson's The American Republic," The Review of Politics, IV (January, April, 1942), 77-90, 173-193.

Corcoran, J. "In Memoriam: Orestes A. Brownson," The American Quarterly Review, I (1876), 56-66.

Cross, Robert. "Origins of the Catholic Parochial Schools in America," The American Benedictine Review, XVI (1965), 194-209.

Day, Edward. "Brownson and the Motherhood of Mary," The American Ecclesiastical Review, CXXIX (July, 1953), 20-27.

_____. "Brownson's Quest for Social Justice," The American Ecclesiastical Review, CXXXI (1954), 90-111.

Donovan, Joseph P. "Brownson, the Philosophical Expounder of the Constitution," American Catholic Philosophical Association: Proceedings of the Seventh Annual Meeting (1931), 148-165.

Donovan, Joseph P. "Matchless Interpreter of a Peerless Constitution," The Homiletic and Pastoral Review, XLVIII (1948), 494-502.

_____. "Why a Brownson Revival," Acolyte, III (1927), 6-7.

Ellis, John Tracy. "Short History of Seminary Education," Seminary Education in a Time of Change. Edited by James Michael Lee and Louis J. Putz. Notre Dame, Indiana: Fides Publishers, 1965.

Fitzsimons, M. A. "Brownson's Search for the Kingdom of God: the Social Thought of An American Radical," The Review of Politics, XVI (January, 1954), 22-36.

Frese, Joseph R. "Brownson on Know-Nothingism," Historical Records and Studies of the American Catholic Historical Society, XXVIII (1937), 52-74.

Gildea, W. "An English View of Brownson's Conversion," Catholic World, LXIX (1899), 24-31.

Gleason, Philip. "American Catholic Higher Education: A Historical Perspective," The Shape of Catholic Higher Education. Edited by Robert Hassenger. Chicago: University of Chicago Press, 1967.

Harson, M. "Orestes Brownson, LL.D.," Catholic World, LXXIX (1904), 1-21.

Hecker, Isaac T. "Dr. Brownson and Bishop Fitzpatrick," Catholic World, XLV (1887), 1-7.

_____. "Dr. Brownson and the Workingmen's Party of Fifty Years Ago," Catholic World, XLV (May, 1887), 200-208.

_____. "Dr. Brownson in Boston," Catholic World, XLV (1887), 466-472.

_____. "Dr. Brownson's Road to the Church," Catholic World, XLVI (1887), 1-11.

_____. "The Transcendentalist Movement in New England," Catholic World, XXIII (1876), 528-537.

Hewit, A. F. "Dr. Brownson," Catholic World, XXIII (1876), 366-377.

Hoffman, Ross J.S. "The American Republic and Western Christendom," Historical Records and Studies, XXXV (1946), 3-17.

Hollis, C. Carroll. "Brownson on George Bancroft," The South Atlantic Quarterly, XLIX (January, 1950), 42-52.

Kirk, Russell. "Brownson and a Just Society," The Month (1954), 348-365.

Krummel, Carl F. "Catholicism, Americanism, Democracy, and Orestes Brownson," American Quarterly, VI (Spring, 1954), 19-31.

Ladu, Arthur I. "The Political Ideas of Orestes A. Brownson, Transcendentalist," Philological Quarterly, XII (July, 1933), 280-289.

Lannie, Vincent P. "Alienation in America: The Immigrant Catholic and Public Education in Pre-Civil War America," Review of Politics, XXXII (October, 1970), 503-521.

_____. "The Emergence of Catholic Education in America," Notre Dame Journal of Education, III (Winter, 1973), 297-309.

Lannie, Vincent P. and Bernard C. Diethorn, "For the Honor and Glory of God: The Philadelphia Bible Riots of 1840 / sic /," History of Education Quarterly, VIII (Spring, 1968), 44-106.

Lathrop, G. P. "Orestes Brownson," Atlantic Monthly, LXXVII (June, 1896), 770-780.

MacCarthy, John. "Dr. Brownson: A Fireside Sketch of a Great Man," Ave Maria, XVIII (December 2, 1882), 941-945.

Maynard, Theodore. "Orestes Brownson, Journalist," Commonweal, XXXVII (1943), 390-393.

McAvoy, Thomas T. "Brownson's Ontologism," Catholic Historical Review, XXVIII (1942), 376-381.

_____. "The Catholic Minority in the United States, 1789-1821," Historical Records and Studies, XXXIX-XL (1952), 33-50.

_____. "The Formation of the Catholic Minority in the United States, 1820-1860," Review of Politics, X (1948), 13-34.

_____. "Orestes A. Brownson and American History," Catholic Historical Review, XL (October, 1954), 257-268.

_____. "Orestes Brownson and Archbishop John Hughes in 1860," Review of Politics, XXIV (1962), 19-47.

_____. "Public Schools vs. Catholic Schools and James McMaster," Review of Politics, XXVIII (January, 1966), 19-46.

McLoughlin, J. "A Study of Dr. Brownson," Catholic World, LXXVII (1903), 310-319.

McMahon, "Brownson and Newman," America, XXIX (1953), 45-47, 79-80.

_____. "Orestes Brownson," Commonweal, LXXXIII (1965), 260.

McMahon, "Orestes Brownson on Church and State," Theological Studies, XV (1954), 175-228.

Messerli, Jonathan. "To Broaden Schooling Was to Narrow Education," Notre Dame Journal of Education, I (Spring, 1970), 5-16.

Michel, Virgil. "Brownson, A Man of Men," Catholic World, CXXV (1925), 755-762.

_____. "Brownson's Political Philosophy and Today," American Catholic Quarterly Review, XLIV (April, 1919), 193-202.

_____. "Orestes A. Brownson," Catholic World, CXXV (1925), 499-505.

Mims, Helen S. "Early American Democratic Theory and Orestes Brownson," Science and Society, III (Spring, 1939), 166-198.

"Orestes A. Brownson as a Philosopher," American Quarterly Church Review, XIX (January, 1868), 532-547.

Parry, Stanley J. "The Premises of Brownson's Political Theory," The Review of Politics, XVI (April, 1954), 194-211.

Parsons, Wilfrid. "Brownson, Hecker, and Hewit," Catholic World, CLIII (July, 1941), 396-408.

Power, Edward J. "The Educational Views and Attitudes of Orestes A. Brownson," The Records of the American Catholic Historical Society of Philadelphia, LXII-LXIII (June, September, December, 1951, June, 1952), 72-94, 142-171, 221-252, 110-128.

_____. "Formative Years of Catholic Colleges Founded before 1850," Records of the American Catholic Historical Society of Philadelphia, LXV-LXVI (March, December, 1954; March, 1955), 24-39, 240-250, 19-34.

Rowland, James P. "Brownson and the American Republic Today," Catholic World, CLII (February, 1941), 537-541.

Ryan, A. "Orestes A. Brownson: The Critique of Transcendental-ism," American Classics Reconsidered: A Christian Appraisal. Edited by H. Gardiner. New York: Scribner, 1958, 98-120.

Ryan E. "Brownson and Newman," The American Ecclesiastical Review, LII (1915), 406-413.

_____. "Orestes Augustus Brownson," Downside Review, XLIV (1926), 115-124.

Ryan, Thomas R. "Brownson's Love of Truth," Catholic World, CLXVI (March, 1948), 537-544.

Ryan, Thomas R. "Brownson's Technique in Apologetics," American Ecclesiastical Review, CXVIII (January, 1948) 12-22.

_____. "Orestes A. Brownson and Historiography," Irish Ecclesiastical Record, LXXXV (1956), 10-17, 122-130.

_____. "Orestes A. Brownson and the Irish," Mid-America, XXXVIII (N.S.XXVII), (1956), 156-172.

_____. "Orestes A. Brownson on Salvation and the Church," American Ecclesiastical Review, CXXIX (September, 1953), 157-169.

_____. "Whence Comes Freedom?" Catholic World, CLXVII (September, 1948), 491-497.

_____. "Why Continue to Smear Brownson?" Acolyte, XVII (October, 1941), 11-14.

Schwinn, Bonaventure. "Portrait of a Roaring Radical," Commonweal, XXXIX (March 3, 1944), 495-498.

Shelley, T. "Orestes Brownson and Archbishop Hughes," St. Meinrad Essays, XII (1959), 25-39.

Smith, Timothy. "Parochial Education and American Culture," History and Education. Edited by Paul Nash. New York: Random House, 1970, pp. 192-211.

_____. "Protestant Schooling and American Nationality, 1800-1850," Journal of American History, LIII (March, 1967), 679-685.

Soleta, Chester A. "The Literary Criticism of Orestes A. Brownson," Review of Politics, XVI (July, 1954), 334-351.

Stefun, B. "Orestes Brownson: Apologist," The Homiletic and Pastoral Review, LXIII (1962), 40-47.

Tyack, David B. "The Kingdom of God and the Common School: Protestant Ministers and the Educational Awakening in the West," Harvard Educational Review, XXXVI (Fall, 1966), 447-469.

_____. "Onward Christian Soldiers: Religion in the American Common School," History and Education. Edited by Paul Nash. New York: Random House, 1970, pp. 212-255.

Wilson, Henry. "New Departure of the Republican Party," Atlantic Monthly, XXVII (January, 1871), 104-120.

Unpublished Material

Ayo, Nicholas R. "A Study of Brownson's Boston Quarterly Review." Unpublished master's thesis. University of Notre Dame, 1962.

Baron, R. J. "New Light on the Political and Religious Life of Orestes Brownson." Unpublished master's thesis. University of Illinois, 1947.

Bennett, Spencer Clare. "Orestes Brownson: On Civil Religion. Conflicts in the Evolution of a Concept of National Faith." Unpublished doctoral thesis. Case Western Reserve University, 1973.

Carrico, James. "Faith and Reason as Reconciled in the Philosophy of Orestes A. Brownson." Unpublished master's thesis. University of Notre Dame, 1934.

Collier, M. "The Educational Principles of Orestes Augustus Brownson." Unpublished master's thesis. Catholic University of America, 1948.

Conroy, Paul R. "Orestes A. Brownson: American Political Philosopher." Unpublished doctoral dissertation. St. Louis University, 1937.

Deye, Anthony H. "Archbishop John Baptist Purcell of Cincinnati: Pre-Civil War Years." Unpublished doctoral dissertation. University of Notre Dame, 1959.

Diffley, Jerome. "Catholic Reaction to American Public Education, 1792-1852." Unpublished doctoral thesis. University of Notre Dame, 1959.

Faddoul, Germain. "The Harmonizing of Faith and Reason in Brownson's Pre-Catholic Experience." Unpublished doctor dissertation. University of Notre Dame, 1963.

Flynn, Austin. "The School Controversy in New York, 1840-1842, and Its Effect on the Formulation of Catholic Elementary Policy." Unpublished doctoral dissertation. University of Notre Dame, 1962.

Francella, Sister Mary. "Brownson's Idea of Progress." Unpublished B.A. thesis. University of Notre Dame, 1927.

Gleason, Philip. "The Reorganization of Catholic Higher Education." Unpublished paper delivered at a conference on Saint Mary's College in the Seventies: Its Christian Dimensions. Notre Dame, Indiana, April 6, 1974.

Hollis, C. C. "The Literary Criticism of Orestes Brownson." Unpublished doctoral dissertation, 1954.

Hueston, Robert F. "The Catholic Press and Nativism, 1840-1860." Unpublished doctoral dissertation. University of Notre Dame, 1972.

Ireland, Robert E. "The Concept of Providence in the Thought of William Ellery Channing, Ralph Waldo Emerson, Theodore Parker, and Orestes A. Brownson: A Study in Mid-Nineteenth Century American Intellectual History." Unpublished doctoral thesis. University of Maine, 1972.

Kenny, Gregory D. "An Historical Theological Study of Orestes Brownson's Thought on the Church and the Progress of Civil Society." Unpublished doctoral dissertation. Catholic University of America, 1966.

Kriner, Marie Bernadette. "Henry Francis Brownson As a Lay Catholic Leader." Unpublished master's dissertation. University of Notre Dame, 1944.

Kunkel, Norlene Mary. "Bishop Bernard J. McQuaid and Catholic Education." Unpublished doctoral dissertation. University of Notre Dame, 1974.

Lannie, Vincent P. "Church and School Triumphant: The Historio-graphy of Catholic Education in America." Unpublished mono-graph, 1975.

Leliaert, Richard M. "Orestes A. Brownson (1803-1876) Theological Perspectives on His Search for the Meaning of God, Christology and the Development of Doctrine." Unpublished doctoral thesis. Graduate Theological Union, 1974.

Marshall, Hugh. "Orestes Brownson and the American Civil War." Unpublished doctoral thesis. Catholic University of America, 1962.

McCarthy, Jay David. "Orestes A. Brownson, A Catholic Voice on the Civil War, 1861-1864." Unpbulished master's thesis. University of Notre Dame, 1956.

McDonald, Lloyd Paul. "The Seminary Movement in the United States 1784-1833." Unpublished doctoral dissertation. The Catholic University of America, 1927.

McGrath, James W. "The Catholicism of Orestes A. Brownson." Unpublished doctoral dissertation. The University of New Mexico, 1961.

Meiring, Bernard J. "Educational Aspects of the Legislation of the Councils of Baltimore, 1829-1884." Unpublished doctoral thesis. University of California at Berkeley, 1963.

Mitchell, Philip J. "A Study of Orestes A. Brownson's Views on the Know-Nothing Movement." Unpublished master's thesis. University of Notre Dame, 1945.

Morrissey, Timothy H. "Archbishop John Ireland and the Faribault-
    Stillwater School Plan of the 1890's: A Reappraisal."
    Unpublished doctoral dissertation. University of Notre Dame,
    1975.

Murphy, F. E. "Orestes A. Brownson's 'The Convert' as a Record of
    American Spiritual Experience in the 1840's and 1850's."
    Unpublished master's thesis. University of Notre Dame, 1945.

Plunkett, De Vere T. "The Concept of Sovereignty in the Writings
    of Orestes A. Brownson." Unpublished master's thesis.
    University of Notre Dame, 1936.

Raemers, Sydney A. "A Critical Examination into the Alleged
    Ontologism of Orestes A. Brownson." Unpublished doctoral
    dissertation. University of Notre Dame, 1929.

Sanfilippo, Mary Helena. "The New England Transcendentalists'
    Opinions of the Catholic Church." Unpublished doctoral dis-
    sertation. University of Notre Dame, 1972.

Shaughnessy, Sister Jerome. "Dr. Orestes A. Brownson's Philosophy
    of Nationalism and Some Contemporary Political Problems."
    Unpublished master's thesis. University of Notre Dame, 1926.

The Heritage of
American Catholicisim

15. ALFRED J. EDE
THE LAY CRUSADE FOR A CHRISTIAN AMERICA:
A STUDY OF THE AMERICAN FEDERATION OF CATHOLIC SOCIETIES, 1900-1919
New York 1988

16. JO RENEE FORMICOL
THE AMERICAN CATHOLIC CHURCH AND ITS ROLE IN THE FORMULATION
OF UNITED STATES HUMAN RIGHTS FOREIGN POLICY, 1945-1978
New York 1988

17. THOMAS J. JONAS
THE DIVIDED MIND:
AMERICAN CATHOLIC EVANGELSTS IN THE 1890s
FOREWORD BY MARTIN E. MARTY
New York 1988

18. MARTIN J. KIRK
THE SPIRITUALITY OF ISAAC THOMAS HECKER:
RECONCILING THE AMERICAN CHARACTER AND THE CATHOLIC FAITH
New York 1988

19. NORLENE M. KUNKEL
BISHOP BERNARD J. McQUAID AND CATHOLIC EDUCATION
New York 1988

20. JAMES M. McDONNELL
ORESTES A. BROWNSON AND NINETEENTH-CENTURY CATHOLIC EDUCATION
New York 1988

21. ELIZABETH McKEOWN
WAR AND WELFARE:
AMERICAN CATHOLICS AND WORLD WAR I
New York 1988

22. BARBARA MISNER, S. C. S. C.
"HIGHLY RESPECTABLE AND ACCOMPLISHED LADIES:"
CATHOLIC WOMEN RELIGIOUS IN AMERICA 1790-1850
New York 1988